Canada and the World since 1867

NEW APPROACHES TO INTERNATIONAL HISTORY

Series editor: Thomas Zeiler, Professor of American Diplomatic History, University of Colorado, Boulder, USA

New Approaches to International History covers international history during the modern period and across the globe. The series incorporates new developments in the field, such as the cultural turn and transnationalism, as well as the classical high politics of state-centric policymaking and diplomatic relations. Written with upper-level undergraduate and postgraduate students in mind, texts in the series provide an accessible overview of international, global and transnational issues, events and actors.

Published:

Decolonization and the Cold War, Leslie James and Elisabeth Leake (2015)

Cold War Summits, Chris Tudda (2015)

The United Nations in International History, Amy L. Sayward (2017)

Latin American Nationalism, James F. Siekmeier (2017)

The History of United States Cultural Diplomacy, Michael L. Krenn (2017)

International Cooperation in the Early Twentieth Century,
Daniel Gorman (2017)

Women and Gender in International History, Karen Garner (2018)

The Environment and International History, Scott Kaufman (2018)

International Development, Corrina R. Unger (2018)

Scandinavia and the Great Powers in the First World War,
Michael Jonas (2019)

Forthcoming:

The International LGBT Rights Movement, Laura Belmonte

Reconstructing the Postwar World, Francine McKenzie

Canada and the World since 1867

ASA MCKERCHER

BLOOMSBURY ACADEMIC
LONDON • NEW YORK • OXFORD • NEW DELHI • SYDNEY

BLOOMSBURY ACADEMIC
Bloomsbury Publishing Plc
50 Bedford Square, London, WC1B 3DP, UK
1385 Broadway, New York, NY 10018, USA

BLOOMSBURY, BLOOMSBURY ACADEMIC and the Diana logo are trademarks of
Bloomsbury Publishing Plc

First published in Great Britain, 2019

Series design: Catherine Wood
Cover image: Map of the Shipping Lanes of the Empire. Copy negative C-109415.
(© Library and Archives Canada)

A catalogue record for this book is available from the British Library.

A catalog record for this book is available from the Library of Congress.

ISBN: HB: 978-1-3500-3676-5
PB: 978-1-3500-3677-2
ePDF: 978-1-3500-3675-8
eBook: 978-1-3500-3678-9

Series: New Approaches to International History

Typeset by Newgen KnowledgeWorks Pvt. Ltd., Chennai, India
Printed and bound in Great Britain

To find out more about our authors and books visit www.bloomsbury.com
and sign up for our newsletters.

This one's for Calvin

Nunc scio, quid sit Amor

Contents

Acknowledgements ix

Introduction: Canada and the world since 1867 1

1 Dominion-building and empire-building 7

2 Canada and Greater Britain 23

3 Canada and the first age of globalization 41

4 Canada's Great War 59

5 North Americanism and the search for peace 77

6 Canada and the descent to war 99

7 The North Atlantic Triangle from world war to cold war 119

8 The middle power and the end of empire 139

9 From colony to nation to colony? 159

10 Canada and the emerging global village 181

11 War and peace in the new world order 205

12 Globalization redux 229

Notes 257
Index 327

Acknowledgements

This book is the result of four things. First, an invitation from Tom Zeiler to contribute to the New Approaches to International History series. My thanks to Tom for the invite, and to making sure that this excellent series has some Canadian content. On a related note, my appreciation to the editorial team at Bloomsbury: Emma Goode, Maddie Holder, and Dan Hutchins have been ever so patient and helpful.

Second, this book has its genesis in courses on Canadian international history that I taught during two pleasant years at the L.R. Wilson Institute for Canadian History at McMaster University. My gratitude to the Wilsonians: Red Wilson, for his support of Canadian history; Viv Nelles, John Weaver, and Ian McKay, for their direction; Debbie Lobban and Max Dagenais, for their administrative assistance; Amanda Ricci, Ian Mosby, Stacy Nation-Knapper, and Colin McCullough, for being excellent colleagues; the students of History 3CG3 and 4CM3, for their engagement with Canada's international history; and Phil Van Huizen, for his friendship.

Third, I have benefitted from the inspiration and support of a rogues' gallery of Canadian international historians: Stephen Azzi, Stephanie Bangarth, Jen Bonder, Bob Bothwell, Jeff Brison, Kevin Brushett, Mike Carroll, Janice Cavell, Adam Chapnick, Susie Colbourn, Jack Cunningham, John Dirks, Greg Donaghy, Karen Dubinsky, Serge Durflinger, John English, Norm Hillmer, Jack Granatstein, Moe Labelle, Whitney Lackenbauer, Dan Macfarlane, Laura Madokoro, Steve Marti, Francine McKenzie, David Meren, Galen Perras, Tim Sayle, Kevin Spooner, Michael Stevenson, Ryan Touhey, David Webster, and Matt Wiseman.

Finally, my son, Calvin, provided the motivation to finish this project, in part because his early arrival delayed its completion. He and my darling Kendall are fonts of inspiration.

Introduction: Canada and the world since 1867

In 2009, amid the global economic crisis, Canadian prime minister Stephen Harper characterized Canada as the envy of the G8 countries, possessing 'all of the things that people admire about the great powers but none of the things that threaten or bother them'. Among many attributes, he noted that Canada had 'no history of colonialism'. Seven years later, Harper's successor, Justin Trudeau, made a similar statement. In commenting on the prospects of future Canadian involvement in peacekeeping missions, he praised his country's capacity to act abroad 'without some of the baggage that so many other Western countries have, either colonial pasts or perceptions of American imperialism'.[1] The point both leaders had emphasized was that in a world in which the legacies of colonialism are still keenly felt, Canadian foreign policy benefitted from the country's lack of overseas colonies. Grounded in self-aggrandizing views, both statements drew the ire of commentators who pointed to the practice of colonialism within Canada itself, though unlike Harper, Trudeau had admitted that Canadians had 'consistently marginalized, engaged in colonial behaviours, in destructive behaviours, in assimilationist behaviours' towards indigenous people.

The notion of a Canada free of colonialism has a potent hold. Praising former governor general Michaëlle Jean's appointment as secretary general of La Francophonie in 2014, the *Toronto Star* assumed that the Haitian-born Canadian's candidacy was helped 'by Canada's lack of baggage as a colonial power', a selling point with Africans mindful of past French conduct.[2] This viewpoint was especially common during the mid-twentieth-century wave of decolonization. At its 1960 national convention, the social democratic Cooperative Commonwealth Federation resolved that as 'a nation untainted by colonialism', Canada was well positioned to assume UN peacekeeping duties. Asian and African countries, a young Liberal Party activist wrote soon after, admired Canada because 'unlike many Western nations, we have no past record of imperialism or colonialism'.[3] Indeed, Canada was once a colony, a point officials were keen to emphasize as a means of building bridges to what was then called the Third World. Perhaps taking this position too far, Arnold Smith, a Canadian diplomat who served as the first Commonwealth secretary general, was fond of referring to 'a string of leaders of successful national liberation movements, starting with Canada's Sir John Macdonald and running up through Nehru and Nkrumah and Kenyatta'.[4]

The first Canadian prime minister, Macdonald, is famous for his campaign slogan 'A British subject I was born, a British subject I will die', words certainly never uttered by Kenyatta, Nkrumah, or Nehru. Moreover, Macdonald was white, as were most Canadians during his time in office, and their experience of empire was very different from that of colonial subjects in Africa, Asia, or the Caribbean. Or of indigenous people in Canada. Although later generations were happy to overlook Canadian colonialism, Macdonald and the other so-called Fathers of Confederation had been clear that their goal was to create not only a new country but, through westward expansion and a trans-continental railway, a new empire, a 'Great Britannic Empire of the North'.[5] Control of this vast territory required the Canadian government to negotiate treaties – by definition, international agreements – with the indigenous people who lived in this region, a process that casts dark light on the nature and conduct of Canadian external relations. Macdonald's nation-building effort rivaled that of Otto von Bismarck, just as his skills at empire-building exceeded those of Cecil Rhodes, who failed to build his own transcontinental railroad. While it is true that Canada did lack overseas colonies, certain Canadians eyed the West Indies as a potential colony (and continue to hold thoughts of bringing Turks and Caicos into Confederation) just as they also considered running a League of Nations mandate – a quasi-colony – in Armenia after the First World War. Furthermore, soldiers from Canada participated in British colonial campaigns, most notably the Boer War, and at the height of European imperialism many Canadians, viewing themselves as citizens of a British World, gloried in the achievements of their empire. There was opposition to these developments, just as there are opponents today of what some Canadians, largely on the left, see as Canada's support for American imperialism, or Canada's neocolonial involvement in the Global South through multinational corporations, global economic institutions, and military intervention. Since the 1960s it has even been common to see critics of the economic, cultural, and political status quo contend that Canada has come full circle – from a colony of Britain to a 'colonial dependency' of the United States.[6] The story of Canada and colonialism is rich and complex, connecting internal and external affairs, and bringing the Canadian experience into play with larger currents in international history.

Examining important and multifaceted issues such as Canadian experiences with colonialism is at the heart of *Canada and the World since 1867.* My focus in this book is on Canadian international relations, broadly defined. As part of the New Approaches to International History series, this study takes a wide approach accounting for developments in international history, a venerable field of study that, despite what its critics may think, has advanced far from its origins of analysing 'what one clerk wrote to another'.[7] From traditional diplomatic and military issues, to questions of immigration and human rights, to the influence of culture and finance, my aim is to showcase the complexity of Canadian interactions with the world. However, while incorporating transnational perspectives and placing Canada within global frameworks, this book, as a work of international history, stays primarily centered around international relations. Yet, as I emphasize – to the extent that word limits permit – it is important to look beyond officials and diplomats and incorporate other Canadians whose actions or ideas took them beyond Canada's borders. At the same time, it is vital not to ignore the foreign policymakers within government. Similarly, while this is a book about international affairs, it seeks to connect Canada's foreign and domestic politics. Elsewhere, I have made the case for why this type of wide-ranging analysis matters to the future of Canadian international history.[8] Briefly put, Canadian political history has undergone an essential revitalization and now incorporates a broad range of viewpoints and issues. While not losing its focus on international relations, Canadian international history is benefitting by following suit. Herein, I offer a stab in this direction.

Canada and the World since 1867 focuses on four broad themes. First, it looks at Canada's complex relationships with Britain and the British World, by exploring the more-than-century-long process of Canadian decolonization. While Canada gained control over its domestic affairs in 1867, London retained formal control of Canadian foreign policy until 1931. Other ties to Britain – a separate court system, control over Canada's constitution – were broken over subsequent decades. Decolonization took so long because imperial allegiances retained a strong hold on Canadians, as did notions of Canada as an inheritor of a British imperial ethos. Through migration, culture, and economics, many Canadians identified as British and lived within a British World, an interconnected polity stretching across the globe. Such ideas led to continued support for British imperial ventures well into the middle of the twentieth century and drove Canada's own empire-building initiatives abroad and at home. Indeed, traces of these concepts continue to infuse notions of Canada as part of the Anglosphere, the club of English-speaking peoples, and as a power that deploys military and diplomatic assets in support of nation-building ventures in the Global South.[9] Resistance to such notions was apparent, whether from Canadians who wanted to forge their own independent country or those who objected to British imperialism.

Second, this book analyzes Canada's vital connections with the United States, a country that looms large thanks to its economic, cultural, and political power. As consumers of American culture and goods, as exporters of natural resources, and as major participants in US military and security initiatives, Canadians rank as Americans' foremost trading partners and allies. This situation did not develop overnight, but occurred through the intermingling of peoples, ideas, cultures, economies, and institutions. The process did not go uncontested. In common with people around the world, Canadians have confronted the onslaught of American civilization with varying degrees of hostility, acceptance, and adaptation.[10] A major theme developed here is how Canadians sought to manage their relations with a country that, over the course of Canada's history, rose from a continental power to a global empire.[11] Canadians' own trajectory, emphasized below, has been toward acceptance of Canada's fate as a North American country.

Third, while Canada's relations with Britain and the United States are important, this study examines Canadians' interactions with the non-Western world, the new point of emphasis in Canadian international and transnational history. As this recent scholarship attests, Canadians took seriously their contacts with the Global South, where they wrestled with issues of racism, human rights, and development. As with relations with the British World and the United States, dealings with the colonial world, and later the Third World, were reciprocal, with Canadians drawing upon examples from abroad. Student radicals protesting American economic penetration of Canada and Québécois nationalists demanding an independent Quebec drew upon the language of anti-colonialism. Moreover, attention to anti-colonial conflicts abroad focused attention on colonialism at home, and a theme running throughout the book is the Canadian state's international relationships with aboriginal peoples. Historians have devoted mounting attention to this settler colonialism, which in its Canadian context has meant challenging the view that 'colonialism happened elsewhere'.[12] It is here that Canadian international history appears in a most critical light.

Finally, *Canada and the World since 1867* explores the evolution and impact of various ideas about Canada's place in the world, the nature of Canadian foreign policy – including colonialism – and various internationalisms, from the liberal internationalism guiding belief in multilateralism to the fascism popular in the 1930s.[13] Some of these concepts are almost uniquely Canadian – the idea of Canada as a middle power and the concept of North Americanism – while white supremacy and human rights are global phenomena that have received growing attention in international history as has the connection between immigration and foreign relations.[14] An emphasis, too, is how Canadians have managed the interplay between the local and the global, especially during the two periods of globalization at the start and end of the twentieth century. Yet

Canadians have always been buffeted by global currents. Again, this book is not a true transnational history as its focal point remains Canada's international relations. A final caveat: while incorporating primary research, the bulk of this book draws upon the rich and evolving history of a country deserving of greater attention within the field of international history writ large.

1

Dominion-building and empire-building

In 1884, the Canadian government arranged for one thousand members of the British Association for the Advancement of Science to visit Canada. This motley collection of scientists from various disciplines traversed the Dominion to see for themselves 'Anglo-Saxon, British-Canadian enterprise spreading' from Montreal to the Pacific. Soon after, journalist George Ham trekked from Manitoba across the prairies and over the Rocky Mountains, a trip eased by the completion of the transcontinental Canadian Pacific Railway (CPR) in 1885. To Ham, the vast area of the west was 'tenantless and silent, only awaiting the Anglo-Saxon race to be transformed into a prosperous and thriving country'. Addressing Canadians in the east, he appealed for an infusion of investment and manpower as 'the required element in developing the young, but sturdy, Dominion into the Greater Britain of the West'.[1] Full of enthusiasm, these comments showcase a sense of promise about what might become of Canada; in imagining themselves as the inheritors of British imperialism in North America, these men saw the new country as an empire in its own right. Coming at the height of Victorian-era imperialism, appeals for Canada to embark on its own empire-building project highlight that Canadians were no strangers to colonialism. Not only did Sir John A. Macdonald and other Canadian politicians set out, quite successfully, to build a new federation of provinces, but, as these characterizations attest, they also built an empire. For good reason one British historian listed the Fathers of Confederation 'among the greatest of Victorian empire-builders'.[2] The point is worth dwelling upon because recent efforts to describe Canada in colonial terms, specifically as a settler colony, have been pooh-poohed by detractors as faddish tripe.

In reviewing Canadian nation-building efforts in the first few decades following Confederation, this chapter makes clear that what Canada's government and its supporters achieved was colonial expansion, complete with a subject population. British imperialism – and French colonialism before it – had been central to the settling of eastern and central Canada as well as the Pacific Coast. But settlement of the West and expansion into British Columbia's (BC's) interior were Canadian efforts, conducted by the new Dominion government, and part of a wider process that occurred across the 'Anglo-World'. In Australia, South Africa, New Zealand, the United States, and Canada, settlers fanned out into territory supposedly empty of people and ripe for development. As writer Stephen Leacock put it, 'The continent was, in truth, one vast silence, broken only by the roar of the waterfall or the cry of the beasts and the birds of the forest.'[3] Of course, these territories were not empty and so the drive for expansion and the acquisition of land for settlement led to confrontations between settlers and indigenous people.[4]

Whereas other types of colonialism have centred around the exploitation of subject people, territory is settler colonialism's central element, requiring the 'elimination of the native'.[5] In Canada's case, this process involved the subjugation, segregation, and attempted assimilation of indigenous peoples and the assertion of control over their land. Aboriginals were not passive in this process, but, ultimately, Canadian dominion was established from sea to sea to sea. Given that indigenous peoples constituted sovereign nations with whom Canada's government concluded treaties – by definition, international agreements – colonial expansion casts a new light on the conduct of Canadian diplomacy. Moreover, the treatment of these subject people raises troubling questions about ethnic cleansing and genocide, politically fraught terms that I shall avoid.[6] Rather, I take historian Margaret Jacobs's point that settler colonialism is a preferable phrase, 'not because what happened to Indians was not egregious but because it was different from what happened to Jews in Europe, Muslims in Bosnia, or Tutsis in Rwanda'.[7] For indigenous people, Canadian nation-building came at a cost. As for Canada's government, it gained a huge expanse, advertised to would-be settlers as the Last Best West.

Canadian Confederation in 1867 occurred against a backdrop of momentous events that tested the federal model of government, including the US Civil War, the Wars of German Unification, and the unification of Italy. Canada's creation as a merger among three British colonies was decidedly more low-key, the result of negotiation and statute. Canadian colonists were mindful of this difference. 'We are striving to do peacefully and satisfactorily what Holland and Belgium, after years of strife, were unable to accomplish', stated politician George Brown. 'We are seeking by calm discussion to settle questions that Austria and Hungary, that Denmark and Germany, that Russia and Poland, could only crush by the iron heel of armed force.' Eyeing events to the south, he added, 'We are striving to settle forever issues hardly less momentous than those that have rent the neighboring republic and are now exposing it to all the horrors of civil war.'[8] John A. Macdonald, too, was conscious of the US example, judging that because 'of the fratricidal war, Canada had every prospect of being the great nation on this continent'.[9] The American union's fracture and the resulting conflict influenced Macdonald's thinking about the need for a strong federal government, though on this point he faced pushback from other colonial politicians, who sought to preserve provincial interests.

For the British North American colonies, the US Civil War proved vitally important. Driven by a mix of economic and political motives, roughly forty thousand Canadians – including several thousand black people – fought during the conflict, mainly for the Union, while around fifteen thousand Union deserters fled north to find refuge, just as thousands of freed slaves had done via the Underground Railroad. Britain's support of the South, and the actions of Confederate spies and agents in the British colonies, outraged Union officials. Mounting Anglo-American tension generated fears that the victorious Union army would march north and annex the colonies.[10] Although cancelling its 1854 reciprocity treaty with the colonies, military annexation was not on the minds of officials in Washington. A related notion did appeal to several hundred Irish American veterans and members of the Fenian Brotherhood, a transnational group committed to Ireland's independence. Aiming to seize Canada and ransom it to London in exchange for Ireland, in 1866, they mounted several raids, even scoring a minor win over Canadian militia at Ridgeway, the only victory for Irish independence between 1798 and 1919.[11] Fenian attacks continued until 1871; what they mainly accomplished was the union of three of Britain's North American colonies, which banded together not only to create a common market in the face of the loss of reciprocity with the United States but for mutual self-defence against military threats from the south.

The British North America Act, passed by Britain's Parliament, united New Brunswick, Nova Scotia, and the Province of Canada – comprising Canada East (Quebec) and Canada West (Ontario) – and on 1 July 1867, a new country was created, albeit one with limited powers. Preferring to protect local interests, the colonies of Prince Edward Island (PEI) and Newfoundland opted out of Confederation, a reminder of the divisions among the colonial governments. One historian put it well in noting that in creating Canada, the Fathers of Confederation took each other 'not by the hand but rather by the throat'.[12] The year 1867 was not an end point. PEI became a province in 1873, and occasional efforts were made to bring Newfoundland into the federation, though this effort took until 1949.

What captured the attention of leading Canadian politicians, especially those from Ontario, was the West. This territory, George Brown proclaimed, had to be 'opened up to civilization'. His newspaper, the *Globe*, urged the creation of 'the most magnificent empire on the face of the earth, which yet remains in a state of nature'.[13] Thomas D'Arcy McGee – assassinated by a Fenian in 1868 – affirmed that the Dominion's future 'depends on our early occupation of the rich prairie land', a judgement supported by Edward Blake, who saw that Canada's future 'as a distinct state, the representative of British power on this continent, largely depends upon our success in colonizing that region'.[14] Much like the later scramble for Africa, Canadian officials saw an imperial competition with the United States – a scramble for the West. 'I would be quite willing, personally, to leave that whole country of wilderness for the next half-century', Macdonald had admitted in 1865, 'but I fear if Englishmen do not go there, Yankees will.' Five years later, he remained convinced that Americans were 'resolved to do all they can, short of war, to get possession of the western territory and we must take immediate and vigorous steps to counteract them'.[15]

The sense of competition with the Americans likewise fuelled Dominion politicians' interest in absorbing the colony of British Columbia into the federation. Animating them were US Secretary of State William Seward's statements about annexing the colony, a concern magnified by the acquisition of Alaska in 1867, and the activities of some vocal, though not particularly numerous, annexationists within BC. Only days after Confederation, the *Globe* warned Seward against thoughts of northern expansion – Canadians would 'stand by the old flag to the last man and to the last cartridge' – and urged Ottawa to work with BC politicians in 'building up a new nationality on this continent', one 'superior' to the United States.[16] Terms were eventually negotiated, and BC entered Confederation in 1871. This development, one Canadian senator noted, created 'one great country stretching from the Atlantic to the Pacific'. 'Our country has expanded into a broad empire', wrote another commentator.[17] Among the terms was the requirement that Canada build a railroad linking the Pacific province to the east. Macdonald and other eastern politicians wanted a transcontinental railroad to reach BC and to provide the means of peopling the West.

By the time BC became a Canadian province, Ottawa's plans for developing the plains were already in train. In 1869, in one of the largest land deals in history, Canada had purchased Rupert's Land – the sweeping territory from Northern Ontario to the Rocky Mountains – from the Hudson's Bay Company. Yet, the newly named North-West Territories were inhabited already. Following the logic of settler colonialism, the Canadian government's goal of acquiring territory meant eliminating indigenous control. One advocate of Western expansion put this position plainly: 'Canada must ere long attain to a high position in the scale of nations, and thus leave little room for regret that the possession of her soil has been transferred to the Anglo-Saxon race, and that the rule of the fierce Indian has for ever passed away.'[18] Later commenting on the westward flow of 'the Anglo-Saxon wave of civilization' over land that was 'too valuable to be kept as mere buffalo preserves', Methodist missionary E. R. Young spoke in glowing terms of colonial progress. Where there were once 'rude native-made boats manned by human muscles', now there were the 'shrieks and shrill whistles' of steamboats and railways, which had 'awakened the echoes amid the' solitudes of centuries, and now everything in that land seems to feel the throbbing pulse of a new and active life'.[19] Colonial expansion did not go uncontested.

Within Rupert's Land lay Red River, a fur-trading settlement populated largely by the Métis, a distinct people of mixed indigenous and European – mainly French and Scottish – ancestry. With the Canadian government's purchase of the territory, Red River residents rightly feared for their future. When land surveyors and a governor arrived at the edge of the territory, an armed Métis party turned them back. Soon, the Métis took control of the administrative hub of Fort Garry, founded a provisional government, and, under the leadership of Louis Riel, entered negotiations with Canada about their future status. Tensions rose, however, when armed members of the Canadian Party – an anti-Catholic, anti-French group – sought to seize control of Red River. The execution of one of the coup plotters outraged opinion in Ontario, and Ottawa arranged for the dispatch of military forces, whose putative purpose was to secure Red River against American encroachment.

Given the lack of a Canadian military, the contingent consisted of the remaining British garrison under Colonel Garnet Wolseley, a hero of British imperial adventures, later celebrated as Gilbert and Sullivan's very model of a modern major general. Praising the despatch of this force, Toronto's mayor told a rally of five thousand people of his confidence 'that the same power which had been able to make itself felt at Lucknow and Delhi would be sufficient to put down that miserable creature (cheers) who attempts to usurp authority at Fort Garry and establish again the supremacy and glory of the British flag'.[20] The military force trekked overland from Ontario to Red River, arriving too late to accomplish much beyond showing the flag. Riel, held responsible for the killing, fled to the United States, where he became a citizen.[21] Meanwhile, Ottawa had agreed to most of the Métis demands, and the province of Manitoba entered Confederation in July 1870. Among the rights extended – and not fully honoured by Ottawa – were linguistic and religious protections, as well as a land, which Macdonald characterized as 'a reservation for the purpose of extinguishing the Indian title grant', recognition that such title existed in the minds of Canadian officials if only long enough to get rid of it.[22]

With suzerainty established over Red River, the Canadian government began demonstrating its authority over the North-West Territories. Between

1872 and 1874, Canadian, British, and American surveyors set about physically demarcating the Canada–US border along the 49th parallel (established by an 1818 treaty), from the Lake of the Woods to the Rockies. Unlike in the east, the western border lacks natural barriers, and the placing of boundary markers did little to close what remained a permeable frontier.[23]

On the Canadian side of the line, the surveyors were joined by the North-West Mounted Police (NWMP), a paramilitary force formed in 1873 on the model of the Royal Irish Constabulary. 'With emigrants of all Nations flowing into the country, we are in constant danger of an Indian war', Macdonald worried in 1871. 'This may be prevented only by an early organization of a mounted police.'[24] The NWMP's first task was establishing Canadian sovereignty vis-à-vis the United States. Following its march west in 1874, the force expelled American traders operating in Canada. Initially, indigenous groups welcomed the Mounties' presence for there had been attacks by American traders, including a massacre in the Cypress Hills. Natose-Onista (Medicine Calf) of the Kainai Nation (Blood Tribe) told Alexander Morris, the territorial lieutenant governor, that 'before the arrival of the Police, when I laid my head down at night, every sound frightened me; my sleep was broken; now I can sleep sound and I am not afraid.' Similarly, Isapo-Muxika (Crowfoot), chief of the Siksika (Blackfoot), remarked to a missionary that 'he was much pleased with the change that the coming of the Mounted Police had brought in all the west'.[25] Feelings of relief were fleeting. A missionary informed Morris in 1875 that indigenous people on the plains 'have an awful dread of the future. They think that Police are in the country not only to keep out whiskey traders, but also to protect white people against them, and that this country will be gradually taken away from them without any ceremony.'[26]

The Mounties' main focus was enforcing sovereignty internally and by 1880s, protection of settlers was key. In 1882, the NWMP commissioner ordered that it was 'imperative' that settlers 'receive good police protection from such a large body of Indians ... as well as that order should be kept among the Indians themselves', and as Macdonald reiterated, 'the business of the Mounted Police is principally to keep peace between white-men + Indians.'[27] Meanwhile in the Pacific Northwest, Royal Navy gunboats continued to impose order as they had prior to Confederation, policing intertribal conflict, and enforcing Canadian sovereignty and laws. The gunboats' reach was limited by their inability to project power beyond coastal and interior waterways, and so these vessels constituted the 'armed might of the fragile system' of Canadian rule in BC in the years leading up to the railroad's completion.[28]

Establishing Canadian sovereignty over the North-West Territories and BC meant denying the sovereignty of indigenous groups. The creation of the Canada–US border was a facet of this process, one that, from an indigenous and Métis perspective, created a false divide separating groups whose own boundaries extended beyond the 49th parallel.[29] The surveying work aside, the border remained open, and, in 1877, a minor crisis ensued when three thousand Očhéthi Šakówiŋ (Sioux) under Tȟatȟáŋka Íyotake (Sitting Bull) crossed into Canada after having defeated Colonel George Custer's cavalry. At a time when Prime Minister Alexander Mackenzie's government was working to control the indigenous population within Canada, the presence of this large, armed contingent was unwelcome. Lacking the military forces necessary to assert itself in the West, Ottawa urged London to press the US government to repatriate the Očhéthi Šakówiŋ, but to little avail. In response, Mackenzie dispatched a special mission to Washington to lobby on Canada's behalf, a brief Canadian foray into diplomacy independent of Britain. As for Tȟatȟáŋka Íyotake, with Ottawa unwilling to grant land or rations, he and his people departed Canada in 1881.[30] Over the course of the following two decades, whether through the NWMP's policing efforts on the plains or the imposition of territorial boundaries over waterways in coastal BC, the border effectively thickened, upsetting indigenous patterns of life.[31]

Of greater impact to indigenous peoples than the closure of the border was the loss of territory. The Dominion Lands Act of 1872 and the formation of the Department of the Interior were attempts to create a western land boom; without a rail link, few settlers took up the opportunity of cheap land particularly in such a forbidding climate. Macdonald's plans to construct a transcontinental railroad were foiled by his own corruption, with a bribery scandal leading to the collapse of his government and the election of Alexander Mackenzie's Liberals in 1873. A tight-fisted Scot, Mackenzie had little interest in the railroad because of its exorbitant cost, so when Macdonald returned to office in 1878, the project was stalled. Macdonald launched his National Policy of high tariffs on British and US imports, and mounted a new push for a transcontinental railroad. The goal was to build up industry in central Canada and to create a large market for manufactured goods in the West, with a railway the key to encouraging settlement. The National Policy was presented as being more than a simple economic policy. 'Until this great work is completed, our Dominion is little more than a geographical expression', Macdonald explained.[32] In 1881, construction of the main portion of the railroad across the prairies was begun by the newly created CPR. By that point, Canada had established its control over the region through treaties with indigenous groups.

In 1871, Canadian officials had begun negotiating the Numbered Treaties, a series of eleven treaties with indigenous groups in the North-West. Concluded between 1871 and 1877, the first seven treaties solidified Canadian control of the bulk of the prairies; the remaining treaties, negotiated between 1899 and 1921, covered land in northern Canada. In BC, no treaties were signed over control of the mainland portion of the province, a fact that did not prevent settler encroachment over lands, waterways, and resources.

Since the Numbered Treaties were international agreements, in effect the treaty-negotiating process marked Canada's first major, independent foray into international diplomacy, though here Ottawa was bound to follow the British model, established with the Royal Proclamation of 1763, of recognizing indigenous land tenure and sovereignty by making treaty with them. As scholars have long noted, Canadian and indigenous cultural differences tended to produce different understandings of the treaties.[33] Ottawa's main concern with these agreements was land and so from this perspective the Numbered Treaties were a success.

Indigenous negotiators recognized the Canadian government's goal, and from their perspective, the treaties were meant to establish the terms by which sovereign entities would coexist on shared land. During the Treaty 6 negotiations, Pîhtokahanapiwiyin (Poundmaker) a young Nêhiyawak (Plains Cree), affirmed, 'This is our land, it isn't a piece of pemmican to be cut off and given in little pieces back to us.' 'The sound of the rustling of the gold is under my feet where I stand', stated Chief Mawedopenais of the Saulteaux band of the Ojibwa amid talks over Treaty 3 in 1873, 'where we stand upon is the Indians' property'.[34] Land was not the treaties' only aspect. The agreements carried the promise of farming implements, seed, livestock, medical assistance, and annuities, all obligations that, as shrewd bargainers, indigenous leaders forced the Canadian government to accept. As for why indigenous groups on the plains entered into and accepted the Numbered Treaties, disease was devastating their communities; bison, a source of food, fuel, and clothing had been driven near extinction; and the example of the US wars against aboriginals south of the 49th parallel provided a vivid example of what organized state violence could accomplish in the pursuit of territory.[35]

With the Numbered Treaties in place, indigenous groups were herded onto allotments of land held in trust by the federal government. Some individuals moved to reserves willingly, others for reasons of basic survival: the years 1878–80 saw the collapse of the bison herds. While the smattering of government officials in the region scrambled to distribute rations, starvation provided an opportunity for Ottawa to assert its will. The Macdonald government used food as a cudgel to force recalcitrant indigenous groups to take treaty and move to reserves. Although thousands died of starvation and disease, there was only the barest sense of a humanitarian crisis. Macdonald put the issue plainly: 'we cannot allow them to die for want of food', but yet his officials were 'doing all they can, by refusing food until the Indians are on the verge of starvation, to reduce the expense'.[36] The policy of 'clearing the plains' worked, and by 1883, the last holdout chief, Mistahimaskwa (Big Bear), had taken treaty and most of the surviving indigenous people on the prairies were on reserve.[37] Macdonald, who served concurrently as prime minister and minister of the interior, a post giving him oversight of indigenous policy, was not wrong when he stated, in comments recognizing the process of settler colonialism, that, 'We must remember that they are the original owners of the soil, of which they have been dispossessed by the covetousness or ambition of our ancestors.... At all events, the Indians have been great sufferers by the discovery of America, and the transfer to it of a large white population.'[38] What emerged from the famine was a disconnect between the diplomatic response to indigenous communities in the North-West, which had recognized them as sovereign entities, and the administrative one, which treated them as subject people.

Government policy transformed indigenous people into colonial subjects. On reserve, individuals were expected to take up farming, but other than 'two acres and a cow' they were given little instruction or assistance.[39] Traditional governance systems were ignored, and indigenous lives were managed by the Department of Indian Affairs, created in 1880 to oversee the reserves and enforce laws pertaining to indigenous people. Government-appointed Indian agents governed the reserves; like the district officers of the British Empire, they were responsible for the management and protection of subject peoples under their watch. They punished individuals who acted out and rewarded those who were quiescent. Indian agents imposed the pass system – introduced in 1885, in the midst of an uprising on the plains, and in place for decades thereafter – which prohibited people on reserve from leaving without approval.[40] Further, the federal government banned a variety of religious ceremonies, though they continued to be practiced in secret.[41] The crackdown on cultural practices and the pass system reflected the duality of Canadian policy: on the one hand, the government sought to assimilate indigenous people into the wider population; on the other, they were to be segregated from the general populace. These notions were enshrined in the Indian Act of 1876, which remains in place nearly a century and a half later.

Applying to indigenous people throughout the country and not just to those on the prairies, the Indian Act allowed the federal government to manage the lands, resources, and money of those people defined as 'Indians'. This categorization was important, for not only did it create a group of subject peoples, it created a single race, Indians, out of what was a diverse array of groups living across a continent. Individuals given Indian Status were denied most rights, with the legislation holding out the possibility that in exchange for the franchise Indians could gain equal rights by giving up their status, thereby no longer being 'Indian'; female Indians would lose their status by marrying non-Indians. This policy – 'a human, just and Christian' one in the words of Alexander Mackenzie, whose government implemented it – created a subclass of people who were the responsibility of the government until they had advanced to the level of white Canadians.[42] Bringing civilization to North America's indigenous population extended back to early contact, but it found new impetus in the Victorian-era high tide of empire. Missionaries who fanned out across the prairies, BC, and the Arctic in the decades after Confederation fancied themselves ' "path-finders" for multitudes to follow; we were foundation builders of empire; we were forerunners of a Christian civilization.' 'The great aim of our civilization', Macdonald explained in 1887, 'has been to do away with the tribal system and assimilate the Indian people in all respects with the inhabitants of the Dominion, as speedily as they are fit for change.'[43]

The civilizing mission, with its goal of assimilating and thereby eliminating indigenous people, drove the development of industrial schools. Modelled after institutions in the United States and begun by the Catholic and Anglican churches in the early 1800s, the schools aimed to transform indigenous children into civilized Canadians. Once the reserve system was in place, government interest in the idea grew, and a partnership was formed with the churches. 'When the school is on the reserve', Macdonald stated publicly, 'the child lives with its parents who are savages, and though he may learn to read and write, his habits and training and mode of thought are Indian. He is simply a savage who can read and write.' The solution was to remove indigenous children and place them into schools away from reserves, 'where they will acquire the habits and modes of thought of white men'.[44] The Inspector of Indian Schools in the west voiced an added bonus, namely that it was 'unlikely that any Tribe or Tribes would give trouble of a serious nature to the Government whose members had children completely under Government control'.[45] From the 1870s to 1997, when the last school closed, 30 percent of indigenous children in Canada passed through the residential school system, and of the 150,000 students, roughly 6,000 died of disease and malnutrition. Students were subjected to various forms of abuse as well as to medical experiments. In its emphasis on assimilation, the Indian Residential School system was 'an instrument of attempted cultural genocide', as indeed is the Indian Act, measures both meant to eliminate indigenous language, culture, and, in effect, people. 'Our objective', an administrator later explained, 'is to continue until there is not a single Indian in Canada that has not been absorbed into the body politic, and there is no Indian question, and no Indian Department'.[46] Rare is it to see a civil servant hope for the elimination of their department, but that is the logic undergirding Canada's indigenous policies.

Starvation, segregation, and the seizure of children belie a positive view that many Canadians take of their treatment of indigenous people, largely because they compared themselves to the United States, where warfare was a dominant factor on the plains. The peaceful frontier, noted a military historian, is 'one of these self-congratulatory myths which bind a nation together', and it has a ring of truth, for between 1866 and 1895 the US Army fought 945 engagements against indigenous people, while Canada's military fought seven; throughout the 1870s, the US government spent $20 million per year on these campaigns, whereas Canada's total budget during this decade averaged $19 million.[47] As has been the case on so many issues, Canadians were keen to draw a favourable comparison with the Americans. The Mackenzie government justified the expenditures made via the Numbered Treaties as a preferable alternative to 'the deplorable war' against aboriginals in the United States. American policy towards indigenous people, for the *Globe*, was 'a dark record of broken pledges, undisguised oppression and triumphant cruelty'. One Manitoba journalist added that there would be no 'Indian war in Canada' since Canada's aboriginals knew that they were 'under the protection of the Great Mother' and that the Canadian government would 'faithfully carry out the agreements made under the Treaties by which his title to the soil was surrendered'.[48] Canadian policy was hardly virtuous, and in 1885, there was an armed conflict in the North-West. Yet, few indigenous people on the plains took part in this revolt even as they had every reason to fight against Canada's government.

The 1885 North-West Rebellion – or Resistance, depending on one's taste – was largely the work of Métis who had left Manitoba and moved west following the federal government's failure to abide by guarantees given following the Red River standoff. Concerns about land and political rights motivated Métis protest in 1884 and violent action early the following year. Under the leadership of Louis Riel, who had been convinced to return to Canada, the Métis were in open revolt in the hopes of repeating what they had done in 1870: force Canada to accede to political demands and the creation of a new province in which Métis rights would be guaranteed. The Métis sought indigenous assistance in their confrontation with Ottawa, but leading chiefs were reluctant to fight. Instead, Mistahimaskwa and Payipwat pressed the Canadian government to live up to its treaty obligations and sought a diplomatic solution. There was sporadic and even accidental indigenous participation in the events, largely the result of youth who ignored the wishes of their elders and of the overzealousness of Canada's military forces. There was no large-scale indigenous uprising except in the minds of worried settlers who expected the worst from the 'savages'. Indigenous quiescence was helped along by the deployment of Canadian soldiers to reserves and by increased rations.[49]

Canada of 1885 was not Canada of 1870 and the federal government was now capable of confronting the Métis challenge. Opting for a military response, Macdonald likened the uprising to the current British campaign in Sudan against forces led by the Mahdi, a Muslim fundamentalist. Riel, he told the House of Commons, was 'a sort of half-breed Mahdi' who had to be dealt with sternly.[50] Five hundred Mounties and over 5,300 volunteer militia from the provinces left to secure the region, moving quickly along the completed portions of the new railway, a testament to how, as in Africa, railroads allowed the projection of imperial power. In another sign of technological prowess, the Canadians carried with them a Gatling gun on loan from the US Army. Overall command of the Canadian forces fell to Colonel Frederick Middleton, a British veteran of imperial campaigns in India and New Zealand. The ensuing fighting was scattered and smallscale, with the Métis forces effective in waging guerrilla-style attacks on the larger Canadian forces, whose record in the field is best summed up by the title of one participant's campaign memoir, *Reminiscences of a Bungle, by One of the Bunglers*.[51] Still, Canadian forces captured Batoche, the Métis capital, and the Métis fighters and the smattering of indigenous warriors were brought to heel. When the Canadian volunteers returned home, they were feted as imperial heroes, who, in the words of the *Toronto Mail*, had 'sustained the warlike traditions of their race' and so 'received the warm welcome which British subjects always give to soldiers when they return from those services of danger which we have learned to consider invariably the occasion of victory'.[52]

Imperial justice was swift. Although few indigenous fighters had taken part in the events, Pîhtokahanapiwiyin and other chiefs were compelled to surrender. The assumption in Ottawa was that the uprising was the work of indigenous people writ large. 'I have not hesitated to tell this House, again and again', Macdonald stated after the fighting had ceased, 'that we could not always hope to maintain peace with the Indians; that the savage was still a savage, and that until he ceased to be savage, we were always in danger of a collision, in danger of war, in danger of an outbreak.'[53] Given this assumption, there was a disproportionate breakdown in the prosecution of rebels: forty-six Métis were charged with treason, with seven imprisoned; eighty-one indigenous men were charged and forty-four imprisoned. In one of the most controversial decisions in Canadian history, Macdonald allowed Riel to be hung for treason – although at the time he was a US citizen – a move that outraged French Canadian opinion. Also, Macdonald permitted the hanging of eight indigenous men, in the largest mass execution in Canada since the killing of pro-American traitors during the War of 1812. The prime minister's reasoning was clear: 'The execution of Riel and of the Indians will, I hope, have a good effect on the Métis and convince the Indians that the white man governs.'[54] To ensure that point was not lost, indigenous observers, among them students from the local industrial school at Battleford, were brought to see the executions.[55]

The North-West Rebellion marked the end of large-scale and armed resistance to the spread of Canada's dominion over the continent. The hangings at Battleford occurred on 27 November; Riel was hung on 16 November, fittingly, perhaps, in Regina, named for Queen Victoria, the British empress; and on 7 November financier Donald Smith, the future Lord Strathcona, had driven the last spike of the CPR into the ground at Craigellachie, BC. The following year, Macdonald travelled on the CPR, surveying the Dominion on what was his only cross-country trip. In the end, judged the historian Goldwin Smith in 1891, the Métis had been in the way of 'British and Protestant colonisation' and their small numbers would be 'merged in a great inflow of English-speaking settlers'.[56] As Smith's comment attests, westward expansion had made space available for Anglo-Saxon settlement, yet, initially, re-peopling the plains did not turn out as planned.

Until the 1890s, settlement of the North-West was far from a success. Little wonder given fears of attack by indigenous people, the inhospitable climate and terrain, a poorly performing Canadian economy, and the fact that, until the completion of the railroad, the region was largely inaccessible. Despite cheap land available through the 1872 Dominion Lands Act, few whites lived on the prairies. In a continuation of a tradition going back to the arrival of the Loyalists at the end of the American Rebellion, many of those settlers who did come to Canada's west from the 1870s through to the 1890s were refugees of one sort or another, including Russian and German Mennonites and a group of Icelanders permitted to form their own autonomously governed settlement, New Iceland. Leo Tolstoy helped arrange for the settlement of 7,500 Russian Doukhobors seeking refuge, and Alexander Galt, the Canadian high commissioner in London, convinced Lord Rothschild to sponsor the travel of 1,500 Russian Jews fleeing pogroms. Additionally, there was an influx of several thousand Mormons, recruited from the United States in the mid-1880s for their skill at farming in arid conditions. Anglo-Saxon immigration to the plains proceeded at a slow pace, though by 1886, the North-West Territories were judged to have a sufficient white population that the franchise was extended to all non-indigenous male residents.

An acceleration of Western settlement came with the election in 1896 of a Liberal government under Wilfrid Laurier. Making immigration a major priority, his minister of the interior, Clifford Sifton, launched a massive overseas campaign to encourage immigration. His ideal settler was 'a stalwart peasant in a sheep-skin coat born on the soil, whose forefathers have been farmers for ten generations, with a stout wife and a half-dozen children'.[57] To this end, Canadian immigration agents sought migrants from Russia, Germany, Sweden, and Austria-Hungary and their pamphlets boasted of *The Wondrous West*, of *The Last Best West*, and of *Canada: Land of Opportunity*. The result of Sifton's policies was 'a great Exodus' to the region, although immigrants came not just to fill the West but also to provide workers for central Canada's booming factories as well as cheap, unskilled labour for mining, timber, and the other extractive industries that dotted the country.[58] The numbers are startling: whereas just 17,000 immigrants had come to Canada in 1896, in 1913 there were more than 400,000 newcomers.[59] Cities grew exponentially and the economy boomed. By 1905, enough settlers lived on the prairies that two new provinces, Alberta and Saskatchewan, were created out of the North-West Territories. Conversely, only in the 1930s did Canada's indigenous population experience growth.[60]

Not all immigrants brought into Canada under Sifton's policy were viewed favourably, and non-whites were excluded under his immigration program. Reflecting the prevailing racial hierarchy, preferred immigrants hailed from 'the sturdy races' of northern Europe, who thrived in cold climates, a marker of superiority at the time. 'By the vigour of the North-West winter', wrote one booster of westward settlement, 'the country is preserved from the overflow of Southern Europe.'[61] Eastern Europeans, too, were viewed in an unfavourable light, particularly ethnic Ukrainians, roughly 170,000 of whom came to Canada between 1896 and 1914. 'One look at the disgusting creatures', stated Sir Mackenzie Bowell, a leading Orangemen who served briefly as Conservative prime minister, 'has caused many to marvel that beings bearing the human form could have sunk to such a bestial level.'[62] One British journalist reported that 'the scum of the earth' had come to Canada, and Stephen Leacock warned of a political danger posed by immigrants who were 'mere herds of the proletariat of Europe, the lowest classes of industrial society, without home and work, fit objects for philanthropic pity, but indifferent material from which to build the commonwealth of the future'.[63] Anarchist Emma Goldman's visit to Winnipeg in 1907, prompted the city's mayor to warn that within the city's 'large foreign population' lurked people with 'undesirable elements in their character' that made them susceptible to radical ideas.[64]

Winnipeg became the epicentre of a post-Great War wave of strikes that gripped Canada and led to a nativist backlash against Eastern Europeans, who, in the wake of the Russian revolution, were increasingly suspect in the eyes of government officials and Anglo-Saxon Canadians. A pushback had begun under Sifton's successor, Frank Oliver, who barred further Ukrainian immigration. Presaging concerns voiced a century later by those Canadians worried that Third World immigrants were ill-suited to life in a Western country, Oliver judged that Ukrainians had not reached a requisite 'degree of liberty, civilization, progress or prosperity'. His solution to Canada's population needs was to 'look to our own people and to kindred people upon whose identity and loyalty we can depend'. Socialist politician J. S. Woodsworth agreed, writing in *Strangers within Our Gates*, his tract on immigration, that what Canada required was 'more of our own blood to assist us to maintain in Canada our British traditions and mold the incoming armies of foreigners into loyal British subjects'.[65] If the idea of the British immigrant was welcome, actual British immigrants were sometimes less than ideal. Or, rather, English immigrants were a problem, particularly those hailing from the middle and upper classes, who were viewed as effete and unsuited for work in the hardscrabble economy.

' "No Englishman need apply" ', was a common-enough feature in many early twentieth-century job advertisements that the British press took note.[66] Still, for turn-of-the-century exponents of Canadian Britishness, immigration was one of many issues on which British was judged to be best.

Creating a space for British settlement was at the heart of the empire-building project upon which John A. Macdonald and other politicians had embarked. In the end they were successful, and later generations of Canadians could boast that 'Older Canada sent out her sons to possess the new lands', and that 'these first settlers belonging to the stronger races from which the older portions of Canada were colonized', had settled the new land.[67] The process of settlement came at a cost for those people who occupied the West, reinforcing a prominent assumption that aboriginals were a dying race. 'The Indian tribes are passing away', wrote one missionary, 'and what is done must be done quickly. On the western plains, native songs, wafted in the evening breezes, are the dying requiem of the departing savage.' After touring the plains in 1893, the wife of Canada's governor general wrote of the 'poor folk', whose 'race is yearly diminishing and that bye-and-bye all traces of their existence will have vanished'.[68] Some observers saw this development as natural, but also there was recognition of settler colonialism. Captain William Francis Butler, a British officer who had served in the Red River expedition, reflected on a process that he had seen 'from the Atlantic to the Pacific. First the white man is welcome guest, the honoured visitor; then the greedy hunter, the death-dealing vendor of fire-water and poison; then the settler and exterminator.' 'Poor creatures!', exclaimed George Monro Grant, principal of Queen's University and a leading imperialist. 'Not much use have they ever made of the land; but yet, in admitting the settler, they sign their own death warrants!'[69]

As Grant and Butler recognized, in setting out to transform the world, Anglo-Saxon settlers displaced indigenous people. To varying degrees, what occurred in Canada happened in the United States, Australia, New Zealand, and South Africa. In *The Expansion of England*, historian J. R. Seeley wrote of 'the great English Exodus' and the 'unopposed occupation of empty countries by the nation that happened to have the greatest surplus population and the greatest maritime power'.[70] Of course, the land that the British occupied was not empty, but that view prevailed among those who fanned out to the colonies of settlement. This expansion paralleled the wider march of European imperialism at the end of the nineteenth century. Canadians were no strangers to imperialism, not only because they constructed their own colonial space in the West and established control over subject peoples across the country, but because even after Confederation they remained part of the British Empire and continued to think in terms of this wider imperial framework. Colonialism came easily to nineteenth-century Canadians, many of whom inhabited a

British World. The North-West, George Grant wrote, had developed into 'an integral and important part of the grandest Empire in the world', and for one of Macdonald's political allies, the CPR had established 'an unbroken line of road and railway from the Atlantic to the Pacific through British territory'.[71] These proud statements indicate how imperial-minded Canadians envisaged the Dominion and its early development through the lens of an ongoing connection with Britain.

2

Canada and Greater Britain

Speaking on the campaign trail in 1891, John A. Macdonald denounced his Liberal opponents' proposed policy of free trade with the United States by declaring, 'A British subject I was born – a British subject I will die. With my utmost, with my last breath, will I oppose the veiled treason which attempts by sordid means and mercenary proffers to lure our people from their allegiance.'[1] Among Macdonald's most famous utterances, this emotional appeal to British loyalty resonated with the sizeable portion of the electorate that identified as British. In the later nineteenth century, many Canadians, Macdonald included, viewed their country as a part of Greater Britain, or of the British World.[2] Greater Britain was the polity within which many Canadians lived, at once real and imagined. Trade, investment, migration, and culture were all tangible elements connecting Canada and Canadians not only to the imperial metropole but to a global empire. The British, in the words of French Premier Georges Clémenceau, were '*un peuple planétaire*', and Canadians numbered among them.[3]

Within this global firmament, Canadians saw their country, touted as the first self-governing Dominion, shining brightest, even if Canada still moved within Britain's orbit. Although Confederation in 1867 gave the new Dominion authority on a host of issues, Canada lacked formal autonomy let alone independence, a situation that suited many Canadians just fine. Whether because it was a source of nationalism or, more likely, because European imperialism was at its apogee and in vogue, English Canadians' fervour for the empire only increased in the nearly five decades from Confederation to the start of the Great War.[4] Canadian imperialists sometimes seemed more supportive of the idea of Greater Britain than their counterparts in the United Kingdom. 'The besetting racial sin of the Englishman of the present generation', complained the Toronto *Globe*, 'is that he has not come to realize that the British community includes the Britons of Greater Britain.'[5] Membership in the empire was a source of seeming strength and influence – as participation in the US-led international order after 1945 would be for later generations of Canadians – and whether in Sudan, South Africa, or Flanders, Canadians were willing to spend blood and treasure to protect their empire. Examining Canada's place within the British World from Confederation to the run up to the Great War, this chapter explores how Canadians conceived of their relationship towards the British Empire and how the mindset of imperialism translated itself into Canadian politics and policy. Further, it looks at two central tensions that arose from this worldview.

First, Greater Britain existed not just on maps but in the minds of its adherents. An imagined community, it linked people across the globe who saw themselves as a part of something greater than Canada or Australia or the Raj, thereby allowing Canadians to feel commonalities to Australians or Indians. Like any form of nationalism, the idea of Greater Britain involved defining who belonged and who was to be excluded. In this regard race was central, not simply white and non-white, but the added layer of a belief that to be British was to be Anglo-Saxon. Reinforcing the sense of superiority over indigenous people at home and non-white colonial subjects abroad, the racial categorization deeply ingrained in this worldview also generated ethnic tensions with non-British Canadians.

Second, Greater Britain clashed with a more parochial if still nascent Canadian nationalism. Macdonald himself, for instance, beat the drums of imperialism when it suited him at election time, but he was otherwise cautious to involve Canada in imperial affairs. The period examined here saw efforts by successive Canadian governments, Conservative and Liberal, to eke out some measure of autonomy from London. Yet, politicians only went so far: public opinion seemingly favoured the imperial tie, and Macdonald and his immediate successors saw Canada as a part of Greater Britain. For a century after Confederation, many Canadians viewed their place as being within the British World, and the process of Canada's decolonization – the ballyhooed move from colony to nation – was a long one indeed.

Confederation in 1867 was not an act of independence. Rather, as Macdonald had put it during the debates over a colonial merger, 'a different colonial system is being developed – and it will become, year by year, less a case of dependence on our part and of overruling protection on the part of the Mother Country, and more a case of a healthy and cordial alliance. Instead of looking upon us as a newly independent colony, England will have in us a friendly nation – a subordinate but still a powerful people – to stand by her in North America in peace or in war.'[6] Created with the encouragement of the Colonial Office in London, the new Dominion of Canada – 'Kingdom' had been considered, but was rejected as too offensive to American sensibilities – gained control of internal matters, the regulation of trade, and oversight of defence, but it remained within the empire.[7] The Judicial Council of the British Privy Council stood as the final appellate body in civil and criminal cases, Canada lacked control of its constitution (a responsibility held by the Parliament in London) and of its foreign policy, Canadians remained British subjects as Canadian citizenship did not exist, and a British governor general sat as the representative of the monarch and as the 'human link in the imperial chain' between the Dominion and the Colonial Office.[8] The governor general's role had to be defined. When Prime Minister Alexander Mackenzie complained to Lord Dufferin of his overreach into domestic matters, Dufferin agreed with Mackenzie's affirmation that Canada was not a Crown Colony, but, he tersely added, 'neither are you a Republic'. Still, the Canadian point was made. When the Marquess of Lorne, Dufferin's successor, was appointed, various viceregal powers were eliminated and Lorne was instructed to avoid involvement in internal matters.[9] Mackenzie, meanwhile, founded both the Supreme Court of Canada and the Royal Military College (RMC) of Canada, two small steps towards autonomy, though, as cases could still be appealed in Britain and as Canada's miniscule army functioned as an imperial contingent, these moves were more shadow than substance. Ultimately, Dominion status mattered in that it denoted that Canada, and eventually the other colonies of settlement, differed from the dependant territories of the empire, places that lacked self-government and, not coincidentally, were full of non-white people.

Confederation signified Britain's willingness to turn over most responsibilities of governance to the Canadians, a process that had begun two decades earlier. In London, a group of financiers lobbied for Confederation in the hopes that unification of the colonies would improve their investments, but the decisive factors on the British side were a short-lived wave of imperial retrenchment and a long-term belief that a federation was inevitable.[10] By the 1860s, British politicians were looking inward and the costs of overseeing Canada were judged to be exorbitant. Reflecting popular attitudes, in *Phineas Finn*, Anthony Trollope had his fictional protagonist, serving as colonial undersecretary, declare, 'Not one man in a thousand cares whether the Canadians prosper or fail to prosper', but they did care 'that Canada should not go to the States because, though they don't love the Canadians, they do hate the Americans'.[11] With self-government granted, between 1869 and 1871 Britain withdrew its frontier garrison along the Canada–US border, the last contingent leaving after having asserted Ottawa's authority over Red River. 'An Army maintained in a country which does not permit us even to govern it!' Benjamin Disraeli had grumbled. 'What is the use of these colonial deadweights which we do not govern?'[12] London retained two naval bases, at Esquimalt and Halifax, part of the imperial defence network.

Beyond the withdrawal of British forces, in 1871, Macdonald sat as a British delegate to an Anglo-American conference in Washington. Called to resolve differences stemming from London's support for the Confederate cause during the Civil War, the British saw an accord with the United States as a means of improving Canada–US relations, thereby ruling out the need for the departing garrison. Macdonald, too, wanted improved relations, including a renewed reciprocity deal with the United States, but the issue was a non-starter. The failure to achieve a trade agreement, and a clause in the 1871 Washington Treaty granting Americans fishing rights in Canadian waters, strained the Canada–Britain relationship. The British, Macdonald complained, sought only 'to go home to England with a treaty in their pockets, settling everything, no matter at what cost to Canada'.[13] On a positive note, via the Washington Treaty the US government gave de facto recognition of Canada's existence.

That the British looked out for their own interests no doubt came as little surprise to Macdonald, a consummate politician, and he himself placed the interests of the new country above those of the empire. With a floundering economy, in 1879, he introduced the National Policy, which increased tariffs not just on US goods but on manufactured imports from Britain, hardly a move fostering intra-imperial trade. The tariffs sparked increased US and British investment into the country, and cemented the importance of the City of London to early Canadian economic development. However, the financial taps did not always flow. Outlining for Macdonald the difficulty in securing funding for the CPR, George Stephen complained that 'Jumbo, the big elephant brought by Barnum, is a matter of ten times more interest to London than twenty Colonies.'[14] Beyond economic concerns, Macdonald had little interest in imperial defence. He told the Commission on the Defence of British Possessions and Commerce Abroad, set up by the Colonial Office to review empire-wide defence issues, that Canada wished to stay away from colonial wars.[15] As a politician, he recognized that public opinion might force the government into contributing troops to a conflict. 'I think if war were imminent', he wrote, 'the spirit of the people themselves will force on the Legislature and the Government of the day the necessity for taking an active part in it.'[16] Macdonald was not wrong on this point, for imperial sentiments ran high in Canada on matters of warfare, as he, and later Laurier, were to find.

By the 1880s, British enthusiasm for empire recovered from its decline two decades earlier, with growing competition from other European powers generating imperial fervour. In this light, in 1884, the British turned to Canada for assistance in Sudan. As part of the effort to relieve British forces besieged at Khartoum, London sought Canadian canoeists for the task of transporting a relief force down the Nile. In considering the request, Britain's first appeal for help from the Dominion, Macdonald analysed the strategic picture and struck a note of narrow self-interest. 'We do not stand at all in the same position as Australasia – The Suez Canal is nothing to us – and we do not ask England to quarrel with France or Germany for our sakes ... Why should we waste money & men in this wretched business?'[17] Not for the last time did a Canadian policymaker judge that the protection of British interests in North Africa was none of Canada's business. Nonetheless, with public sentiment demanding a contribution Macdonald allowed a volunteer force to be raised at Britain's expense.

While the dispatch of this contingent sent English-Canadian hearts aflutter with imperial pride, many of the volunteers – indeed, the volunteers that London wanted most, given their skill – were indigenous. As long-time British allies, the Mohawk of Kahnawà:ke sought to contribute to the imperial campaign, as did warriors from several other aboriginal groups.[18] Confusing matters, by the time the Nile volunteers left for Africa, Macdonald's government was engaged in its own colonial campaign in the North-West Territories against Métis forces led by Louis Riel, whom the prime minister likened to the British foe in Sudan.[19] At the very moment Britain was enlisting indigenous people from Canada in Africa, the Canadian government was reinforcing its own colonial suzerainty on the plains.

For all his unwillingness to prioritize the empire's interests over those of Canada, Macdonald did nothing to upset the status quo in terms of Canada's lack of autonomy internationally. He opposed the establishment of any sort of foreign service, affirming, with a touch of fiscal prudence, that being 'cast upon our own resources' would be the 'ruin of Canada'.[20] An exception of sorts was the 1869 appointment of a Canadian representative in London to act largely as a commercial agent in the British capital, where Canada had opened an immigration office the previous year. This position was given official sanction in 1880, when Alexander Galt, a former finance minister, was named to the newly invented position of high commissioner. Meant to promote trade with and immigration to Canada, the position's title denoted the fact that the high commissioner was not representing a foreign government in the same way as an ambassador. As Galt lacked diplomatic status and avoided diplomatic negotiations there was no hint of separatism. The establishment of a high commission in London, Macdonald stated, was 'a very important step towards asserting the importance of the Dominion of Canada as a portion of Her Majesty's Empire'.[21]

The other Dominions would come to appoint their own high commissioners both to Britain and to one another. Meanwhile, political relations between Ottawa and London were conducted via the governor general, and the British Foreign Office continued to represent Canadian issues with foreign governments. In 1893, for instance, Sir Charles Tupper's brief government negotiated a trade agreement with France, but the document itself was signed on Canada's behalf by the British ambassador in Paris. On foreign policy issues, there was little room for manoeuvre. In the wake of Russian pogroms in 1905, Laurier spoke out in deploring the killing of Jews, but he forced the withdrawal of a resolution in the House of Commons to formally condemn the violence, noting, 'we have not at this moment the right to interfere in foreign matters as to which the crown of England alone is responsible.'[22]

There was diplomacy of a kind conducted within the empire in the form of colonial conferences, the first held in 1887, with Sandford Fleming, the famous Canadian engineer, representing the country. With the 1897 conference, the heads of government of the self-governing territories were permitted to attend, allowing the various prime ministers and British colonial officials to attempt to settle on common policies. The imperial conferences, as they were known after 1907, became a mainstay of intra-imperial relations, with fifteen meetings held from 1887 to 1937. There were other international conferences at which Britain represented the empire, with modest changes made in 1912, when Dominion delegates sat separately from the British delegate to the International Radiotelegraphic Conference; the feat was repeated the following year at the Conference on Safety of Life at Sea. Overall, these were minor technical conferences. On major issues of peace and war, the empire spoke with one voice.

Trade and immigration were the exceptions to Canada's extra-imperial presence. Much of the activity on these issues came from the provinces. In 1882, Quebec sent Senator Hector Fabre to Paris to represent the province; Ottawa employed him to represent Canada's interests too. Like the high commission in London, the Paris commission had official sanction but lacked diplomatic status.[23] As for the other provinces, in 1885, Nova Scotia opened a trade and immigration office in London, New Brunswick followed suit two years later, and by the early 1900s most provinces had representatives in the imperial capital. The federal government, meanwhile, employed quasi-official commercial agents throughout the 1880s mainly in Europe and the Caribbean, and in 1887, Macdonald passed a bill creating a trade ministry. However, due to an economic downturn and austerity drive, the Department of Trade and Commerce formed in 1892. Two years later, the department established its first trade commission in Sydney. That same year, Minister of Trade and Commerce Mackenzie Bowell convened a Colonial Conference in Ottawa attended by representatives from the self-governing colonies of New Zealand, New South Wales, Queensland, South Australia, Tasmania, Victoria, and the Cape Colony. Under the watchful eyes of a British observer, the conferees agreed to increase trade with one another, but they signed no formal agreement on this score as Britain's colonial secretary saw this move as 'equivalent to breaking up the Empire'.[24] On trade, both within the empire and without, Canada acted swiftly, and by 1911, there were twenty-one trade commissions, from Durban to Berlin and from Yokohama to Havana. Trade, then, was a major Canadian outlet to the world in a period in which Canada lacked the legal authority to conduct diplomacy. It was not until 1909 that a Department of External Affairs (DEA) – not foreign affairs, for there was nothing foreign about relations with Britain and other parts of the empire – was created. With little policy to be made, it was little more than a glorified post office.[25]

Other than promises to boost intra-imperial trade, Bowell's 1894 Ottawa conference had resulted in an agreement to construct a Pacific telegraph cable, part of a network, the 'All Red Line', linking together the British Empire – the red smudges on the map. In championing the telegraph network, completed in 1902 (the Atlantic cable had been laid in 1865), Sandford Fleming was certain of the importance of 'welding the British Empire by the great and subtle force of electricity'.[26] The cable network tied together the British World, spreading news and information. The All Red Route of railroads and steamships was another important tie, moving people, goods, and mail. Traversing a continent and with steamship service to Asia, the Canadian Pacific Railway formed a critical part of this system. In the common parlance of the time, technology had annihilated time and space, reinforcing the sense that Greater Britain was global. In commenting on the 'geographical unity of the British empire', Canadian educator George Parkin offered a glowing description of the possibilities opened by this network. 'You meet a friend in London', he wrote, 'as he shakes hands with you in farewell, he hails a cab to catch a P. and O. boat for Singapore, or an Allan Liner for Vancouver. You see a familiar face, and you remember that you last saw it a few weeks ago in Montreal or Melbourne. These are not exaggerations, but the ordinary facts of daily life to men of business and travel.'[27] As the first organizing secretary of the Rhodes Trust from 1902 to 1922, Parkin played an important role in fulfilling Rhodes's intent of building a network centred upon the British World, with British universities the nexus of an academic web extending across Greater Britain. Alongside telegraph cables and intra-imperial mail, these schools comprised one of the informal links that bound together British subjects.[28] The turn of the century world was a globalized one, with empire helping to connect disparate parts of the globe.

Imperialists like Parkin saw the empire as a sort of organism, 'the greatest aggregation of human beings that ever was joined together in one body politic'. Keeping this creature together was a major goal of the imperial federationists.[29] In 1884, the Imperial Federation League held its inaugural meeting in London, and branches soon spread across the empire. Its members sought to ensure that as the white self-government colonies gained Dominion status a new mode of imperial unity could be found via a federation of imperial states. Through adaptation, the empire would not only survive but thrive. In a lecture supporting this notion, Queen's University's George Monro Grant advocated for a British-Canadian union 'that would give to Canada not only the present full management of its own affairs, but a fair share in the management and responsibilities of common affairs' of the empire. Canadians would have a stake in the wider imperial project, though he was careful to add that imperial federation would not mean 'taking away our sons to fight in Burmah [sic] and Afghanistan'.[30] The proposed federation's grandiosity did not prevent its proponents from drawing up plans for a vast imperial parliament and for establishing Dominion rule over various dependent colonies, such as the West Indies. Given the example of Canadian confederation and the creation of countries like Germany and Italy, it seemed natural to conclude, as Parkin did, that 'the aspect of the whole world irresistibly suggests the thought that we are passing from a nation epoch to a federation epoch'. Although the Imperial Federation League lasted less than a decade, the idea of imperial unity through a federal arrangement lived on and served to inspire groups like the Round Table, which included a who's who of influential early twentieth-century English Canadians who believed in closer union between Canada and the metropole.[31]

As the federationists' outlook attests, many Canadians saw the British Empire as something to be championed. They thrilled to its exploits and celebrated its ethos of bringing order to far flung corners of the globe. 'Imperialism in its last and highest development', opined a leading voice of Canadian liberalism, 'imperialism as it possesses and controls the race at the present moment, is not only no breeder of wars, but it is the greatest agency for peace the world contains.'[32] Conservative MP George Foster praised Britain for having 'mothered nation after nation, people after people, continent after continent, brought them out of darkness and slavery and set them upon the path of a better civilization'.[33] For white Canadians the experience of colonialism was very different than it was for black workers on sugar plantations in Jamaica, for Indian labourers in Bengal, or for indigenous students in Canadian residential schools, and they shared in British attitudes towards supposedly inferior peoples.[34] George Grant, among the foremost Canadian imperialists, applauded an empire that had 'brought order out of chaos, given peace to warring creeds and races, chained human tigers, introduced civilization, established justice, opened wide the doors for all the forces of Christianity to enter'. India, in his view, was 'perhaps the greatest monument of [Britain's] fitness to govern races unfit for self-government'.[35] Grant praised the efforts of 'our sons' who were 'taking their part in introducing civilization into Africa, under the aegis of the flag, and in preserving the *Pax Britannica* among the teeming millions of India and South-Eastern Asia'.[36] Like many of his contemporaries, he saw a role for Canada in managing this empire.

Canadians took part in campaigns of empire. During the Crimean War, Canada's colonial legislature had allowed Britain to recruit local volunteers, and the first Victoria Cross awarded to a Canadian was won by Alexander Dunn during the 1854 Charge of the Light Brigade. William Hall, a black Canadian sailor in the Royal Navy, won a Victoria Cross for his actions at Cawnpore and Lucknow during the Indian Rebellion in 1857–8, a conflict in which the British raised a regiment of Canadian volunteers. Meanwhile, given the miniscule size of the Canadian military, many of the early graduates of Canada's RMC served throughout the empire. 'What better place to exercise a man of action's talents than under the vast open skies of Africa', wrote William Stairs, an RMC alumnus who fought in colonial campaigns in the 'dark continent', where he earned a reputation for savagery. Two RMC engineers went on to highly distinguished imperial careers: Major General George Macaulay Kirkpatrick served in the Royal Engineers and in the early twentieth century held senior military positions in Australia, India, and China; Sir Édouard Percy Cranwill Girouard built railways in British Africa before becoming governor of Nigeria and Kenya.[37] These were individual contributions to furthering British imperial interests abroad.

Girouard's involvement in managing the empire exemplifies how, within the British World, there were opportunities open to privileged and well-connected Canadians – in his case, his father was a wealthy lawyer, Conservative MP, and Supreme Court justice. Also, Girouard stands as an interesting figure given that he was French Canadian, and adherents of Greater Britain were increasingly inclined to view non-Anglo-Saxons with suspicion, just as many French Canadians were reluctant to take part in imperial initiatives. French-English relations in Canada were a perennial source of tension, but for French Canadians there was some grudging respect for British rule, under which they were permitted to retain Catholicism, French civil law, and, ultimately, their own culture and language. In welcoming the Prince of Wales to Quebec's 1908 tercentenary celebrations, politician Adélard Turgeon had declared that it was 'British liberty which had allowed national dualism to thrive' in Canada.[38] French Canadians accepted British rule, Henri Bourassa affirmed, because they had made it work successfully in advancing their own interests and so they 'claimed the benefits with the same pride that characterizes all British citizens'. Bourassa, who founded the nationalist and anti-imperialist *Ligue Nationaliste Canadienne*, even claimed a British intellectual lineage, noting, 'I am a Liberal of the British School. I am a disciple of Burke, Fox, Bright, Gladstone.'[39] There was respect, even, for British institutions. Visiting Quebec's provincial legislature, French academic André Siegfried was taken aback by parliamentary debate: "Monsieur l'orateur, l'honorable membre pour Québec a dit ..." Approbation is signified by sonorous guttural cries of "Hear, hear!" The whole impression is thoroughly British.'[40] Further, French

Canadians saw British overseas imperialism as a source of order, though, as imperial feeling swelled in English Canada, this appreciation waned. What they did not want, as Bourassa explained, was 'to follow the British world in a movement of evolution that would lead them to assume new obligations towards the Empire'.[41] Bourassa viewed Canadian interests in national not imperial terms. So did Montreal's *La Presse*, which put a domestic cleavage over the Boer War into perspective: 'We French Canadians belong to one country, Canada. Canada is for us the whole world; but the English Canadians have two countries, one here and one across the sea.'[42] As much as these sentiments reflected a French Canadian viewpoint, they also encapsulated a nationalist outlook that abutted with imperial sentiments.

Attitudes about the superiority of the British abroad were translated into anti-Francophone political action at home, a situation worsened by the anti-Catholicism popular in North America in the late nineteenth century. For members of the Orange Order and other groups who believed strongly in making Canada an Anglo-Saxon, Protestant bastion, French Canadians were a threat on religious and racial grounds. 'In order to build up a great nation', stated Charles Mair, a fervent Francophobe and imperialist, 'minor nationalities are no doubt called upon to make heavy sacrifices'.[43] Orangeman Alexander Muir penned 'The Maple Leaf Forever', a de facto national anthem emphasizing Britain's conquest of New France. In 1890, Muir's political ally and fellow Orangeman Dalton McCarthy, a leading imperial federationist, told the House of Commons of the need to abolish French in the North-West Territories, for 'we cannot have, and never will have in this country, two nationalities'. In response, fellow Conservative MP Joseph-Adolphe Chapleau pointed out that Britain's empire was 'composed of a greater variety of nations and creeds than was the Roman Empire', and he wondered, 'Do the Imperial Federationists think they are going to help on their scheme by prosecuting a minority?'[44] Increasingly, Macdonald's Conservative Party had less room for French Canadians and fewer MPs from Quebec. The great British imperial statesman Alfred Lord Milner could write in 1913 that a French Canadian 'may be a British soldier or administrator all the same, and he will have absolutely the same scope and opportunities as his competitors of British blood', but few Anglo-Saxon Canadians of a similar pro-empire mindset likely agreed.[45]

Liberal Prime Minister Wilfrid Laurier – Sir Wilfrid in 1897 – was representative of some French Canadian opinion. He saw much to admire in Britain and in British institutions. Canadians, he noted positively, had 'the blessing of living under British monarchical institutions, and we appreciate them to the full'.[46] He accepted a knighthood while attending Queen Victoria's diamond jubilee, a visit to Britain during which he also received honorary degrees from Oxford and Cambridge. However, increasingly uncomfortable with the growing trend of militant Anglo-Saxonism, Laurier resisted London's attempts to involve Canada in imperial ventures.

During the 1897 Colonial Conference, Laurier opposed Joseph Chamberlain's plans for a centralized imperial foreign policy, not the last time a Chamberlain would see hopes for closer imperial cooperation frustrated by a Canadian prime minister. Laurier, Chamberlain judged, was 'not a man with whom to go out tiger-hunting'.[47] Despite his resistance to imperial centralization, that same year Laurier's government implemented the first of several preferential tariffs benefitting Britain – imperial preference – a reversal of the Macdonald government's restrictive policies. Moreover, as Laurier proclaimed in a rousing speech to the Royal Colonial Institute, 'England has proved at all times that she can fight her own battles, but if a day were to come when England was in danger, let the bugle sound, let the fire be lit on the hills, and in all parts of the Colonies, though we may not be able to do much, whatever we can do will be done by the colonies to help her.'[48] This was no one-off statement, made in the heady days of Victoria's diamond jubilee. Three years later, having committed Canadian soldiers to fight in South Africa, Laurier affirmed that Canada would defend 'England were she engaged in a life and death struggle'. What he was less sure of, was whether Canadians should take part 'in the secondary wars of England'.[49] With South Africa, Laurier faced this question, one that Macdonald had confronted on Sudan. Public opinion forced both leaders' hands.

In 1899, Laurier was questioned over whether Canada should contribute troops to the British effort to assert authority over the Boers of South Africa. Privately, he confided to Frederick Borden, the minister of militia and defence, that 'we have too much to do in this country to go on military adventures'.[50] However, he felt public, press, and parliamentary pressure to advance Greater Britain's interests. Likewise, Canada's Protestant churches backed the war, viewing it as part of Britain's civilizing mission, even though the conflict would be to the benefit of British mining companies.[51] Laurier agreed to a Canadian contribution to the imperial war effort. Mindful of opposition from French Canadians and other groups less enthused by imperialism, and reflecting his own coolness towards involvement in secondary wars, only volunteers would go abroad to the Canadian military's first overseas campaign.

In a declaration reflecting the war's supposed noble purpose, Laurier assured departing soldiers that the conflict was 'not a war of conquest', adding that they were going to fight for 'the cause of justice, the cause of humanity, of civil rights and religious liberty'.[52] In all, between 1899 and 1902, over seven thousand Canadians volunteered for service in South Africa, some in units organized by Canada's government, others in a privately raised contingent, Strathcona's Horse, bankrolled by Lord Strathcona (Donald Smith), Canada's high commissioner in London. Also, Britain recruited and paid for the formation of mounted Canadian units and brought Canadian horsemen into the South African Constabulary, a paramilitary force policing areas captured from the Boers. Given that it was a war for empire in which rugged Anglo-Saxons fought against foes who one Canadian characterized as being 'as ignorant of the outside world as the Hudson Bay Indians', the British rejected offers of volunteers from Vancouver's Japanese community and the Haudenosaunee, traditional allies of the British.[53] This conflict was cast as a white man's war, and despite the bombast of a civilizing mission, much of it involved counter-insurgency warfare that included confining civilians to concentration camps and burning the farms of insurgents, real or suspected.[54]

The unpleasant realities of empire-building did not deter Canadian imperialism's advocates from viewing the war through the glowing rhetoric of imperial solidarity. For George Grant, with the British call for assistance 'an electric current flashed ... from Halifax to Victoria, thrilling all English-speaking hearts ... and a cry went up that the war was Canada's as well as England's'.[55] The *Globe* viewed the despatch of Canadian soldiers as 'a national declaration of Canada's stake in the British Empire', and the *Military Gazette* praised this development for removing 'the old stigma that Canada, while enjoying all the benefits and protection, was reluctant or indifferent to assume the duties and sacrifices of Empire'.[56] A war correspondent, meanwhile, characterized Canada's contribution as the result 'of centuries of colonizing effort, of generations of a colonizing policy whose aim had been to bind ever closer in one high destiny the new and growing nations of the earth'.[57] The Canadians even recorded a significant victory to match these high expectations. At Paardeberg in February 1900, Canadian soldiers won the first major British action of the war. Laurier praised news of the victory, which 'revealed to the world that a new power had arisen in the west'. For one commentator, the war had a nation-building effect and fit a pattern in which Canada's 'whole life has been stimulated, the standard of its manhood built up, the national character strengthened by the achievements of its sons in the Fenian Raids, the Red River Expedition, the Nile Campaign, the North-West Rebellion, and the South African war'.[58]

The references to manhood and national character were deliberate, for the Boer War provided an opportunity for displays of muscular imperialism, and Canadian soldiers proved themselves to be effective soldiers, physically well-equipped for campaigning in rugged conditions. British failures at the outset of the conflict left many Canadians content with their own performance and convinced that 'the slum-born, undernourished, British Tommy lacked the stamina and initiative to defend the Empire, and effete, supercilious "Piccadilly Aristocrats" lacked the vision and will to provide the leadership'. In the war's wake, Rudyard Kipling criticized his countrymen, for while 'the Younger Nations' like Canada and Australia had produced 'men who could shoot and ride',

Britons had conducted themselves poorly.[59] Their failings led to the creation of the Boy Scouts and other organizations aiming to overcome the apparent degeneracies caused by urban life. There were few such concerns regarding the Canadians, who, in the words of one MP, had helped the country awaken 'to the possibility of having an active and aggressive national life'. Through the war, Canada had 'gained an enviable position in the world'.[60] Upon their return, Canadian soldiers were feted, parades were held, and monuments built. Paardeberg Day, 27 February, became the date on which Canadians honoured veterans and soldiers – that is, until the end of the Great War. As for the Boers, they soon became fellow members of Greater Britain, with many Canadians coming to view them as a civilized presence in Africa.

All this praise aside, there were opponents to Canadian involvement in the war. While farmers and labourers were generally uninterested in the conflict, Irish and German Canadians opposed it. So did French Canadians, some of whom identified with the Boers as a repressed minority group, and Bourassa broke with Laurier.[61] These opponents earned the ire of jingoes. Reporting on 'a bad day for the pro-Boer' in March 1900, the *Globe* described how factory workers in Toronto rounded up Boer sympathizers and 'gave their erring brothers a mock trial and made them kneel on the Union Jack and beg pardon'. In Montreal, three days of clashes between English and French university students led Governor General Lord Minto to observe that it would take but 'a very small spark to make a racial blaze here'.[62] The blaze did not come, but the Boer War left smouldering embers, and the English-French divide on foreign policy issues only grew. For ardent Canadian imperialists, who saw themselves as part of the British World, the French fact in Canada was something to be ignored or wiped away. It was no coincidence that in his work praising Canadian involvement in the South African war, one young Conservative politician wrote that in Canada, British traditions 'are the only common national traditions'.[63] French Canada was viewed, not incorrectly, as a negative force when it came to developing intra-imperial ties. The British general who commanded Canada's small permanent army blamed the Laurier government's 'ill-disguised French and pro-Boer proclivities' for preventing Canada from taking a greater part 'in the great movement which has drawn the strings of our Anglo-Saxon British Empire so close'.[64]

There was English Canadian opposition to the Boer War and imperialism though calls to sever empire's bonds were largely muted. Prominent exceptions were lawyer and constitutional expert J. S. Ewart and Goldwin Smith, a transplanted British historian. 'All the power which we have comes from a statute passed at Westminster', noted Ewart, a tireless advocate of independence. 'It does not depend in any way upon our own declaration'. Herein lay a danger, for in Ewart's judgement, because Canada's political authority was 'the gift of the Imperial Parliament', it could easily be taken away. In his view, it was necessary for Canada to have control of its own constitution and that meant severing ties with Britain, a radical proposition during a time of robust imperial sentiment.[65] Amid the Boer War, meanwhile, Smith was one of the few vocal English Canadian opponents of involvement. Also an advocate of independence, he criticized how Canada was 'simply swept in the train of the dominant part in the Imperial country', into fighting in South Africa.[66] Smith's anti-imperialism might have found more adherents were he not also an apostle of annexation to the United States.

For imperialists, the empire provided protection, particularly from the United States, which loomed large in Canadian thinking. 'Canada separated from Britain could not be independent', warned Grant. Rather, Canada 'would be treated as if we were in the position of Mexico', a country subservient to the Americans. Colonel George Denison told the British Empire League that 'If we Canadians desire to be free and safe, it must be in that Empire to which we are attached.' Predicting that 'independent, we could not survive a decade', Stephen Leacock added, in one of his most famous statements, 'I ... am an Imperialist because I will not be a Colonial'.[67] Nor was British protection confined to military matters. As Laurier's Liberals found in the 1891 election, Macdonald's appeals to imperial patriotism were successful in rallying opposition to free trade with the United States. This thinking about Britain's importance for Canada as a counterweight to American influence endured well into the twentieth century.

The British had their own interests, which often prioritized improving relations with the United States even if that meant disadvantaging Canada. Macdonald had discovered this problem with the 1871 Treaty of Washington. Three decades later, a dispute over the Canada–US boundary at Alaska again laid bare Albion's perfidy. To resolve the border issue, in 1903, a six-person arbitration commission was struck, and in the end the British commissioner sided with the three American commissioners in deciding that the United States be given the bulk of the claim. The US side was in the right. Nonetheless, Canadians felt betrayed, particularly since Canada had rallied to the flag over South Africa. Bourassa was quick to connect Alaska to the recent war, noting that while Canadians 'were shedding their blood for the empire on the soil of Africa, Mr. Chamberlain was coldly sacrificing the interests of Canada'.[68] Laurier, too, struck a tough note, complaining 'that so long as Canada remains a dependency of the British crown the present powers that we have are not sufficient for the maintenance of our rights'. Privately, like Macdonald before him, he recognized that 'the Empire's interest and the Empire's policy were in most cases Great Britain's interest and Great Britain's policy'.[69]

Any public disappointment caused by Alaska was fleeting, for in the decade leading up to the Great War, English Canadian sentiments were overwhelmingly pro-empire. Toronto, a visiting Brit observed in 1905, was 'the most ultra-British city on earth ... Englishmen suffering from a laxity in loyalty should hasten to Toronto, where they can be so impregnated with patriotism that they will want to wear shirt fronts made of the Union Jack'.[70] Part of the reason why imperialist fervour ran so high in Toronto and other central Canadian cities was the huge influx in immigration from the British Isles, which meant that during the 1890s and early 1900s, Canada became more British.[71] As immigrants often do, these British newcomers provided a flow or remittances back to the home country, even as the City of London continued to be a vital source of foreign investment in Canada.[72] What is interesting to consider is whether much of the pro-imperial sentiment in Canada was the result of British diaspora politics, though homegrown, Canadian enthusiasm for empire should not be discounted.

During the Boer War, imperial-minded women had formed the Imperial Order Daughters of the Empire, a patriotic organization modelled after the Daughters of the American Revolution. Guided by their mantra 'One Flag, One Throne, One Country', members worked to support Canadian soldiers overseas and, as a vocal pressure group, the IODE preached closer imperial ties. By the Great War, the organization counted fifty thousand members, and, along with the Dominion Order of King's Daughters, it was one of several organizations of Canadian women who saw themselves as living within and contributing towards the British World.[73] Female imperialism and patriotic maternalism also lay behind the formation of the Canadian Red Cross Society, a branch of the British Red Cross. In a sign of women's support of the British civilizing mission, Red Cross nurses accompanied Canada's Boer War contingent and Canadian women went to South Africa to provide education to Boer children confined to concentration camps. Canadian women also found a role in empire through missionary work, a vital outlet of female imperialism.[74] Missionary activities, nursing, and patriotic groups attest that interest in empire was not bound by gender. Empire Day, an empire-wide holiday established by Clementina Fessenden, was first celebrated on 23 May 1899 in Hamilton, Ontario, and journalist Agnes Christina Laut praised Canada as *The Empire of the North*.[75]

The Girl Guide movement, which spread to Canada soon after the founding of the main British organization, was another outlet for female imperialism, and it exemplified a wider emphasis on preparing young people for bearing empire's burdens and on ensuring the good health of the future of the Anglo-Saxon race. The Boy Scouts, too, came to Canada, and Newfoundland, from Britain; likewise, it promoted the martial values of character, strength, and discipline. The group's popularity led the YMCA to create its own Canadian scouting organization, which emphasized similar values with the addition of a heavier emphasis on muscular Christianity. In selling the virtues of his organization, Lord Baden-Powell proclaimed, 'if Canadian boys rise to men worth their salt, Canada will have the place of honor in that Empire.'[76]

Similar desires to prepare boys for service drove the cadet movement and the National Defence League's effort to make military training compulsory in schools. The campaign was unsuccessful, but six provinces did incorporate cadet training into their curricula. The move was controversial. Some parents objected to the militarism; others, primarily in rural areas, opposed having their sons spend less time on the farm, a sign of 'pacifism of the pocketbook rather than principle'.[77] The chief inspector of Toronto schools gushed over the importance of cadet training, which gave 'training in patriotism to the young people of the country – not hatred of other lands, but love of his own land, the consciousness of the glory of being a Canadian and of being associated with the grand old British Empire'.[78] In this era, Canada itself was viewed as an adolescent, though following the Boer War there were some commentators who saw 'Jake Canuck' as 'the grown-up son in the firm of John Bull and Sons'.[79] Others would later credit the Great War with prompting Canada's coming of age, through representations of an adolescent Canada continued to be a staple of editorial cartoons well into the 1920s.

Cadets and scouts were signs of a desire to mould young imperialists and of a wider concern with military preparedness. In the years preceding the Great War, what Laurier called 'the vortex of militarism' was a popular force globally.[80] In Canada, while past military achievements may have thrilled the imperially minded, actual spending on a peacetime military had traditionally been negligible, though between 1903 and 1911, Laurier's government had increased the defence budget. In this environment, there emerged a variety of groups – the National Defence League, the Canadian Defence League, the Canadian National Service League, the Navy League of Canada – pressing for a larger military capable of contributing to the empire. British officials hoped for such a commitment. 'The Canadian army is Canadian', stated Sir Edward Hutton, the British commander of Canada's forces, 'but it is also British.'[81] At the 1902 Colonial Conference, Chamberlain likened Britain to a 'weary Titan' and appealed for help. When New Zealand's prime minister responded by proposing the formation of an Imperial Reserve force made up of Dominion soldiers, Laurier opposed the suggestion, unwilling to allow for measures that smacked of imperial centralization. In 1904, his government's Militia Act opened overall command of the Canadian military to Canadians, a move looked upon by officials in London as a species of 'separatism'.[82] Apart from a brief interlude from 1908 to 1910, a British officer commanded Canada's army until 1919.

Matters came to a head over a Canadian navy. In 1906, the British withdrew their naval forces from Halifax and Esquimalt; First Sea Lord John Fisher's judgement was that London should 'not spend one man or one pound in the defence of Canada'.[83] Given growing Anglo-German naval competition, what the British sought was money from Ottawa for the construction of Royal Navy ships, which would be Canada's contribution to the defence of the realm. Given his own opposition to imperial centralization, Laurier's solution was to found a Canadian navy. At the 1909 Imperial Conference, the British accepted a Canadian and Australian proposal for separate navies, and in May 1910, the Naval Service of Canada was created. This move placated neither imperialists nor nationalists; the latter delivered a by-election loss to the Liberals in a Quebec riding. Laurier's next move was to delay plans for a large Canadian navy, instead acquiring two old British cruisers, the HMCS *Niobe* and the HMCS *Rainbow*, the latter vessel no doubt terrifying the German Kaiser by name alone. Imperialist critics dismissed this meagre force as a 'tin-pot navy', and urged a commitment to Britain. As an 'integral part of the British Empire', a Navy League spokesperson thundered, it was Canada's duty to contribute to the navy because 'whatever is vital to that Empire is vital to Canada, and we have shown that the maintenance of Britain's supremacy at sea is vital to her'. Also appealing for a naval commitment, Robert Borden, leader of the Conservative opposition, reminded listeners that the British ensured the 'safety of our commerce, the security of our shores'.[84]

The issue was tied up in the 1911 election, which centred around a free trade agreement that the Laurier government had concluded with Washington. In opposing the trade deal, Borden played to pro-empire sympathies and presented the choice before voters as 'the Union Jack and British connection as opposed to the Stars and Stripes and Yankee Domination'.[85] In addition to the accusation that the Liberals were disloyal to Britain on economic grounds, the Conservatives highlighted Laurier's opposition to an imperial navy. Together, these issues, plus general fatigue with a party that had been in power for fifteen years, resulted in a Tory victory. Borden put a halt to further spending on the Canadian navy. Instead, after attending meetings in London in 1912, he agreed to contribute $35 million to the Royal Navy for battleship construction, a sum approaching a quarter of annual Canadian government expenditures. However, Laurier had the last laugh, for Borden's Naval Aid Bill authorizing the spending failed to pass the Liberal-controlled Senate, and both major parties in Canada established the tradition of making a cock-up of military procurement.[86]

The scuttling of the naval bill ended a deflating chapter in Canadian politics. However, the issue, with its partisan squabbling over military spending, laid bare questions of loyalty to Britain and of Canada's place within the British World. Should Canadians follow Britain's lead or pursue more narrow interests? Macdonald and Laurier had wrestled with these matters and in doing so had felt public pressure bear down upon them, particularly over warfare. For those Canadians who saw Canada as part of Greater Britain, it was axiomatic that Canada would involve itself in British conflicts. Speaking at a meeting of the Committee of Imperial Defence in 1911, four months before being voted out of office, Laurier told British officials that they did 'not appreciate the different conditions in which we stand in the Dominions beyond the seas compared with the centre of the Empire here'.[87] Yet, for many Canadians of British stock, there was no such geographical distinction to be made. The British World was indivisible and not simply because in the early twentieth century Canada lacked legal independence from Britain. For reasons of identity, culture, kinship, and economics, Canadians looked to Britain and to the empire. A successful politician, Laurier knew this fact and he himself felt a fondness for Canada's British heritage as well as a sense of loyalty that led him to pledge support for Britain at the outset of the Great War. That conflict tested Canadian commitment to the empire and exposed societal fissures. In the run up to the war, nationalist sentiments in the belligerent nations were high, and the pro-Empire feeling among Canadians was a sign of a wider British nationalism that helped fuel the conflict of 1914–18. Before considering the war, however, we next turn to Canadian links with the world beyond Greater Britain.

3

Canada and the first age of globalization

In supporting the Canadian government's plans to bring the colony of BC into Confederation in 1871, a Halifax newspaper contended that acquiring this new territory would 'give British North America its true position in the British Empire as the great central link uniting those Islands that constitute the "Motherland" with those great dependencies of India, Australasia and New Zealand'.[1] Creating this link required not just an outlet to the Pacific but a transcontinental railroad, the completion of which established Canada, in the words of George Monro Grant, as 'the natural keystone between the old world of northern Europe and the older world of China and Japan'.[2] Canada's perceived importance in connecting the Atlantic and the Pacific serves as a reminder that the country has been oriented not just eastward towards Europe but westward towards Asia. Canada's future, wrote George Parkin, was 'as a Pacific Power'.[3] For Parkin, Grant, and other imperialists, the geographical fact of Canada's connection to two oceans – the Arctic, at this point, was terra incognita for most Canadians – only enhanced the country's role within Britain's empire. Beyond the Pacific lay a world of economic possibility, a consideration that appealed to a wider swathe of Canadians. Vancouver, historian and anti-imperialist Goldwin Smith observed, 'hopes to have a great Asiatic trade and become a mighty city', a development he supported fully.[4] In the pre-Great War era of globalization, Asia loomed large as a destination for Canadian investment, as a market for goods, and as a source of migrants. Moreover, there was the United States, emerging as a world power in economic, military, and cultural terms, and captivating, as always, Canadian admirers and detractors alike. In 1902, British journalist W. T. Stead warned of *The Americanization of the World*; five years later, American journalist Samuel

Moffett celebrated *The Americanization of Canada*.[5] So even as they remained a part of Greater Britain, Canadians wrestled with their position within both North America and an increasingly globalized world.

This chapter examines Canadian interactions beyond the British World in the roughly five decades following Confederation. These years were marked by growing global connectivity, a result of European imperial expansion, new transportation networks built around steam power, new forms of communication such as the telegraph, and the spread of investment and people. Whether in Asia and the circum-Caribbean, or with the United States, Canadians took advantage of these connections. As much as it was lauded, globalization was a source of tension. While appreciative of the flow of investment and goods to and from Asia and the West Indies, some Canadians feared the arrival of non-white migrants, a reaction apparent in other British settlement colonies and the United States.[6] 'Canada should remain a white country', stated William Lyon Mackenzie King, the deputy minister of labour. Socialist politician J. S. Woodsworth agreed, adding a warning about importing 'non-assimilable elements' into the country.[7] Fundamentally, concern about immigration revolved around the question of who was Canadian. Proximity to the United States only compounded the issue. Were Canadians, as Moffett put it, just 'Americans without knowing it'?[8] An ongoing challenge throughout Canada's history, in this era the issue of defining a Canadian took on added importance given globalization's challenge to physical and cultural boundaries.

True to its promoters' hopes, the Canadian Pacific Railway (CPR) became an important link between Canada and the world. During the railroad's construction, Canada's government had given tens of millions of dollars to the CPR, a sign of Ottawa's interest in economic development. A goal for the company and its backers both in and outside of government was to transform Canada into the 'Greater Britain on the Pacific'.[9] In 1886, only weeks after its first train reached Port Moody, east of Vancouver, the company began chartering vessels from Cunard – the great shipping firm begun by Halifax's Samuel Cunard – that brought goods from Japan and China. Within five years, under the leadership of its American-born president, William Van Horne, what was now the Canadian Pacific Steamship Company had secured a contract with the British and Canadian governments to carry mail to Hong Kong. Next, the company began operating its own steamships, the Empress Line. Carrying mail, express cargo, and passengers, these vessels formed a key part of the 'All-Red Route' of ships and rail lines tying together both the British World and the Atlantic and the Pacific. These vessels and the railway itself established the CPR as a major presence in global trade, communication, and travel networks, with the Empress steamers travelling to and from the railhead at Vancouver and the major port cities of Yokohama, Shanghai, and Hong Kong, and later, to Manilla, Honolulu, and British India. Affiliated with CPR, the Canadian–Australasian Steamship Company began operating in 1893, offering service between Victoria and Vancouver and British possessions in the South Pacific. At the other end of the CPR, the terminus at Montreal – at the time Canada's industrial and financial hub – was the gateway to Europe and the rest of the Americas. CPR marketing was not wrong in branding the company as 'The World's Greatest Highway'.

Under the British North America Act, Canada was given freedom in its trade and commercial policy, but the federal government was slow to embrace new trade possibilities beyond the United States. In the 1870s and 1880s, Ottawa had employed informal trade agents, with the Department of Trade and Commerce formed only in 1892. Canada's forays into global trade began with the establishment of a trade commission in Australia in 1894, the same year in which Ottawa hosted a conference of British territories that produced agreements to boost trade, establish common guidelines for intra-imperial mail, and construct undersea telegraph lines. Canada's Pacific presence was enhanced with the opening of trade offices in Yokohama (1904) and Shanghai (1906), and by direct steamship service between Vancouver and Vladivostok (1913), with Canada establishing trade commissions in Petrograd and Omsk in 1916.[10] Canadian trade with the Asia-Pacific grew slowly if steadily, but failed to meet the admittedly grandiose expectations of government officials and other boosters. For instance, attending the 1903 National Industrial Exhibit in Osaka, Canada's agriculture minister made a big push for Canadian grain sales in the hopes of switching the Japanese away from rice as a staple foodstuff.[11] There was greater success for Canadian financial companies, especially Montreal's Sun Life Insurance. By the dawn of the twentieth century, Sun Life had offices in China, Japan, Singapore, India, and North Africa. The spread of capital was a central feature of this and other periods of globalization, and Canadian companies benefitted from Canada's status as both an importer and exporter of investment.

Beginning with the opening of an office in Barbados in 1879, Sun Life established a major presence in the circum-Caribbean, which, more than Asia, stood as an important outlet for Canadian investors, a market for exports, and a source of commodities. Canada–West Indies trade was long-standing, having occurred since the French colonial period. The modern trading relationship started in 1866, the year before Confederation, when Britain's North American colonies jointly despatched a commercial mission to the British West Indies and Brazil (a stop in Mexico was cancelled due to revolutionary violence).[12] This visit led to direct Canada-West Indies steamship service and blossoming trade, especially Canadian exports of fish and imports of sugar. Trade commissions were later opened in Barbados, Havana, and Mexico City, and in 1882 the Merchants Bank of Halifax – later the Royal Bank of Canada – opened a branch in Bermuda; the Bank of Nova Scotia did the same in Jamaica in 1889. Canadian bank branches soon dotted 'those colonies in the sunny south'.[13]

The circum-Caribbean became the first major outlet for Canadian finance, including investment in utilities, insurance, and transport in Cuba, Puerto Rico, Bermuda, Jamaica, British Guiana, and Trinidad. Having developed street car lines in Toronto, William Mackenzie set up operations in São Paulo in 1899; a decade later the Brazilian Traction, Light and Power Company was a major presence in Brazil. Touting investment in the region, the *Journal of Commerce* boasted that Canadians sought 'fresh fields and pastures to prove that neither snows nor tropic suns could check the onward march of well-directed energy'.[14] After overseeing the CPR's construction, William Van Horne set about building railways in Cuba and Guatemala; two other CPR contractors founded Jamaica's West Indian Electric Company, and future newspaper baron Max Aitken amassed a fortune through investments in tramway and electric companies across the Caribbean. In an era of Anglo-American domination of Latin America and the West Indies, Canadian investors benefitted from association with the region's economic and military powers. In Van Horne's case, he secured his Cuban rail line following the US-imposed end of Spanish rule on the island, an event that led to the influx of Canadian banks to Cuba.[15]

The significant presence of Canadian capital in the British West Indian colonies led some figures to entertain dreams of expansion. 'A Dominion stretching from South America to the Pacific Ocean!' proclaimed one Nova Scotia journalist and advocate of a Canada–West Indies union. 'It would give Canada just that which is needed to round off the Confederation. All we lack now is a bit of tropical territory.'[16] Imperial federationists and the proto-Canadian nationalist group Canada First had nurtured hopes of expanding into the Caribbean since the 1880s, and the idea gained traction in the early twentieth century. In 1909, Prime Minister Wilfrid Laurier considered a proposal by the president of the West India Electric Company to administer Jamaica, and the London-based West India Committee postulated that 'Canada may be in a position to do for the West Indies what the United States is doing for Cuba and Puerto Rico.' Sun Life president T. B. Macaulay led the Canadian-West Indies League, an annexation lobby group. Macaulay's hopes of a merger were dashed, but a 1911 economic conference in Ottawa produced a Canada–West Indies trade agreement.[17] Annexationist sentiments peaked during the Great War, when there were talks between Canadian and British officials over the possibility of Canada administering Jamaica, Antigua, and Trinidad.

Although outside of the timeframe of this chapter, the question of wartime Canadian annexation of the West Indies encapsulates the themes central to Canada's dealings with the non-white world. Canadians valued British possessions in the Caribbean on economic grounds, hence the interest in taking over these territories. In 1916, Robert Borden advanced the idea because it would see an increase in Canadian territory, population, and importance, especially since administering the far-flung islands would require Canada to become a naval power. Furthermore, Canadians could participate in empire's civilizing mission. 'The responsibilities of governing subject races', he speculated, 'would probably exercise a broadening influence upon our people.'[18] At Borden's behest, Sir Joseph Pope, the undersecretary of Canada's Department of External Affairs, analysed the matter. On one hand, Pope listed the economic benefits that would accrue, adding that annexation would reward Canada for 'the blood and treasure' being expended in Europe. On the other, he highlighted the 'negro question', which was twofold: black West Indians would want to vote, as they were already permitted to do locally, and they would want to travel to Canada, a reversal of Canadian immigration policy.[19] Even though British officials, including Prime Minister David Lloyd George, backed the idea, in 1919, Borden ruled out annexation, citing the potential difficulty 'of dealing with the coloured population'.[20] During the post-Second World War wave of decolonization, it became common for Canadian officials to declare that Canada had never held overseas colonies; here, though, was a moment in which it came close.

West Indian annexation showcased the importance of people to the story of globalization. The circuits of relatively quick and cheap transportation allowed for the flow of goods and people, a process in which Canada was both exporter and importer. Whether serving religious, humanitarian, or imperial purposes – or a combination thereof – Canadian missionaries traversed the world beyond North America, forming an important outlet at a time in which Canada's diplomatic presence was nil. Drawing together Protestants, mainly from Anglo-Ontario, and Catholics, largely from Quebec, missionary work was one of the few ways for Canadians to visit Japan, China, or India.[21] For women especially, missionary work was a liberating experience and a legitimate way to work outside the home and to travel abroad.[22] In an era of evangelizing Christianity, missionary activities held a wide appeal among both those actually going abroad and those Christians supporting their efforts from home. It was a global enterprise, in which Canadians took a prominent role; by one estimate, by 1925, Americans and Canadians comprised half of the world's twenty-nine thousand missionaries.[23]

The reasons for missionary activity were varied. For some, spreading Christianity to Asia and Africa was about advancing a civilizing mission, with missionaries serving as handmaidens to empire. *The Globe* praised missionaries for their 'journeyings, martyrdoms, voluntary surrenders of self and all the human heart holds dear for the sake of sharing with remote and unsympathetic peoples the Christian ideal and life'.[24] Among indigenous people in Canada, missionaries extended Canadian rule west and north, and by seeking to alter local customs and cultures, they enhanced the Canadian state's assimilationist efforts. The same civilizing spirit motivated missionary activities beyond Canada. Canadian missionaries operating in Trinidad and British Guiana served alongside British colonial administrators in seeking to help subject peoples. 'England has given the people of Indore an organized army, protection, wise administration of law and education', recorded one proponent of mission work in India. 'To Canada is left the distinguished honour of sending the gospel'.[25] Given its association with imperialism, missionary activity created animus among local people, perhaps most famously during the Boxer rebellion in China. In a melding of imperial and missionary spirit, George Monro Grant told a British Empire League meeting that he regretted that Canada had not sent troops to China where 'civilization itself was at stake'.[26]

Missionaries held sincere desires to help foreigners, both in the present and in the afterlife. In an appeal for missionary service in China, James Hudson Taylor, founder of the China Inland Mission, remarked during a conference at Niagara-on-the-Lake, that in Asia there was 'a great Niagara of souls passing into the dark'.[27] Beyond this spiritual quest, like aid and development workers in the latter half of the twentieth century, missionaries sought to improve people's daily lives. By building and running schools or engaging in medical work, these charitable activities did more concrete good than did evangelizing. Toronto's Donald MacGillivray, an influential Presbyterian missionary in China, was involved in educational work and in combating opium addiction, goals pursued by his wife, Elizabeth, who worked with the YWCA's Chinese branch.[28] Whether due to religious conviction, human compassion, or exposure to and interaction with foreigners, many missionaries came to deplore Canadian discrimination towards non-whites living in Canada.[29] Such discrimination was particularly strong in BC, Canada's gateway to the Pacific.

The province's coastal cities Victoria and Vancouver were the main points of entry for Asian migrants. Although it grew into a quintessentially British city, like all entrepôts Victoria attracted traders and travellers from across the globe. One visitor described encountering people of 'almost every nationality ... Greek fishermen, Jewish and Scottish merchants, Chinese washermen, French, German and Yankee officeholders and butchers, Negro waiters and sweeps, Australian farmers and other varieties of the race, rub against each other, apparently in the most friendly way'.[30] Victoria had a sizable indigenous population, as did BC, where contact and settlement had come relatively late. Over the course of the late nineteenth and early twentieth centuries, Victoria was steadily anglicized: immigrants from Britain arrived, among them retired military officers and civil servants from India and other parts of the Asian empire, and cricket clubs, private schools, ornamental gardens, and other trappings of upper-class English life popped up across the city.[31] This effort to transplant England to BC came at a cost for non-white people, who were viewed as a threat by local, provincial, and federal politicians engaged in making BC into a white man's province. 'When Frenchmen, Italians, and even Germans come to British Columbia it is only a question of time before they are absorbed into the Canadian commonwealth', stated an Anglican minister. 'Not so with the Japanese and Chinese, who are Mongolian, Yellow, Asiatic, and non-Christian people.'[32] Migrants from across the Pacific, warned one local MP perhaps with some self-awareness of settler colonialism, meant that BC risked becoming 'a colony, and ultimately a possession of a united Orient'.[33]

Fears of the 'Yellow Peril' were common during the 'Coolie era', when, in the mid to late nineteenth century, millions of Chinese migrants became part of a world-spanning, mobile labour pool. A gold rush in 1858 drew upwards of thirty thousand people to BC, among them thousands of Chinese. Many stayed in Victoria, working as fishers and labourers, especially as Vancouver Island and mainland BC were developed. Chinese labour was particularly valued, though the same could not be said for the labourers themselves. This fact was made explicit during the CPR's construction. From 1881 to 1885, roughly fifteen thousand Chinese men were brought to Canada as cheap, expendable labour, many of them recruited by Yip Sang, a CPR employee.[34] Employing Chinese labour was politically controversial, but as John A. Macdonald explained, 'At present it is simply a question of alternatives. Either you must have this labor or you cannot have the railway.' Although defending cheap labour as a necessity, Macdonald offered the assurance that he would not permit 'Mongolians becoming permanent settlers'.[35]

Matters came to a head in 1885, with the railroad's completion. To prevent male labourers from bringing family members, especially females, to Canada, Macdonald's government imposed an exorbitant fee on Chinese immigrants. The move was necessary, the prime minister explained, to avoid creating 'a mongrel race' endangering Canada's 'Aryan character'. In addition to this Head Tax, his government stripped the federal franchise from Chinese people, who, in Macdonald's view, had 'no British instincts or British feelings or aspiration, and therefore ought not to have a vote'.[36] The only limits to Macdonald's goal of creating a white Canada were that Chinese in Canada were not deported and that immigration was not banned entirely. A total ban, he explained, would upset China's government thereby 'killing future business with that country'.[37] As with the West Indies, trade with distant people was to be encouraged, their movement to Canada discouraged.

Although Canada's Chinese community protested, the Head Tax was increased exponentially at several points, and remained until 1923, effectively putting a stop to legal Chinese immigration. The measure remained popular with white workers, whose fears of labour competition fuelled racist sentiments. It was no coincidence that the Vancouver Trades and Labor

Council warned Prime Minister Laurier – who twice increased the Head Tax – that 'white supremacy could not continue in the face of Asian immigration'.[38] In contrast, Canadian industrialists, seeking a larger pool of workers and lower wages, supported Asian migration. 'What we want is population', affirmed William Van Horne. 'Labour is required from the Arctic Ocean to Patagonia, throughout North and South America, but the Governments of other lands are not such idiots as we are in the matter of restricting immigration.'[39] With Chinese immigration banned, when the Grand Trunk and Pacific Railway began construction in 1905, the company procured temporary workers from Russia.[40] Rumours that Grand Trunk would import Japanese labourers led to an outbreak of racist violence.

For white Canadians, Japanese immigration was viewed in the same negative terms as immigration from China. The problem for Canada's federal government was that Japan was a British ally, and in 1906 Canada acceded to the 1894 Anglo-Japanese Treaty of Commerce and Navigation, which allowed the Dominion to begin trading with the Japanese. Further complicating the matter was that unlike China, Japan was a rising great power with growing international clout. Some Canadians had a measure of grudging respect for Japan. Paying the country a compliment, Manitoba MP Nicholas Flood Davin characterized Japan as 'the England of those eastern seas, inhabited by the Anglo-Saxons of the yellow races'.[41] Japan's victory over Russia in a 1905 war left a positive impression, with Laurier noting that 'the Japanese has adopted European civilization, has shown that he can whip European soldiers, has a navy equal man for man to the best afloat, and will not submit to be kicked and treated with contempt, as his brother from China still meekly submits to'.[42] Due to the Anglo-Japanese alliance, Ottawa disallowed various pieces of anti-Japanese legislation passed by the BC legislature. Sir Oliver Mowat, federal justice minister, warned that British Columbians 'might seriously interfere with international relations and federal interests'.[43] That was the case in 1907.

In addition to a sharp uptick in Japanese migration to BC in 1906 and 1907, Indian and illegal Chinese immigration had increased too. Class-based racial anger in BC was stoked further by an economic downturn. At the same time, mounting Asian migration to the states along the US Pacific Coast led to an explosion of violence in Bellingham, Washington, and other coastal cities. Within days, Vancouver's Asiatic Exclusion League staged a parade protesting rumours that Grand Trunk sought to import ten thousand Japanese. The march descended into mob violence. Over one thousand marchers rioted through Vancouver's Chinatown and set upon the Japanese section of the city, where residents beat them back. Canada's governor general blamed the incident on 'agitators coming from the United States', but the violence was homegrown.[44]

Laurier's response was twofold. First, since Japan was an ally, he agreed to pay recompense to Japanese Canadians whose property had been damaged;

no such restitution was given to the riot's Chinese victims. Second, Laurier addressed the issue of Japanese immigration. Given the Anglo-Japanese alliance and Canadian firms' hopes of breaking into Japan's market, Laurier ruled out banning immigration or imposing a head tax, steps sure to offend the Japanese. His solution was to despatch Rodolphe Lemieux, his minister of labour, to Japan to hammer out a deal. Through the so-called Gentlemen's Agreement, Japan's government agreed to restrict annual outmigration to Canada to 400 male labourers and domestic servants. The Japanese assented because they, too, restricted immigration. In defending this first Canadian foray into quasi-diplomacy in the Pacific – Britain's ambassador in Tokyo had been present during the talks – Lemieux explained to the House that this measure was preferable to asking a British ally 'to brand themselves before the whole world, as an inferior race – which they are not. They are, on the contrary, the rising power in the Far East.' 'It seems to me', retorted a French Canadian nationalist MP, 'that we have been sacrificing Canadian interests for the Imperial policy of Great Britain'.[45]

The Gentlemen's Agreement solved one problem only to create another. US President Theodore Roosevelt was upset that Canada had struck a deal without American participation. By happenstance, William Lyon Mackenzie King, Canada's deputy labour minister, was in Washington, conducting research for a report on Asian immigration. Summoning King to the White House, Roosevelt held forth on the need to bar Asian immigrants, even musing about a desire to use military force against Japan should it refuse to prevent its people from heading to the United States. He appealed for the creation of an Anglo-American alliance against Japan and asked King to carry this message to British officials. In London, King found little sympathy for Roosevelt's suggestion, especially because the president sought to target Indian immigration, which raised a host of intra-imperial issues for both the British and Canadians.[46] The president's proposal, while rejected, gives some insight into the racial thinking that predominated in this period, including the practical limitations to ideas about Anglo-Saxon solidarity.

The fin de siècle saw a flurry of interest in the idea of an Anglo-Saxon-dominated world, a notion of racial solidarity and superiority appealing to some Canadians. Looking at Canadian and British involvement in South Africa and American fighting in the Philippines, one writer exulted that 'both branches of the Anglo-Saxon people are engaged in subduing inferior races' and that 'progressive civilization' was being established in these far-flung territories, 'where the Boer and Filipino have been made to realize that the Anglo-Saxon race never errs, that it makes war only for the benefits of humanity'.[47] Inspired by the US guerrilla war in the Philippines, Rudyard Kipling penned 'The White Man's Burden' to urge Americans to take up an imperial role alongside Britain. One Canadian academic agreed, 'Should the United States decide on an expansive policy the world will no doubt benefit.' 'I embrace the United States as a part of the Anglo-Saxon community', wrote another Canadian.[48] The French Canadian fact was the most obvious sign that Canada was not an Anglo-Saxon polity, though in the 1880s, the Toronto *Daily Mail* advocated annexation with the United States because it would mean the creation of a large Anglo-Saxon Protestant bloc that could dominate French Canadian Catholics.[49] The Anglo-Saxon idea was fantasy, but no less important for that: it reflected the race thinking of the time – with Anglo-Saxons at the apex of a racial hierarchy – with the uptick in its popularity indicating the unease created by immigration from Asia and continental Europe.

As for Roosevelt's concern with Indian immigrants, just as efforts to restrict Japanese immigration had to account for other factors, Indian migration posed a practical problem for Canadian officials in that Indians were fellow British subjects, deserving of the same rights and freedoms – including freedom of movement – as Canadians. Yet, between 1904 and 1908, the arrival in BC of five thousand South Asians led white British Columbians to demand an end to this movement of people. King had studied the matter as part of his investigation of immigration policy. Concluding that Indians were unsuited to life in Canada given the climate, nonetheless, because of the imperial tie he recommended against barring Indian immigration outright. At his suggestion, in 1908, the Laurier government amended the Immigration Act to require potential Indian migrants to make a continuous voyage to Canada, a difficult task made harder by the fact that this service was only offered by CPR, and Ottawa barred the company from selling the requisite tickets. The regulation affected not only potential Indian migrants but also Japanese migrants travelling to Canada via Hawaii, a route that could be used to bypass the Gentlemen's Agreement. The measure was effective: during 1910–20, only 112 Indians gained admittance to Canada.[50] As for the Indian population within Canada, Ottawa mulled a scheme to move them to British Honduras to work as labourers, but abandoned the plan as impractical.[51]

Indian resistance to Canadian discrimination emerged soon after the continuous voyage requirement was enacted, and it melded into protests against both American restrictions and British imperial rule. 'You drive us Hindus out of Canada and we will drive every white man out of India', proclaimed one protestor.[52] Vancouver's Hindustani Association promoted immigration rights and demanded an end to the continuous journey rule. Its efforts were closely monitored by William Hopkinson, a British police official from India hired by Ottawa to investigate Indian political activity. Given the transnational nature of Indian resistance, his actions carried him across the Pacific Northwest to both sides of the Canada–US border. In North America, South Asian protests crystalized behind the Ghadar (Revolt) Party, formed in 1913 to challenge immigration restrictions, the curtailing of citizenship rights, and British rule in India. Monitoring the organization, British, American, and Canadian authorities grew increasingly worried as Ghadar members forged links with radical socialists who shared anti-imperialist goals. There was violence: Hopkinson was assassinated, comeuppance for having supported the killing of several Ghadar members by rival Indians. Once the Great War began, the Ghadar movement received support from the German government, prompting a further crackdown by Canadian, American, and British authorities.[53] Overall, what the movement achieved was Anglo-Saxon cooperation.

Meanwhile, in the spring of 1914, Vancouver area newspapers warned of 'Hindu Invaders'.[54] In protest of the continuous voyage rule, Sikh entrepreneur Gurdit Singh had chartered the *Komagatu Maru* to carry 376 Indian migrants to Canada. 'We are British citizens', Singh declared, 'and we consider we have a right to visit any part of the Empire.'[55] The ship arrived at Vancouver after having made stops at Hong Kong, Shanghai, and Yokohama. Twenty-two passengers who were returning to Canada were allowed ashore; the rest were barred entry and confined to the overcrowded ship, which sat in port for nearly two months. In Vancouver, there were protests for and against letting the men leave the vessel. With government authorities set on enforcing immigration restrictions, the *Komagatu Maru* was compelled to return to India, escorted from Canadian waters by the HMCS *Rainbow*, one of Canada's two newly acquired naval vessels. The incident laid bare the hypocrisy in how notions of British imperial citizenship were applied in practice.[56] Despite the high tide of imperial feeling in pre-Great War Canada, Indians were held in contempt. One academic, O. D. Skelton, warned of the dangers inherent in the clamour 'for a white Canada', namely that it 'will not lessen the unrest in India when from Johannesburg and Vancouver come reports of how nominal is the Hindoo's share in imperial citizenship'.[57] Skelton, who went on to become an important figure in Canadian foreign policy circles in the 1920s and 1930s, was a lonely advocate of tolerance.

Even though they too were fellow British subjects, black West Indians were barred from Canada. So were black Americans, as several hundred migrants seeking to escape segregation in Oklahoma found after trying to emigrate to Canada in the early twentieth century. The Canadian colour bar was formally erected in 1911, with the passage of an Order-in-Council – use of the Immigration Act was avoided because of imperial citizenship – that prohibited 'any immigrants belonging to the Negro race, which is deemed unsuitable to the climate and requirements of Canada'.[58] The resort to weather was a convenient fiction ignoring the fact that black people had been living in the territory that became Canada since the first slaves were imported under the French colonial regime. Beyond its use for restrictive purposes, the notion stemmed from a prevailing view that people from colder climes were superior to those from the tropics. 'In the northern zone', wrote journalist James Macdonald, 'the thermometer is on the side of the white man.' A cold climate, contended imperialist George Parkin, allowed Canada to avoid 'the great colour problem'. On this point, he found agreement with socialist J. S. Woodsworth, who wrote, 'we may be thankful we have no negro problem in Canada.'[59]

Parkin and Woodsworth were contrasting Canada with the United States, a past-time reaching back to 1776. The Canadian readiness to obscure inconvenient similarities and to magnify slight differences was a central ingredient in the making of Canadian identity. This anti-American, or un-American, aspect to Canadian life is less the product of genuine antipathy than of self-preservation, a recognition that many Canadians share with Americans a common language, cultural habits, and even lineage. Indeed, some figures asked, why should Canada even be a separate country? For transplanted British historian Goldwin Smith, Canada was an artificial creation of a railroad and a tariff that tried in vain to orient the country along an east-west axis, when its natural orientation was north-south. His solution to Canada's stunted economic growth was a union of the two North American countries. This outcome was inevitable, for in Smith's view, Canada and the United States were already one polity, the result of 'geography, commerce, identity of race, language, and institutions, with the mingling of population and constant intercourse of every kind'.[60] Smith's prescription found little traction publicly, a testament to the practical limits of Anglo-Saxon racial rhetoric. Yet he made sound observations about the sorry state of the Canadian economy and the interchange of people and ideas across the Canada–US border.

There was little to commend about the Canadian economy of the 1870s and 1880s. In these decades, poor economic growth resulted in poor population growth as more people left the country than arrived as immigrants, with a high birth rate being the only reason for any uptick in Canada's population. Most migrants left for the United States: the 1880s saw 825,000 Canadians head south, a shocking figure given that Canada's population in 1891 was just 4.8 million.[61] Even once the economy picked up in the 1890s, this southward flow continued, though the Laurier government's immigration drive in 1896 made up for these losses. By 1900, former Canadians comprised 10 per cent of the US population. This number included hundreds of thousands of Maritimers and French Canadians, who fled sluggish local economies for booming mill towns across New England. As Catholics and as francophones, French Canadians were suspect in the eyes of many Americans; in 1881, Massachusetts's governor likened them to the 'Chinese of the Eastern States'. Yet, most Canadian immigrants adjusted seamlessly to life in the United States.[62]

During the Laurier immigration boom, some 400,000 Americans came north. If non-white immigrants were a problem, American immigrants were welcomed, for they ensured the new country's 'Anglo-Saxon character'.[63] This easy interchange of people – white people it should be emphasized – across the border is signified by questions around confused allegiances. Chicago-born William Van Horne was a driving force behind the CPR; his opposite number, the Canadian-born James Hill, was the architect of the Great Northern Railway that stretched across the United States. With Hill, an historian noted, it is difficult to identify 'where the Canadian stopped and the American began', and one might ask the same about Van Horne.[64] Similarly, the physical educator James Naismith was born in Ontario but invented basketball in Springfield, Massachusetts, in 1891, leading to endless debate about whether basketball is an American or Canadian creation.

Such questions indicate the complex intimacy of Canadian–American relations. However, close ties were also a source of insecurity. Canadian thirst for American culture raised concerns about the spread of American ideas. Rodolphe Lemieux, responsible for negotiating the Gentlemen's Agreement with Japan, was perturbed that 'our theatres, sports, magazines, newspapers, are all more or less of the Yankee sort'.[65] Not just a matter of the influx of American material, the issue boiled down to what it meant to be Canadian. 'Our Art is not Canadian', complained one critic, while another warned, 'No one, and this is the gravest charge our literature has to bear, has yet synthesized for us the meaning of our Canadian life, nor revealed us to ourselves.'[66] For many English Canadians, identity was found in the British connection. 'It counts for something that Canada has to-day a King Edward', wrote historian George Wrong.[67] The British counterweight was important, leading to worries that it was being degraded as Canadians became more North American. Journalist and imperialist J. Castell Hopkins sounded the tocsins over 'the gradual but steady development of a non-British view of things'.[68] In 1907, French sociologist André Siegfried concluded from his travels in Canada that 'at bottom, by taste and tradition, English Canadians are very English still'. Nine years later, he wondered, 'Is it possible that a Dominion which is American in its way of life can remain attached to Britain?'[69]

Some Canadians embraced connections to the United States. Even before Confederation, American political movements had attracted and repelled in equal measure. This process accelerated in the late nineteenth century, thanks to the spread of mass media and connections forged by relatively inexpensive, easy travel via railroad. The social gospel movement and progressivism both found a ready audience among Canadian academics, politicians, civil servants, and activists who shared their American counterparts' concerns with industrialization, urbanization, and unbridled capitalism. Canadians drew inspiration from US campaigns for urban planning, consumer protections, labour rights, social policies, eugenics, prohibition, and women's suffrage, though importantly, these networks of reformers were not simply North American, but often stretched across the English-speaking world. Leading British and Australian suffragists, for instance, travelled to Canada in the years leading up to the Great War.[70] Like American culture and American capital, American unions – the Knights of Labor and the American Federation of Labor (AFL) – expanded north. 'We are more than neighbors; we are kin', declared AFL chief Samuel Gompers. 'There is no 49th parallel of latitude in unionism', added a member.[71] This observation was true enough, because the Canadian economy was increasingly developing along US lines.

Washington's termination of its 1854 reciprocity treaty with Britain's North American colonies was one of the spurs to Canadian Confederation. During the 1871 Washington Treaty discussions, Macdonald had sought a new agreement, but the Americans were uninterested. Under Alexander Mackenzie's brief Liberal government, the very liberal-minded George Brown had begun trade talks with Ulysses Grant's administration, but no treaty was forthcoming. When Macdonald returned to government, he implemented the National Policy, a huge tariff on imported American and British goods, with the goal of building up industry in Ontario and Quebec, and in this regard the policy was a success, even if industrialization proceeded in fits and starts and resulted in the gradual deindustrialization of the Maritime provinces, with companies consolidating operations in central Canada. Furthermore, protectionism damaged Canadian living standards, part of the reason for outmigration to the United States in the 1880s. The National Policy made for good politics, as Macdonald's hold on Canadian political life indicates. 'You cannot get anything by kissing the feet of the people of the United States', he had stated in the 1878 election.[72]

The tariff had the effect of encouraging American and British investment, which financed the takeover of Canadian companies and the formation of Canada-based subsidiaries of US and British firms, a prudent means of getting past the tariff wall. It helped, no doubt, that there was a common language at play and that – for American investors – Canada was so close.[73] Standard Oil purchased Imperial Oil, American Bell Telephone bought a stake in Bell Canada, and J.P. Morgan and Carnegie Steel's Charles Schwab financed the creation of the International Nickel Company in Sudbury. Westinghouse, Singer, and International Harvester each opened plants in Canada. Because of these investments and despite the tariff, in 1907, a visiting British journalist marvelled that 'Canadians, who are only 5,500,000 in number, buy more goods from the United States than are purchased by all the inhabitants of all the Central and South American Republics.'[74]

There were opponents of the National Policy. In 1887, in the face of an ongoing economic slump and the flood of outmigration, the Liberal Party resolved to pursue reciprocity with the Americans. Within the party, proponents of a customs union formed the Commercial Union League, with Goldwin Smith as president. During the 1891 election, Macdonald campaigned against free trade, and with Smith involved with the Liberals, it was easy for the old Tory to label his opponents as annexationists.[75] Defeated by Macdonald's protectionism, the Liberals subsequently dropped reciprocity from their platform; when they formed government in 1896, free trade with the United States was an afterthought. By 1910, however, the issue was back in play. The Laurier government had overseen an economic boom and there was a sense that Canadian firms could now compete with their US counterparts. Also, there was considerable pressure from Canadian farmers, upset at their lack of access to the well-protected American market. Facing similar domestic demands for a reduction in tariffs, William Howard Taft's administration was happy to negotiate with Ottawa, and in January 1911, a deal was inked. Next, the agreement had to be ratified. Surprisingly, it sailed through both houses of Congress, thereby raising suspicions among some Canadians. Fears were confirmed when Speaker of the House James 'Champ' Clark declared: 'I hope to see the day when the American flag will float over every square foot of the British North American possessions clear to the North Pole.' 'I fear the Greeks when they are bearing gifts', Conservative MP George Foster stated the very same day.[76]

The floodgates of anti-Americanism opened. Robert Borden and the Conservatives accused Laurier of treason. The choice, he stated, was 'whether the spirit of Canadianism or continentalism shall prevail on the northern half of this continent'.[77] Prominent Liberals in industry turned on the prime minister and there was a public outcry. 'The feeling in Montreal and Toronto against the Agreement', the governor general observed, 'could hardly be stronger if the United States troops had already invaded our territory'.[78] Given the controversy, Laurier opted to put the issue to the electorate. Pro-British elements of the populace had two issues to focus on: selling out to the Americans, and Laurier's unwillingness to contribute to the Royal Navy. 'Which will it be?' asked the Toronto *World*, 'Borden and King George, or Laurier and Taft?' The Montreal Women's Anti-Reciprocity League put the issue simply: 'Reciprocity means Annexation.'[79] The agreement had its defenders. Henri Bourassa critiqued the protectionists for ignoring 'the elements of Northern American geography', and liberal political economist O. D. Skelton questioned the logic that 'when a Canadian farmer sells a bag of potatoes to a New Yorker he throws in his country to boot'.[80] Farmers backed free trade, and in the election Liberals swept Alberta and Saskatchewan. But the Conservatives dominated throughout the rest of the country, especially in Ontario, where fervour for Britain and suspicions of the United States were highest and where the Tories won seventy-two of eighty-six seats. Macdonald's National Policy was reaffirmed.[81]

Three points are worth noting. First, the protectionists had a point. Taft admitted as much, telling Theodore Roosevelt that the agreement 'would produce a current of business between Canada and the United States that would make Canada only an adjunct of the United States'.[82] Second, whatever anti-American rhetoric may have been stirred up, much of it was purely political. Within weeks of becoming prime minister, Borden – a believer in Anglo-Saxon unity – affirmed that 'Canada's voice and influence should always be for harmony and not for discord between Europe and the great Republic.' Beyond the cancellation of the agreement, there were no follow up actions to suggest any anti-Yankee platform on his part.[83] Third, the rancour over trade aside, the international relationship between Canada and the United States – while lacking formal diplomatic relations – proceeded well and the 1911 trade agreement was only one side of a productive bilateral arrangement.

Between 1908 and 1916, Canada and the United States signed three comprehensive wildlife protection agreements: the Inland Fisheries Treaty (1908), the North Pacific Fur Seal Convention (1911), and the Migratory Bird Treaty (1916). This successful foray into 'conservation diplomacy' stemmed from shared environmental concerns among progressives on both sides of the border. It showed, too, early recognition that environmental issues crossing political boundaries required international cooperation.[84] The same attitude guided the completion of the Boundary Waters Treaty (1909). This agreement created the International Joint Commission (IJC), a permanent body, equally divided between Canadians and Americans, designed to resolve issues that arose from North America's shared waterways. A prudent idea, the IJC put potentially sensitive matters into the hands of specialists rather than politicians. Over the next three decades, the commission became celebrated, by Canadians at least, as the exemplar of the cooperative Canada–US relationship, principally because the United States, a great power, agreed to treat a smaller power as an equal.[85] Also, there was the International Boundary Commission, established in 1908 to settle outstanding questions surrounding the boundary line between the two countries. Arbitration at The Hague produced the North Atlantic Coast Fisheries Agreement (1910), ending an issue that had plagued North American relations for three quarters of a century.[86] These various agreements testify to the harmonious nature of much of Canada–US relations and to the efforts of officials in both countries to establish legal instruments to resolve disputes.

Not that there was perfect harmony, even through these sorts of arrangements. During the Alaska boundary dispute, the commission's decision favouring the US territorial claim upset Canadians, though much of their ire was directed towards the British commissioner, who had sided with the American commissioners against Canada. Furthermore, the Americans were in the right, though it did not help Canadian amour propre that Theodore Roosevelt spoke loudly while wielding his big stick.[87] The power differential between the two neighbours was obvious. As Laurier remarked to US Secretary of State Elihu Root, 'we are a small ctry & cannot resist, you can force us but it is not fair or just.'[88] Despite American power, Canada was largely treated well. Furthermore, militarily, the border was undefended, especially in comparison to Europe. Here was the basis for the notion that North America was different from other parts of the world, an idea that gained traction amid the Great War. On the eve of the conflict journalist James Macdonald, a central advocate for what he would later call the 'North American Idea', praised the 'unprecedented and unparalleled fact of 4,000 miles of civilized internationalism', which stood as 'a message to all continents, the supreme message of North America to all the world. What has been done by those proud and ambitious Anglo-Saxon peoples ought not to be impossible in Europe or elsewhere in the civilized world.'[89]

Macdonald's lauding of the peacemaking abilities of the Anglo-Saxon peoples was no mistake. Canada's first five decades were marked by efforts to ensure that the country's population was white. Worth remembering is that Ottawa's efforts to bar non-white people came at the same time as it was encouraging mass immigration. Support for racial exclusion was not confined to government. A popular song that warned of the 'oriental grasp' concluded with the declaration 'White Canada Forever'.[90] This attitude led to policies enforcing Canadian borders against the inward flow of unwanted peoples. Additionally, boundary enforcement appealed to Canadians concerned with the United States, economically and culturally. The period of globalization preceeding the Great War – like the late twentieth-century iteration – was a source of insecurity, especially so for citizens of a new country.

Canada benefitted from its connections abroad. In 1891, amid more than a decade of sluggish economic growth, with tens of thousands of Canadians leaving for the United States each year, Wilfrid Laurier wrote to Liberal Party leader Edward Blake, who had faced a drubbing at the hands of John A. Macdonald over the issue of reciprocity. 'We have come to a period in the history of this young country', he worried, 'when premature dissolution seems to be at hand'.[91] Thirteen years later, Laurier, now prime minister, boasted: 'The nineteenth century was the century of the United States. I think we can claim that Canada will fill the twentieth century.'[92] What changed in that time was an industrial and agricultural boom helped along by a huge influx of immigrants. 'Prosperity', in the view of one journalist, 'has brought the self-confidence and the initiative that were lacking during the long lean years'.[93] The Dominion's turn of the century growth drew the attention of government officials as far afield as Argentina, where there were hopes of developing the pampas along Canadian lines, and Russia, where Canada's westward expansion was viewed as a model for Siberia.[94] Canada's political system attracted attention too. Living in the country from 1907 to 1914, John Monnet gained insight into federalism, lessons he later applied as the intellectual force behind the European Union.[95] And over the summer of 1914, celebrations were held to mark the centennial of the Treaty of Ghent, which had ended the War of 1812. With tensions rising in Europe, commemorations of a century of relative peace in North America seemed poignant indeed.

4

Canada's Great War

'The country went mad!' was how one Canadian described the public mood when war was declared in August 1914. There were celebratory bonfires in Regina, a military parade in Winnipeg, and in Toronto, '"Rule Britannia" and "God Save the King" filled the air . . . [and] Union Jacks appeared in windows and storefronts'.[1] Given popular imperialism and militarism in early twentieth-century Canada – and in the combatant countries more broadly – this public outpouring of support is hardly surprising. Nor, given the factors that drove Canada into the conflict, is it a surprise that the Great War exposed tensions 'between French and English, between new and old Canada, between classes, and between city and country'.[2] What is surprising, perhaps, is that by the end of four years of brutal fighting on Britain's behalf, many Canadians, even those who were imperially minded and who had championed Canada's combat role, sought greater autonomy for their country. As Prime Minister Sir Robert Borden told the Imperial War Cabinet in July 1918, as the war entered its final months, 'unless [Canada] could have the voice in the foreign relations of the Empire as a whole, she would before long have an independent voice in her own foreign affairs outside the Empire'.[3] Although it is too much to credit the conflict as Canada's war of independence, it did mark a stepping stone in the long process of Canada's decolonization as there were many Canadians who demanded vindication for the sacrifices that had been made during four years of slaughter. Yet, the war's utility as a nation-building event was limited, for it divided as much as it united.

Focusing on diplomatic and political issues surrounding the Great War and Canada's role in what was an imperial war effort, this chapter looks at the ways in which Canadians reacted to the conflict. A clash among rival imperial powers, the war led to the collapse of four empires and mounting calls for self-determination on the part of dozens of ethnic groups and subject colonial peoples. Canadian attitudes reflected this wider trend, differing only in terms of degree. Growing autonomy from Britain and a sense of nationalism especially in English Canada were but two reactions to the conflict. Four years of grinding warfare led Canadians, variously, towards increased nativism, socialism, internationalism, and isolationism. 'The world has drifted far from its old anchorage', Borden reflected on the day the armistice was declared, 'and no man can with certainty prophesy what the outcome will be.'[4] As was true globally, tremendous wartime dislocation exposed a variety of fault lines, which continued to shake and shape Canada long after the guns fell silent.

In 1914, the British World went to war. Dependent on Britain, Canada was automatically committed to the imperial war effort, and Canadian blood and treasure were expended on a world-spanning campaign to advance British interests. For Canada, there was little at stake in the fate of Serbia or Belgium except as these areas affected Europe's balance of power and then only because Britain cared about European events. With the metropole at war, the Dominions responded. 'The democracies of Greater Britain stand together in all parts of the world to support the traditions of British liberty', wrote historian and Round Table member George Wrong. Borden, meanwhile, appealed to 'a common resolve to put forth every effort and to make every sacrifice necessary to ensure the integrity and maintain the honour of the Empire'.[5] Or, as one propaganda poster from the period had it, the British lion had called its cubs to its defence and the young whelps were readily responding. What really mattered, then, was the Canadian response to the declaration of war. Although automatically involved, the nature and extent of this involvement was for Ottawa alone to decide. The Conservative government, in power thanks to the 1911 election in which they had campaigned on the naval issue and the British tie, had no compunctions about sending troops overseas. For Canadians who identified themselves as a part of the British World, Britain's war was Canada's war.

Like previous Canadian campaigns in Sudan, the North-West, and South Africa, in 1914, the government appealed for volunteers. The response was overwhelming. An initial goal of 25,000 volunteers was quickly met, and then surpassed: in October, 31,000 Canadians left for Europe, and the government announced plans to raise a second contingent. Most in the first cohort were British-born, and so flocking to the colours was a natural response for men who had only recently come to Canada. Recruitment numbers were helped, too, by an economic downturn. Still, the outpouring of Canadian support was neither the result simply of diaspora politics nor necessity. Militarism was popular, so was the Empire, and there was an incipient nationalism characterized by Wilfrid Laurier's boast that the twentieth century belonged to Canada. The war was an opportunity to showcase the young country abroad, to test Canadian mettle and manhood against the Hun – the popular pejorative for Germans, a barbaric threat from the East. As Colonel George Denison, an imperial federationist, proclaimed in 1914, 'We have been children long enough, let us show the Empire that we have grown to manhood.'[6]

A limitation on the war's potential as a nation-building event lay in its imperial nature. Loyal service to King and Empire did not appeal to all Canadians, and the conflict raised the spectre of internal strife along ethnic, linguistic, and religious lines. Observers had only to look back at the Boer War and the naval wrangling to see the potential for problems. At the conflict's outset, Borden and Laurier struck a truce and even Henri Bourassa accepted that Canada had to contribute soldiers to the war effort. The government pledged to send only volunteers abroad – British liberty ruled out conscription, something done in autocratic societies like Germany or, problematically given that it was an ally, Russia – and Laurier issued a declaration steeped in imperial patriotism: 'Canada, a daughter of old England, intends to stand by her in this great conflict. When the call comes our answer goes at once and it goes in the classical language of the British answer to the call of duty: "Ready, aye, ready." ' Given France's involvement, he implored French Canadians to recognize that 'We of French origin had a double duty to perform.'[7] Staunchly Catholic, few French Canadians agreed with this appeal to support the decadent Third Republic. Still, French Canadian men did volunteer for service albeit at lower rates than in the rest of the country and while some coalesced into the francophone 22nd and 69th battalions, others filtered into other units.

Signs of Canada's involvement in the British World at war were apparent in economic and material terms. Unlike the other self-governing Dominions, Canada contributed food and munitions to Britain, a sign of Canadian devotion and of the relatively short distance across the North Atlantic. Initial Canadian munitions production was marked by corruption and inefficiencies. So, in 1915, R. H. Brand, a British civil servant and ardent Round Tabler, assisted Canadian pork baron Joseph Flavelle in establishing the Imperial Munitions Board, the Canadian branch of Britain's Ministry of Munitions.[8] Their efforts at creating an integrated imperial production network were highly successful: Flavelle – an archetypal war profiteer, a reputation he carried with him – was knighted, and, by 1917, Canada produced between one-fourth and one-third of all the shells fired by the British artillery in Northern Europe, an important contribution given artillery's impact on the war's conduct. Meanwhile Canadian food production proved vitally important to the imperial war effort, particularly as British farmers were pressed into military service. Canada took up the slack, and in 1917, 'Canadian wheat stood between Britain and starvation.'[9] The imperial connection worked in other ways. Prominent Canadians in London served in the wartime British government. Sir George McLaren Brown, an executive who headed Canadian Pacific's European operations was seconded to the British War Office, handling logistics. Max Aitken, the Canadian-born financier, owner of the *Daily Express*, and British MP, served as the minister of information in 1918. Andrew Bonar Law, Aitken's political ally and a New Brunswicker by birth, was a wartime cabinet minister. These individuals testify to the elite network binding together the British World. Aitken, who received a peerage, becoming Lord Beaverbrook in 1917, did much to popularize notions of Canadian loyalty to the imperial cause, writing of the 'willing but untrained civilians who came rushing from the Pacific Coast, the Rockies, the grain-belt, the Western Prairies, and the fields and forests and cities of the East, to offer themselves to the Empire in her hour of need'.[10]

Manpower was Canada's most direct and consequential contribution. The Canadian Expeditionary Force (CEF) operated as an imperial contingent under the British Army Act and was directly commanded by a British officer until June 1917, when the soon-to-be-knighted General Arthur Currie was put in charge.[11] Throughout the entirety of the war, Britain oversaw the higher direction of Canadian military operations, a source of growing resentment for Borden and other Canadians. The CEF's first major action came in April 1915, at Ypres, which marked Canadians' introduction to industrialized warfare, with the battle notable for the Germans' first use of poison gas. During the month-long engagement, 6,500 Canadians were killed, wounded, or captured, a total nearing the whole of Canada's commitment to the Boer War. That the battle lasted so long – not simply a day or two – and that the casualties were so high, was an early sign that this war differed from the colonial campaigns in South Africa or the North-West. The losses here 'transformed the war from a great adventure to a great crusade' and sparked a 'Canadianization process' in how Canadians saw the war. Increasingly, they took ownership of the war effort rather than viewing it in imperial terms. Ypres, one newspaper proclaimed, was 'Canada's Birthplace as a Nation', one of several instances during the conflict that attempts at nation-building were found amid the mud and blood.[12]

As an imperial contingent, Canadians – and Newfoundlanders – took part in many of the major British engagements on the Western Front and shared in the terrible losses. Soon, questions arose about British leadership and Canada's lack of input on strategy. In mid-1915, on his first wartime visit to Britain, Borden found Herbert Asquith, his British counterpart, loath to give even basic information about the war. 'Procrastination, indecision, inertia, doubt, hesitation and many other undesirable qualities have made themselves entirely too conspicuous in this war', the Canadian prime minister thundered in 1916, adding that he agreed with a British politician who had quipped that the major problem facing the British army was not a shortage of munitions, but a shortage of 'brains'.[13] Despite his complaints, the reality was that however much Borden groused about these issues, he continued to meet Britain's pressing manpower needs. In October 1915, Borden committed to raising 250,000 men; four months later, he doubled this commitment.

The announcement of half a million men came as Britain was taking the unprecedented step of implementing conscription and so Borden felt pressure to increase Canada's contribution. Given casualty rates, maintaining 500,000 troops in the field would require 300,000 new recruits annually, an unattainable goal. As Canada's finance minister later recalled, in opting for this move, the Cabinet 'simply went on faith'.[14] Whatever faith he possessed in Britain or in the need for victory, within days of making this decision, Borden expressed his upset with being denied any say over the war's conduct. 'It can hardly be expected that we shall put 400,000 or 500,000 men in the field and willingly accept the position of having no more voice and receiving no more consideration than if we were toy automata', he told Canada's high commissioner in London. 'Any person cherishing such an expectation harbours an unfortunate and even dangerous delusion. Is this war being waged by the United Kingdom alone, or is it a war waged by the whole Empire?'[15] Here was the root of Borden's growing desire for a greater Canadian role in the world, one that would place Canada alongside Britain.

For whatever reason – patriotism, a desire to see victory over the Germans – a spike in recruitment followed Borden's January 1916 announcement of the goal of half a million men. The boost lasted several months but volunteer rates declined sharply, even as hundreds of recruiting leagues with thousands of volunteers, combed the country for men. As the final two years of the war began – a momentous period that saw the CEF engage in its most successful and costliest operations – the flow of reinforcements dried up, leading the government to conscription. Here it is worth considering that even with manpower shortages, a country of almost eight million, with a pre-war permanent army of only 3,110 soldiers, 74,000 poorly trained militia, and several hundred sailors, put over 630,000 men into uniform; an additional 50,000 were rejected on medical grounds.[16] The majority who served were volunteers, constituting roughly one-third of eligible military-age men. Doubtless, the more than one million men who did not serve in uniform included opponents of the war, but among those on the home front, certainly there were farmers, machinists, and longshoremen who saw their labours as contributing to victory. Also, there was the involvement of several thousand women who, for reasons of patriotism, professionalism, or a sense of adventure, served via the only way open to them: as nurses. Women formed the backbone of voluntary societies like the YWCA and the Imperial Order Daughters of the Empire, which ran charities for wounded soldiers and carried out massive production drives to knit thousands of soldiers' socks and roll millions of cigarettes.[17] The voluntary effort included assistance to civilians overseas. The Commission for Relief in Belgium helped people caught in the warzone, and the Canadian Red Cross raised and shipped supplies for French, Belgian, Romanian, and Serbian refugees.[18] By supporting soldiers or assisting civilians, thousands of Canadians were engaged in the global conflict in ways that extended beyond the battlefield. Indeed, throughout the war, Canadians contributed tens of millions of dollars annually to the war effort via Victory Bonds – 'fight or pay' was a prominent slogan.

As for the imperial war effort's higher direction, the other Dominion prime ministers shared Borden's insistence that if London wanted more men, then it should allow for their input. British hesitancy about any diminution of control changed somewhat once David Lloyd George became prime minister in December 1916. Wanting their soldiers, he placated the Dominions by setting up an Imperial War Cabinet and an Imperial Development Board, consultative bodies with little formal power, but that allowed the Dominion leaders to gain information and offer advice. The Imperial War Cabinet met twice, in March–April 1917 and June–July 1918. The first meeting occurred against the backdrop of Russia's revolution and doubts about the Russians continued involvement in the war, giving a sense of urgency to the proceedings. In exchange for promises of increased support, Lloyd George agreed to a resolution classifying the self-governing Dominions 'as autonomous nations of an Imperial commonwealth' and establishing that after the war a conference would be held to work out how the Dominions could be given an 'adequate voice in foreign policy' and 'autonomous consultation' in foreign relations. Along with South Africa's Jan Smuts, Borden had pressed the resolution, as well he might, for by this point Canada had taken seventy thousand casualties.[19] A milestone on the road of decolonization, this statement – lacking any constitutional machinery behind it – was a quid pro quo: more men for the promise of greater autonomy. Control of strategy remained with the British.

Borden's desire to increase troop levels sprang from his commitment to Lloyd George and because of his meetings with Canadian officers and encounters with wounded soldiers. Beyond the ongoing daily attrition among Canadian units, throughout 1917 Canadians were involved in an increasingly costly series of operations. In April, for the first time, the four Canadian divisions overseas fought together, and in a well-planned offensive they captured German defences along Vimy Ridge. Commemorated in Canada as a significant event, the battle was a tactical victory, but the wider Arras offensive of which it was a part was a failure. Vimy left 3,600 dead and 7,000 wounded Canadians. Suddenly, casualty rates exceeded recruitment levels. Similar losses came at the Battle of Hill 70 in August, another stunning Canadian tactical success. That same month Borden introduced the Military Service Act to implement conscription. Parliament descended into bitter acrimony, as French Canadian and rural MPs denounced this move. Farmers feared the loss of sons who were critical to their production, and francophones had little desire to be compelled to fight in what they viewed as a British war. Ernest Lapointe, a Liberal backbencher who went on to influence interwar Canadian foreign policy, saw the measure as the 'very opposite of democracy'.[20] The Liberal Party fractured largely along linguistic lines, with English-speaking, pro-Empire MPs leaving to join with Borden in a Union Government that formed in October. Whatever the declarations of growing autonomy agreed to earlier in the year, to an embittered Laurier these events made it clear that 'Canada is now governed by a junta sitting in London, known as "The Round Table" ... with Tories and Grits receiving their ideas from London and insidiously forcing them on their respective parties.'[21] As Canadian politicians bickered that autumn, overseas the CEF experienced tremendous losses in the months-long grind at Passchendaele.

In December, Borden submitted the Union Government to an election, essentially a vote on conscription. What ensued was the most vicious campaign in Canadian history: Borden was depicted as the adjutant of Death, Laurier as the Kaiser's stooge. Lieutenant Colonel John McCrae, whose poem 'In Flanders Fields' was used on Union election posters, was blunt: 'I hope I stabbed a Fr. Canadian with my vote.'[22] To help along his side, earlier in the year Borden had passed two pieces of legislation: the Military Voters Act allowed soldiers overseas to choose the riding in which their vote would be counted or to allow the party for which they voted to make this decision; the Wartime Elections Act stripped the vote from an estimated 50,000 conscientious objectors and Canadians born in enemy countries while enfranchising female relatives of servicemen. The latter move carried a touch of progressivism, for it marked the first time that women could vote federally in Canada. Yet, it was a naked political ploy: 'Vote to save your kin', was the message delivered to female voters.[23]

The Union Government won a sizeable majority and a significant majority of the popular vote, but Quebec gave sixty-two of sixty-five seats to the Laurier Liberals, and Borden's side lost all four Acadian constituencies.[24] With victory in hand, Borden set about enacting conscription, eventually raising nearly 100,000 troops, almost half of whom were sent overseas. However, in April 1918, when too many of those men called up for service were exempted and, with withering losses occurring at the front, Borden ended an exemption for farmers, outraging this constituency. That spring also saw anti-conscription riots in Montreal and Quebec City, with violent clashes between protestors and government troops.[25] As far as wartime insurrection went, these developments and the squabbling over conscription paled in comparison to the mutinies in the French Army in 1917, to the insurrection in Ireland, and to Russia's revolutions. Still, the internal divides created here were foremost in the minds of Canadian politicians during later foreign policy crises.

Conscription went into effect just in time, for throughout the first half of 1918, the Germans launched withering offensives along the Western Front to wear down the British and French before the arrival of American soldiers – the United States having entered the war in April 1917. The Germans overstretched themselves: in July, the French and Americans scored huge successes at the Marne, and in August British and Dominion forces launched a successful offensive at Amiens. The Hundred Days campaign had begun, with the Canadian Corps playing a pivotal role in beating back the Germans and ultimately helping to secure an armistice. On 11 November, Canadian soldiers entered the Belgian city of Mons, where British forces had first engaged the Germans in 1914. As the guns fell silent, the *Globe* exulted that 'tyranny has been dethroned, the world breathes once more the air of liberty, and humanity looks on the future again with eyes of hope and gladness'.[26] Canadian successes during the Hundred Days came at a terrible cost, a crippling 45,000 casualties out of roughly 100,000 men. Early the next year, there were mutinies among impatient troops desperate to go home, a sign of the same discontent that was roiling Canadian society.

Before turning to issues of post-war diplomacy and political tumult, we might briefly consider international aspects of Canada's wartime experience that go beyond the fighting on the Western Front or wrangling over Canadian autonomy. In terms of the Pacific World, racialist-minded Canadians confronted the problem of Japan, a British ally. At the conflict's outset, BC Premier Richard McBride urged Borden and British officials not to allow Japan into the war because he feared a Japanese betrayal. What proved particularly galling for McBride was that due to the poor state of Canada's navy, Japanese vessels guarded BC's coast. His solution was to purchase two submarines from the United States, the first and only time that a Canadian province possessed its own naval forces, though the vessels were quickly transferred to Canada's navy.[27] McBride aside, the Japanese acquitted themselves well against the Germans and there were words of gratitude in BC for 'the presence of the Japanese fleet on the Pacific'.[28] Canada's position within the Pacific World led to further racial complications involving roughly 85,000 members of the Chinese Labour Corps, recruited by the British government to fill manpower shortages. Secreted from Vancouver to Halifax en route to the Western Front in sealed train cars lest their presence upset white Canadians, armed guards ensured that these labourers did not abscond.[29]

Across the Pacific and in Eastern Europe, Canadians were embroiled briefly in the upheavals of the Russian revolutions. Although it was readily admitted that Imperial Russia was the most 'barbaric' state in Europe, the autocracy was an important ally against Germany.[30] A growth of wartime contacts between the two northern countries, especially Russian purchases of Canadian arms and munitions, led Canada to open trade commissions in 1916. The two revolutions there the following year alarmed Canada's government, but it was the communist coup that proved fateful. In an unfortunate blunder, in 1917 Leon Trotsky, detained in Halifax while travelling from New York to Russia, was released by Canadian authorities and he went on to play a significant role in the eventual Bolshevik victory in the Russian civil war.[31] Canada sought to prevent such a victory when, in August 1918, just as the war on the Western Front moved into its final phase – an uncertain development at the time – Borden agreed to Lloyd George's request for soldiers for an international coalition backing anti-Bolshevik forces. A handful of Canadians were deployed to the port cities of Murmansk and Baku, 500 Canadians went to Archangel, and a much larger force of 4,200 soldiers, plus Red Cross nurses, was sent to Vladivostok. Raymond Massey, an officer in the Siberian contingent, recalled their intentions: 'The expedition was to help complete what Winston Churchill had termed the "Cordon Sanitaire", which was to contain the Bolshevik revolution.'[32] Bizarrely, given the ongoing civil war, Ottawa hoped to advance economic interests in the region. To this end, accompanying the Canadian soldiers were trade officials and representatives of the Royal Bank of Canada who were tasked with opening a local branch. The Canadian forces accomplished little and in February 1919 Borden announced their withdrawal, telling the British that 'Russia would have to work out her own salvation'.[33] The intervention marked the first Canadian clash with Russian communism, but at the time it was the domestic struggle against Bolshevism that caught Canadian authorities' attention.

Russia was one important neighbour, the United States another. The American decision to remain neutral in the conflict for nearly three years rankled some Canadians. 'America counted her profits while Canada buried her dead', one Canadian diplomat bitterly recalled.[34] Incidents of German submarines operating out of US waters, fears of German saboteurs sneaking into the country, and a desire to ensure that enlisted Canadian soldiers did not flee south, led to increasing border security and customs enforcement, a thickening of the border that upset the daily lives of people living in the Canada–US borderlands.[35] American neutrality also benefitted the Canadian war effort. With British investors, a traditional source of foreign capital in Canada, focused on production at home, the Borden government found financing the war difficult. To fill the breach, Canada turned to the United States. A 1917 agreement with Washington allowed Britain to use money loaned to it by American sources to purchase materiel in Canada so long as parts manufactured in the United States were included in the final product – a similar arrangement, the Hyde Park agreement, would be worked out in the next war. In this way, the war saw a drawing together of Canada and the United States, a process that accelerated after the conflict ended. Signifying this development, in 1918, a Canadian War Mission opened in Washington to better coordinate production and supply. Although the mission closed in 1921, and while it was a proto-diplomatic post serving a very specific function, it was a wartime marker on Canada's winding road to autonomy.

That road went through Paris. In terms of the peace talks and the setting up of post-war institutions, Borden and other Canadians pressed to be involved.

At the December 1918 Imperial War Cabinet meetings, Lloyd George opposed separate Dominion representation at Paris, instead proposing that a single British delegate represent the Empire. Borden and Australia's Billy Hughes objected, contending that Dominion sacrifices justified their presence at the negotiating table. Lloyd George relented, and a British Empire Delegation attended the peace talks, with the Dominion leaders taking part alongside Britain's prime minister.

Canada had little impact on events in Paris. At one point, after Borden complained of being kept out of high level deliberations, French premier Georges Clémenceau reminded him of Canada's place, snapping, 'I make no mystery of it, there is a conference of the Great Powers going on in the next room.'[36] Still, Borden involved himself where he could, attending most of the meetings of the British Empire Delegation and serving as vice president of the Commission on the Greek Question. Lord Milner, Britain's colonial secretary, saw Borden as the only Dominion leader, 'who, without ceasing to be a good Canadian, is capable of taking the wider view and whose judgment and influence are really useful on Imperial and International questions'.[37] On the issues up for debate, Canada's delegation took a light stance on reparations, seeking to balance the sense that Germany be punished with the fear that German economic disaster could foster Bolshevism. The Canadians displayed little enthusiasm for self-determination, a major element of Wilson's platform for the peace talks, and one that inspired delegates from dozens of oppressed ethnic groups and subject colonial peoples. Sir George Foster, chair of the Canadian delegation, worried that self-determination, 'if logically carried out, would erect a chaos of incapable and impossible communities, and spell ruin and disorder and possible anarchy'.[38] Nor did the Canadians support a Japanese resolution proposing racial equality. While not outright hostile to the proposal, and indeed, seeking compromises to overcome steadfast opposition from the Australians and Americans, Borden had little desire to support a motion that challenged Canadian immigration restrictions.[39] Canada's representatives preferred an ordered, imperial world that largely maintained the status quo.

In ensuring their place in post-war international institutions and in buttressing their case for participation, Canadian officials drew upon attitudes that assumed a racial hierarchy and an ordering of states in which Canada was more than a minor power as befitted its wartime record. Retired Liberal politician Sir Clifford Sifton informed Borden that in pushing back against international opposition to Canada's status within the emerging League of Nations, Canadians would 'see the Japanese and Italian delegates and their respective governments individually and collectively sizzling in the lowest depths of Hell before they will agree to accept a standing inferior to the negroes of Liberia'.[40] Borden needed little convincing. Not only had Canadians sacrificed much during the war but there stood the prevailing belief that as a white man's country, Canada was superior to countries in Latin America and to the smattering of independent states in Africa and the Middle East. 'Shall *these* be the arbiters of Canada's future?' asked a cartoonist in the *Halifax Herald* above an image of a handsome Jack Canuck being judged by a panel of swarthy goblins representing Cuba, Haiti, Honduras, and Panama. In making the case for Canadian membership in the International Labour Organization (ILO), Borden contended that Canada should be accorded a seat given its relative power. Canadians, he emphasized, would 'not tamely submit to a dictum which declares that Liberia or Cuba, Panama or Hedjaz, Haiti or Ecuador must have a higher place in the ILO than can be accorded to their country which is probably the seventh industrial nation of the world'.[41] Here, in a prototypical form, was an articulation of Canada as a middle power, a notion that achieved prominence following the next world war.

A separate seat in the League and separate representation in the ILO signified growing autonomy. Further, in June 1919, the Treaty of Versailles was signed on behalf of the British Empire, with representatives from the Dominions and India then signing below the British signature; Canada and the other Dominions ratified the treaty on their own. Loring Christie, legal adviser in the Canadian Department of External Affairs, saw that, with the developments at Paris, Canada had become 'in some degree an international person'.[42] International recognition was important, as were British concessions to the Dominions. Although the planned post-war conference on Dominion autonomy was shelved, Canadians such as journalist John Dafoe, attached to Canada's Paris delegation, saw that the war had taken 'the traditional Empire and replaced it with a brotherhood of nations'. Likewise, Sir Arthur Currie praised the move afoot to make the empire 'a constellation of nations, free, equal, united ... under one flag and one King'.[43] That same month, when Britain and the United States negotiated a treaty with France guaranteeing that country's border with Germany – ultimately, the US Senate killed the agreement – the British included an article that the undertaking 'shall impose no obligation upon any of the Dominions of the British Empire unless and until it is approved by the Parliament of the Dominion concerned'.[44] What was emerging, though it lacked formal constitutional changes, was an imperial federation, whose members were equal in status, yet united under Britain.

For imperially minded Canadians, the war for empire became a war for autonomy within the empire, a sign that developments at Paris were matched by changing mindsets regarding Canada's place within the British World. 'Out of the torture of war', wrote George Wrong, 'have come the free, equal, and united states of the British Commonwealth.' 'The war has brought Canada out into open', added University of Toronto President Sir Robert Falconer. In his view, the Dominions now stood 'as a recognizable unit alongside Britain'.[45] Both Wrong and Falconer were imperial federationists, and so Canada's evolving status must have seemed like the fulfilment of their designs. Borden, especially, saw the connection between events overseas and developing Canadian autonomy. As he explained to the House of Commons in May 1917, in his statement introducing the conscription bill, wartime sacrifices were worthwhile because 'the battle for Canadian liberty and autonomy is being fought to-day on the plains of France and of Belgium'.[46] In 1918, Borden told Lloyd George that 'the idea of nationhood has developed wonderfully of late in my own Dominion: I believe the same is true of all the Dominions.' Privately, he reflected that 'in the end and perhaps sooner than later, Canada must assume full sovereignty. She can give better service to GB & the US & to the world in that way.'[47]

Is this evidence that the Great War was Canada's war of independence? The meaning of the war for Canadians, and the question of whether any good came of the conflict, has been subject to considerable debate. There were those Canadians who were disgusted by the slaughter and the futility of the war. *Generals Die in Bed* was the title of a popular anti-war novel, and one of the country's leading war artists bitterly explained, 'You in Canada ... cannot realize at all what war is like. You must see it and live it.'[48] Then again, 'In Flanders Fields' is not only the most famous Canadian war poem but it is an ardent statement in favour of continued wartime sacrifice. In the search for meaning, much attention has focused upon Vimy Ridge. With understatement perhaps, one historian noted how difficult it must have been for 'most of the Canadians engaged at the sharp end of the historic battle to realize that Vimy was a victory, let alone a nation-building event'.[49]

Certainly, some Canadians quickly seized on this view of the battle. For poet Alfred Gordon, it was clear that 'henceforth we shall lift a higher head / Because of Vimy and its glorious dead.' Visiting Vimy in 1919, on a 'pilgrimage' to Canadian battlefields in Europe, Dafoe wrote that the events of April 1917 held 'a unique place in the Canadian consciousness' just as the war itself was important for Canada's 'national consciousness'.[50] There were other battles, too, that seemed to herald changes. Having visited various Canadian battlefields while taking part in the Paris Peace talks where he played an instrumental role in the ILO's formation, James Shotwell, the Canadian-born Columbia University historian, reflected that when Canadian soldiers 'smashed the German front at Amiens and the Hindenburg Line between Arras and Cambrai, in that most heroic chapter of the war, it ended for all time the colonial period of Canada's history'.[51] Shotwell was no militarist: he helped author the Kellogg–Briand Pact of 1928, which renounced war. His views encapsulated a sense of worthwhile sacrifice that prevailed among some Canadians and certainly fit the war of independence theme.[52]

For some Canadians, then, the war was a nation-building event. Not long after the conflict ended, one veteran, Frank Underhill, wrote that the conflict provided 'the visible demonstration that there has grown up on her soil a people not English nor Scottish nor American but Canadian – a Canadian nation'.[53] The absence of French Canadians is notable but so too is the sense of Canadian nationalism, a force that began to more fully emerge during the 1920s. In part, the sense of Canadian accomplishment sprang from disillusion or dissatisfaction with Britain. A future Ontario premier, who served in the trenches, ruminated over the imperial connection: 'Let Canada raise her own army, feed it, and officer it and it will be better than having Englishmen, who think we are backwoodsmen, run it. It's all right to talk Imperialism in Canada but come across and give England a great big dose of Imperialism and it would do more good. Then perhaps they would cease regarding us as "colonials".'[54] There is truth, then, to the war of independence notion, though by no means had the imperial tie to Britain been broken.

Certainly, Americans were unconvinced by notions of Canada's autonomy. US participation in the war, and Wilson's involvement in the peace process, raised the hopes of Canadians who looked warmly upon notions of an Anglo-Saxon-led order. The war, one commentator noted in the same month as the United States entered the conflict, was consolidating the 'interests of the English-speaking peoples', and hastening 'the day when a mutual understanding between Britain and America will bring with it an official guarantee for the peace and prosperity of all mankind'. Borden, too, believed that Britons and Americans bore a 'responsibility and duty for the world's peace', which was 'not less than their world-wide power and influence'.[55] An irony, then, is that the Canadian presence at Paris was a sore spot between London and Washington, and Canada and the other Dominions' membership in the League of Nations was one of the reasons why the US Congress rejected League membership. While Woodrow Wilson made the case that an autonomous Canada was 'more likely to agree with the United States than with Great Britain', for Anglophobic Americans, the Dominions' presence seemed to give more votes to Britain.[56] There were real-world limits both to romantic notions of Anglo-Saxon comity and to international recognition of growing Canadian autonomy.

Whatever nation-building occurred during the war was limited by war-induced sectional strife. Within several months of Vimy – partly due to losses incurred there – Borden had plunged the country into the battle over conscription. Animosity between French and English was palpable. 'The racial chasm, which is now opening at our feet', Laurier lamented, 'may perhaps not be overcome for many generations.'[57] Beyond the French–English divide, the war saw increased discrimination directed towards minority groups, though an exception were Irish Catholics, whose participation in the war led to greater acceptance within the Canadian polity.[58] Roughly half a million Germans lived in Canada at the start of the war. Some, like Joachim von

Ribbentrop – later Adolf Hitler's foreign minister – returned to Germany to fight for the Kaiser. Rumours of German spies and saboteurs were rife, generating a public backlash against Germans: businesses were attacked or boycotted, orchestras refused to play music by German composers, patriotic hooligans in the town of Berlin, Ontario, defaced a statue of Kaiser Wilhelm in a local park, and the Saskatchewan towns Koblenz, Prussia, and Bremen disappeared.[59] As for Berlin, it was renamed Kitchener in honour of Britain's war minister. The federal government acted as well. Passed shortly after the war began, the War Measures Act allowed Ottawa to censor the press and suspend habeas corpus. Using this authority, 80,000 recent émigrés from enemy countries were compelled to register with the federal government under pain of imprisonment. Only a few of this number were German or Austro-Hungarian reservists, and yet roughly 8,000 'enemy aliens' – Germans, Turks, Bulgarians, Ukrainians – were interned on security grounds and placed into work camps.[60] Most of the internees were Ukrainians, from the Austro-Hungarian province of Galicia, who had long been viewed in a negative light, and the war created the permissive environment in which government officials acted upon these sentiments.

Prejudices were evident, too, in the treatment of non-whites. Indian, Chinese and Japanese Canadians were barred from enlisting even when members of these communities offered to create their own segregated units. Also, Black Canadians were prevented from joining the CEF. As a group of black recruits was told, they had no place in 'a white man's war'.[61] However, protests regarding their exclusion, and the eventual need for recruits, led the government to relent, and in 1916 a segregated construction battalion was formed, with over 1,000 black Canadians eventually serving during the war. Pressure from Chinese and Japanese Canadian groups also led to a policy change, and several hundred Chinese and Japanese were recruited.[62] Military service did not alter their citizenship status, however, and so although Canadian authorities could conceive of an evolving relationship with Britain on the basis of wartime service, they did not support such a development at home in terms of racial minorities who fought alongside their white countrymen.

Indigenous people faced discrimination in their attempts to fight. Despite being traditional allies of the Crown, the Six Nations were initially turned away, as were indigenous recruits in general. In 1916, this policy was reversed, and between 3,500 and 4,000 indigenous men served abroad. Just as the war stimulated some English-Canadians' sense of nationalism, it spurred activism among indigenous veterans.[63] Lieutenant Frederick Loft (Onondeyoh), a Mohawk veteran, returned from Europe keen to press for greater rights. Specifically, he was galvanized by two pieces of legislation: the Oliver Act of 1911, allowing the federal government to relocate reserve land located near growing municipalities, and the Soldier Settlement Act of 1919, letting

Ottawa apportion reserve land to reward non-indigenous veterans. In framing his protest, Loft pointed to aboriginal peoples' record of service and to the values for which the war had been fought, namely 'the sacred rights of justice, freedom and liberty so dear to mankind, no matter what their colour or creed'.[64] In 1919, he founded the League of Indians of Canada. Although short-lived due to its members' competing political agendas, the League's formation marked the first effort to unite indigenous people across Canada into a collective political group and an early moment of political activity, presaging later activism. As a sign of how seriously it viewed this development, Ottawa sought to forcibly enfranchise Loft, thereby eliminating his Indian status, and in 1927, federal authorities amended the Indian Act to make it illegal for status Indians to organize publicly or retain legal counsel.[65] Praising indigenous participation in the war, Duncan Campbell Scott, who oversaw Indian Affairs, wrote, 'The Indians deserve well of Canada, and the end of the war should mark the beginning of a new era for them.'[66] In reality, Canadian policy favoured stiffening the status quo in response to indigenous pressure.

Beyond race, the war exposed fault lines around class, though here, also, there was an ethnic component. While the wartime economy had produced full employment, the shift to a peacetime economy led to falling production and a concomitant loss in jobs and wages. Compounding the situation were temporary workplace closures and illness caused by the Spanish flu, which claimed upwards of 50,000 Canadians, nearly as many deaths as Canadian losses during the war. Societal strains increased when several hundred thousand veterans returned in search of work. What ensued – indeed, what had begun while the war was still on – was a workers' revolt, a series of strikes across the country.[67] The year 1919 was an especially testy one, with the five-day Seattle General Strike that February providing a vivid example of what determined workers could accomplish. From 15 May to 25 June, Winnipeg saw its own general strike: roughly 30,000 private and public sector workers left their jobs, unemployed workers, including veterans, joined them and the city shut down. Employment issues were top of mind, but for many of those involved in the Winnipeg events and in sympathy strikes across the country, the revolutions in Russia loomed large. 'To be a leftist in the atmosphere of 1917–1920', one historian has written, 'was to breathe a very special atmosphere, one in which a top to bottom reconstruction of society had seemingly gone from being a utopian dream to a real possibility.'[68]

For government officials and other elites, this possibility was a nightmare. 'In some cities', Borden recalled in his memoirs, 'there was a deliberate attempt to overthrow the existing organization of the Government and to supersede it by crude, fantastic methods founded upon absurd conceptions of what has been accomplished in Russia.'[69] Fears of Bolshevik-inspired revolts led Ottawa to ban a host of left-wing groups in 1918, but ongoing labour radicalism generated demands for further 'defensive measures of a drastic sort against those who would reproduce in Canada the conditions now existing in Russia'.[70] In Winnipeg, the strikers were opposed by the Citizens' Committee of 1,000, an elite-led counter-protest group that warned that 'nothing less than Bolshevism has raised its ugly head'. Justice Minister Arthur Meighen agreed on the danger posed by the 'revolutionists of various degrees and types, from crazy idealists down to ordinary thieves'.[71] In the end, the government opted for stern measures: strike leaders were arrested, and, in response to protests against this move, the Mounties charged rioting crowds. Federal troops then occupied the streets of Winnipeg; faced with force, the strikers returned to work. The aftershocks of Russia's revolutions were keenly felt in Winnipeg and reverberated throughout Canada.

In the wake of ongoing labour unrest, Canadian authorities looked for culprits, and attention focused squarely on Eastern Europeans. In January 1919, Royal North-West Mounted Police Commissioner A. B. Perry had urged the monitoring of immigrant communities 'susceptible to Bolshevik teaching and propaganda' and a federal inquiry into the labour revolt concluded that Eastern European immigrants had left vital industries 'thoroughly saturated with the socialistic doctrines which have been proclaimed by the Bolsheviki'.[72] Overseeing the trials of the Winnipeg strike leaders as presiding magistrate, Hugh John Macdonald, the son of Canada's first prime minister, inveighed against East Europeans 'in our midst', who adhered to 'Bolsheviki ideas ... it is absolutely necessary that an example should be made'.[73] What followed was a broadening of the Criminal Code's definition of sedition and amendments to the Immigration Act in June 1919 allowing for deportation of those promoting activities undermining law and order.

The anti-Bolshevik backlash was not just a reflection of long-standing Anglo-Canadian bigotry towards Eastern Europeans, for there were communists in Canada with links to the ugly regime emerging in Moscow. Socialism and its more radical cousins were popular with immigrant workers. Furthermore, founded in 1921, the Communist Party of Canada (CPC), counted many foreign-born Ukrainians, Finns, and Jews as members and many of the party's early activities were targeted towards immigrant groups. Membership was never large, but members were committed to revolution.[74] Moreover, via the Communist International, which coordinated international communist activities in Moscow, the CPC had strong links with the Communist Party of the Soviet Union. Undoubtedly, while many communists adhered neither to the party line nor to the dictates of CPC headquarters, the COMINTERN connection was an important one that shaped the actions of Canada's official communist party for decades to come, giving credence to authorities' fears of an international communist conspiracy.[75] In defending the economic and political status quo, authorities were not wrong to look suspiciously at

Eastern Europeans, though as was so often the case, the involvement of a few individuals from a minority group in a suspect political movement led to overblown fears of the minority as a whole.

More generally, fears of Eastern European Bolsheviks, real and imagined, and ongoing economic dislocation, triggered a post-war uptick in nativism. One MP who favoured limiting immigration worried that the country would otherwise become 'a nation of organ-grinders and banana sellers', while in the view of one academic, European immigrants were 'disposed to retain their mother tongue, maintain old customs, harbor ancient prejudices, and make little educational progress'. Jews, too, were a target of hate.[76] What made the supposed immigrant threat even more potent for concerned Anglo-Canadians was their sense that many of the best of their race had died in Flanders and Northern France. As one journalist put it, Canadian sacrifices during the war left the country 'stripped of much of the good old Anglo-Saxon stock', leaving open a vacuum to foreigners.[77] A result was an uptick in support for eugenics, spawning a variety of policies, including forced sterilization, meant to keep white Canada pure.[78] Nativism and poor economic conditions together drove a new immigration policy. Announced in 1923, it prohibited immigration except for a few preferred classes of people from the white Dominions and Western Europe – including erstwhile enemy Germany – with limitations on the number of migrants from Eastern Europe. Immigration from the British World was a point of emphasis, in the hopes of building up English Canada's racial stock.[79] Also, a new law effectively barring almost all Chinese immigration was implemented, a move in line with actions taken elsewhere in the Anglo-Saxon world. 'Nothing was more striking', one commentator observed, 'than the instinctive and instantaneous solidarity which binds together Australians and Afrikaners, Californians and Canadians, into a "sacred Union" at the mere whisper of Asiatic immigration'.[80] To protest the limitations inherent in the emerging sense of Canadian nationalism, in 1924, Chinese Canadians across the country began marking Dominion Day as 'humiliation day'.[81]

Perhaps it had been a pyrrhic victory, but at the end of four years of fighting, Canada had been on the winning side in a war spanning the globe, and by the time the members of the Siberian expedition arrived home in 1919, Canadians had fought at both ends of the Eurasian landmass. For some Canadians, the incredible cost of this effort had been worth it, for what emerged from the terrible fighting was a growing sense of nationalism and growing distance from Britain. Increased nativism, ethnic divisions, and economic dislocation were the ugly after effects of a brutal war, one that had produced little good. As Borden himself feared, the Great War was 'the suicide of civilization'.[82] In each of the belligerent countries fractures had been exposed, and while Canada had its problems, it avoided the internecine violence that occurred in Russia, Germany, and Ireland. 'The world cannot be torn up by the roots for five years without destroying much of the old stability and acquiescence in the established order', observed university professor O. D. Skelton.[83]

After the war, Skelton became an influential figure in the emerging Canadian foreign policy establishment, with a goal of pushing the limits of Canada's autonomy from Britain. His quest to isolate Canada within a North American cocoon was but one of the ways in which Canadians reacted to the war. There was a push, too, for Canada to embrace internationalism. Within days of the armistice, the *Globe* had struck a hopeful note, urging the creation of a new order in which the 'venerable bogey the "Balance of Power" will have no place'. The following year, it stressed the need to ensure that the League of Nations could 'exert a far more powerful influence in the direction of world peace and the enforcement of international law than could any voluntary concert of the Great Powers'.[84] Internationalism, isolationism, and lingering imperialism each had a significant place in post-war Canada, with proponents of these viewpoints certain that their preferred course was the best way to steer the country through a world transformed by the Great War.

5

North Americanism and the search for peace

Lecturing on the theme of 'The British Empire and World Peace' in Toronto in 1921, sometime lawyer and politician Newton Rowell addressed the lessons of the Great War and the promise of the road ahead. War, he mused, was 'no longer a sane or practicable method of permanently settling disputes between nations', and as for the nation-state, he was of the view that 'human thought and activity transcends national boundaries'.[1] As his lecture's title suggests, Rowell was not unenthusiastic about Canada's British connection. Nor, as a Liberal who had joined the Union Government in 1917, was he averse to supporting military causes. Yet with the war over, Rowell, a strong supporter of missionary activity, was thinking in terms of an internationalism that would negate the need for force. Along with Robert Borden, Rowell was a founding member of the British Institute of International Affairs, later the Royal Institute of International Affairs, which had its origins in discussions between American and British officials during the Paris peace conference regarding the need for learned study and interchange on international affairs. The Americans went on to found the Council on Foreign Relations, and in 1928, a separate Canadian Institute of International Affairs (CIIA) was created, with links to the Institute of Pacific Relations (IPR), another post-war think tank. Rowell co-founded the CIIA as well as the League of Nations Society, the Canadian offshoot of Britain's League of Nations Union. In explaining his sense of the importance of promoting knowledge of international affairs via such organizations, Rowell put the matter simply: 'trouble in the Balkans set the world in flames'. Further, serving as a Canadian delegate to the League's inaugural meeting, he spoke strongly against 'European policy, European statesmanship, European ambition', which had 'drenched this world in blood and from which we are still suffering and will suffer for generations'.[2]

Rowell's views and activities are reflective of the interrelated themes examined in this chapter. His hopes for peace were echoed variously by an emerging peace movement, by a variety of groups intent on steering Canada away from imperial conflicts abroad, and by isolationists who wanted to confine the country within continental boundaries. Then there were internationalists, who contended that the best way to achieve peace was to support a rules-based world order centred around the League of Nations. Other Canadians rejected the League, believing that by being bound to enforce the organization's key collective security principle, Canada would find itself embroiled in far-flung conflicts, a commitment that flew in the face of the country's emerging autonomy. For many Canadians, it was vital to guard Canada's autonomy from the League and London alike.

An evolving Anglo-Canadian relationship was at the heart of many of the post-war developments in Canada's position in international affairs. Although they both sprang out of British organizations, the CIIA and the League of Nations Society signified a growing Canadian interest in the world beyond Britain. People in many countries wrestled with these questions of peace and internationalism, but what made the Canadian experience unique was a thread that one can trace through these various issues: Canada's increasing North Americanization.[3] Many Canadians who thought about foreign affairs during the interwar decades conceived of a unique brand of internationalism, North Americanism, and saw Canada and the United States as countries distinct from Europe and destined to follow their own path. Overall, this chapter emphasizes the ways in which Canadians dealt with the fallout of the Great War and with how they envisioned their country's role in the post-war world.

Funded by donations from Canadians and Americans, the Peace Arch between Blaine, Washington, and Surrey, BC, was dedicated in September 1921. Marking the end of the War of 1812, the arch was one of many public commemorations of the century of peace between Canada and the United States. Beginning in 1912, across the borderlands between the two neighbours, there had been a variety of memorials, statues, and plaques. However, the Great War put many celebrations on hold. 'That terrible storm of war', Borden told a Canadian Peace Centenary Association meeting, 'brings into clearer relief the more excellent way which these two great powers have found and followed.'[4] The notion that Canada and the United States had worked out a unique relationship, providing a lesson for other countries, had begun to emerge prior to the war, thanks to the profusion of commissions and treaties employed by Ottawa and Washington to resolve disputes over their shared continent. The war gave a boost to the concept, particularly in the writings of

Canadian journalist James Macdonald, who proselytized 'The North American Idea'. Macdonald saw the bilateral relationship characterized by the peaceful resolution of disputes and by the fact that, despite the vast power differential between the two neighbours, they interacted as equals, with the Americans abiding by these agreements, resorting to arbitration where necessary, and avoiding threats and the use of force. To Macdonald, this interaction was 'civilized internationalism'. North America, he proclaimed, was 'more than a continent of Geography: It is also a World Idea'.[5] Whatever the accuracy of Macdonald's analysis, it had definite salience given the slaughter of 1914–18.

The North Americanist viewpoint – that the Canada–US relationship was a model for the world – gained prominence in the post-war years along with a related distaste for European-style diplomacy. A tour of war-shattered Europe in 1919 left newspaperman J. W. Dafoe 'more than ever glad to live in North America' and separated from the world's trouble spots. 'Not only have we had a hundred years of peace on our borders', Canadian Senator Raoul Dandurand told the League of Nations in 1924, 'but we think in terms of peace, while Europe, an armed camp, thinks in terms of war.' In a lecture series, University of Toronto President Sir Robert Falconer contrasted North America with 'the plight of Europe: country set against country, race against race, frontiers watched by suspicious guardians'.[6] For North Americanists, the exemplar of their idea was the 1909 International Joint Commission (IJC), where Canada and the United States sat as equals. The IJC, Liberal Prime Minister Mackenzie King stated, was 'the new world answer to old world queries' and could have been a model for what emerged out of the Paris Peace Conference rather than the League, which he saw as a flawed body.[7] Americans, too, shared the North Americanist outlook. Visiting Vancouver in 1923, Warren Harding – the first sitting US president to visit Canada – contemplated, 'If only European countries would heed the lesson conveyed by Canada and the United States, they would strike at the root of their own continuing disagreements.'[8]

North Americanism was one of several ways in which Canadians reacted to the Great War. There was a resort to isolationism, a view linked to the North American idea. Canadians' destiny lay 'not on Continental Europe but here on the free soil of America', affirmed Liberal MP Charles Power, who put his isolationist call plainly: 'let Europe be the arbiter of its own destiny.' Famously, Dandurand explained that Canadians 'live in a fireproof house, far from inflammable materials'.[9] There was a broader internationalism too, whose adherents looked beyond North America to the League of Nations, and, relatedly, a peace movement, two viewpoints that gained in popularity thanks to the wartime horrors.

The search for peace was a central preoccupation for many Canadians in the post-war era, and, as in Britain and the United States, pacifism found a constituency among progressives, socialists, and other idealists who wanted to ensure that the Great War was indeed the war to end all wars.[10] A variety of women's groups had formed during the war to advocate for peace, most prominently the Women's International League for Peace and Freedom (WILPF), which mounted a small but vocal opposition to the conflict.[11] After the war, WILPF's Canadian members rallied against military spending and cadet training, and championed the League. WILPF provided an important outlet for Canadian women at a time in which their political options were limited, and there was an overlap between members of this peace group and suffragist organizations. Agnes Macphail, a WILPF member and Canada's first female MP, served as a League delegate in 1929. Before arriving in Geneva, she attended a WILPF meeting in Prague. 'Blessed are we who live in the North American continent', Macphail concluded after travelling through central Europe, a 'seething mass of unrest'. No isolationist, she believed that 'because of our happy position we owe leadership to the world'.[12] Macphail's outward facing North Americanism was typical of many internationalists and pacifists. An advocate for Canada to fully embrace the work of the League, J. S. Woodsworth, the country's leading socialist, took the North Americanist view that since 'many of our forefathers came here to escape the military burdens of Europe', Canadians should take little interest in war.[13] This blend of North Americanism and pacifism resonated in post-war Canada.

Canadians, especially on the left, involved themselves in a host of other homegrown and transnational organizations with an internationalist and pacifist bent: the World Alliance, the Fellowship of Reconciliation, the League for Social Reconstruction, and the Fellowship for a Christian Social Order. In 1932, the latter two organizations came together with the Quakers and the United Church of Canada – created in 1925 through a merger of four mainline Protestant denominations – to found the Institute of Economic and International Relations at Lake Couchiching in Orillia, Ontario. Decades later, the annual Couchiching conferences remained a forum for figures from Canada and abroad to discuss pressing international and public policy issues.

Similarly, the CIIA was formed in 1928 as a forum for debate about the direction of Canada's foreign policy, to publicize information on international affairs, and to advocate for Canadian engagement in the world. The form of that engagement was a source of disagreement within the organization. Its founders, Borden, Sir Arthur Currie, Vincent Massey, John Dafoe, and Sir Joseph Flavelle, tended to be more imperially minded, while Escott Reid, a young academic who became the CIIA national secretary in 1932, was, at the time, an isolationist. Individual CIIA branches across Canada chose their own points of consensus, and, overall, the institute developed a particularly anti-British outlook given its affiliation with the IPR, headed by Winnipeg insurance magnate Edgar Tarr, a fierce critic of British imperialism. A transnational organization with branches across the Asia-Pacific – the CIIA was the Canadian affiliate – the IPR brought members together for semi-annual meetings to discuss international matters of mutual interest to Pacific Rim countries.[14] For Canadian participants, these conferences showcased the international tensions gripping the Pacific world, especially the grim realities resulting from Japanese aggression against China. Following Japan's invasion of Manchuria, the 1931 IPR conference scheduled to meet in Huangzhuo was moved to Shanghai. The next two conferences in Banff (1933) and Yosemite (1936) were marred by continuing Sino–Japanese strain, a reminder that Canadian engagement in Pacific, like broader engagement in the world, carried certain dangers.

Eventually affiliated with the CIIA, the League of Nations Society also marked Canadian interest in the world. Among its leading founders were Rowell, Borden, Falconer, and Currie, individuals whose instincts leaned more towards imperialism than the liberal internationalism embodied – in theory – in the League. The Society held meetings and distributed literature promoting the League's activities, but initially there was little enthusiasm for its works, perhaps a reflection of its founders' views. However, in 1925 a new, broader-based leadership was brought in, transforming the organization. Branches were founded across the country, student organizations held Model League Assemblies, and through the Society's efforts, secondary school curricula in every province save Quebec were amended to include mandatory discussion of the League's works. Membership grew steadily as did circulation of its journal *Interdependence*, edited by Graham Spry. A socialist and broadcast pioneer who co-founded the League for Social Reconstruction and organized Canadian anti-fascist forces during Spain's civil war, Spry typified the internationalist shift in the Society's leadership. 1928 saw a peak of 13,407 members in seventeen branches.[15] This high tide did not last, and with the Great Depression membership ebbed considerably as many Canadians focused inward on the economic crisis.

Within government circles, there was little support for an active role in the League and Canadian officials had conspired at several points to neuter the organization. At the Paris peace talks Borden opposed Article X of the proposed League covenant – the key collective security provision – because they viewed the clause as an infringement on Canada's growing autonomy and rejected being automatically committed to war in far-flung destinations, a reasoning that John A. Macdonald and Wilfrid Laurier might well have applauded. This stance made Borden's involvement with the League of Nations Society incongruous. Subsequently, Canada embarked on a three-year campaign to have League members amend Article X to allow individual countries to decide the nature and extent of how they would enforce collective security, but in 1923 a resolution on this score failed.[16] By that point, a Liberal government was in power. Commenting on the poor state of Canada's internal politics thanks to the war, Charles Power urged an effort to 'conciliate Quebec and Ontario before we start conciliating Roumania and Ukrainia'.[17] King's position on collective security resembled that of his Conservative predecessors. In a stance he would stick to right up to Canada's declaration of war against Nazi Germany, in 1923 he proclaimed, 'it is for the parliament to decide whether or not we should participate in wars in different parts of the world'.[18] This view guided his thinking on Canadian commitments to the League and – his chief concern – commitments to Britain.

Canadian government hesitancy towards the League extended beyond collective security. In response to the Ottoman slaughter of Armenians during the Great War, through the Colonial Office – Canada's official outlet to the world – Ottawa had condemned Turkish actions. After the war, as the League considered the fate of surviving Armenians, British Colonial Secretary Lord Curzon suggested that Canada administer the newly created enclave of Armenia as a League Mandate, a quasi-colonial solution employed by the victorious powers to oversee territory from the German and Ottoman empires. There was some support in Canada for the country to do its 'duty' in administering Armenia, but speaking for the government, Rowell, who had been among the foremost voices condemning Turkish atrocities, pointed out that the region was 'somewhat remote from Canada's sphere of influence'. Responding to an additional League request for Canadian assistance in reducing tensions between Turkey and the short-lived Armenian republic, Prime Minister Arthur Meighen contended that Canadians 'could not undertake the responsibility' of overseeing diplomatic talks.[19] Canada was one of eight states to vote in favour of Armenia's League membership; although the motion failed, Ottawa's position was opposite that of London, a sign of some Canadian independence in foreign affairs. As the Armenian incident shows, however, whatever their wartime claims to nationhood, Canadian officials did not yet entertain desires for an expansive role in the world.

Although Ottawa was loath to act in response to the Armenian genocide, individual Canadians reacted to the crisis with greater urgency. The press had covered the Turkish slaughter of Armenians, publishing worrying reports from journalists and missionaries in the region. After the war ended, there were calls for Canadians to assist the survivors. 'Civilisation failed to save the Armenians from massacre', intoned the *Globe*. 'It should save the remnant from starvation.'[20] Relief funds were raised and supplies were collected and distributed by various Christian organizations, the Canadian Red Cross, and the newly formed Armenian Relief Association of Canada. No doubt members of these groups were motivated by the fact that the Armenians were fellow co-religionists facing persecution from the 'Bestial Turk', long a bugbear in Western thought.[21] There were other Canadians involved in international relief efforts. Under the auspices of the US charity Near East Relief, nurse Sara

Corning assisted Armenian refugees and other minority groups targeted by Turkish forces. Through the League's Commission on Deported Women and Children, doctor W. A. Kennedy helped to return Armenian orphans to next of kin.[22] Furthermore, 100 orphan refugees were housed in Georgetown, Ontario. However, in a reminder of humanitarianism's limits, particularly in a period in which human rights had little currency in international affairs, between 1919 and 1930, Canada's government took in just 1,250 Armenian asylum seekers, well below the numbers taken in by other Western countries.[23]

Aboriginal involvement with the League, meanwhile, was an area where Canada's government proved unyielding. Despite their participation in the fight against Germany, Ottawa had little interest in granting rights or privileges to Canada's indigenous population. 'The Indian is a ward of the Government still', affirmed Meighen.[24] In 1921, Levi General Deskaheh, spokesperson of the Six Nations of Grand River Territory, visited Britain in a failed attempt to get King George V to deal with him as the representative of a traditional ally. Three years later, the Grand River council petitioned the League to mediate what it viewed as an international dispute with Canada's federal government, which was moving to impose a new governance structure and dismantle the Six Nations Hereditary Council.

In mounting this petition, the Grand River band sought international recognition of their political and territorial sovereignty, thereby reaffirming a nation-to-nation relationship with Canada. The petition, which cited the 'aggression of our Canadian neighbours', found support from the Dutch government, an ally since the 1600s.[25] Subsequently, Levi General contended that the Six Nations deserved League membership because they fit the definition of a state and 'are, and have been for many centuries, organized and self-governing peoples, respectively, within domains of their own, and united in the oldest League of Nations, the League of the Iroquois'. As a sign of statehood, he tried, as one observer sniffed, to 'register with the League several strips of wampum representing treaties his ancestors had concluded' with the Dutch, French, and British.[26] In response to this challenge, the British and Canadian delegations lobbied other countries to withhold support from the Six Nations' complaint and eventually the League Secretariat rejected the petition. Beyond showing the Canadian government's hostility towards indigenous activism, the fate of Levi General's initiative stands as one of many examples of the League's failure to meet the aspirations of subject peoples who had embraced the rhetoric of self-determination promulgated by Woodrow Wilson. In 1928, two years after Canada won its autonomy from Britain, a group from Grand River sent a 'Declaration of Independence from the Crown and the British Empire' to Ottawa and petitioned Britain's Foreign Office to have the Royal Canadian Mounted Police (RCMP) removed from the reserve so as to protect their 'sovereign and political autonomy'.[27] The move went nowhere, but it signified indigenous efforts to achieve international recognition.

Where Canadian officials displayed enthusiasm for the League was in establishing Canada's own international presence distinct from Britain. In 1927, Ernest Lapointe, King's influential Quebec lieutenant, pushed for Canadian representation on the League Council, the organization's executive body. Lapointe's reasoning was less to support the League than to 'advertise Dominion status' abroad. Canada won the seat, a marker of growing autonomy. Lapointe, though, was clear that Canada should do little on the council or in terms of international security commitments, announcing, for instance, that he did 'not see that Canada should assume obligations in connection with the boundaries between France and Germany'.[28] Council membership was its own reward.

There were Canadians invested in the League's work. Various experts served on the Child Welfare Committee, the International Labour Organization, the Advisory Committee on the Traffic of Women and Children, and the Health Committee.[29] O. D. Skelton, the academic turned senior foreign policy advisor to Canadian prime ministers as undersecretary of the Department of External Affairs from 1925 to 1941, relished how, at the League, Canadians met officials from the world beyond the Empire. Attending the 1924 League, he marvelled that the meetings in Geneva brought 'together in one room representatives of practically every nation on earth, brown & black & white, Europe & America & Asia'.[30] For Skelton, who sought to broaden Canada's international presence and build a foreign policy independent of Britain, the League was an outlet for new relationships. Still, in Ottawa there was little enthusiasm for collective security, the League's raison d'être, a fact that did little to stop politicians from mouthing false pieties about its value. 'Canada perhaps as much as any country in the world is united in its efforts to further the work of the League of Nations', King affirmed in 1929. 'It is united in that effort because this country holds strongly to the cause of peace and desires to see peace furthered not only within its own borders but amongst the nations of the world.'[31] Certainly, King wanted peace, a hope that led him to spurn collective security and, therefore, the League, which was only as good as its members' adherence to its provisions.

Canadian caution about the world beyond North America extended to international security writ large. In 1925, the European great powers concluded the Locarno Treaties, a settlement that guaranteed Belgian, French, and German borders, thereby bringing a modicum of continental stability. Like a similar, abortive agreement in 1919, Locarno exempted the Dominions from automatically participating in this arrangement. Canadian policymakers opted against signing on to it. Skelton applauded the agreement, but, as he put it to King, a European security guarantee was a matter in which Canada, unlike

Britain, had no direct interest as the two countries were 'separated by three thousand miles of sea and incalculable differences in culture, in problems, in outlook. We are British North America; Britain is British West Europe.' Canada's security, he added in a further flourish of North Americanism, rested 'in her own reasonableness, the decency of her neighbour, and the steady development of friendly intercourse, common standards of conduct, and common points of view'. Reflecting his desire to disentangle Canada from Britain, he concluded, with coincidental prescience, 'We cannot give a blank cheque to whatever statesmen will be in power in London in 1940.' King agreed with this stance.[32] The mix of North Americanism and scepticism of overseas commitments was typical of King and Skelton's outlook.

King's stance on Locarno had been foreshadowed by Borden and Meighen. At a December 1918 Imperial War Cabinet session, Borden had urged Britain to 'keep clear, as far as possible, of European complications and alliances'. Canada, he added, would not support future policy that 'meant working in co-operation with some European nation as against the United States'.[33] Here was a statement of isolationism from Europe's problems and of a desire to keep North American relations in good repair. After stepping down as prime minister in 1920, Borden stuck to this position while serving as the Canadian representative to the 1921–2 Washington Naval Conference. The issue here was Pacific security, with the conference producing several historic agreements on naval arms limitation, on cooperation in maintaining open access to China's economy, and on resolving disputes through mediation rather than force. The latter move, meant to lessen regional tensions, took the place of the Anglo-Japanese Alliance of 1902. Fuelled by the same reasoning that had motivated Borden's statement to the Imperial War Cabinet, Prime Minister Meighen had pressed Britain to annul the alliance with Japan lest it upset Anglo-American relations. Instead, Meighen sought 'an English speaking concord' and the convening of a Pacific conference to settle outstanding issues.[34] The Washington treaties met Meighen's goals, though his influence on British policy remains a point of historical debate. As tensions between Japan and the Western powers mounted throughout the 1930s, some commentators fingered Meighen for having blundered by sinking an alliance that might have prevented or contained Japanese aggression.[35] In any event, Canadian policy at the Washington Conference paralleled that of the Americans, who had wanted an end to the Anglo-Japanese agreement. 'It is not surprising that Canadian interests and policies revealed themselves to be quite similar to the interests and policies of the United States', observed J. B. Brebner, 'for they sprang from a North Americanism'.[36]

Brebner, a Toronto-born Columbia University historian, was a proponent of North Americanism who pooh-poohed Canadian nationalist concerns about American encroachment. Fears of Americanization, he contended, were overblown, for Canada, too, was North American. Perhaps self-referentially, he observed that 'Canadians have played probably somewhat more than their proportionate part in designing the continental pattern of life. Scientists and inventors from Quebec and California sell their ideas, whether they be of ginger ale or preventative medicine, in New York or pills in Chicago.'[37] Brebner's Columbia colleague James Shotwell was another transplanted Canadian North Americanist. Having played an important role in the creation of the League-affiliated International Labour Organization, Shotwell provided the inspiration behind the 1928 Kellogg–Briand Pact, which bound signatories to avoid the use of war in resolving disputes. King signed the agreement for Canada, viewing his invitation to do so as 'the high water mark' of international recognition 'of Canadian nationality'.[38] Kellogg-Briand represented the high tide of post-Great War internationalism.

Beyond his contributions to Kellogg-Briand, Shotwell did much to promote North Americanism. Through ties to the Carnegie Endowment for International Peace, he convinced the think tank to sponsor four conferences on Canadian–American relations, two at Queen's University, in Kingston, Ontario, and two at St Lawrence University, in Canton, New York. Under his guidance, Carnegie sponsored a twenty-five-volume series on Canadian–American relations. Published between 1936 and 1945, and written mainly by Canadians, the series produced several landmark historical studies.[39] Both the Carnegie Corporation and the Rockefeller Foundation took a major interest in Canada, donating millions to universities, libraries, museums, art galleries, and government-run programs, an effort that signified the growing American presence north of the 49th parallel.[40] For North Americanists such as Shotwell, that presence was welcome, for it promoted the intertwining of the two countries and the seemingly unique internationalism of the Canadian–American relationship. 'In the intimacy of their contacts rather than in the "unfortified frontier"', he wrote in 1934, 'Canada and the United States have something more than theory or administration to offer the world.'[41]

The 1920s saw growing intimacy between Canadians and Americans. North Americanism sprang from the very real profusion of economic, cultural, and political ties between the two neighbours, a result of technological developments, market forces, and geopolitical shifts. Diplomatically, during the war, Canada had operated a wartime mission in the US capital and in 1920, under the Conservatives, Ottawa commenced trilateral negotiations with the British and Americans to appoint a Canadian minister to serve as the second-in-command of Britain's Washington embassy. When King came to office in December 1921, he abandoned the plan, not wanting a Canadian attached to a British mission.[42] King himself was North Americanism personified – he had worked as a labour consultant for the Rockefeller Foundation during 1914–18 – and once remarked to a US official that he wanted to put Canada on 'the

American road' rather than the British path, and bring the two North American neighbours be 'closer in every way, political as well as economic'.[43]

In July 1922, King travelled to Washington, where he met with Warren Harding in what was the first summit between an American president and a Canadian prime minister; Harding visited Canada the following summer. In Washington, King negotiated a draft update of the Rush–Bagot treaty, the 1817 agreement limiting naval arms on the Great Lakes and the basis of North Americanist cant about the undefended border. King's goal was to sign the agreement as a means of testing Canadian autonomy from Britain, but he abandoned the idea. In March 1923, however, Lapointe, serving as fisheries minister, and American Secretary of State Charles Evans Hughes inked the Halibut Treaty, a landmark agreement managing fish stocks. Like other Canada–US agreements, it led to the formation of a commission to oversee this shared resource. Its true importance, however, came from the fact that Canadian officials had independently negotiated the agreement with the Americans, and Lapointe signed it without the accompanying signature of Britain's ambassador. How inspiring that a marker on the road to Canadian independence should be something so simple as a fisheries agreement.

As for diplomatic representation, in 1927, Canada and the United States exchanged ministers, doing so despite President Calvin Coolidge's characteristic disinterest. While it was another sign of imperial devolution, when Canada's appointee, Vincent Massey, presented his credentials in Washington, he did so alongside Esme Howard, Britain's ambassador, a move meant to showcase London's approval of this development. The British did indeed approve, in part because a third of the business conducted at their Washington embassy concerned Canada. Despite this development, Howard noted that a certain 'solidarity' existed between British and Canadian diplomats in the US capital. Moreover, Massey was hardly an anti-British republican and he served as minister in Washington at a time in which pressing bilateral issues pertained to what he referred to as 'fence-line disputes' that resulted from the shared continent, such as immigration, smuggling, extradition, and resource sharing. The two neighbours, he observed, 'had not yet begun to consider ways to handle trouble in far-away places, such as Egypt or Laos, or even in places not quite so far away, such as Cuba'.[44]

In these disputes, there were various signs of North Americanism at work. A 1925 agreement made the International Boundary Commission, formed in 1908, a permanent body overseeing the joint management of the border, and one that accorded the two countries equal status. In a milestone in environmental law, a series of arbitration decisions required Consolidated Mining and Smelting Company of Canada to pay compensation to American farmers whose land had been poisoned by the company's Trail Smelter and to curb future emissions.[45] Moreover, important transborder infrastructure was constructed, including the Peace Bridge at Niagara Falls (1927), the Ambassador Bridge between Detroit and Windsor (1929), the Detroit–Windsor Tunnel (1930), and the Thousand Islands International Bridge (1937). These road links, taking advantage of the improvement and spread of automobiles, further entrenched transnational links in various border regions, and in Detroit–Windsor and Niagara, they created integrated regional economies and workforces. There were other transnational links: Franklin Delano Roosevelt (FDR) maintained a summer home at Campobello, New Brunswick, and John Foster Dulles, the future secretary of state, owned a cottage on Duck Island, near Kingston, which lay in the heart of the Thousand Islands region, where many wealthy Americans built vacation homes.

Intensification of a North American economy proceeded apace. Even as Canadian exporters faced the hurdle of the 1922 Fordney–McCumber Tariff, in 1927, Canada surpassed Britain as the Americans' largest trading partner. Studebaker and Packard assembled cars in Canada, while Ford, Chrysler, and General Motors – in partnership with Canadian industrialists – built vehicles at plants in Windsor and Oshawa, two of many Ontario cities where American investment proved important to economic development. Unable to compete with engineering advances and economies of scale, Canadian automakers either disappeared outright, or else partnered with US manufacturers. Canadian merchants fared better, with Hudson's Bay Company and Eaton's competing with Sears and Roebuck and Woolworth. Coca Cola, Kraft, and Kellogg discovered that Canadians tastes mirrored those of Americans, with prohibition in the United States meant that Hiram Walker and Seagram's spirits found their way into speakeasies south of the border.

Prohibition signified the possibilities and pitfalls of Canada's propinquity to the United States and the fact of what Ernest Hemingway, then a reporter for the *Toronto Star,* called the 'long unguared frontier'. During the Great War, Canadians had tried prohibition, a move praised by American teetotalers. 'I congratulate you people on the progress which you have made', William Jennings Bryan told a Toronto audience, 'and hope that the United States soon will overtake you.'[46] Finding that it was not to their taste, Canadians largely phased out prohibition in the immediate post-war years, doing so just as the US government banned the production, importation, transportation, and sale of alcohol. On the plus side, Canadians benefitted from the smuggling of alcohol and from cross-border tourism that, annually drew tens of thousands of thirsty Americans to Canadian hotels and bars, many of them built just across the border. Winnipeg's mayor suggested advertising touting his windswept municipality as 'the city of snowballs and highballs', and Montreal, a relatively short train ride from urban centres in the populous Northeast, became the 'Paris of North America'.[47] Given this cross-border traffic, Canadians well understood the inanity of American prohibition. One journalist noted that a good way to make Canada 'unpopular with the influential and powerful people of the United States' would be to ban liquor exports. Massey recalled that, as a foreign diplomat, if offered cocktails one 'had to choose between criticizing by implication his host's attitude to the law by refusing to drink, or helping break the law by accepting it'.[48] The smuggling of alcohol created a transnational crime network. Al Capone's statement, 'I don't even know what street Canada's on', was no reflection of the typical American ignorance of their northern neighbours for he knew well Canada's importance to his bottom line. Smuggling led to violence and sovereignty concerns. In 1929, a Canadian vessel, the *I'm Alone*, was sunk by a US naval ship off Louisiana. The issue was put to arbitration and a settlement was reached, but the case was simply the most sensational of a variety of incidents involving the actions of American law enforcement. Prohibition showcased the problems for Canadians in adopting a position askance from their southern neighbour. In 1930, after enjoying a decade of profiting off of parched Americans, Ottawa prohibited liquor exports to the United States.

In terms of primary resource exports, the 1920s were a boom period for Canada – 'the Dominion dominates the earth', gushed one journalist.[49] These resources helped fuel the surging US economy, and American investors poured money into Canadian timber, minerals, and hydro power. North Carolina tobacco and electricity baron James B. Duke took an interest in hydroelectric development in Quebec, and in the most extreme cases of US investment, company towns were founded: Arvida, Quebec, based around an Alcoa smelter, and Baie-Comeau, Quebec, where the *Chicago Tribune*'s owner founded a pulp and paper mill.[50] Interestingly, American company towns in Canada thrived, while similar projects outside of North America, such as Henry Ford's Fordlandia in Brazil, flopped. Canadian companies were engaged in the same process themselves, with the 1920s witnessing a continuation of investment in Latin America and the Caribbean, including the development of large mining projects in Nicaragua by newly incorporated Noranda. Indeed, while some Canadians worried about US investment in Canada's primary resource sector, Canadian investors were busy sinking money into mining operations abroad. Mining became a business synonymous with Canada, and the leading industry publication, the *Northern Miner*, was published in Canada and read in boardrooms and private clubs around the world.

To get past Canadian tariffs, US investors set up subsidiaries and branch plants north of the border. While some figures objected to the infusion of foreign money – A. A. Heaps, a Labour MP, complained that Canadians had become 'hewers of wood and drawers of water to American capitalists' – overall there were few complaints.[51] Later generations of Canadians lamented foreign ownership, but one Quebec premier was blunt: 'Import dollars, keep our children.'[52] Even so, a booming US economy drew a flood of migrants south, leading Canadians to worry, as they would in later decades, about a 'brain drain', the loss of highly educated and skilled people to the United States.[53] In overall economic terms, Canada was an important outlet for US investment and trade, though in a pattern that played out globally throughout the century, Canadian nationalists feared that American ideas came with imported American dollars.

For Canadians, proximity to the United States has been a continual and simultaneous source of opportunity and threat. In the 1920s, longstanding anxieties over economic domination mixed with concerns over cultural assimilation, the result of the influx of American mass media, from magazines to radio to film. Historian Archibald MacMechan saw danger in 'the subjection of the Canadian nation's mind and soul to the mind and soul of the United States'. Americanism was 'like baldness', observed an art critic, 'once caught there is no escape'.[54] Language heightened this problem, though French Canadians, too, feared American culture, which promoted, complained a future diplomat, 'the glorification of cinema stars and baseball aces', over more worthwhile heroes.[55] Dynamic and with mass appeal, American civilization provoked unease among foreigners, doubly so for concerned Canadians who were mindful that the undefended border did little to protect them against the delights of Broadway, Hollywood, and Tin Pan Alley.

American magazines became a major fixture in Canada, with *Ladies Home Journal*, *Saturday Evening Post*, *McCall's*, and *Pictorial Review* outselling their Canadian competitors, whose publishers successfully pressed for tariffs, doing so on nationalistic grounds that masked their financial reasoning. With a larger print run, American publishers did have an economic advantage. Also, they had a more appealing product. One opponent of the magazine tariff was not wrong in observing that on cultural grounds, 'If you could drop the United States into oblivion to-morrow by an earthquake, the greatest sufferer in the world would be Canada.'[56] Real problems with American magazines lay in the fact that Canadian readers received little news about Canada, and what news they did receive through these sources was filtered through American lenses. The same issue played out in Canadian newspapers, which relied upon American wire services.[57] Ditto radio, only to a greater degree given the difficulty in stopping Canadians from tuning into American stations. Furthermore, Canadian stations affiliated themselves with US networks, broadcasting mostly American programs. Radio, lamented one critic, was 'throwing us all the more under United States influence'.[58]

As with magazines, American radio was popular because of the product on offer. The same was true of film, an industry dominated by US studios, which treated Canada as a domestic market. Conservative politician George Drew – an ardent imperialist – had to admit that 'the Hollywood production was on the average vastly superior to the British' and so the mother country could provide no countervailing force.[59] Nationalist groups such as the IODE urged censoring US films for supposedly American themes of sex and violence. There were complaints, too, about US on-screen depictions of Canada, with one critic asking, 'are there nothing else in our Dominion but Indians, French–Canadian lumberjacks, and North West Mounted Police?'[60] A century later, the historian is tempted to point out that little has changed. Importantly, it seems mistaken to view American radio and film simply in terms of a foreign/domestic binary, for in the 1920s, as today, Canadians – and other foreigners – dotted American screen, sound, and page, including studio executives Louis Mayer and Jack Warner; actors Mary Pickford, Fay Wray, and Raymond Massey; band leader Guy Lombardo; and cartoonist Joe Shuster. Then, as now, there was 'a veritable army of Canadians' in the American cultural industry.[61]

There were other American imports. The Rotary, Lions, and Kiwanis service clubs came to Canada in the 1920s, bringing with them their commitment to charity and promoting North Americanism. The Kiwanians, for instance, organized an annual Canada-US Goodwill Week. Concerned with anti-black racism throughout the western hemisphere, Marcus Garvey opened chapters of his Universal Negro Improvement Association in Canada, though he himself was deported by Canadian officials, who feared his message of black empowerment. Despite Canadian immigration restrictions, black migration to Canada continued, and black Canadians forged links with anti-racist activists in the United States, thereby developing 'a tangible transnational race consciousness'.[62] Conversely, the heightened nativism of the early 1920s provided a propitious climate for the Ku Klux Klan (KKK) to spread to Canada, with subsidiaries set up during the early 1920s. Tending to avoid violence, and working within the law to affect local politics in its anti-Catholic, anti-immigrant, anti-Jewish, and anti-black crusade, Canada's Klan, reported the New York Times, 'lacks the robes and goods and militancy of its southern brethren but bristles with Klegles and wizards and above all well-paid organizers'. At its root, the Canadian KKK – one of several post-war nativist groups – was interested in promoting Canada's British heritage and the interests of Anglo-Saxon Protestants, and thereby constituted a 'somewhat more extreme version of what most people thought'.[63] One unwelcome Canadian export to the United States was Father Charles Coughlin, the repellent radio preacher, whose anti-Semitic and anti-communist harangues against the FDR administration made him a popular fixture on the conservative fringe.

The growth of North Americanism did not go uncontested. William Phillips, who served as the first US minister in Ottawa, returned home from his posting mindful that the 'much-talked-of "invisible border" was in fact a very real barrier'.[64] Canada's existence was a testament enough to Canadian desires to remain separate from the United States, plus, anti-American sentiment formed a powerful if not essential glue in many forms of Canadian nationalism. As Graham Spry quipped, 'if the fear of the United States did not exist, it would be necessary, like Voltaire's God, to invent it.'[65] Among Spry's many causes was a national radio station to counter American radio. 'Britannia rules the waves', his Canadian Radio League noted, 'shall Columbia rule the wavelengths?'[66] Lobbying efforts paid off in 1932, when R. B. Bennett's Conservative government, which had imposed magazine tariffs, created the Canadian Radio Broadcasting Corporation (CRBC). Later becoming the Canadian Broadcasting Corporation (CBC), the CRBC was modelled on the BBC as a state-run broadcaster, which meant, Bennett boasted, 'complete Canadian control of broadcasting from Canadian sources, free from foreign interference'.[67] In this context foreign did not mean British, and the CRBC and its successor featured British news and programs and British royal events, though, of course, Britain's monarch was Canada's monarch. The broadcaster, Bennett stated, was 'a dependable link in a chain of Empire communication'.[68] The CBC was one state-run response to American media; another was the National Film Board (NFB), created in 1939. Hardly an answer to Hollywood, the NFB produced documentaries, its staid nature perfectly encapsulating the differences in the media landscape between the United States and Canada.

There were other signs of growing Canadian nationalism, developments not strictly linked to efforts to differentiate Canadians from Americans, though that factor played into a developing sense of distinctive Canadian identity. Several national organizations were founded: the Canadian Authors Association (1921), the Canadian Historical Association (1922), the CIIA (1928), and the Royal Canadian Geographical Society (1929), which sought 'to make Canada better known to Canadians and to the world'. In terms of art, the Group of Seven, a Canadian art collective, saw their characteristic style of landscape art as a means 'to make us at home in our own country'. Commenting approvingly on this goal, author Frederick Housser explained that in terms of creative expression, Canadians' 'British and European connection' was 'a millstone about our neck'.[69] Here, nationalism served the purpose of differentiating Canada from Britain, a strain of thought that grew throughout the 1920s. In 1921, nationalists promoting a break with Britain formed the Native Sons of Canada. Quickly expanding across the country, the organization opposed Asian immigration, hoping that the new Canadian nation of their dreams would be white. Other Canadians saw Britain as 'an effective counter weight' to American influences, and one strain of nationalism in Canada, popular among conservatives, had a pro-British, anti-US basis.[70] Canadian nationalism, like Canadian identity, is contested ground and often an amalgam. 'Canada is British-American', wrote one mid-1920s observer, 'economically more American than British, spiritually more British than American'. A decade later, constitutional scholar Frank Scott discerned a similar mix. 'The Commonwealth', he concluded, 'provides the Sunday religion, North America the week-day habits'.[71]

The post-war period did see growing distance from Britain, though many Canadians continued to inhabit the British World. Was the result a more North American Canada? In a sense, yes. The Washington Naval Conference, for instance, saw Arthur Meighen's Conservative government prioritize relations with the United States over considerations of Britain's position in the Pacific. However, the situation was not zero-sum, as if growing independence from Britain was matched by dependence on the United States. Mackenzie King sought to differentiate between Canadian and imperial interests and to prioritize the former. He had an opportunity to do so over the small Ottoman seaport of Chanak, occupied by British forces at the end of the Great War.

Throughout 1922, the Turkish military had pushed occupying forces out of western Turkey. With the Turks threatening the British position in Chanak, Colonial Secretary Winston Churchill appealed to the Dominions for assistance. Australia and New Zealand offered troops; Canada and South Africa rejected Britain's entreaty. King sensed that Canadians were tired of war, and what upset him personally was that in threatening to fight Turkey, the British government had failed to consult with the Dominions and so he suspected that London was playing an 'imperial game', seeking to 'test out centralization vs. autonomy as regards European wars'. In a position he stuck to throughout the crises of the 1930s, he resolved that 'No contingent will go without parliament being summoned.'[72] King's evasion in pointing to Parliamentary authority was a deft manoeuvre, for the crisis occurred when Parliament was out of session and, by the time it reconvened, the situation was resolved. 'I am sure we have done right & aided the cause of peace by holding back', he reflected.[73] This position was controversial, and in the press and among Conservatives there were calls for Canada to back Britain, a reminder that, despite the nation-building of Vimy Ridge, pro-British sentiments remained strong. 'The minute there is any war or threat of war in Europe in which Great Britain might be involved', groused Charles Power, 'the Jingoes will so stir up the Country that in a Plebiscite or Referendum 75% of the people would immediately vote for war.'[74]

King exemplified the tensions surrounding post-war Anglo-Canadian relations. He was fond of Britain, of Canada's British heritage, and of the monarchy. Commenting, for instance, on a 1929 speech by Churchill, he thought it 'very good' in stressing the importance of intra-imperial trade and 'closing with a very fine & very true peroration re "united we stand, divided we fall" re British Empire'. Yet, he had opposed Churchill over Chanak, and later characterized the cigar chomping statesman as 'one of the most dangerous men I have ever known'.[75] Like Laurier, his political mentor, King was fond of the British Empire, but wary of imperialism. Remarking on an encounter with one Tory peer who presumed Canadian backing for Britain's overseas campaigns, King noted that he was the type of effusive imperialist who would 'be responsible for the break up of the British Empire'.[76] Although King's position appeared to favour breaking Canada's imperial links to Britain – certainly that is how his political opponents presented it – his stance had much in common with the position that Borden had enunciated in 1917: that the Dominions be part of the empire yet autonomous. Commenting on J. S. Ewart's advocacy of outright independence, King noted that Ewart was for total separation, 'I am not. I believe in British Empire as a "Co-operative Commonwealth".[77]

Beyond wariness of being drawn into imperial wars, King had little time for the military. A visit to Canadian naval facilities at Esquimalt in 1920, left him convinced of the waste of 'these military & naval fads'.[78] Following the Great War, Canada's army shrank to a permanent force of 4,125, with 50,000 militia, though the government had difficulty meeting the latter target, a sign, perhaps, of Canadians' weariness of war.[79] Like his predecessors going back to Macdonald, King saw little need to maintain much of a peacetime military, and so spending remained minimal. Given his views, King was doubtless little impressed when, during a 1923 visit to Britain, arch-imperialist Leo Amery, the First Lord of the Admiralty, took the Dominion prime ministers to review the fleet at anchor at Spithead. The Royal Navy, Amery reminded King, 'is why you are Prime Minister of Canada and not, at best, one of the Senators for the American State of Ontario'.[80]

King's 1923 visit to Britain was notable for his clash with British imperialists at the Imperial Conference. The convening of these conferences – triennial by happenstance, not design – was just one sign that the infrastructure of the British World remained intact, and the decade or so following the Great War saw an expansion of these intra-imperial links: an Imperial Wireless Committee, an Imperial Economic Committee, an Imperial Shipping Committee, the Pacific Cable Board, and the Imperial War Graves Commission. The first British Empire Games – the precursor to the Commonwealth Games – was held in Hamilton, Ontario, in 1930.[81] As for the 1923 Imperial Conference, the British, Australian and New Zealand delegations sought a united foreign policy. Like Laurier three decades earlier, King opposed this measure, arguing that Dominion foreign policy should be subject to their respective parliaments, a stance supported by the South Africans and Irish. Since there was no resolution favouring a united position, by default, the conference reaffirmed Dominion autonomy. In staking out his opposition, King had promised that in a serious crisis, 'Canada may be expected to do in the future as she has in the past'. Otherwise, London officials should not assume that they had 'a blank cheque' from Ottawa.[82] This distinction was important to make as the British had acquired more territory as a result of the war and yet had fewer resources with which to police an increasingly restive empire. Depressing Whitehall imperialists, King's stance pleased Skelton, who saw the conference as 'a notable day in the history of Canadian self-government'.[83]

Change in Canada-Britain relations proceeded apace. In 1925, Amery, now colonial secretary, took the sensible step of setting up a Dominions Office, separate from the Colonial Office, since the Dominions were 'wholly different in character' than dependent colonies.[84] With the Dominions neither colonies nor foreign countries, in a sign of the unique intra-imperial diplomacy that existed – high commissioners rather than ambassadors – the new ministry was also separate from the Foreign Office. That same year, Canada House, the Canadian high commission in London, opened its doors at its fabulous location at Trafalgar Square. While the Canadians had generally led the other Dominions in such matters, here Canada trailed Australia and South Africa, which had opened commissions in 1909 and 1911, respectively. Further north at Wembley Park, visitors to the British Empire Exhibition, which ran from 1924 to 1925, could view the Canadian pavilion, whose designers had chosen to project an image of Canada as a united, self-governing Dominion.[85] These were small signs of the changing imperial relationship. It was in 1926 that several leaps were taken.

In June, King's scandal-plagued minority government faced defeat and the prime minister sought an election. Rather than following King's advice, Governor General Julian Byng gave opposition leader Arthur Meighen the opportunity to form a government. Meighen's Conservatives required the support of the Progressives, hardly a stable match and, predictably, the Tory government was short-lived. In the resulting election, King struck a nationalist note, questioning whether a British governor general should be permitted to ignore the advice of a Canadian prime minister. Whether this issue resonated with voters, the Liberals won a majority. Fresh off this victory, King arrived at the 1926 Imperial Conference, where the Irish and South African leaders sought a radical statement of independence and a constitutional change to boot. Despite his clash with Byng, King opposed these moves as too politically fraught – a declaration of independence had a decidedly American ring to it – and in committee meetings he pushed for a compromise statement. The resulting report, the Balfour Declaration, named for the conference chair, established what was already occurring in practice: that the Dominions were autonomous in foreign and domestic policy, equal in status to Britain and one another, and united in a Commonwealth, the term now frequently used to describe the arrangement between Britain and the Dominions. Further, the conference certified that the governors general were no longer to be regarded as the British government's agents. In a stroke, the Dominions had won their independence, though autonomy was the preferred word, and through the Commonwealth a patina of imperial unity was maintained. Legal confirmation of the Balfour Declaration came with the 1931 Statute of Westminster. This act of the British Parliament granted the Dominions legal freedom from Britain except in areas where they chose to remain subordinate, such as British control of Canada's constitution. Although the Balfour Declaration and the Statute of Westminster were significant steps towards decolonization, Canadian colonial attitudes and pro-imperial sentiments did not suddenly disappear. For King and his successor, R. B. Bennett, Canada still had a place within the British World.

The changes in the governor general's position meant that Canada's Department of External Affairs became the transmitter and recipient of messages to and from London, and in April 1928, Sir William Clark arrived in Ottawa as British high commissioner, Whitehall's representative in Canada. King, meanwhile, wasted no time in seizing upon Canada's newly won status: the League Council seat and Massey's appointment as minister in Washington in 1927, a commissioner general appointed to Paris in 1928, and in 1929, a Canadian embassy opened in Tokyo.[86] Canada's government had reached out to important places beyond Britain, and, in the case of Japan, gained a diplomatic foothold in Asia. Other than the opening of a post in the Low Countries in 1939, a move forced upon Ottawa by the Belgians, in the period between the Balfour Declaration and the Second World War, these three missions, the League, and the high commission in London were the extent of Canada's diplomatic presence abroad.

Though Skelton pushed for a greater presence in the world, King and Bennett saw no need for an exchange of high commissioners with the other Dominions, nor, despite a high tide of pan-American sentiment, did they seek out a role in Latin America. Highlighting the limited foreign understanding of Canada's changing status, Washington opposed Canadian participation in the Pan-American Union out of a belief that Canada would simply be a stalking horse for British interests.[87] American concerns were only slightly far-fetched, for in 1927, King cut relations with the Soviet Union – Ottawa's recognition of the Moscow regime had come in 1924, the result of Canadian adherence to a British–Soviet agreement – following revelations of a Soviet subversive network in Britain. 'I have wished to cancel all along and this gives a fine opportunity to do the right thing and help Britain and show the unity of the British Empire', stated King. He added, 'We do not want communism flourishing in our country.'[88] Despite the mix of interests at play, the desire to stand in solidarity with Britain shows the limits of Canada's post-Balfour foreign policy. In reacting to the break with Moscow, Labour's A. A. Heaps was on the right track in suggesting that, at one of its first opportunities to show its 'new status', Canada had 'weakly followed' Britain's lead.[89]

On more important matters than relations with Josef Stalin's totalitarian state, Canadian officials displayed independence from Britain, and it was not King, the North Americanist, but Bennett, the imperialist, who struck harsh blows against imperial unity. Bennett's Conservatives won power in 1930 as the Great Depression pummelled Canada's economy. A catalyst of the economic crisis was the collapse of global trade, sparked by the American Smoot–Hawley tariff. Against the tide of American protectionism, King had vowed that, 'If the United States, or any other country, does not want to trade with Canada, except on unequal terms, then surely we can look as never before to the rest of the world, and particularly to the rest of the British Empire.' 'Let Uncle Sam Go His Own Way', the liberal *Globe* thundered, 'Our Way is With John Bull.'[90] Pro-empire sentiments were magnified among Conservatives. As with Macdonald and Borden, however, Bennett's imperialism was tempered by Canadian nationalism. 'I have a record', he asserted in the House of Commons, 'which will yield to that of no hon. Gentleman opposite in my love and devotion to that empire, but I would be indeed a poor Britisher if I were not a Canadian first.'[91]

Assuring voters that reviving trade was the means to restoring the country's economy, Bennett promised to 'blast' his way into foreign markets. Backed by a majority government, he had an opportunity to do so at the 1930 Imperial Conference in London, where trade talks dominated. Bennett's 'Canada first' stance left little room for reciprocal trade arrangements with Britain and the other Dominions. At the end of the conference, though, he extended an invitation to the imperial delegates to attend an economic summit in Ottawa. A major initiative for a minor power, this conference, Bennett declared, would 'lay the foundation of a new economic Empire in which Canada is destined to play a part of ever-increasing importance'.[92]

The 1932 Imperial Economic Conference in Ottawa imparted a sense of solemnity – there was a national day of prayer for the summit to produce a beneficial outcome – and a sense of excitement. 'London in its vastness is accustomed to such events', observed CRBC President Hector Charlesworth, but a conference of this sort was new for Ottawa. 'Here were delegates from the banks of the Zambesi', he rhapsodized, 'and the Ganges, the Shannon and the Thames; men born and bred under the Southern Cross and North Star; men who had traversed all the seven seas, who knew the hot plain of the Australian interior; the lovely waters and mountains of New Zealand; the kopjes of South Africa; the teeming cities of India; the pastoral vistas of the British Isles'.[93] Ultimately, such high hopes were largely misplaced. The Ottawa conference resulted in the signing of a dozen bilateral trade deals establishing preferential tariffs – imperial preference – among the signatories. Yet, there was no overarching agreement creating an empire free trade zone. Despite his imperial rhetoric, Bennett had played spoiler, guarding Canadian interests and seeking to squeeze concessions out of the other delegates. Neville Chamberlain, the British chancellor, complained of Bennett's narrow nationalism, noting that, 'Instead of guiding the conference in his capacity as chairman, he has acted merely as the leader of the Canadian delegation.'[94] For the second time in fifty years, a Chamberlain had had his imperial dreams crushed by a Canadian prime minister. As for the agreements made in Ottawa, they did little to reverse Canada's slumping economy or spark new trade opportunities with other Commonwealth countries.[95] Ironically, then, Bennett the imperialist turned to the United States, seeking a free trade deal with Canada's North American neighbour.

At the same time, as the imperial delegates were meeting in Ottawa, across town hundreds of unemployed labourers, union members, progressives, socialists, and communists were convening a Workers' Economic Conference. 'One feature which distinguished the Workers' Conference from the Imperial Conference', wrote a reporter, 'was the absence of pot bellies at the former.'[96] Meant to provide a counterpoint to Bennett's summit, the gathering of left-wing forces was one of many challenges mounted to the Canadian status quo as the Depression ravaged the country's economic, political, and social fabric. In 1933, Bennett reflected on Canada's economic status, noting that 'ten and a half million people were only a drop in the world bucket, and this depression was universal in extent, and what might overtake a situation that was local could not be applied to a situation that had become world-wide'.[97] Abroad, the crisis of capitalism consolidated illiberal forces in Germany, Japan, Spain, and Italy that sought to upset the fragile peace and overturn the tenuous liberal order based around the League. We turn to examining how depression-ravaged Canadians responded to this tumult. North Americanism, isolationism, and internationalism were evident in Canadian reactions to the international crises of the 1930s. Yet, it was the connection with Britain that proved of utmost importance, for just eight years after the Statute of Westminster, Canada went to war. In the view of the IODE, the Dominions' emergence 'from colonies into six self-governing national groups is especially significant in a world where a number of nations are asserting that democracy is out of date'.[98] Canadians prided themselves on having won their independence through evolution, not revolution, an important fact in the 1930s as the British Empire faced existential threats from Nazi Germany and Japan.

6

Canada and the descent to war

In looking back upon international history in the 1930s, one feels a sense of inevitability about the coming of the Second World War. Certainly, that is how the situation occurred to people at the time, especially as the decade wore on. In 1937, Escott Reid, national secretary of the Canadian Institute of International Affairs (CIIA), judged, 'we are living in the shadow of an impending war.'[1] The next year, Lester Pearson, a young diplomat and Great War veteran, sensed 'the disappearance of all post-war hopes of a new international order'. Despite his fondness for Britain, and the years he spent at Oxford, Pearson put great stock in post-Westminster independence in foreign policy. 'I am not going to be impressed if next year I am asked to fight because of Tanganyika or Gibraltar', he wrote of the possibility of being drawn into a British war. Although toying earlier in his career with isolationism, Pearson sensed that Canada could neither seal itself off from nor prosper in a world dominated by Nazi Germany: 'If I am tempted to become completely cynical and isolationist I think of Hitler screeching into the microphone, Jewish women and children in ditches on the Polish border, Goering, the ape-man and Goebbels, the evil imp, and then, whatever the British side may represent, the other does indeed stand for savagery and barbarism.'[2] Pearson's comments are revealing of a growing distance between Britain and Canada but also of the ideological and emotional ties that continued to bind the two countries together, for the British World did not come to an end with the Statute of Westminster, and many Canadians joined Britons in sensing the Nazi threat to liberal democracy. Reid, too, flirted with isolationism, but ultimately came to reject this view, particularly given threats such as Nazism. Going on to stellar careers in the Canadian foreign service, both men drew lessons from the 1930s as they set about fashioning a more internationalist Canadian foreign policy in the Second World War's wake.

Pearson and Reid were mere diplomats in the 1930s. During that 'low, dishonest decade', responsibility for foreign policy fell to R. B. Bennett, and then to Mackenzie King, neither of whom put much stock in collective security, nor relished the prospect of Canadian participation in a war, whether in some far corner of the world or in the heart of Europe, and whether fought on behalf of Britain or the League of Nations. In considering the Canadian government's response to the collapse of the tenuous international order, one finds little glory. Rather, what one sees is two politicians seeking to avoid involvement in a second global conflagration within two decades. Bennett and King acted in the pursuit of peace. In doing so, they were not lagging behind public opinion, for few Canadians greeted the prospect of another war even if that meant looking the other way as Germany gobbled up Czechoslovakia or Japan bulldozed through China.

For Canadians, the horrors of the Great War were still fresh, as were strains wrought by the Great Depression. This chapter explores Canadian reactions to the economic, political, and ideological dislocations of a decade of depression and demagoguery. These were issues that King himself highlighted in 1936, when he warned of the 'real danger' posed by 'Fascism vs. Communism, Capital vs. Labour – class warfare in all the European countries, & who will say not also in America'.[3] War seemed set to magnify these fissures, and yet in September 1939, despite the decade's domestic upheaval, and notwithstanding the Statute of Westminster, King chose to come to Britain's aid.[4] His descision was backed by nearly all of Canada's parliamentarians and, eventually, by the over 1 million Canadians who donned uniforms and the millions more who contributed to the war effort at home. Examining this choice against its international and internal context is the focal point of what follows.

Canada was among the countries hit hardest by the Depression. Its export-driven economy, reliant on US and British investors, was crippled by the retraction of global trade and the drying up of investment. Factories, mines, and lumber camps closed, and many of those thrown out of work were unskilled labourers with few opportunities in a collapsed job market. In 1933, the unemployment rate peaked at 30 percent. Compounding the situation was an ecological disaster on the prairies as the drought that famously transformed the US Midwest into a dustbowl had the same effect north of the 49th parallel. Harvest failure only increased unemployment. Across the country, provincial and municipal governments faced severe budgetary constraints. With bankruptcy imminent, in 1934, Newfoundland gave up Dominion status and returned to colonial administration. As despair spread, so too did demands for government assistance, a novel break from the prevailing economic orthodoxy. Like Herbert Hoover in the United States, Bennett had little enthusiasm for handouts. Government relief, he believed, would be spent on 'candy and beer'.[5] Instead, Bennett opted for fiscal prudence, seeking a balanced budget and expanded trade.

In 1931–2, Bennett's efforts to revive intra-imperial trade were somewhat successful but ultimately hamstrung by parochial interests, and he had little initial luck with the Americans. Tariffs imposed by the Republican-led Congress had been an issue for Canada long before the infamous Smoot–Hawley tariff of 1929. Still, the prospect of the latter measure had been alarming enough to the King government that it had sought an exemption. The White House had agreed to do so in exchange for Canadian cooperation in constructing the St Lawrence Seaway. However, after President Hoover leaked news of this prospective deal to the press, King, reluctant to appear to yield to US pressure, bowed out of an agreement and imposed countervailing duties against Smoot–Hawley. Together, these tariffs halved Canada–US trade.[6]

When he came to power, Bennett, seeking a compromise, rekindled talks with Hoover. By 1932, they had agreed, at least, to joint construction of the Seaway, which promised to be a public works project and a sign of bilateral harmony. Like many worthy initiatives, the treaty authorizing construction died on the US Senate floor.[7] Eventually, trade talks proved fruitful, and by late 1935, the Bennett government and the Franklin Delano Roosevelt (FDR) administration had nearly reached a limited free trade agreement. However, it was King who signed the deal, just weeks after trouncing Bennett in a federal election. The date was 11 November, and its symbolism was not lost on King. In a flourish of North Americanism, he told the US ambassador that, with the agreement, 'we, in the New World, would be setting an example of what could be accomplished in the arts of peace. If the countries of Europe see that the New World is breaking down these nationalistic barriers, and developing their trade, it will serve more than anything else to bring the European nations to their senses.'[8] With war clouds gathering, thanks to Italian aggression against Ethiopia, the example of Canada–US relations seemed as pertinent as it had following the Great War.

As for the Depression, Bennett bore the brunt of public anger. Just as there were shanty towns dubbed 'Hoovervilles' in the United States, Canadians had their own Bennett-inflected vernacular: the Bennett barnyard (an abandoned farm), the Bennett blanket (a newspaper), Bennett coffee (roasted wheat), the Bennett Buggy (a horse-drawn automobile), and Eggs Bennett (roasted chestnuts). The rotund millionaire was easy to lampoon, and though his government did introduce some relief programs, they paled in comparison to FDR's New Deal, doing little to dispel the view that Bennett was uncaring. Sensing disaster and up for re-election, in 1935, he took the advice of his brother-in-law, the Canadian minister in Washington, who urged him to piggyback on Roosevelt's popularity by implementing his own new deal. In a series of radio broadcasts, Bennett outlined plans for social programs and government intervention in the economy.[9] Indeed, he had already acted, creating the Bank of Canada, a central bank to coordinate monetary policy. Bennett was not alone in warming to Keynesian ideas, which received increasing support from Canadian economists eager for new solutions to the economic crisis. Through fora such as the Canadian Political Science Association and the CIIA, and via apostles of Keynes such as R. B. Bryce, a Cambridge-educated economist who became a leading civil servant, Keynesian economics gained purchase in Canada.[10] Although Canadian voters might have wanted a more interventionist government, by 1935, they had little enthusiasm for Bennett.

Beyond its impact on Bennett's electoral fortunes, the Depression had a wider influence on Canadian political affairs. Economic hardship fed ideological and political extremism and the status quo was buffeted by the same winds that battered other countries. New political parties emerged. Founded in 1932, and uniting workers and farmers in common cause, the Cooperative Commonwealth Federation (CCF) offered voters a single social democratic option. 'No CCF Government will rest content', the party's 1933 manifesto declared, 'until it has eradicated capitalism'.[11] This was a radical solution indeed, and CCF candidates were soon sitting in provincial legislatures and the House of Commons. Equally radical was the Social Credit movement, a funny money philosophy begun in Britain that called for the redistribution of wealth via small cash payments to consumers as a means of priming the economic pump. A Social Credit Party won power in Alberta in 1935 under the leadership of a bible-thumping, Jew-baiting, press-bashing radio preacher and it continued to hold power provincially until 1971.[12] In Quebec, meanwhile, Maurice Duplessis, another right-wing populist, was elected in 1936 on an anti-Ottawa, anti-union, anti-Semitic, anti-communist, pro-church platform, a winning combination that would see his Union Nationale in power – other than a stint from 1939 to 1944 – until 1960. While the CCF and Social Credit challenged the status quo, Duplessis sought to protect it against the forces of modernism and socialism. In this era of political and ideological ferment, these parties were relatively moderate given the other fare available.

The crisis of capitalism in the 1930s led to increasing popularity not simply for the CCF's social democratic option but for communism. Reflecting wider trends in the international communist movement, in 1928, there had been a purge within the Communist Party of Canada (CPC), with the party chairman and other apostates denounced by Moscow as followers of Leon Trotsky. Happily for the forces of order in Ottawa, the divide between the Soviet-controlled CPC and the Trotskyist movement ensured that over the next sixty years a significant portion of Canadian Marxists' energies were devoted more to battling one another than to agitating against elites. Even so, the Depression was a godsend for the far left. The CPC's slogan 'Fight or Starve' resonated widely, and through a variety of front organizations appealing to veterans and workers, the party saw its membership increase. In addition to countrywide hunger marches, communists organized a huge National Unemployment Conference in March 1932, a sign of strength that led fearful government authorities to deploy armoured cars to Parliament Hill. At Moscow's behest, the CPC sought to build a broad-based popular front of centrist and left-wing groups via the League Against War and Fascism, all to boost the communist cause.[13]

The communist struggle against the far right in the 1930s was international in nature, and while Canada's government remained neutral in the Spanish Civil War, Canadian anti-fascists joined the effort to defend Spain's socialist government against Francisco Franco's German and Italian-backed rebels. Canadians' main contribution to the International Brigades was the Mackenzie–Papineau Brigade, formed in July 1937, and named after rebels from Canada's colonial period. Canadian volunteers had begun enlisting earlier in the year, and in all nearly 1,700 went to Spain; over 400 did not return.

Most Mac–Paps were recent Eastern European immigrants, many had been recruited from government-run relief camps for the unemployed, and three-quarters were communist, though not all of them toed Moscow's line.[14] Perhaps most famously, Norman Bethune, a Great War veteran and surgeon, who converted to communism during the Depression, contributed to the anti-fascist cause in Spain via medical work, though in 1937 he returned to Canada. Then travelling to China in 1938, Bethune served alongside communist forces there until his death in 1939. Other Canadian leftists joined Bethune in the international struggle. The Committee to Aid Spanish Democracy collected assistance for civilians, and the Canadian Committee of the Save the Children Fund raised money to help children in Spain and in China. Referring to the Mac–Paps, one conservative Canadian hoped that the war in Spain would 'rid us of these undesirable people', and a writer in Quebec City's *L'Action catholique* declared that 'If the Nazi dictator and the Fascist Duce have faults on their consciences, it is surely not for having succeeded in halting communist ambitions.'[15] Canada's government, meanwhile, banned Canadians from fighting in foreign wars, though no arrests were made. As for communist anti-fascism, it had its limits. Since it took direction from Moscow, when the Soviet Union and Nazi Germany concluded a non-aggression pact in August 1939, the CPC altered course and opposed Canadian involvement in the war, that is until the Germans attacked the USSR in 1941.

Growing support for communism was a worrying development in elite circles. To Bennett, riots and demonstrations were the work of 'organizations from foreign lands desiring to destroy our institutions', and he implored Canadians 'to put the iron heel ruthlessly on propaganda of that kind'.[16] Canadian Catholics vigorously opposed communism, especially in Quebec, where, as two historians have written, the anti-communist fervour was so potent that 'an uninformed observer landing in Quebec City, in 1937, could have thought that the Bolshevik revolution was imminent'.[17] Across the country police engaged in violent clashes against far-left radicals, and Bennett himself put the heel to the CPC in 1931, arresting its general secretary, Tim Buck, and other party leaders. Applauding this move, the *Montreal Gazette* noted that communists' aims were 'wholly and utterly inconsistent with established principles of government and the organization of society in Canada'.[18] Buck's imprisonment became a cause célèbre for rights activists for he had been convicted under Section 98 of the Criminal Code, a law enacted following the 1919 Winnipeg General Strike that covered a broad scope for what constituted sedition. In 1934, after much publicity, including an attempt on Buck's life while he was incarcerated, he and his fellow prisoners were released.[19]

Fearing revolutionary violence from the thousands of disgruntled unemployed, Bennett authorized the creation of relief camps. Overseen by the military, the first camp opened in 1932, and by 1935 there were roughly two hundred camps through which more than 170,000 men passed. Wages were poor and conditions were harsh, and so the camps bred discontent. Protests ensued, and former camp labourers, egged on by communist agitators, embarked on a cross-country trek by rail from Vancouver to Ottawa. In Regina in June 1935, the Mounties interrupted the voyage and their efforts to arrest protest leaders precipitated violent clashes. While Bennett and other authorities viewed the trekkers as a threat, one member of the organizing committee was less sure of his movement's potency, recalling, 'We couldn't slice a loaf of bread into five bologna sandwiches without appointing a committee to see that it was done according to plan.'[20]

Bennett's hostility towards communism translated into antipathy towards the Soviet Union. As he had explained in 1928, 'there can be no comity between nations when the representatives of one nation are concerned with destruction of the government to which they are accredited'.[21] In 1931, he put this rhetoric into action by embargoing imports from the USSR, a move taken ostensibly because the Soviets were dumping wheat and lumber onto the international market, thereby depressing prices for Canadian exports. To O. D. Skelton, Bennett's policy was wrongheaded, for it was only by supporting trade that Canada could 'do our bit to bring the world back to sanity'. Despite Bennett's views on the Soviets, Skelton convinced him to back the USSR's admission to the League of Nations in 1934, a move that Henri Bourassa condemned as 'kiss[ing] on both cheeks' a country whose leaders were 'the outstanding apostles of atheism'.[22] Yet, what mattered was getting the Soviets to participate in an international system that seemed increasingly on the brink of collapse. In Geneva to oversee Canada's vote on the matter, Skelton dined with the Soviet foreign minister, who threw 'the swankiest lunch', which the

Canadian diplomat took as 'a striking commentary on proletarian principles and practices'.[23]

Those principles were a draw for many Canadians, including some who travelled to the USSR to see communism in action for themselves. They arrived during a period in which the Soviet economy was undergoing massive growth. Impressed with the evident success of a planned economy during a 1935 visit, lawyer and CCF founder Frank Scott saw these achievements as 'islands in a sea of backwardness' and he decried signs of totalitarianism, from 'the fundamental disbelief in individual choice', to the 'reliance on authority and obedience'. Visiting the following year, Agnes Macphail likewise was impressed by signs of economic advancement, but she saw no 'smiling people'.[24] The dearth of smiles aside, the USSR drew thousands of left-wing Finnish Canadians, who opted to leave the reactionary climate in Canada for the chill of Karelia, where they endeavoured to set up their own socialist paradise.[25] As for the clash between communism and Canada's government, in 1936, Mackenzie King reinstated trade with the Soviet Union, closed the relief camps, and repealed Section 98 of the Criminal Code.

Fascism was an international movement too, and in the 1930s it experienced its own popularity in Canada. 'I do not believe there is a city or province in Canada where Nazi propaganda is not being carried on', Macphail warned in early 1939, 'no doubt some of it begun by people who come from totalitarian states, particularly Germany, but too often carried on by so-called Canadians.'[26] One draw to the far right was anti-communism; anti-Semitism was another. In 1931, Canada was home to roughly 150,000 Jewish people who, in the economic climate of the period, were an easy scapegoat for fascists and populists who preyed upon latent anti-Semitism among Canadians. In Quebec, Catholicism and nationalism poisoned the political atmosphere against the province's Jewish population. An *Achat chez nous!* campaign, encouraging French consumers to buy goods from francophone shopkeepers, morphed into a boycott of Jewish businesses. At an April 1933 rally of the French Canadian nationalist *Jeune Canada* youth group, held the month after Hitler consolidated power in Germany, journalist André Laurendeau warned of 'the masters of the metropolis', and other speakers denounced Montreal Jews' 'nefarious power' and warned of 'Russo-Jewish Immigration and Its Consequence: Communism'. Likewise, historian and priest Lionel Groulx saw 'Jewish internationalism as one of the most dangerous forces of moral and social decency on the planet'.[27] Groulx, Laurendeau, and other *nationalistes* felt a 'fascist temptation' and, in reacting to modernity, urbanism, and liberalism, they came to embrace the Catholic corporatism of the Italian, Spanish, and Portuguese fascists. Even a young Pierre Trudeau was tempted.[28] Most infamously, reflecting an extreme nationalist position, Adrien Arcand, a former Union Nationale candidate, formed the *Parti national social chrétien* in 1934.[29]

Adopting the swastika and an anti-Semitic and anti-communist platform, Arcand's 'blue shirts' joined Hitler's brown shirts and Oswald Mosley's black shirts in the rainbow of fascist hate.

Anti-Semitism was not confined to Quebec. In Toronto, far-right hooligans formed Swastika Clubs, fascist gangs that harassed Jews. One group terrorized Jewish bathers at Balmy Beach, and in August 1933, at Christie Pits park, club members unfurled a swastika banner at a baseball game being played by a local Jewish team. What ensued was a six-hour brawl that led Toronto to ban displays of the symbol.[30] In addition to Arcand's blue shirts, a Canadian Nationalist Party was founded in Winnipeg in 1933, and the Canadian Union of Fascists held its first meeting in Regina in 1937. These groups were active elsewhere in the country and, meeting in 1938, they opted to form a united fascist organization, the National Unity Party of Canada (NUP). With six thousand members in 1939, it cast itself as a Canadian party, downplaying any international links even as it drew inspiration from abroad. Under Arcand's direction, the NUP abandoned the swastika – it 'symbolizes the white race', Arcand felt, but 'it does not particularly symbolize Canadian nationalism' – adopting as its insignia a torch surrounded by maple leaves and topped by a beaver, an unfortunate use of the furry creature.[31] Thankfully, once the war began, Canadian authorities jailed Arcand and other leading fascists for its duration.

Beyond homegrown fascism, both the Italian Fascists and the Nazi Party – like the communist movement – found support among Canadian ethnic communities. In the 1920s and 1930s many Italian Canadians looked positively upon Benito Mussolini, his political movement, and its achievements, though this sense of pride was by no means universal.[32] Many Italian Canadians were pleased by Mussolini's anti-communism and by his outreach to the Catholic Church; even today, the fresco on the apse of Montreal's Church of the Madonna della Difesa bears a depiction of Mussolini on horseback. Also, support for Italian fascism sprang from efforts by Italy's government to foster links with the Italian Canadian community via its consulates in Canada.[33] Similarly, for Nazi officials, who conceived of a *Volksgemeinschaft*, or worldwide German community, the half million German Canadians were an important overseas contingent. German consular officials in Canada launched outreach efforts to and distributed propaganda among the German Canadian community and built links to Canadian fascist groups. The Nazi Party itself funded the creation of two front organizations meant to spread propaganda. Both groups had thousands of members in branches across the country, but Nazism appealed to more recent immigrants. Hostile towards Nazism, older generations of German Canadians formed the German–Canadian League as a counter to Nazi propaganda and to the front organizations' efforts to take control of local cultural groups.[34] The fascist powers' efforts to court diasporic opinion signified not only the ideological struggle of the 1930s but that certain governments retained an interest in their former citizens, an attitude apparent nearly a century later with China.

Many Canadians rallied against the far right. Defending his attendance at an anti-Nazi protest for which he was criticized by *Jeune Canada*, Senator Raoul Dandurand affirmed that 'Hitler was condemned by all people of conscience', and a Toronto politician's threat to throw Germany's leader into the city zoo's beaver cage sparked a minor diplomatic tiff with the Nazi government.[35] In terms of more concrete action, the Canadian Jewish Congress picketed fascist speakers and boycott German goods. Jewish and left-wing groups urged Canada to spurn the 1936 Olympics, a propaganda showcase for the Nazi regime. Following the British Olympic Committee's lead, Canada's Olympic Committee opted to send Canadian athletes.[36] Visiting Berlin at the time of the summer games as part of a delegation negotiating a trade agreement with the Nazi government, diplomat Dana Wilgress recalled that the mass events held in the city were 'an impressive and at the same time frightening sight'. Despite public opprobrium, Wilgress and Canadian Trade Minister William Euler concluded a trade pact. Having met with Hitler, Euler offered sceptics the assurance that the German dictator 'expressed an earnest desire for peace and described his fear of bolshevism'.[37] As for trade with the Nazis, that same year King's government established commercial relations with the Soviet Union; when it came to totalitarian regimes, Canada's government was hardly discriminating.

What began to galvanize increasing numbers of Canadians against Nazi Germany was the violence of Kristallnacht in November 1938, which came just months after a war scare over Czechoslovakia. 'The Hitler regime appears to be determined to exterminate the Jews of Germany', warned the *Toronto Star*, while the *Globe and Mail* criticized Ottawa's 'laissez-faire attitude' towards denouncing the violent acts of Jew hatred.[38] In Montreal, 4500 people demonstrated against the 'pogrom', and across Canada, concerned citizens 'packed auditoriums and theatres … to join in protests against the mistreatment of Jews in Germany and to ask that the Dominion government take steps to aid Jewish refugees'.[39] Responding to this criticism, *Völkischer Beobachter*, the Nazi Party organ, asked, 'Why should Canadians look abroad? If Canadian journalists want to see real atrocities they need only go to the Indian reservations of their own country.'[40] As Canadians interested in promoting human rights were to find over the coming decades, Canada's treatment of indigenous people was often deployed by vile regimes interested in reminding Canadians of their own shortcomings.

Tragically, the Canadian government did little to help Jewish refugees fleeing Nazi terror. Norman Robertson, one of Canada's leading diplomats was blunt: 'We don't want to take too many Jews but, in the present circumstances particularly, we don't want to say so.'[41] Anti-Semitism factored into Canadian government thinking, both individually and on a political level, for King feared that a refugee program would spark a backlash in Quebec. His goal, he admitted, was to 'keep this part of the Continent free from unrest', which meant avoiding an 'intermixture of foreign strains of blood' that would create 'an internal problem in an effort to meet an international one'.[42] At the 1938 Evian Conference, where an international solution to the refugee issue was sought, Canadian delegates sided with the overwhelming majority in opting against accepting Jewish migrants. Nor did the events of Kristallnacht change King's views even as he admitted that, 'The sorrows which the Jews have to bear at this time are almost beyond comprehension.'[43] Individual Canadians, such as feminist Nellie McClung, intervened with the government to save friends and acquaintances in Germany. Also, there was organized pressure from Jewish groups, pacifist organizations, and the Canadian National Committee on Refugees and Victims of Political Persecution, whose leadership included prominent figures Senator Cairine Wilson and Sir Robert Falconer. The government was not swayed.[44] Between 1933 and 1945, just five thousand Jews were admitted to Canada. In the most egregious example of Canadian indifference, in the summer of 1939 the SS *St. Louis*, a ship carrying 937 Jewish refugees from Germany, was turned back from Canada after having been barred entry to Cuba and the United States. Sadly, Canada's government had not yet reached the point where it was willing to welcome refugees. The grim words of one immigration official summed up the prevailing view in Ottawa towards that plight of Europe's Jews: 'None is too many.'[45]

The tepid response to Nazi pogroms symbolized Ottawa's reaction to Nazi Germany and its expansionist allies, Italy and Japan. With Canada physically isolated from Europe and Asia, Bennett and King had the luxury of deciding whether to involve the country in overseas squabbles. Their policy, effectively a bipartisan one, was to keep the country away from problems for as long as possible. There were plenty of Canadians who shared similar desires, though for varied reasons. Neutralists urged Canada to avoid all international commitments. Referring to George Washington's farewell address, one historian praised the American president's maxim, 'friendship towards all, but entangling alliances with none'.[46] Conversely, there were appeals for Canadians to 'think internationally', to put aside petty nationalism and support 'World Cooperation'.[47] There were demands, too, for disarmament, a call that came from women's groups, from veterans, from labour, and from conservatives such as George Drew, who denounced the 'Salesmen of Death', and Arthur Meighen, who warned in 1931 that 'civilization has to end war, or war will end civilization'.[48] In 1932, half a million Canadians signed a petition calling for arms control, a document presented to Canada's government, which submitted it to the World Disarmament Conference at Geneva.[49] In 1936, the Canadian

Youth Congress (CYC), an umbrella group formed by various Christian groups, issued a Declaration of the Rights of Canadian Youth: 'We want our country continually, and with all its resources, to struggle to promote collective security and peace among all nations and peoples.'[50] Lobbying politicians, members of the CYC organized a Youth Peace Day, held on 11 November, Armistice Day, and participated in international youth congresses in Geneva in 1936 and Poughkeepsie, New York, in 1938. Backing the League of Nations, the CYC urged Canada's government to sanction aggressors and to 'determine its own participation in war' rather than simply follow Britain's lead.[51]

Canadian diplomats were frustrated both by the lack of action and by Canada's relative impotence as a minor power. Vincent Massey recalled that diplomat Hume Wrong had 'developed a plan for the perfect representation of Canada at conferences. Our delegate would have a name, even a photograph; a distinguished record, even an actual secretary – but he would have no corporeal existence and no one would ever notice that he was not there.'[52] Meanwhile, Lester Pearson, attending the 1932 Disarmament Conference, recorded that the Canadian delegation's 'greatest crisis' occurred 'when someone proposed in a naval sub-committee that the number of warships be reduced by one-half. This put us in an impossible position, politically and mathematically, since our naval strength at that time was three ships. Fortunately, at least for us, the proposal was not taken seriously.' Beyond the League, there was little diplomatic activity. With both Bennett and King, Skelton pressed for the opening of new diplomatic missions in Latin America, in Europe, and in the other Dominions, but his proposals were rejected.[53]

A new mission opened in 1929, in Japan, an expression of Canadian interest in the Pacific World. Yet the Depression hit, dashing Canadian hopes of promoting trade in Asia.[54] For Japan, the economic crisis spurred a policy of expansion into China, and in 1931, the Japanese military engineered a crisis providing a pretext to invade the resource-rich region of Manchuria. Although an act of aggression against a League of Nations member, the international community ignored Chinese pleas to invoke collective security. Given that the Republic of China had only recently been nominally unified under a Nationalist government after over a decade of strife, some Canadians viewed Japanese rule as a source of stability, a display of the same logic that led to support for European imperialism. Lieutenant Colonel Fraser Hunter, a Canadian veteran of colonial service in the British military, saw in China a clash 'between order and chaos', while *Saturday Night* viewed Japan as a source of 'order and good government'.[55] Rather than condemn Japanese aggression, Canada's League representative, C. H. Cahan, blamed China for its own weakness. Overall, Canadian policymakers hoped to conciliate the Japanese and Chinese, with Bennett even suggesting, quite improbably, that the Canada-US International

Joint Commission could serve as a model for resolving differences between the two sides, a sign that North Americanism was alive and well.[56]

While there were calls in Canada for trade sanctions against Japan. CCF leader J. S. Woodsworth warned, perceptively, that a failure to punish Japan was simply 'laying the foundation for a war in the future', but Ottawa followed London's lead and refused to act. 'Every country has too many troubles of its own today to go knight-erranting', wrote Skelton. In a comment outlying an attitude the remains a point of debate with regard to Canadian foreign policy, he added that Canada 'cannot afford to cut off trade even with sinners'.[57] Unchecked Japanese aggression in Manchuria disillusioned some Canadian observers. The *Vancouver Sun* chastised the 'silent League', and the Toronto *Globe* likened the organization to 'a bathing beach life-guard who has a wonderful coat of tan but who cannot swim'.[58] The League's future was put in further doubt when, in 1933, Japan pulled out of the organization in protest at being censured over its conduct in Manchuria. A sign of mounting tension in the Pacific came two years later with the collapse of naval disarmament talks in London.

For some Canadians, increasing Japanese power was evidence of a growing danger. 'Has White Control of World Affairs Ended?' asked one journalist. Two *Maclean's* contributors warned of an 'Oriental Threat' from the Japanese, an 'imperially-minded people'. This characteristic was viewed favourably by one writer, who saw the Japanese as 'temperamentally akin' to Westerners in contrast to the Chinese, who were 'essentially Asiatic', hence Japan's success over China.[59] Such thinking had been a staple of Canadian views on Japan and China, reflected in differing approaches to immigration: Japan, a great power, was subject to a limited quota; China, a country in disarray, faced more discriminatory regulations. Both approaches were predicated on restricting Asian immigration, a stance subjected to criticism for contributing 'to international ill-will'. Having once opposed non-Anglo-Saxon immigration, Woodsworth reversed himself, and by 1934, he was denouncing the 'narrow prejudices' that harmed Canada's image abroad.[60]

The prevailing view favoured barring Asian immigrants. Writing on Canadian foreign policy in the Pacific, Norman MacKenzie defended restrictions on security grounds since Japanese and Chinese immigrants remained loyal to the 'proud and powerful' countries of their birth. Similarly, and with German conduct in Czechoslovakia in mind, historian Arthur Lower warned that the presence of a considerable body of Japanese immigrants would lead to 'a species of Sudetenland coming into existence in Canada', with Japan's government sure to annex British Columbia in order to reunite 'the great body of their folk'.[61] Expressed soon after the Second World War had begun, Lower's fears were fantasy, but they encapsulated basic insecurity with a world that had been upended by Axis aggression. It was this same thinking that led to the Canadian government's decision in 1942 to intern Japanese Canadians.

Collective security took another hit in 1935, when Mussolini, hoping to make Italy great again, invaded Ethiopia. In advising Bennett of the course to take, Skelton explained that Canadians were 'immensely more interested in Alberta than Abyssinia' and warned that economic sanctions could escalate to sterner measures, namely war.[62] However, following Britain's lead, Bennett took a forceful stance. The Canadian League delegation condemned Italy's actions, backed sanctions, and secured membership on a committee considering further action. Briefly, Canada supported collective security. Yet, amid this crisis, Bennett's government was voted out of office, replaced by Mackenzie King's Liberals. Like Skelton, who retained his post, King feared an escalation of the situation, and his Quebec lieutenant Ernest Lapointe bluntly explained that, 'no interest in Ethiopia, of any nature whatever, is worth the life of a single Canadian citizen'.[63]

The new Liberal government backed away from sanctions. In Geneva, Canada's delegate, W. A. Riddell, caused a brief stir when he proposed embargoing oil, coal, steel, and iron, earning himself a sharp rebuke from King. As Riddell later recalled, he had been 'thoroughly convinced that this was the last and best chance that the member states would have of preventing a European collapse and another world war'.[64] Riddell may have been correct, for Britain's recourse was to pursue appeasement, giving Ethiopia to Italy in a secret deal struck with France. To Frank Underhill, an historian and public intellectual, 'the Collective System is dead. It now becomes a subject for learned investigation by professors of history in their PhD seminars.' With such disarray, Underhill, an isolationist and Great War veteran, contended that it was now vital for Canada to affirm 'that the poppies blooming in Flanders fields have no further interest for us'.[65]

King shared Underhill's interest in keeping Canada away from war. 'It looks as though almost without doubt, Japan and China will get into further conflict', he noted privately several months after the Ethiopian crisis had ended. 'This is another reason why Canada should hesitate about advocating sanctions in the League of Nations.'[66] The issue became pressing when, in July 1937, the Japanese attacked China, igniting a conflict that ended only with Japan's surrender in August 1945. A broad spectrum of Canadian organizations – the League of Nations Society, the Trades and Labour Congress, the Canadian Legion, the Canadian Teachers' Federation, the National Council of Women, the Women's International League for Peace and Freedom, church groups, and provincial and municipal governments – called for a boycott of Japanese goods, an embargo on the export of metals, and upholding the League covenant. Meanwhile, the Red Cross and a quickly formed China Medical Aid Committee collected donations for civilian relief, and Chinese Canadians organized their own protests against Japanese aggression, enforced their own boycott of Japanese goods, and sent aid to China.[67] Other Canadians warned of impending war. Summarizing the climate in the House of Commons, Agnes Macphail noted sardonically that, 'all the old fears are being revived – that Canada is not safe from Germany, from Japan and I suppose from Russia. And phrases I never thought to hear again are used repeatedly: "Preparedness brings peace," "Make the world safe for democracy," and even that old boner "We must defend our women and children." '[68]

The efficacy of economic sanctions has long been subject to debate. With Japan, supporters of sanctions criticized King's inaction. Woodsworth judged Ottawa 'guilty' of supporting Tokyo, China's consul in Toronto warned that Canada was 'supplying the sinews of war' to 'a war-mad nation' and Alberta's legislature passed a resolution denouncing the sale of exports 'destined to aid Japan in its ruthless attack upon the innocent, peace-loving Chinese'.[69] These charges upset the prime minister, who feared the risk of escalation. His task, he believed, 'was to spike the guns of war on a world scale' and that meant opposing sanctions. The League, he wrote, was an 'International War Office', and Canada had to steer clear of it.[70] Inaction was hardly an inspiring position in the face of aggression. For King, China was not worth war: Canada had few interests there, meaning that it would be involved only to protect Britain's colonial outposts. 'I am now where Sir Wilfrid was, in a more dangerous time in the world's history', he had stated earlier in the year, 'but still between the devil & deep blue sea in having to steer between Imperialism & Nationalism in extreme forms'.[71] King had no desire to commit Canadian soldiers to the League or to Britain.

What of pro-British sentiment in Canada? Following a tour of the country in 1934, Maurice Hankey, secretary of Britain's Committee of Imperial Defence, came away worried about Canadian support. The CIIA and League of Nations Society were dominated, he judged, by 'extremists of all kinds – "highbrows", isolationists, French Canadians, Irish disloyalists' who discussed 'the gravest matters without any real knowledge of the facts' and assumed the worst about Britain. Although Conservative politicians assured him that Canada would fight as it had in 1914, Hankey found that, in contrast to the 'fervid Imperialism' on display in New Zealand and Australia, Ottawa's 'calculating aloofness ... strikes a chilly note'. Overall, there seemed to be no answer to 'the brutal question' of Canadian assistance in a future war.[72] As Hankey observed, there was a growing distance between Canada and Britain, but it is important not to overstate the extent of the divide. For instance, to avoid being tied up in imperial military planning, Bennett and King prevented officials at the High Commission in London from attending Committee of Imperial Defence meetings. Even so, direct Anglo-Canadian military ties continued, a sign of the British World at work.[73]

The Statute of Westminster may have brought in legal autonomy, but many Canadians continued to think in British terms. If there was one force that symbolized ongoing fervour for the British connection it was the monarchy. Canadians, like people throughout the world, had watched star-struck at the abdication of Edward VIII, and had rallied in celebration of the 1937 coronation of his successor. When George VI and Queen Mary toured Canada in May 1939, an estimated three million Canadians, nearly one-third of the population, came out to see them in person.[74] There were even favourable responses to the royal visit among francophones, particularly since the royals spoke in French during the Quebec leg of their tour.[75] The royal visit came at an important juncture, with Europe on the brink of war, and the positive responses of Canadians – not all Canadians, of course – signified the continuing links that bound the British World together. The Canadian Legion was not alone in viewing the King's dedication of the national war memorial – the centrepiece of his visit – as having 'symbolized the fusion of a people in a nation and a nation in an empire'.[76]

Although Mackenzie King opposed a common imperial foreign policy, he recognized the pull of imperial sentiment, and he made this position evident at the May 1937 Imperial Conference. Among Canadians, he cautioned, there was 'outspoken rejection of the theory that whenever and wherever conflict arises in Europe, Canada can be expected to send armed forces overseas to help solve the quarrels of continental countries about which Canadians know little'. He admitted, however, that affection for Britain was alive and well, and should the British go to war 'a strong pull of kinship, the pride in common traditions, the desire to save democratic institutions, the admiration for the stability, the fairness, the independence that characterize English public life' would drive Canadians into the conflict.[77] Several weeks later, in Berlin, he repeated this view to Hitler, telling the führer 'that if the time ever came when any part of the Empire felt that the freedom which we all enjoyed was being impaired through any act of aggression on the part of a foreign country', then the empire, Canada included, would go to war.[78] Unfortunately, for posterity's sake, King came away from this meeting convinced that the German despot 'truly loves his fellow-men, and his country, and would make any sacrifice for their good', and he accepted Hitler's affirmations that he was a man of peace. 'It is curious', one British diplomat noted after receiving word of King's Berlin visit, 'how easily impressed & reassured Hitler's visitors are when Hitler tells them that Germany needs to expand at somebody else's expense but of course does not want war!'[79]

There was little enthusiasm in Ottawa for tough measures against Nazi Germany. When Hitler remilitarized the Rhineland in March 1936 in violation of the Treaty of Versailles, Skelton urged caution, noting that the peace agreement was 'presumably a treaty to end a war, not a promise to begin another'.[80]

In 1938, Hitler's threats to annex parts of Czechoslovakia home to ethnic Germans, sparked a war scare that lasted for much of the year, eventually prompting diplomatic negotiations in Munich. Here, in September, British prime minister Neville Chamberlain and French premier Édouard Daladier agreed to give Hitler the Sudetenland in exchange for a guarantee that the Germans would not occupy the rest of Czechoslovakia. The move prevented hostilities and was applauded in Canada. Praising Chamberlain, King expressed his 'unbounded admiration at the service you have rendered mankind', while Lapointe credited the British prime minister with having 'saved civilization'. In Ottawa, a local baby was named Neville in Chamberlain's honour and the city council considered following suit by renaming streets connected to the new national war memorial after the 'Peacemaker of the Century'. King himself oversaw a public celebration of the Munich agreement, which included the placing of the figures Peace and Liberty atop the war memorial.[81]

There were opponents of appeasement, but they were few. John Dafoe, long a vocal critic of Nazism, decried how Britain and France had 'approved, sanctioned, certified and validated' German aggression. Dafoe was not wrong, but his clear-eyed analysis prompted a pushback from the public. As one worker at Dafoe's newspaper recalled, 'The switchboard was flooded with calls from irate readers eager to denounce the editor as a war-monger who would not be content until the flower of Canadian manhood was again being slaughtered on the battlefields of Europe.'[82] The Canadian Legion was equally blunt in opposing appeasement. War was 'terrible', the group noted, but there were worse things, namely the 'loss of civil and religious liberties, submission to a debasing tyranny, and dishonour from the betrayal of those who have trusted us', namely Ethiopians and Czechs.[83]

King's pursuit of peace gives a misleading impression that he was opposed to war against Germany. In fact, amid the Sudeten crisis, he admitted that it was 'a self-evident national duty, if Britain entered the war, that Canada should regard herself as part of the British Empire'. His caveat was that Ottawa should define the extent of Canadian participation.[84] That was the result just a year later. Canada's entry into the Second World War occurred on Britain's behalf, an outcome that King both expected and accepted. During the Czech crisis, he told several influential Cabinet ministers that he 'would stand for Canada doing all she possibly could to destroy those Powers which are basing their actions on might and not right'. When Skelton urged neutrality in the event of war over Czechoslovakia, King disagreed, rejecting the idea of North American isolation. 'Our real self-interest lies in the strength of the British Empire' he stated, 'not in our geographical position and resources'.[85] Following the Munich agreement, the Liberal government boosted the defence budget over and above a modest increase in military spending instituted in 1937. Against critics, King defended the move as 'reasonable and almost necessary' in light of international tension.[86] War was not an outcome that King desired, hence his support for appeasement, but it was an outcome that he accepted. With Munich as backdrop – it 'threw a shadow over our deliberations', one negotiator later wrote – Canada, Britain, and the United States finalized a series of limited free trade agreements. At this critical time the British were interested in, and received, a show of support from the Canadians and Americans. As King told Chamberlain, the trade deals demonstrated 'the evident friendship between Great Britain and America'.[87]

By the winter of 1938–9, the war had an air of inevitability. In January, King admitted to himself that German aggression involved a 'threat to freedom the world over which we could not possibly hope to escape'.[88] Two months later, German forces invaded the remainder of Czechoslovakia and Hitler set his sights on Poland, prompting a British and French declaration guaranteeing Polish independence. With the collapse of the Munich settlement, King embarked on a coordinated campaign to prepare the way for Canadian involvement in the coming conflict. In the House of Commons, he took North Americanist swipes at a 'continent that cannot run itself', but affirmed Canada's support for the British. 'A world in which Britain was weak would be greatly worse for small countries than a world in which she was strong', he declared, adding that while Canada would not back a war over 'trade or prestige in some far corner of the world', it would be a different matter if there 'were a prospect of an aggressor launching an attack on Britain, with bombers raining down on London'.[89] Not neglecting French Canadian opinion, King had Lapointe denounce 'The ostrich policy of refusing to face dangers will not keep them away.'[90] When the Germans attacked Poland in August, there was no question of Canadian neutrality.

London declared war on 3 September, Ottawa followed a week later. The delay, King told the British high commissioner in late August, would be to show that Canadians could make their own decisions and that Canada was no mere 'Colonial possession'.[91] His long-standing view, going back to Chanak, was that on the question of war, Parliament would decide. Following three days of debate, a vote was taken in the House of Commons on the evening of 9 September. Opposition was almost nil, helped by King's assurance that there would be no conscription. French Canadian MPs and the CCF supported the government and the sole vote against came from Woodsworth, a pacifist to the end. Among the public, there was 'little of the naked enthusiasm' of 1914 but there was support nonetheless.[92] King, meanwhile, was pleased with the week-long delay. Parliament had demonstrated Canadian independence, making it clear that 'Canada stands as a nation' not only within the Commonwealth but 'among the nations of the world'.[93] Skelton's view differed. The war's 'first casualty', he reflected privately, was 'Canada's claim to independent control of her own destinies'. 'Why was Canada at war?' asked French Canadian nationalist André Laurendeau. 'Because England was at war, and only for that.'[94] He might have added: *Plus ça change, plus c'est la même chose.*

Whether a week's delay is evidence enough that the Statute of Westminster had given Canada its independence is a matter of taste. Certainly, Skelton and Laurendeau's criticism of the reasoning for war has merit, demonstrating Westminster's limitations in an era when Britain retained an emotional, cultural, and familial pull for many Canadians. Yet there was a sense, too, that it was in Canada's interest to come to the aid of the British, the French, and indeed, the Polish, and that Canadians had a role to play in ensuring European stability. That is how the matter appeared to the British high commissioner in Ottawa. Soon after Canada's declaration of war, he reported on a wide cross-section of support for the war effort. From 'the important Ukrainian and other minorities in the middle West' to the 'intellectuals' in the east, Canadians were convinced that confronting Nazism was in their interest. What this showed, he concluded, was that 'equality of status is not incompatible with co-operation in common aims, loyalty to a common allegiance, and the defence of common principles'.[95] That Canada had won its independence in foreign policy in 1931 did not mean that there was something axiomatically mistaken in supporting Britain in 1939.

The Canadian government shared with the British government – and the governments of the other democracies – an interest in a stable Europe and in defending important principles of liberal democracy and freedom, all of which were challenged by a German regime that welcomed war and was bent on European domination. There was a need, one commentator wrote, to take part in the 'grim struggle to defeat the carnivorous nationalism of the Third Reich', and soon after the war began, King noted that 'only by the destruction of Nazism and the resistance of ruthless aggression, can the nations of the British Commonwealth hope to continue to enjoy the liberties which are theirs under the British Crown'.[96] The realization that Hitler could not be appeased, came late to many people, but the realization did come. In early 1939, Agnes Macphail, a staunch North Americanist who voted in favour of the Canadian declaration of war that September, reflected that across the globe, 'we are seeing liberty, freedom and personal security being swept away for thousands, yes even millions of people. We see democracy backing away before the onslaught of fascism'. What surprised her, was 'that the conscience of the world has been scared to such an extent that we can endure the tragedy of China, the betrayal of Czechoslovakia and the unparalleled agony of Spain without doing something about it'.[97] The 1930s had been a decade of terrible tumult for Canadians, not least because it ended with their country again at war, this time against an enemy that was both a military and ideological threat. As we turn to examine Canada's Second World War, it is worth keeping in mind that participation in that conflict was driven not just by loyalty to Britain but by ideas of Canadian interests and values, concepts that then drove efforts to forge a new direction in the country's foreign policy.

7

The North Atlantic Triangle from world war to cold war

In 1945, the Carnegie Endowment for International Peace published *North Atlantic Triangle*, the last in its twenty-five-volume series on Canada-US relations. Setting out to explore the bilateral relationship between 'the Siamese Twins of North America', J. B. Brebner, the Canadian-born Columbia University historian, realized that this history would be incomplete without incorporating Britain. His resulting conception of an Anglo-American-Canadian triangle became one of the most influential frameworks for viewing Canadian foreign relations. With the Second World War nearing its end, Brebner looked ahead to the post-war world, writing of the three English-speaking powers that 'No such group of nations is more experienced or more capable of contributing to collective security.' This view was shared by James Shotwell, who, in the volume's foreword, expressed hope for an international order modelled after the peace achieved within the 'Anglo-Saxon polity', a reminder that the triangle's roots lay in long-standing concepts of racial, cultural, and historical solidarity within the so-called Anglosphere.[1] Brebner's views were very au courant. Three months after Japan's surrender, as the world moved into a new era, William Lyon Mackenzie King mused about the need for 'some larger design to help keep the English-speaking peoples together'. The next winter, in Fulton, Missouri, Winston Churchill cautioned his listeners, not only that an 'iron curtain' was descending amidst Europe, but that the preservation of peace depended upon 'the fraternal association of the English-speaking peoples'.[2] That association appeared rocky. In 1948, Brebner briefly reviewed post-war cooperation within the triangle and found it lacking, for 'once the uncalculating joint enterprise of unlimited war was over', each country had looked to secure separate interests.[3] Unbeknownst to Brebner, as his article went to print, Canadian, American, and British diplomats were meeting in secret to hammer out a transatlantic alliance meant to ensure the security and stability of the international order.

Canada's place within the wartime North Atlantic triangle is at the centre of this chapter, which looks, too, at the Canadian search for security from the end of the Second World War to the early cold war. The interplay among the triangular powers during this period is well known, but our concern is less with the tired question of whether Canada played the role of Anglo-American go-between than with how Canadians managed the wartime transition of power between Britain and the United States. The Second World War was 'The Last Great Imperial War Effort', one in which Canadians took a major role in Britain's defence.[4] By the end of the conflict, British power was kaput. The United States, meanwhile, was ascendant as a global power, with the cold war solidifying its preponderant position.

Canadians found themselves in the middle of this transition in power, which occurred at the same time as officials in Ottawa began to take a more expansive interest in international affairs and to support a revived liberal international order centred around collective security. And no wonder – for the second time in two decades Canadians had been at war. The search for collective security led Canadian authorities to pursue a post-war role of ensuring a measure of stability in a continent threatened again by an expansive, totalitarian power. Just as they had opposed Nazism, Canadians and their government enlisted in containing the Soviet Union. Doing so meant supporting the United States, which pursued containment across the global. The trajectory of this development was clear to Canadian diplomat Dana Wilgress, who observed in 1947 that Canada was moving 'into still greater dependence upon the United States' at the exact moment that 'the Pax Britannica of the nineteenth century' was giving way to 'a Pax Americana'.[5] For Canadian officials, and for many Canadians more generally, US leadership in the cold war and its backing of the wider post-war international order was welcome even as the exercise of American power became a source of concern.

At war's outset in September 1939, King's initial policy was one of limited liability: Canada would prioritize its navy and air force; supply the Allies with food, munitions, and other materiel; and, through the British Commonwealth Air Training Program, train tens of thousands of Allied pilots and aircrew. Limited liability was a shrewd policy, meant to forfend the costly casualties produced by a ground war, thereby avoiding conscription and with it, sectional strife with Quebec and along class lines. This position was put to Canadian voters in March 1940, an election in which King's Liberals increased both their parliamentary majority and their share of the popular vote and won all but three Quebec seats. The vote's timing was propitious: within weeks the Nazi blitzkrieg ended limited liability. As the countries of Western Europe fell to the German onslaught, King feared an 'attack upon Britain which is liable to produce any kind of reaction in this country. It is going to be a terrific job of holding Canada together.'[6]

Luckily the Germans stopped at the English Channel, but France's surrender transformed the war for Canada. New army units were formed and sent to Britain, and recruitment efforts increased as did aircraft production and shipbuilding. The Liberal government implemented the National Resources Mobilization Act, allowing it to mobilize the country's material and human resources. Through this measure and the creation of a Wartime Prices and Trade Board, Ottawa regulated employment, set prices, controlled wages, and rationed food and other goods. For Canada, the conflict had become a total war: the government controlled the economy and it conscripted sixty thousand men, though only for home defence. Canada now stood as Britain's foremost ally, a fact that unsettled King, especially given British weakness. 'It is an appalling day for Britain when she has to seek from one of her Dominions ships, ammunition, aircraft, additional land forces, etc.'[7]

Following France's surrender, Canada opted to maintain relations with the French collaborationist regime, doing so even after relations between Vichy and London were broken. The King government's position rested, first, on a hope that good relations with Vichy would prevent it from joining the war on the Nazi side, and second, on an appreciation for the regime's popularity among Quebec's conservative, Catholic population. It was not until November 1942 that Ottawa cut this tie; in the interim, Canadian diplomats had acted as go-betweens for London with Vichy. Overall, Canada and Canadians backed the Free French. Free French Committees were formed across the country to provide material and moral aid to the cause, and in July 1942, Ottawa recognized Free France as the administrator of France's overseas territories; formal recognition of Free France's provisional government came in October 1944. Moreover, starting in 1941, Canada supported General Charles de Gaulle as the true leader of the Free French, lobbied Washington and London to support him, and championed the post-war restoration of France as a great power.[8] When de Gaulle stepped ashore onto French soil in Normandy in June 1944, it was on Juno Beach, liberated by Canadian soldiers. With this support for the Frenchman in France's time of need, it is no wonder that the general's later efforts to destroy Canada took on an air of betrayal.

To return to 1940, Canada's sudden upgrade to the front rank of the war against Germany – and fascist Italy, which had been skulking on the sidelines of the war, opting to enter it only once France was nearing collapse – did not go unnoticed in the United States. 'Canada compromises America's isolation', observed one journalist.[9] Franklin Roosevelt's administration agreed with this judgement. In July 1940, US military officials initiated secret staff talks with their Canadian counterparts. Several weeks later, on a sleepy August day, King and FDR met at the border town of Ogdensburg, New York. Here, they resolved to form a military committee 'to consider in the broad sense the defence of the north half of the western hemisphere'.[10] The Permanent Joint Board on Defence (PJBD) seemed to be, as the opening adjective of its name implied, the basis of a Canada–US alliance. What was agreed to here, though, was not a formal signed treaty. Hence King's later assertion that Canada was 'very fortunate' in that this wartime arrangement 'is not in fact a military alliance'. However, Churchill saw it differently, and alarmed that a Dominion had made such an agreement with a foreign power, he informed King that should the Germans fail to conquer Britain then 'all these transactions will be judged in a mood different to that while the issue still stands in the balance'.[11]

Whatever its nature, the Ogdensburg Agreement marked an expansion of US security interests and a shift in Canadian international relations towards a more American orientation, developments that had already been in train. In August 1938, amid the Czechoslovakian crisis, Roosevelt, speaking in Kingston, Ontario, affirmed that although 'Canada is part of the sisterhood of the British Empire' the United States would 'not stand idly by if domination of Canadian soil is threatened by any other empire'. His hope, he told Canada's governor general, was that the declaration would have 'some small effect in Berlin'.[12] It certainly had an effect on King, who told the president that by raising questions about Canadian independence his speech had 'dropped a bomb'.[13] In essence, FDR had placed Canada under the aegis of the Monroe Doctrine, the long-standing US declaration of intent to keep other great powers out of the western hemisphere. King saw danger in reliance upon the United States, leading him to boost defence spending in the lead up to the war. Roosevelt's offer of protection, he told the Cabinet in early 1939, 'would mean that Canada would become a part of America'. While FDR was genial enough, King recognized that a 'change of leaders there might lead to vassalage so far as our Dominion was concerned'. With his mind on Canada's post-Westminster status, he added that 'There was more real freedom in the British Commonwealth of Nations.'[14] Throughout the war and after, Canadian officials wrestled with the defence implications of proximity to the United States.

Beyond the PJBD, there was Canadian-American cooperation in economic matters. In April 1941, King and FDR met at the president's Hyde Park estate to work out an economic arrangement to alleviate pressures on the Canadian economy created by the US Lend-Lease program, instituted weeks earlier. Canada was already short of American dollars needed to purchase US goods; money from Britain improved this situation, but with Lend-Lease, Canadian officials doubted whether the British would continue to buy materiel from Canada when they could acquire items from the United States on credit.

Without protest, FDR accepted King's proposal: Washington would increase purchases in Canada and allow Britain to use Lend-Lease funds to buy Canadian goods. A sign of the friendly King–FDR rapport, the Hyde Park Agreement – a re-do of a 1917 arrangement addressing the same situation – showcased the president's desire to assist the Allies even as his country remained formally neutral. Also, it marked Canada's economic reliance on the United States. Still, a point of Canadian pride during and after the war was that Canada never accepted Lend-Lease aid from Washington. As for bilateral economic ties, they strengthened throughout the war, and in 1947, Canadian and American officials negotiated an expansion of the existing bilateral trade agreement into a full-on customs union. In the end, King nixed this deal, telling his successor, Louis St Laurent, that 'while it might be sound economically ... it would be fatal politically'.[15] The spectre of the 1911 election lingered on, casting a shadow over wartime comity.

Like the United States, Canada benefitted economically from the war. It became a net exporter of war goods, sending nearly two-thirds of its production abroad. As an indication of Canadian economic power, much of the materiel produced for Britain was financed by $2 billion credit, which Ottawa wrote off at the end of the war. In addition, in 1946, Ottawa loaned London $1.25 billion, what amounted to 10 per cent of Canadian GNP. Aid to Britain testified to the Dominion's continuing commitment to the metropole and to its wartime prosperity.[16] The war put an end to the Depression: full employment was reached; the value of the economy doubled; and there was enough money that the federal government began introducing social welfare programs, including unemployment insurance and family allowances. King's way of responding to public demand and undercutting support for the social democratic Cooperative Commonwealth Federation (CCF), these programs, as one journalist put it, were 'the price that Liberalism is willing to pay in order to prevent socialism'. King viewed himself as progressive, and these measures, he told his caucus, were necessary as a 'proper basis on which to construct a new order'.[17] Whatever the reasoning, a more prosperous, equitable, though not perfect Canada emerged from the war. Even the Conservatives came out in supporting of social welfare, changing their party's name to the paradoxical Progressive Conservative Party. In 1945, the Liberals retained power and King avoided Churchill's fate. It helped the Liberals that they had learned the lessons of the Borden government, and with the war winding down they had taken measures – tax incentives, the sale of government-owned factories – to encourage peacetime production and avoid a return to the Depression.[18]

Canada's military commitment was massive in scale and in scope. Beyond significant material costs, a country of 11 million put over 1 million people in uniform, including fifty thousand women, who served not only as nurses, but as mechanics, clerks, radio operators, and in other non-combat roles that freed men for the front. The slaughter of the Great War had occurred within living memory, but Canadian men were not deterred from volunteering for service and the overwhelming majority of those in uniform joined willingly. No doubt the Depression created an impetus to volunteer, but so too did desires to fight for Canada, or for Britain, or against fascism. Canadian air, naval, and ground forces were arrayed against Nazi Germany.

On the North Atlantic, the Royal Canadian Navy ensured that the vital sea lanes to Britain stayed open. In the skies over Germany, the Royal Canadian Air Force rained down 'fire and fury' in a bombing campaign that remains a source of continuing controversy, particularly because in targeting German war capacity, Allied airmen killed several hundred thousand civilians.[19] On land, from Hong Kong and the French coast to Italy and the Netherlands, the Canadian Army experienced its share of snafus and successes. That the capture of one of the five D-Day beaches was assigned to Canada testifies to the country's relative importance to the Allied coalition devoted to Nazism's unconditional defeat. Tellingly, French and Dutch civilians greeted Canadian soldiers as liberators, not conquerors. A variety of Canadian individuals acted in support for the Allied war effort: in China, missionary James Endicott worked for the American Office of Strategic Services gathering intelligence on the Japanese; in Ethiopia, pilot and future federal politician Robert N. Thompson assisted in the building of an Ethiopian air force; and across occupied Europe, Canada agents conducted covert operations.[20] By mid-1945, Canadian attention turned to the Pacific and Ottawa began mustering troops, aircraft, and naval forces for the planned invasion of the Japanese home islands. Thankfully, American use of the atomic bomb and Soviet entry into the Pacific war in August forced a Japanese surrender.

Canadians played a part in the bomb's development. At British insistence Canada became a junior partner to the Manhattan Project, largely because of the country's stores of uranium, a metal, King predicted, that 'in time would unquestionably win the war with its power of destruction'.[21] The atomic blasts helped convince the Japanese to surrender, though at a terrible cost. 'It makes one very sad at heart to think of the loss of life that it will occasion among innocent people as well as those that are guilty', reflected King several days before the Hiroshima blast. 'We now see what might have come to the British race had German scientists won the race', he noted afterwards. 'It is fortunate that the use of the bomb should have been upon the Japanese rather than upon the white races of Europe.'[22] Beyond displaying the grim military logic and racial thinking of the time, King's reaction indicated quick comprehension of this new weapon's devastating power. He was not alone in feeling a sense of relieved accomplishment. Reporting on the Hiroshima blast, the *Globe and Mail* celebrated the 'Anglo-American-Canadian victory'. 'For better or for worse', it added, 'mankind has now reached a new level of authority in its command of nature. The achievement is sublime; the responsibility is awe-inspiring.' The bomb was 'the culmination of a process in which the American-British-Canadian forces have earned for themselves an unchallenged and unchallengeable reputation', wrote the editors of an opinion journal in a piece titled 'Pre-eminence of the Anglo-Saxon'.[23] This sense of accomplishment in what the countries of the North Atlantic Triangle had achieved was matched by feelings of dread, for 'what happened this week in Hiroshima' could 'happen at some remote date to Montreal or Edmonton'.[24] Despite having the raw resources as well as the scientific capacity, for various reasons, successive Canadian governments opted against building an atomic arsenal, instead relying on American nuclear power.[25]

Canada's minimal participation in the Manhattan Project was typical of its limited status within the Allied war effort, the result of the country's relative size and of its leader's inclination. King made no attempt to see Canada represented on the Anglo-French Supreme War Council, which convened from the start of the war to the French surrender. Nor, despite Canada's increased importance during the eighteen months between the fall of France and the entry of the United States into the war, did he seek to affect the direction of British strategy, and he nixed a British and Australian effort to reconstitute the Great War era Imperial War Cabinet. In December 1940, the US ambassador in Ottawa offered the harsh observation that, 'despite the outward trappings of independence', Canada was acting like 'a mere adjunct of British foreign policy as laid down from London'.[26]

In typical King fashion, sometimes he accepted Canada's minor position as only natural, and at other times it upset him. Following FDR and Churchill's August 1941 meeting off the Newfoundland coast he complained to Britain's high commissioner that this apparent snub 'bears out my view that the only real position for Canada to take is that of a nation wholly on her own vis-a-vis both Britain and the United States'.[27] Soon after Pearl Harbor King admitted to the Cabinet that 'the US and Britain would settle everything between themselves'. When hosting Churchill and Roosevelt at the Quebec conferences in 1943 and 1944, he stayed merely for the photo opportunities, later likening his role 'to that of the General Manager of the Chateau Frontenac', the summit hotel.[28] Yet, a week before the 1943 conference, he told British officials that while he agreed that the war's higher direction should remain an Anglo-American affair, 'the Canadian public were increasingly concerned that there should be adequate recognition of the substantial contributions which Canada was making to the total war effort'.[29] Lester Pearson, who divided his wartime diplomatic service among London, Ottawa, and Washington, saw first-hand the ways in which Canada was sidelined. 'The Allies keep us informed as to what has happened', he recorded; 'very rarely as to what is going to happen or what might happen'.[30]

Canada did score some successes on what one diplomat called the 'prestige front'.[31] King pressed and won Canadian membership on the Combined Food Board and the Combined Allied Production Board, minor committees in the grand scheme of the war, but no less important to Canada, a major contributor of food and materiel. Brigadier General Maurice Pope, the head of Canada's military missions first in London and then in Washington, was permitted to sit as a semi-official observer to the Combined Chiefs of Staff, the Anglo-American secretariat coordinating the western Allies' war effort, but he described himself and the other Canadians as 'merely bystanders'.[32] The impetus behind Canada's efforts lay in the Functional Principle, a concept formulated in 1942 by diplomat Hume Wrong, who was dissatisfied with alliance strategy-making. Each alliance member, he contended, 'should have a voice in the conduct of the war proportional to its contribution to the general war effort' and 'the influence of various countries should be greatest in connection with matters with which they are most directly concerned'.[33] King accepted this position to the extent that he was willing to push for Canadian involvement in the logistical committees. However, he avoided involvement in the war's higher direction. Canada should move cautiously, he told Pearson, as it was 'a mistake to take on too many things'. For his part, Pearson complained about King's propensity of loudly protesting Canadian exclusion but then capitulating to the bigger allies, an approach he likened to the 'strong glove over the velvet hand'.[34]

A source of friction was the US military's massive growth and its presence abroad. Military bases and other infrastructure spread from the Caribbean, to Iceland, to the South Pacific. Canada, too, encountered a grasping American military presence. Within weeks of Washington's declaration of war, US engineers began constructing massive infrastructure projects in Canada's north: weather stations; the Northwest Staging Route, an array of airfields to supply the USSR via the Arctic; the Canol pipeline to carry oil to Alaska; and the Alaska Highway, connecting Alaska to the contiguous United States. These projects damaged the environment and displaced and disrupted the lives of indigenous people, but from Ottawa's perspective their worst impact was on Canadian sovereignty. The situation was not helped by one journalist's report that a telephone operator at the US Army headquarters in Edmonton had greeted a senior Canadian officer by announcing – jokingly, no doubt – 'US Army of Occupation'.[35] Such braggadocio upset King. The Alaska Highway, he explained to a British diplomat, was 'one of the fingers on the hand which America is placing more or less over the whole of the Western hemisphere'.[36] King's solution was to pay nearly half the cost and to insist that it be transferred to Canadian ownership within six months of the war's end. Perhaps with some self-awareness of Canadian history, Vincent Massey wrote from London that the Americans had 'apparently walked in and taken possession in many cases as if Canada were unclaimed territory inhabited by a docile race of aborigines'.[37] Meanwhile, in 1941, the United States had built Harmon Air Force Base in Newfoundland on territory acquired from Britain under the Destroyers for Bases agreement; this US facility, which eventually housed nuclear bombers, remained in operation until 1966.

King's worries about American encroachment were matched by his perennial consternation with British intentions. In January 1944, he raged over a speech delivered by Lord Halifax, Britain's ambassador in Washington, who had called for more frequent consultation and cooperation among Commonwealth members. A logical suggestion for a British official to make, to Canada's prime minister it was evidence that London sought a unified imperial foreign policy. In a stunning overreaction, he thundered that 'Hitler himself ... could not have chosen a more effective way' to divide the empire than Halifax's speech.[38] British apologies followed, and with King due to meet Churchill, officials in London prayed 'that Winston does not let loose some passage of old-fashioned Victorian Imperialism' sure to offend Canada's prime minister.[39] Churchill was on his best behaviour and King underlined to his British counterpart his interest in Canada's post-war standing in the future United Nations organization, pointing out that 'after enlisting nearly one million persons in her armed forces and trebling her national debt', Canada would not be treated like 'the Dominican Republic or El Salvador'.[40] In talks with British officials later that year, he made clear what should have been obvious given his long-standing views, namely that Canadians 'could not countenance our men serving in India, Burma or elsewhere to enable Britain to reconquer her colonial possessions'.[41] King wanted a peace dividend. Much to the concern of British officials, when the fighting ended he ordered the withdrawal of Canadian forces from Europe, spurning a role in pacifying Germany.

Later myth-making would play up Canada's part in the creation of the post-war liberal international order, especially its centrepiece, the United Nations. Often, though, Canadian actions were constrained by King's typical caution. Guided by the functional principle, he told a May 1944 gathering of Commonwealth prime ministers that the great powers had the responsibility for 'maintaining political security' and that while the smaller powers should be a part of the future global order, their role should be confined largely to 'the many functional organizations' to administer programs for refugees, agriculture, and public health.[42] Senior diplomats agreed: the 'best hope' for post-war collective security was an 'effective world security organization' with the participation of all of the great powers.[43] In practice that meant that in negotiations over the UN's structure, the Canadians supported vetoes for the five permanent members of the Security Council. This stance pitted Canada against other smaller powers opposed to vetoes. Furthermore, on orders from Ottawa and against the desires of some of its more idealistic members, Canada's delegation to the conference took a minor role in the proceedings, except for socio-economic questions, where in a display of the functional principle in action, Canadians successfully pushed for the creation of the UN Economic and Social Council. Canada's position on the veto led to a groundswell of opposition to the Canadian campaign to win a non-permanent spot on the Security Council, a seat won by Australia.[44] Despite the Canadian government's timidity at San Francisco, the vote to join the UN passed Canada's Parliament unanimously. King's views had evolved little from the League of Nations era. It was 'a great mistake', he remarked in October 1945, 'to develop organizations and agreements which help to relieve the anxieties and consciences of large numbers of people but which in reality are first a delusion and a snare in that they give a positive advantage to a country that does not care a rap about the sanctity of contracts'.[45]

This opprobrium, coming so soon after the war's end, stemmed from revelations of Soviet spying in Canada. Quickly, a sense of betrayal characterized a Canadian-Soviet relationship that had, since 1917, often been marked by hostility. From September 1939 to June 1941, Ottawa and Moscow had been on different sides of the war, until Germany's invasion of the Soviet Union created an alliance of convenience. In October 1942, there was an exchange of envoys between the two governments. Canada became an important supplier to the Soviets of food aid, medical aid, armaments, and munitions, and across the country committees formed to raise funds for the Soviet war effort, which was the vital component of the victory over Nazism.

The situation soured in September 1945, when Igor Gouzenko, a clerk at the Soviet embassy in Ottawa defected, bringing with him evidence of a spy network reaching throughout the Canadian government and into the British foreign service. Initially, King was hesitant about acting on the information lest he do anything to upset the alliance with the Soviets, but arrests soon followed and in March 1947 Canada withdrew its ambassador from Moscow. Spying is a common occurrence between countries, but the fact that this network – including the sole communist MP in Canada – was run by a wartime ally of suspect ideology with a history of supporting subversive groups magnified the importance of Gouzenko's revelations. Certainly, many Canadians both inside and outside government loathed communism. Meeting for security talks with British authorities, Norman Robertson 'feared that public opinion … would be so stirred by the story' that it would ruin chances of post-war cooperation.[46] Opportunities for cooperation with Moscow were put in doubt by Soviet actions in Europe. By early 1946, King had concluded that 'the rest of the world is not in a very different position than other countries in Europe when Hitler had made up his mind to aim at the conquest of Europe'.[47] One threat to European stability had been defeated, but another rose in its place.

The Hitler–Stalin analogy was easy enough to make, and not simply because both despots sported moustaches. After the second invasion by German forces in thirty years, and with 25 million Soviet citizens dead in the recent war, Stalin was set on constructing a security buffer in Eastern and Central Europe. Moreover, as a committed ideologue, he suspected Anglo-American intentions, assuming that there could be no permanent cooperation between capitalist and communist powers. From the perspective of the western Allies, the Soviet formation of puppet regimes backed by the Red Army and secret police, took on a particularly threatening appearance. Compounding fears were a surge of support for Italy's communist party, communist-led strikes in France, a communist insurgency in Greece, and Moscow's refusal to abide by an agreement to pull its troops out of Iran. Worse, was the realization that because of the Soviets' Security Council veto, the UN was toothless in opposing these latter developments.

As early as March 1946, in reacting to Churchill's iron curtain speech, Pearson raised the need to reform the UN to eliminate the potency of the great power veto. Failing that, he suggested creating a new organization 'as the guardian of the peace for *all* nations', one that 'can function without the Russians and, as a last resort, against them'. From Moscow, Canada's ambassador added that 'Anglo-Saxon hegemony is so essential to the maintenance of peace and security', and so Western should not sacrifice their principles for 'the sake of brief vodka honeymoons'.[48] Fear of Soviet aggression grew. By year end, Pearson warned that the UN 'is not now, and is not likely to be for many years, in a position to preserve the peace and punish the big aggressor'. Highlighting Soviet statements about world revolution, he counselled avoiding 'the mistake we made with Hitler of refusing to take seriously the words those leaders utter for home consumption'.[49] A year later, King observed that Stalin sought 'to become the Master of Europe'.[50] The most worrisome development for Canadian officials was the March 1948 Soviet-backed communist coup in Czechoslovakia. Facing this act of aggression. Louis St Laurent, recently appointed as Canada's foreign minister, stressed avoiding 'the fatal repetition of the history of the pre-war years when the Nazi aggressor picked off its victims one by one. Such a process does not end at the Atlantic.'[51] Viewing European events in the late 1940s through the lens of the 1930s, Canada's recourse was to join with other powers in forming a new collective security organization.

In response to the Czechoslovakian coup, Britain, France, Belgium, Luxembourg, and the Netherlands concluded the Brussels Treaty, pledging to come to one another's defence. Next, they sought out Canada and US participation. The Canadians were responsive. To King, the coup had 'proven there can be no collaboration with Communists', and he wrote British Prime Minister Clement Attlee to urge that they act.[52] Collective security was needed, and within weeks Atlee had initiated security talks with Canada and the United States with the goal of broadening the Brussels Pact into a transatlantic alliance. In a sign of the situation's desperate nature, King supported this development, doing so despite his decades-long preoccupations with Canadian independence and with being drawn into wars.[53] Through the North Atlantic Treaty, his government committed Canada to come to Western Europe's defence. Even so, King avoided involvement in the Anglo-American airlift to deliver supplies to West Berliners during the Soviet blockade of the city from June 1948 to May 1949, a reminder of his mercurial temperament.

For Canada's government, the alliance solved several problems. First, it ensured an American commitment to European security, for Canada and the Brussels Pact countries could not repel a Soviet attack without the United States. Second, as a multilateral organization, it presented a means of counterbalancing Canadian reliance on the United States. Pearson justified Canadian participation on the grounds that there was more safety for Canada in a group than in being stuck alone 'in a double bed' with the United States.[54] Third, it offered the allies a measure of control over US actions, something that appealed to Pearson, who admitted that he had 'more confidence' in European diplomacy getting the West out of a crisis than he did in American problem-solving abilities.[55] Press reaction to NATO was mixed, with the alliance dubbed both 'our only present means of salvation' and 'a poor substitute for the one-world dream' of the United Nations.[56] Wherever public opinion stood, St Laurent, who succeeded King as prime minister in November 1948, put the matter bluntly: 'Canada cannot possibly remain neutral in a third world war even if 11,999,999 out of 12,000,000 Canadians want to stay out.'[57] Approval of alliance membership sailed through Parliament in March 1949, with only two French Canadian MPs in opposition.

For Canada, NATO marked a sea change: it was the country's first peacetime alliance and it signified a commitment to collective security in Europe. While King had approved the move, its impetus came from a younger generation of policymakers who rejected the course Canada had pursued during the 1930s. Summing up the new outlook, Pearson, who became foreign minister in 1948, told a reporter that he and St Laurent 'will sink or swim on total internationalism. No retreat. No appeasement.'[58] NATO, Pearson hoped, would form the basis of an Atlantic community, a political and economic union of countries sharing 'the same democratic and cultural traditions'.[59] The Americans had little enthusiasm for this notion, preferring instead an alliance focused purely on military matters. Canada's diplomats overcame this opposition, and Article 2 – known as the Canadian article – of the North Atlantic Treaty committed the allies to work towards greater economic and social cooperation.

Not much came of the idea of an Atlantic community, but it encapsulated a key element in the thinking behind the alliance, namely that it was an organization of Western countries, defined not simply in geographic terms, but in a cultural sense. In pressing for King's support for the project, Pearson stressed that 'it is essential to remember that the purpose of the pact is to rally the spiritual as well as the military and economic resources of western Christendom against Soviet totalitarianism'. *Saturday Night* magazine, meanwhile, praised the development of a pact that brought together 'the great Christian nations'.[60] Europe should be defended, a briefing note for the prime minister urged, because it was a region from which 'Canada has received nine-tenths of its people, both its languages, its religion, and most of its laws and political institutions.' 'For us in North America the shrines of western Europe are no mere items of geography', explained Arnold Heeney, the undersecretary of state. 'In Britain, in France, in Italy are the vital well-springs of our civilization.'[61] This framing of the alliance reflected the cultural orientation of Canadian foreign policymakers and of many Canadians who conceived of the Soviet threat in military and ideological terms. Based on deeply ingrained cultural attitudes about the superiority of Western civilization in contrast to barbaric forces in the East, the idea of the West served as geopolitical signifier throughout the cold war and beyond. Finally, it reflected Europe's importance, for the continent had twice been at the centre of world wars that had dragged in Canada. American officials would take credit for creating the Western alliance, but Canadians were just as invested in its success.

The Soviet march through Eastern Europe and the Gouzenko revelations, revived anti-communist sentiments in Canada, continuing an ideological struggle at home and abroad that had begun in 1917. *Saturday Night*'s editor warned an audience at a public affairs conference that communism was 'a new religion … seeking to displace what has been the dominant religion of the western world'. St Laurent told the Canadian Chamber of Commerce to be wary of the 'theory-crazed totalitarian group' seeking to subvert Canadian democracy.[62] The Canadian Chamber of Commerce issued pamphlets on *The Communist Threat to Canada* and *How Communists Operate! A Brief Memorandum on Communist Tactics*. Labour unions expelled communist members, and civil society groups like the Royal Canadian Legion and the Imperial Order Daughters of the Empire turned from their traditional causes to the fight against communism. In a demonstration of the workings of what would become known as the military-industrial complex, in 1955 aircraft manufacturer Canadair paid for a series of magazine advertisements on the theme 'Do we actually know where to face Communism?' The answer, evidently, was in schools, where educators created model citizens; on the sports field, where young people practiced fitness; through churches, where religion served as a spiritual bulwark; and in dark alleys, where spies and subversives lurked. In the early cold war years, these concerns existed across the political spectrum. Andrew Brewin, a CCF MP and human rights lawyer, expressed a social democratic commitment to 'confining the new Russian imperialism with its dynamic communist faith'.[63]

Cold war fears of spying and subversion fed the growth of a Canadian national security apparatus, with the Royal Canadian Mounted Police (RCMP) front and centre in monitoring not just foreign nationals such as diplomats, but also a variety of left-wing politicians and activists. Their focus even included women's rights and black power groups, organizations that had tenuous links to the struggle against the Soviet Union but that posed a threat to the established order. There were RCMP agents and informers on university campuses, in labour unions, and in genuine communist front organizations, and there were a variety of programs monitoring Canadians. Operation Picnic involved wiretapping Canadian individuals and organizations, as well as foreign embassies. Operation Featherbed saw investigations into possible spies within Canada's government; by the time it was cancelled in the 1980s, it had turned up no results. More fruitful were counterintelligence operations against communist bloc spies seeking to steal Canadian and allied secrets.[64] Operation Profunc, meanwhile, was a contingency plan in place from 1950 to 1983, to round up and intern thousands of communists and left-wing sympathizers in the event of a third world war.

Targeting Canadians for their beliefs or individual actions tested the application of civil liberties. Most egregious was a crackdown on gay and lesbian civil servants and military personnel, who were fired from their jobs; those caught in the dragnet included several leading Canadian diplomats, notably John Holmes, who salvaged his reputation and became a leading commentator on Canadian foreign affairs.[65] In comparison to the McCarthyite purges in the United States, the Canadian investigations of supposed sympathizers and security risks were far more *Canadian*: quiet and lacking the hoopla of Congressional hearings. Indeed, the public shaming of Canadian diplomat E. H. Norman by US congressmen led Norman to take his own life. Too often, though, the results were the same in terms of destroyed lives and trammelled rights.

Given the chilled ideological climate as well as the looming Soviet menace, challenges to Canadian foreign policy in the early cold war were few and far between. The CCF remained largely supportive of Canada's international position, though as the cold war progressed, divisions within the party emerged more fully.[66] During the Second World War, when the USSR was an ally, the Canadian-Soviet Friendship Society had experienced relative prominence, but this situation changed markedly with the cold war. With only several dozen committed members, the organization soldiered on, and through meetings and newsletters, and, with direct Soviet support – a foreign influence campaign by a hostile power – it sought to improve the Russian image in Canada. Among its publications was *Moscow: As Two Canadian Saw It*, the travelogue of Frank and Libbie Park, two communists who lived in the Soviet Union, and, later, in Cuba, where they worked for the communist government's media arm.[67]

A more significant and vocal force against the cold war consensus was the Canadian Peace Congress (CPC), formed in May 1949 under former missionary James Endicott's leadership. In China's Civil War, his sympathies lay with the communists, and after returning to Canada in 1947 he became a vociferous critic of the Chinese Nationalists and an outspoken advocate for China's Communist Party.[68] Through the CPC, Endicott challenged Canada's cold war orientation, a position that garnered support from Canadian peace advocates. In a sign of interest in the CPC's message, a May 1950 rally at Maple Leaf Gardens was attended by twelve thousand people. Given the status quo, the Congress was naturally left-wing. However, its lack of criticism of Soviet and Chinese actions, and the prevalence of communists among its leadership – Endicott held the dubious distinction of being among the final recipients of the Stalin Peace Prize, the despot's answer to the Nobel Committee – led to waning support over the course of the 1950s, particularly as new peace groups emerged.[69]

Beyond monitoring spies and subversives, the national security state emerged in other ways. In 1951, Canada's government made the decision not to establish a covert foreign intelligence service. Instead, Ottawa would rely on information provided by its allies. During the war, however, to monitor the Vichy regime's diplomatic mission in Ottawa, Canada's National Research Council had created a signals intelligence station that became the Communications Security Establishment (CSE). The CSE remains the anchor of the Canadian contribution to the Five Eyes network, the US-led intelligence partnership along with Britain, New Zealand, and Australia – the English-speaking peoples.[70] Beyond this intelligence gathering capacity set up to monitor foreign governments' communications, the cold war transformed Canada's military. While large forces had been raised during both world wars, they had been temporary in nature, with a small peacetime military the rule since 1867. The permanent sense of crisis pervading the cold war created a need to have forces on hand, either in Europe to deter a Soviet offensive, or in the air or off the coast of Canada to defend against attack. Furthermore, Canada would gain the ability to deploy forces to deal with crises abroad. The result was the creation of a standby military capable of contributing to allied efforts and collective security.

Brooke Claxton, minister of national defence from 1946 to 1954 was responsible for much of this development. The ongoing Soviet threat, he noted, 'has produced an attitude in Canada towards defence which is quite different from any that we ever had before in peacetime'.[71] In late 1950, at the height of the Korean War, Claxton and Pearson warned Cabinet that, given the likelihood of a third world war, forces had to be sent to Europe to meet Canada's NATO commitment. In this light, a moderately sized, well-funded peacetime military was 'essential'.[72] The next year, in more colourful language, Pearson justified increased military spending by contending that Canadians were 'faced now with a situation similar in some respects to that which confronted our fore-fathers in early colonial days when they ploughed the land with a rifle slung on the shoulder. If they stuck to the plough and left the rifle at home, they would have been easy victim for any savages lurking in the woods.'[73] As part of its NATO commitment, Ottawa despatched ten thousand military personnel to Western Europe, an open-ended deployment establishing Canada's commitment to its allies. In a sign of lingering British ties, Canadian ground forces were attached to the British Army of the Rhine.

The decision to ramp up spending and to send a military contingent to Europe came in the wake of the Korean War, an event that transformed the cold war into a global conflict. Canada briefly served on the United Nations Temporary Commission on Korea (UNTCOK), formed to oversee unification of the country, which was divided into a Soviet-backed North and a US-backed South. King opposed involvement in a country of which Canadians 'knew nothing'. Worse, he sensed that Korea was a 'really dangerous part between the Americans and the Russians', where the two powers were likely to clash. St Laurent and several other ministers favouring participation on UNTCOK threatened to resign on the issue and King relented. This standoff marked the transition from King to more internationalist-minded policymakers. However, Canadian involvement with the commission was short-lived as Canada left UNTCOK in protest over American plans to form a separate government in the South.[74] Canadian policymakers held concerns over the direction of US foreign policy, concerns magnified by the Korean War.

Coming within less than a year after the Soviet test of a nuclear bomb and the communist victory in China's civil war, North Korea's invasion of the South in June 1950 jarred Western authorities. The Harry Truman administration responded by pledging to save South Korea. In the House of Commons, to applause from the assembled MPs, Pearson praised the United States for having 'recognized [its] special responsibility' to confront aggression. To the US ambassador, who appealed for assistance, he added that 'Canada [would] not "let [the] US down." '[75] However, Pearson, St Laurent, and other senior ministers were wary of contributing to a purely American mission; rather they resolved to give 'help to the United Nations, fulfilling our obligations under the Charter, and *not* help to the United States'. At the same time, Pearson warned against going 'too far' in pressing for a UN label because the Americans might insist on using the organization in ways that Canada would not approve.[76] Here was a defence of Canada's collective security responsibilities mixed with a note of caution about US belligerency. This consideration became more important as the fighting in Korea worsened.

Ottawa dispatched naval vessels followed by an infantry brigade, which served alongside British, Australian, New Zealander, and Indian troops in a Commonwealth Division. With this force sent under UN auspices, Pearson's mind turned to creating an international police force to enforce the UN Charter. 'If Canada emphasized this principle in announcing its decision', he told St Laurent, 'we might be initiating something new in the way of backing up the United Nations which could have important consequences.'[77] This hope came to nothing – Pearson would return to the idea later in the decade – and the UN intervention was subsumed within an American-dominated war. The situation turned bleak in autumn 1950 when US forces provoked Chinese intervention. In response to the widening war, the American authorities indicated that they might employ nuclear weapons against Chinese targets, a development that, in Pearson's view, would risk 'destroying the cohesion and unity of purpose of the Atlantic community' and weaken the remaining ties between Asia and the West.[78] Mercifully, the use of these weapons was avoided, but the incident left many Canadian officials worried about American bellicosity. As US diplomats recognized, Canadian forces had been committed to Korea 'only because of Canada's faith in the United Nations and active support for its principles'.[79]

Canada's infantry brigade did not arrive in Korea until early 1951. By then Pearson had sought to bring about an armistice, lobbying Washington to pursue negotiations to end the fighting, a suggestion that angered his US counterpart Dean Acheson.[80] Alarmed by the division created between the United States and its allies, Pearson complained to Hume Wrong, Canada's ambassador in Washington, of the need to have the Americans agree 'that our objective in the Far East is the defeat of aggression and not the use of the United Nations to overthrow Communist Governments'.[81] He made his frustrations public, stating that it was 'as dangerous, for the generals to intervene in international policy matters as it would be for the diplomats to try to lay down military strategy'. In separate comments several days later, he added that it was imperative to ensure that the UN 'does not become too much an instrument of any one country'.[82] These statements were perceived, rightly, as a rebuke of US handling of both the war and the UN. Behind the scenes, meanwhile, Pearson and other Canadian diplomats assisted their Indian counterparts in laying the groundwork for the Korean Armistice in 1953. Outraged by Canadian support for the Indians, Acheson dismissed Pearson as 'an empty glass of water'.[83]

The unhappy Korean experience did little to interest Canadian officials in Asian security. 'Korea is but a "side show" in the over-all struggle between the

USSR and the Western world', Arnold Heeney told Pearson. On the question of whether Canada should support Washington in creating an Asian version of NATO, Canada's foreign minister mused that doing so would mean following policies that had produced 'such unhappy consequences in China; and which are not working out too well in Korea'. The United States followed through, creating SEATO, but Ottawa spurned membership. 'Militarily', the head of Canada's armed forces confirmed, 'we have no more interest in South East Asia than we would have in a case of communist aggression in Iran or Pakistan.'[84] The point was important given later US involvement in Vietnam, Laos, and Cambodia and indeed American overt and covert involvement across what was soon called the Third World. Collective security, meanwhile, generated early enthusiasm in Canada: other than a few Quebec MPs, the House of Commons had backed the UN intervention in Korea and the Canadian press was largely supportive. 'The United Nations has suddenly acquired new vigor and importance', boasted one newspaper, while *Maclean's* contended that for all its faults that UN had proven itself 'worthwhile'.[85] Always sardonic, Hume Wrong came to a different conclusion, quipping to Pearson that the sorry state of the war effort would deter other states from becoming 'victims of collective security'.[86]

Beyond generating disquiet over US foreign policy, the Korean conflict put a stop to Ottawa's plans to recognize the communist regime in Beijing. In the waning years of the Chinese nationalist republic, Canada's government had extended loans to the regime for it to purchase surplus Canadian military equipment, which was used for its war against the communists. Soon Canadian diplomats at the embassy in Nanjing concluded that the Nationalists were fated to lose. 'The disease is bad and the cure may be worse than the disease', Ambassador T. C. Davis noted with reference to the two warring sides, 'but I think we may as well realistically face the fact that sooner or later [the communists] are going to control all of China.'[87] The communist victory in 1949 was not a shock to Canadian officials, but the development was alarming nonetheless. Guidance for Canada's Cabinet labelled China 'a potential enemy state' likely to side with the Soviets in a war. Even so, it might be possible to prevent 'a thorough-going totalitarian Communist system' from developing by influencing the new government through trade and other contacts.[88]

The United States ignored the new regime, and Britain established diplomatic relations with it, while for Canada, the issue languished, and sporadic talks between Canadian and Chinese diplomats dragged on throughout 1950. With the Korean War Ottawa shelved plans to recognize the Beijing government. In early 1951, when Canada backed a UN resolution condemning China as an aggressor in Korea, Chester Ronning, the Canadian representative in China, was expelled from the country and Canada shuttered its diplomatic mission. Over the next few years, Canadian missionaries withdrew in the face of communist agitation.[89] For two decades, Canada refused to recognize China's government and there was little contact between Canadians and Chinese. Exceptions included the occasional communist peace activist, such as Endicott, or intrepid travellers, such as journalist and lawyer Pierre Trudeau, who visited the country in 1960 and left convinced of the inanity of 'refusing to recognize the existence of those who rule a quarter – soon to be a third – of the human race'.[90] A decade later, as prime minister, Trudeau established relations with Beijing. Importantly, the end of non-recognition preceded a similar move by the Americans and came amid a cold war thaw.

Isolation of China was an outlier, for throughout the cold war, Canadian diplomats sought to establish links with Soviet bloc countries. After Stalin died in 1953, the warming international climate led to the resumption of Canada–Soviet relations and the conclusion of agreements on trade and cultural exchanges. Canadian performers, scientists, and athletes travelled to the USSR with their Soviet counterparts paying reciprocal visits. The goal of this cultural diplomacy – whether displays of Inuit art, broadcasts by CBC's International Service, or Glenn Gould's piano concertos – was to break down barriers while also waging ideological combat against communism.[91] Outreach efforts were extended to countries throughout the Soviet sphere and Pearson himself became the first Western statesman to tour post-Stalin Soviet Union during a 1955 visit notable also for a drinking contest between the Canadian and Russian delegations. Committed to waging the cold war at home and abroad, nonetheless Canadian officials were mindful of the need to lessen international tension, for as Pearson pointed out to John Foster Dulles, President Dwight Eisenhower's hawkish secretary of state, 'there was a real danger of actions by the superpowers converting small wars into world wars'.[92] In such a conflict, Canada occupied an unfavourable piece of geography.

In reacting to North Korea's invasion of the South, Canadian officials looked to the recent past. Collective security, Pearson stated, demanded a response because otherwise Western powers would be repeating 'the performance of Abyssinia and Munich'.[93] The same thinking drove support for NATO. Whatever one might think of the notion seventy years later, the analogy had a definite resonance to the generation who had lived through the confrontation with Nazism. Drawing the same lesson, US authorities committed to containing the Soviet Union. In doing so, the United States began to construct a new type of imperial rule through its alliances, what historians have called an 'empire by consent' or an 'empire by invitation'.[94] Like the Western Europeans, the Canadians welcomed American participation in the post-war international order and leadership of the Western alliance. After all, the United States had a massive military, a booming economy, and the atomic bomb. In the tense climate, many Canadians greeted American protection. This process had begun during the Second World War, and it accelerated with the cold war.

At the same time as they welcomed the United States as a protector and guarantor of international stability, Canadian officials expressed unease about their reliance on American power. King, for instance, judged that the 'long objective of the Americans was to control the continent [and] to get Canada under their aegis'. Several months after NATO was formed, Pearson received a briefing by senior State Department officials on long-range US plans for an expansion of ties between Canada and the United States that would lead, effectively, to a merger between the two countries. Commenting on Pearson's reaction, an American noted, 'he was mildly shocked by it, to say the least'.[95] Beyond the American embrace, there were worries, too, about the direction of American foreign policy, with the Korean experience making clear that the US could be overly belligerent and that it was not necessarily concerned with its allies' views. 'Our preoccupation is no longer whether the United States will discharge her responsibilities', Pearson stated in a speech that drew considerable criticism from US officials and columnists, 'but how she will do it and how the rest of us will be involved.' His comments, he explained privately, stemmed from 'our feeling of dependence on the United States and the frustration over the fact that we can't escape this no matter how hard we try'.[96] NATO had been conceived in part to give the allies some measure of control over US foreign policy, even as it cemented American hegemony in the West. As for the Atlantic alliance, it soon posed its own set of problems for Canadian policymakers as they sought to deal with the collapse of European colonialism.

8

The middle power and
the end of empire

Addressing the 1958 Couchiching Conference, Lester Pearson touched on major currents in international affairs, noting that when it came to flashpoints in countries throughout what was then the Third World, it was instinctive that 'our minds, or perhaps more often, our emotions, relate it to the struggle between Moscow and Washington'. Urging his listeners to question this automatic assumption, he counselled that many international crises were 'the reflection of something deeper than the "cold war" '.[1] As Pearson well knew from his time as foreign minister during the so-called golden age of Canadian foreign policy in the late 1940s and 1950s, there was both a world beyond the North Atlantic and a series of policy issues that, while intertwined with the cold war, were the result of the decolonization of Europe's empires. 'It may be that in the verdict of history a hundred years or so from now', he once reflected, 'it will be agreed that of the communist revolution in Russia in 1917 and the emergence of independent Asian countries after World War II – the latter revolution will be considered in its long-range impact as more important than the former.'[2]

The end of empire, the emergence of dozens of new states, and the growth of the Third World had a profound impact on international affairs. Canadian responses to decolonization were decidedly mixed, for Canada's interest in backing its Western allies, who sought to retain their imperial holdings, clashed with Ottawa's general sympathy for colonial demands for self-determination. Just eight months before the Suez crisis, Pearson had asked reporters, 'if we hold colonial territories against the wishes of their inhabitants are we going to be stronger or weaker in the long run?'[3] Decolonization had a transformative impact on Canadian foreign policy, leading to the creation of development assistance, to the innovation of peacekeeping, to the expansion of Canada's diplomatic presence, and, eventually, to alterations in immigration policy.

This chapter interrogates the golden age of Canadian foreign policy, but rather than focus on the cold war, its lens is the post-war wave of decolonization. The rise of the 'darker nations' exposed deep concerns in Ottawa, where there was recognition that with the waning of formal European imperialism, Canada, as a Western state, was in a shrinking minority within both the UN and the Commonwealth, forums in which battles over racial discrimination and continuing colonialism gained prominence.[4] Reporting on events at the UN in 1959, the influential journalist Blair Fraser observed that while the West's attention focused on the struggle against communism, most of the organization's time dealt with the 'not-so-cold war between the colored and white', a seeming problem for Canada, he admitted, because the UN served as a reminder 'that the whites are a minority of the human race'.[5] In Fraser's judgement, Canada, a middle power, could bridge racial divides, a common assumption in foreign policy circles. For instance, John Holmes, a former diplomat and head of the CIIA, offered the assurance that having spurned 'imperialism and racial discrimination', Canadians were trusted by Third World peoples.[6] Ignoring forms of discrimination within Canada as well as colonial practices towards indigenous people, these views encapsulated a popular notion of Canada as a relatively benign actor in global affairs and an exceptional country, that was itself a former colony. Given the interplay between the cold war and decolonization, finding a positive role for Canada in relation to the Third World took on considerable importance.[7] Increasingly, as decolonization proceeded apace, as international power shifted from the West to newly independent countries, and as an international human rights regime emerged more fully in the latter half of the twentieth century, Canadian exceptionalism came increasingly under attack both at home and abroad.

Within Canadian foreign policy circles, the decade and a half following the Second World War became a mythical period in which Canada – stable, secure, and relatively undamaged by the fighting – possessed inordinate international influence. The notion had begun during the war, when The Economist opined that Canada, though not a great power, had 'made a category for herself all of her own. Relative to her resources her effort is second to none. In absolute terms the distance which separates Canada from the Great Powers is less than that between her own achievements and that of any other of the smaller powers.'[8] Here was an articulation of Canada as a middle power, a concept that recognized the country's relative importance. 'The evidence of Canada's new position in the world is unmistakable', wrote academic Lionel Gelber. 'Henceforth in world politics she must figure as a Middle Power.'[9] The idea came to reflect not just capability but activity, the belief that Canada had an important role to play in fostering a liberal, multilateral world order that stood in sharp contrast to the policies pursued during the interwar period. 'Canada's part in the last war raised her to the status of a nation', gushed Brooke Claxton in the conflict's closing months, and 'Canada's part in this war has given her the opportunities and responsibilities of world-wide interests', especially 'furthering international co-operation'. Journalist Grant Dexter was more concise: 'the Canada of 1939 no longer exists'.[10]

This idealistic rhetoric clashed with the reality of Ottawa's continued pursuit of a limited set of interests, with William Lyon Mackenzie King maintaining influence over Canada's foreign policy until stepping down as prime minister in 1948. Delivering an important 1947 address in which he called for a more internationalist outlook, Louis St Laurent, King's eventual successor, added the caveat that, 'There is little point in a country of our stature recommending international action, if those who must carry the major burden of whatever action is taken are not in sympathy.'[11] St Laurent had become secretary of state for external affairs (SSEA) in 1946 – until that point this position had been held concurrently by the prime minister – and his caution matched King's view of Canada's relative stature. Still, there were changes in Canada's approach to the world with an emphasis on multilateralism. Canadian officials showed far more eagerness for the United Nations than they ever did for the League of Nations and although the UN did not fulfil early hopes as an instrument of collective security, Ottawa turned to NATO to meet the same purpose. There was new enthusiasm for an invigorated Commonwealth and for involvement with recently formed international organizations. Also, quite simply, there was more foreign policy than before the war. During the conflict, new diplomatic posts were opened in the Dominions, in Latin America, and in Russia and China, and this trend continued after the conflict, when, in 1947 – the same year women were permitted to serve as foreign service officers – missions were opened in Turkey, Sweden, Poland, Switzerland, Denmark, Italy, and India. Beyond this expansion of Canada's diplomatic reach, in Ottawa the Department of External Affairs (DEA) became the premier ministry in the federal government. Among its members was a younger generation of diplomats, who had joined the DEA in the late 1930s and 1940s, and, as one of them put it, 'sought for things Canada might do rather than things Canada might avoid doing'.[12]

Beyond official Canadian channels, a host of Canadians worked as international civil servants. In 1951, Hugh Keenleyside, a long-time diplomat, was appointed director general of the UN Technical Assistance Administration after having served in UN-sponsored development projects in Bolivia. Jurist John Read sat on the International Court of Justice from 1946 to 1958, General Howard Kennedy was the first director of UN Relief and Works

Agency for Palestine Refugees, and Brock Chisholm, a leading medical practitioner, was the first director general of the World Health Organization.[13] Canadian nurses, administrators, and healthcare and welfare service professionals worked for the UN Relief and Rehabilitation Administration, and there were Canadians in the UN Food and Agriculture Organization, the UN Atomic Energy Commission, and the International Civil Aviation Organization, which was based in Montreal.[14] Canadian economists could be found in the International Monetary Fund and the International Bank for Reconstruction and Development. Canadian officials, especially the Bank of Canada's Louis Rasminsky, had played an important part in bridging Anglo-American divides over the creation of these two financial organizations and in working to set up agreements for the reciprocal reduction and removal of trade barriers, something which a 1945 Canadian government White Paper on post-war reconstruction saw as the key to 'security and freedom from threat of war'.[15] For the post-war generation of international civil servants, there was much to learn from the interwar years in terms of putting in place a rules-based liberal international order, where trained professionals, working through various organizations, could improve global conditions.

Support for multilateralism manifested in other ways. The CIIA experienced a boost in popularity and launched a series of publications, including its flagship *International Journal* in 1946. Then there was the creation of the UN Association (UNA) of Canada. Like the defunct League of Nations Society, its members – many of whom had been League backers – organized meetings to discuss international affairs, petitioned the government to support the UN's work, and raised money to advance UN initiatives, most notably the Trick-or-Treat for UNICEF campaign. The organization supported the formation of Model United Nations clubs at universities and high schools and one branch even held women's beauty pageants to raise awareness about international cooperation. In 1946, the UNA had nineteen branches with two thousand members; fifteen years later, there were twenty-nine branches and membership topped ten thousand. The group was not an oppositional force, for it shared the same broad goals as Canada's government, and the DEA provided funding to the UNA just as Canada helped to fund the United Nations. Summing up her reasons for supporting the UN, association president Kay Livingstone affirmed that the world body was 'the only organization today which attempts to speak for mankind'.[16] For many Canadians, support for the UN became an article of faith particularly with the innovation of peacekeeping in the 1950s.

There were early limits to the Canadian government's enthusiasm for multilateralism, particularly when it came to human rights. The war against Nazism had spurred an international human rights movement: the 1941 Atlantic Charter committed the Allies to the pursuit of a more just world and the UN Charter was infused with rights language. This movement reached its apogee with the 1948 Universal Declaration of Human Rights (UDHR). John Humphrey, a Canadian jurist who drafted this document – what he called the 'Magna Carta of Mankind' – lamented that his efforts had not been supported by Canada's government and that promoting human rights internationally was not a priority in Canadian foreign policy.[17]

Jealous of sovereignty and mindful of provincial jurisdiction, Ottawa was concerned, too, as St Laurent put it, that the UDHR could become 'a source of embarrassment' for Canada's government given issues such as immigration restrictions. Ottawa was set on opposing the international bill of rights until it became clear that Canada was placing itself 'in a rather undesirable minority' with apartheid South Africa and the Soviet bloc. So, reluctantly, Canada backed the UDHR.[18] Futher, Ottawa lagged in adhering to the UN Refugee Convention and to the UN Declaration of the Rights of the Child, signs that, at the state level, the Canadian human rights revolution did not begin in earnest until much later in the century.[19] There was little interest, too, in other innovations in international law that came out of the war. Canadian jurists did not participate at the Nuremberg trials and the Canadian judge who did preside at the Tokyo war crimes trials considered resigning in protest at what he felt was victor's justice. Canada's first independent war crimes prosecution saw SS General Kurt Meyer convicted of killing Canadian prisoners of war; regrettably Meyer's prison sentence was far too short. Moreover, Ottawa proved lax in allowing the detritus of the Nazi regime and its European collaborators into the country, though there were later efforts to prosecute some of these individuals for war crimes and crimes against humanity.[20]

Human rights were a contested topic in post-war Canada, where pressure mounted from groups and individuals concerned by wartime excesses by government authorities, who had targeted conscientious objectors, critics in the press, and ethnic minorities. During the war, several hundred German and Italian Canadians were interned, but it was the treatment of Japanese Canadians, that proved particularly egregious. As in the United States, wartime hatreds mixed with long-standing racist views, leading to pressure on the government to act. While meeting with British Columbia politicians, who were at the forefront of lobbying Ottawa, one senior Canadian military officer was told that war with Japan had spawned 'a Heaven-sent opportunity to rid themselves of the Japanese economic menace for ever more'.[21] King, with little affection for Canada's Asian population and with an interest in boosting his political support, acted. Not only were eight hundred men of military age interned, but the remainder of BC's Japanese Canadian population – including women, children, and the elderly – was 'evacuated' from the coastal region and sent to work camps in the interior. This move came days after similar action was taken in the United States. The timing was no coincidence, for as Norman Robertson explained, 'the policy we have pursued since Pearl Harbor has been largely influenced by what we understood the policy of the US to be'.[22] Yet, Canada's government surpassed the United States in its cruelty, seizing and auctioning off these people's property and, following the war, encouraging Japanese Canadians to emigrate to Japan. Nearly four thousand people were expelled from Canada by this method before protests from human rights activists forced Ottawa to end the program.

In response to these actions, and to the noble sentiments of the Atlantic Charter and the UDHR, Canadians began advocating for a bill of rights and other legal protections. 'You cannot fight for freedom with one hand and strangle it with the other without making yourself look ridiculous', one writer had noted during the war.[23] Jewish and black activists pushed for equal rights for minority groups and, in a famous rights case, worked to integrate the town of Dresden, Ontario. Also, there was pressure from without. Indian officials protested the denial of voting rights to Indians in BC, contending that as British subjects they deserved equality with other Canadians.[24] As the offending laws were those of a provincial government, Ottawa demurred. Facing pressure from a variety of domestic groups, BC relented, allowing non-white provincial residents to vote. Pleased, Jawaharlal Nehru, India's quasi-foreign minister, thanked the Canadians for what he hoped would be the 'forerunner of increasingly friendly' bilateral relations.[25] In a move of its own, in 1947, Canada's government repealed the exclusionary Chinese Immigration Act and implemented a Citizenship Bill giving citizenship to all naturalized residents, except for Japanese Canadians, for whom voting rights and naturalization came the following year. A response to pressure from both China's government – a wartime ally – and domestic activists, these steps also reflected officials' worry that Canada could be called to account internationally. As King feared, UN members' interest in racial discrimination posed a 'great danger'.[26]

Citizenship rights were a sign of progress, but little changed on immigration, with racial restrictions remaining in place. Despite a growing refugee crisis that saw thousands of Chinese migrating to Hong Kong in search of freedom, first, from the civil war, and then, from the communist regime, Ottawa did little to help. This inaction was in stark contrast to the welcome given to tens of thousands of European refugees escaping communism and the dislocation of war-shattered Europe. 'It is not a "fundamental human right" of any alien to enter Canada', King made clear, adding that it was vital to avoid any 'fundamental alteration in the character of our population'.[27] Anti-Asian sentiments died hard.

In 1948 and 1949, independent India amplified its criticism of Canadian immigration restrictions, again pointing out that, as British subjects, Indians should be equal to citizens of white Commonwealth countries. Nehru, now prime minister, went so far as to propose the creation of Commonwealth citizenship to link the disparate peoples of Britain's collapsing empire.

Ottawa opposed the proposal, which, given immigration restrictions, could 'prove embarrassing'.[28] Instead, Canada's government opted for a slight shift. Pearson, as foreign minister, concluded that a quota be instituted. Involving 'no substantial' change in immigration policy, a quota would avoid damaging relations with India, 'which are more important now than ever before'.[29] In January 1951, Canada agreed to admit 150 Indians annually; concurrent agreements were concluded with Pakistan and Ceylon. This option negated altering Canada's immigration regulations thereby allowing discriminatory provisions to remain intact – the same solution used with Japan in 1908. An incremental step, it was hardly a shining moment for racial equality. Indeed, that December the Cabinet voted to continue barring entry to black West Indians.[30]

Immigration aside, Indo-Canadian relations were quite good. Ottawa and London had implemented a solution allowing India to remain in the Commonwealth despite its republican constitution, doing so over objections from South Africa. Newly anointed as Canada's prime minister, in 1949 St Laurent told the Cabinet that this matter 'was one of great concern to the whole world', for it was vital to maintain channels of interaction with India.[31] Wrangling over Indian accession to the Commonwealth occurred concurrently with NATO's creation. The growing cold war drove Canadian interest in building links to the newly decolonized world. The Commonwealth, Pearson asserted, was 'a vital and almost the only bridge between the free West and the free East'.[32] Bridging the old, white Commonwealth and the new, multicoloured Commonwealth underlay newfound interest in a grouping toward which Canadians had been wary given fears of being drawn into British colonial conflicts.

Efforts at bridge-building were a sign of Canadian officials' forward-thinking attitude, but as Canada's experiences at the UN made evident, the cold war tempered sympathy for decolonization. From 1948 to 1949, Canada occupied a non-permanent Security Council seat, and Dutch repression of Indonesia's nationalist movement was a pressing issue. For Ottawa, the overriding concern was to avoid offending The Hague and prejudicing Dutch involvement in the nascent NATO pact. 'North Atlantic imperatives' meant that Canada found itself on the opposite side of its Commonwealth partners India, Pakistan, and Australia, all of which supported the Indonesian nationalists. Although a Canadian-brokered resolution paved the way for Indonesia's independence, it occurred on Dutch terms. Canada, an Australian official complained, was acting as 'the mouthpiece of Holland'.[33] Still, a resolution was passed, evidence of Canadian negotiating skill. By preventing a 'dangerous cleavage' between the West and newly independent countries, John Holmes boasted that he and his fellow Canadian diplomats had shown themselves to be 'honest brokers'.[34] This notion, like the middle power concept with which it was associated, became a dominant characterization of Canadian diplomacy during the golden age, even as, in the case of Indonesia, Ottawa had been working to safeguard Western interests. As it did with India, Canada pursued warm relations with Indonesia. An embassy was opened in Jakarta in 1953 – Canada's first Southeast Asian diplomatic mission – and Ottawa hosted President Sukarno in June 1956, a trip during which Canadians emphasized the benefits of Western-style development in contrast to the Soviet model, a reminder of the cold war struggle for Third World hearts and minds.[35]

In the early 1950s, Southeast Asia was embroiled in anti-colonial violence, as nationalists fought for independence against the British in Malaya and against the French in Indo-China. Canada steered clear of military involvement in these conflicts; despatching military forces to enforce collective security in Western Europe or Korea was different than committing troops to prop up colonialism even in this region, where there was a communist threat. Indirectly, Ottawa turned a blind eye to the fact that its NATO allies, receiving millions of dollars of military equipment from Canada each year, diverted some of this materiel away from Western European defence toward maintaining their overseas possessions. The Canadian government played a careful game, resisting French efforts to involve NATO militarily in North Africa and Indo-China just as it resisted British entreaties over imperial defence. Beyond a desire to avoid becoming bogged down in savage wars of peace, Canadian policymakers sought to avoid damaging Canada's reputation in the expanding Third World.

Fear of communism spreading throughout Asia led Canada to participate in its first real aid program, though billions had been gifted to Britain during the Second World War and over $90 million had been offered to China's Nationalist government for a reconstruction program dismissed by one critic as 'Operation Sinkhole'.[36] Launched in 1950, the Colombo Plan was organized loosely under Commonwealth auspices and aimed largely at the region's Commonwealth countries. 'The undertaking is admittedly new and experimental', Pearson informed Canada's finance minister in an appeal to support the program. 'At the same time I am convinced that it is in the Canadian interest.' Through development spending Ottawa sought, in the words of its program administrator, to give Asian countries, 'a sense of really belonging to our free world'. Colombo Plan programs were important, Pearson added, 'to prevent the spread of communism' and to build up aid recipients' 'economies and therefore their free institutions'.[37] Via the Colombo Plan, most of Canada's development spending went to Asian Commonwealth members, Indonesia, and Burma, and included, variously, the sale of locomotives to India, the construction of a Pakistani cement plant, vocational training for Malayan technicians, and the building of a fishing port in Ceylon.

For supporters of development spending, the programs appeared mutually beneficial. Development in Third World countries alleviated poverty and promoted stability while creating unparalleled opportunities for promoting people-to-people contacts, with volunteers 'setting out from Canada to teach – and to learn – in the centres of the developing world'. The seeming selflessness of aid programs reinforced Canadian exceptionalism. Fresh off a tour of Asian Commonwealth countries, Liberal cabinet minister Paul Martin informed Canadians that it was 'remarkable that a country such as Canada, so far removed from Asia and with no selfish motive to serve', was taking an interest in the region's development. 'But it is because our motives are not suspect', he contended, 'that Canada can wield an influence for sane relations between Asia and the West'.[38] Government sceptics, meanwhile, felt uncomfortable with the Third World, which was distinctly foreign territory. One Finance Department official explained that he and his colleagues 'felt on familiar grounds when dealing with the Europeans, but hundreds of millions of Asians, diseased or starving or both, raised questions of a different type and seemed to involve amounts of a different magnitude that stretched interminably into the future'.[39]

Development, whether through technical assistance (skills transfer, scholarships, and expert advice) or capital spending (money for major projects), was a testament to liberal internationalism's influence on golden age Canadian foreign policy as one can hardly imagine Mackenzie King – reluctant to spend money to alleviate the plight of Canadians during the Depression – sending aid to the developing world. Although subject to increasing criticism by the 1960s, the developing/developed binary was a dominant notion, grounded in the assumption in the West and elsewhere that newly decolonized countries could follow the Western model of modernization. 'We cannot hope to raise the standards of living of these people', affirmed one Canadian development specialist, 'except by using the methods by which we ourselves have become wealthy, we must aid these men by the machine.'[40] Ottawa was not selfless, for beyond the goal of winning hearts and minds and combatting the temptations of communism, much of Canada's aid was 'tied' to the purchase of Canadian products, providing economic stimulus at home.

Canadian officials' conviction that economic development should follow Canada's capitalist course paralleled a belief that the Canadian model of political development was best. In the early 1950s, as the French colonies of Tunisia and Morocco sought independence, their cause became the focus of UN squabbles pitting Western powers against the newly decolonized states. Canada's stance was in the middle: support for debate on this issue, but opposition to resolutions condemning France or to intervention by the UN into what officials saw as French internal affairs. Explaining Canada's opposition to a resolution to form a three-nation committee to facilitate talks between

Paris and Tunisian independence groups, Paul Martin, serving on the Canadian UN delegation, acknowledged that Canadians 'knew the irresistible strength – because we have felt it ourselves – of the urge for freedom which develops in all national groups subject to external control'. Two months later, he told the UNA's Ottawa branch that Canada was well-positioned to play a helpful role in colonial matters because of 'its own comparatively recent emergence to full nationhood'.[41] This reasoning, with its emphasis on Canada as a post-colonial country, was central to the self-image of the honest broker.

At this time, the leading Canadian history text was *From Colony to Nation*, and a variety of Canadian authorities were keen to highlight this trajectory, using Canada's colonial past as justification for guiding new nations.[42] Senior diplomat Dana Wilgress informed university students that they could not be indifferent to calls for self-determination because 'We ourselves have progressed rapidly along the path of self-government, commencing as a colony of one race [the French] conquered by men of another race [the British] and ending as a nation in which the two races are welded together, in complete mastery of their own destiny.'[43] While touring Asia in 1954 – the first visit by a Canadian prime minister to the continent – St Laurent told India's parliament that Ottawa welcomed decolonization, but that 'partly because our own evolution toward complete independence was no less successful for being gradual, we see a certain merit in proceeding in these matters at a pace which allows a firm foundation for self-government to be established'. 'Eastern countries', the editors of the Halifax *Chronicle Herald* noted in a leader welcoming Sukarno to Canada, 'tend to see in the history of Canada's gradual and peaceful growth to independence and national maturity an earnest example of what they can achieve.'[44]

This notion that Canada was an exemplar of a stable, multi-ethnic, federation that had achieved independence though gradual evolution was not entirely correct and its central flaw in the context of post-war decolonization was race, in that the vast majority of Canadians were white and their experience of empire was very different from that of non-white colonial subjects, including Canada's indigenous population. But guiding it, and the affirmations of Canada's own postcolonial status, were two notions: that Canadians understood African, Arab, Asian, and West Indian concerns and could be trusted by newly independent peoples to work with them in a positive manner; and that the process from colony to nation should proceed at a slow, *Canadian* pace, through evolution, not revolution.

Canada's position of balancing support for non-white UN delegations' efforts to raise, discuss, and criticize colonialism while avoiding direct condemnation of Canadian allies was difficult. In the view of Canada's UN ambassador, the organization was becoming a 'wailing wall', with much of its time taken up by colonial issues rather than more pressing matters of international security. Worse, it was Canada's close allies – including its two mother countries – who were in the dock.[45] The sense that the UN was transforming, perhaps for the worse, was deepened in 1955 with the addition of sixteen new members, from the Communist bloc and the decolonized world. This expansion, negotiated by Paul Martin and Canada's UN delegation, meant that the Western powers no longer held a majority in the General Assembly.[46] The emergence of the Afro-Asian bloc – the loose coalition of decolonized states – was signified by the Bandung Conference, a gathering of leaders from twenty-nine Third World countries in April 1955. Recognizing Bandung's importance, St Laurent sent a congratulatory message to the delegates, making Canada the only Western country to reach out to the conference. This receptive attitude – 'How different the Canadians are from other Western countries', stated one Indonesian diplomat – contrasted sharply with the position of Canada's allies.[47] Among Canadian officials there was a tendency to draw such contrasts. In assessing policy on colonial issues, Undersecretary Jules Léger advised Pearson that 'if mistakes and fumblings by our allies remain the order of the day, we have a definite duty to be imaginative in seeking solutions to situations which have so markedly deteriorated in recent weeks'.[48] By then – November 1956 – Ottawa had already offered an imaginative response to its allies' fumbling.

During the Suez crisis, alone among the white Commonwealth members, Canada refused to back the British and French invasion of Egypt. In supporting the creation of a UN peacekeeping force as a means of helping to resolve the situation, Pearson and other Canadian diplomats sought to extract their allies from a mess. Although Egyptian strongman Gamal Nasser received little sympathy in Ottawa, Canadians well understood his importance. As Pearson had put it in early 1956, 'Arab nationalism is clearly one of the key battlegrounds in the new competition which is emerging between the Soviet bloc and NATO.'[49] With Nasser's nationalization of the Suez Canal, Pearson and St Laurent worried about the implications of any British or French use of force – in August, the Cabinet judged that military action would mean that 'the whole Arab world would rally in support of Egypt, and the Commonwealth would be split as would the United Nations' – and like John A. Macdonald in 1885, they had no interest in sending combat troops to the region.[50] The gulf between the Suez Canal and the Rideau Canal was massive, with Canada lacking direct stakes in Egypt. What mattered for Ottawa was the changing UN dynamic, the Commonwealth's cohesion, NATO's future, and Anglo-American relations – a veritable witch's brew stirred up by French and British adventuring, which distracted world attention from the Soviet Union's suppression of an uprising in Hungary. Explaining why Ottawa had not snapped to attention at Britain's side like 'a colonial chore boy', Pearson emphasized that the 'Arab and Asian countries, including the Asian members of the Commonwealth were watching us'. 'Canada's attitude on Suez', remarked an Indian diplomat, 'was the only thing that saved the Commonwealth from dissolution'.[51]

The Suez crisis became a storied event, with Pearson's peacekeeping initiative – the UN Emergency Force (UNEF) – garnering him a Nobel Peace Prize. 'We cannot claim him as an American diplomat', gushed the *New York Times*, 'although we would like to do so.' Canada's involvement in the Middle East was recent, although to many Canadians, the region held religious significance. As Pearson stated, 'we were dealing with the Holy Land – the land of my Sunday School lessons. At one stage in my life I knew more about the geography of Palestine than I did about the geography of Canada.'[52] Chairing the UN subcommittee that drafted a detailed partition plan for Palestine in 1947, Pearson had been intimately involved in Israel's creation, spearheading through the General Assembly a compromise resolution to create separate Jewish and Arab states, an act reflective of post-war hopes that the UN machinery could be used to solve international problems. Canada steered clear of the 1948 war from which Israel emerged, though Canadian Jews raised funds and even sent recruits.[53] Over the subsequent decades, as Arab and Jewish lobby groups emerged in Canada to influence government policy, Canadian officials considered pursuing various peace plans including an effort to internationalize Jerusalem, implemented a scheme that resettled 100 Palestine families in Canada, and slowly expanded diplomatic relations with countries in the region. Often taking an approach that one diplomat likened to 'a plague on both your houses', when push came to shove Ottawa, having helped bring Israel into existence, tended to favour it over its neighbours. While Canada should not pursue 'blind support of Israel against the Arabs', a senior diplomat wrote in 1956, the Jewish state 'remains the only democracy, the only Western-oriented, and the only well-organized state in the Middle East, and one on which we can rely'. In the run-up the Suez crisis, Pearson had approved the sale of fighter aircraft to Israel; delivery of the planes was suspended due to the events of autumn 1956.[54]

The pro-Israeli position, but especially Canada's British ties, made the country suspect in Nasser's eyes, and even though Pearson had created UNEF, initially, Egypt blocked Canadian participation. Meeting with Nasser, Canada's ambassador in Cairo delivered a brief history lesson, pointing out the Chanak crisis, the Washington Naval Conference 'and other significant moves in the growth of our nationhood' that meant that Canada was not a stalking horse for British interests. 'What was needed', Pearson quipped, 'was the First East Kootenay Anti-Imperialistic Rifles!'[55] A compromise was found and a force of 1,100 Canadians deployed as UN peacekeepers.

In this crisis, Canadian policy aimed to save Britain and France from their own folly, and both countries remained important to Canadians. Indeed, post-Suez Canada backed British policy in the Middle East, though there were some objections to the British and American interventions in Jordan and Lebanon in 1958. 'The Canadians were deplorable', fumed Britain's foreign secretary in reporting on his efforts to secure Ottawa's backing.[56] Yet, it was true that with Suez, Ottawa had refused to support London at a critical juncture at which Britain's great power status ended. St Laurent offered a telling turn of phrase when outlining that he did not back the Anglo-French invasion 'because the members of the smaller nations are human beings just as are their people; because the era when the supermen of Europe could govern the whole world has and is coming pretty close to an end'.[57]

It was precisely because of decolonization that peacekeeping became an important aspect of Canadian foreign policy during the cold war. Worries that 'brushfire wars' in the Third World might spiral out of control and draw in the superpowers led to international support for the use of UN forces to keep warring sides apart and allow time for diplomatic negotiations to resolve disputes. Seldom was lasting peace achieved – Egypt expelled UNEF in 1967, paving the way for the Six-Day War – but that was not the fault of the peacekeepers themselves. Due to conflicts that grew out of decolonization, in the 1950s and 1960s Canadians were deployed to Kashmir, the borders between Israel and its neighbours, Congo, and Cyprus. Thanks to peacekeeping, Lieutenant General E. L. M. Burns, who headed, first, the UN Truce Supervision Organization monitoring the Israeli-Arab border and then UNEF, 'learned something about the attitude of Asian, Middle Eastern and South American peoples towards the monster of the age, Imperialism'.[58] As a result, care was taken to distinguish Canadian forces from those of the waning imperial powers. The Congo mission, for instance, had heavy racial overtones of which Canadian officials were assiduously aware. As Norman Robertson highlighted, deploying white peacekeepers to an African country would make it difficult 'to persuade the Congolese masses that the United Nations force was not another form of white domination', and so Canadian troops participated in a supporting role. Congo represented a perfect storm, with both superpowers backing warring parties in a multisided war. Sharing Western goals, nonetheless Canada supported the UN mission, thereby positioning itself 'just West of neutral'.[59] UN difficulties in Congo made clear that peacekeeping was neither easy nor particularly peaceful.

Beyond serving specific interests, peacekeeping appealed to Canadians because it embodied the early idealism behind the UN and the liberal international order more broadly. As prime minister in the mid-1960s, Pearson sought to create a permanent UN police force, his goal since the Korean War. The initiative came to naught, but enthusiasm for peacekeeping remained. 'Whatever else this force may be', one Canadian serving on UNEF recorded, 'it does foster the belief that the UN is a working reality and that editorialists are both wrong and foolish to forecast its demise. Gaza HQ is a hodgepodge of more than two dozen countries. It's quite a sight on Sunday nights to see saris, turbans, business suits, fezzes, etc. A very good feeling. The brotherhood of man.'[60] This idealism led many Canadians to champion a peacekeeping role, particularly as the 1960s wore on and as there grew a desire to differentiate a peaceful Canada from a militaristic United States. As a result, peacekeeping became part of Canadian identity.[61] As for Suez, the peacekeeping force may have been meant to help London and Paris save face, but many Canadians saw the move differently. Howard Green, a Progressive Conservative MP, attacked the Liberals for their 'disgraceful' conduct in 'knif[ing] Canada's best friends in the back'.[62] A large enough swathe of Canadians agreed that Ottawa should have backed the old, white Commonwealth that feelings of betrayal contributed to a Tory victory in the 1957 Canadian federal election.

Surprisingly, despite the Progressive Conservatives' pro-British rhetoric, the new prime minister, John Diefenbaker, adopted a more revolutionary approach on colonial matters. The Tories, Britain's high commissioner in Ottawa complained in 1963, were 'easily flattered about their non-involvement in colonialism' and so had displayed 'a slightly puritanical self-righteousness' towards Canada's European allies.[63] Diefenbaker, and Green – who became SSEA in 1959 – shared the Liberals' sense of exceptionalism. 'There are few that can speak with the authority of Canada on the subject of colonialism', Diefenbaker reminded the General Assembly in 1960, 'for Canada was once a colony of both France and the United Kingdom. We were the first country which evolved over 100 years ago by constitutional processes from colonial status to independence without severing the family connection.' In Kuala Lampur in 1958, he pointed to the fact that 'Canada is the first of the confederations, Malaya the latest'.[64] This was no offhand comparison. At this point, Britain was busy creating federations in the Malay Peninsula, the West Indies, and Central Africa, and Diefenbaker believed that Canada was an excellent model for constitutional development, hence his interest in supporting fellow federal governments via development spending and the dispatch of constitutional experts. Also, to Canadians anyway, the profusion of postcolonial federations was proof that Canada's own federal model was a success, an important point given rising Québécois nationalism. When it came to models, Diefenbaker was clear that decolonization should follow the Canadian example of 'the orderly achievement of freedom and independence' rather than 'hasty and impractical measures'.[65] Underlying this position was a desire to avoid disorder, which could be exploited by Canada's cold war foes.

To counteract the communist threat and promote development, Diefenbaker's government boosted spending on foreign assistance both bilaterally and through multilateral channels, expanded the geographic scope of aid to include French Africa and the Caribbean, and created the External Aid Office, Canada's first stand-alone aid agency. There was military assistance to Ghana, Nigeria, Malaysia, and later Tanzania, as well as cadet programs for Jamaica and Zambia. Ottawa and London created Commonwealth Scholarships to allow students from former British colonies to study abroad. Furthermore, in 1961, Canada launched the Canadian University Service Overseas (CUSO). Although they rejected the comparison for nationalist reasons, like the US Peace Corps, CUSO sent student volunteers to work on Third World development projects. Much of its membership was female, with the program providing a unique outlet for Canadian women to see the world and serve abroad.[66] There were other Canadian development organizations, with little government affiliation, including the Rotary Club, the World University Service of Canada, and various religious denominations. Although missionaries still went abroad, many church groups rebranded themselves and dropped much of their overt evangelization efforts in favour of a focus on development.[67] As for CUSO, many of its members were radicalized by their experiences overseas, becoming sharp critics of Western economic and foreign policy. 'CUSO respects each country and its people's right to self-determination', one volunteer affirmed, 'which can take many unpredictable and un-Canadian forms'.[68] By the mid-1960s, this changed attitudes towards development had become commonplace.

Self-determination presented Diefenbaker's Tories with considerable headaches. At the UN, Canada's position remained set on the 'middle course' of supporting anti-colonial delegations' right to debate colonial issues while opposing measures that would interfere in what the colonial powers maintained was their internal affairs.[69] By supporting debate, Canada set itself apart from many of its Western allies. More active Canadian support for self-determination occurred in 1960, the Year of Africa, when over a dozen countries gained independence and joined the UN, swelling the Afro-Asian bloc's ranks and increasing the anti-colonial pressure. A seminal moment came in December 1960, with the passage of Resolution 1514, the declaration on the granting of independence to colonial countries and peoples. Despite opposition from most of its NATO allies, and in spite of Diefenbaker and Green's concern over anti-colonial criticism of Western powers, Canada supported this resolution, and, over the next two years, it backed a wide range of anti-colonial measures. Canada's goal, as Green put it, was to be in 'seeming alignment' with the Afro-Asians, allowing the Canadian delegation to steer anti-colonial activists towards moderate initiatives. Moreover, a strong supporter of nuclear disarmament, Green wanted Third World support for his arms control efforts. By late 1962, Canada abandoned the middle course, largely because more radical elements among the Afro-Asian bloc sought to pass resolutions sanctioning Canadian allies, steps beyond what Ottawa would countenance.[70] For all their talk of sympathy for colonial peoples and of commonality between a postcolonial Canada and other postcolonies, Canadian policymakers favoured the West. Hence the complaint of a Tunisian reporter who upbraided

Green: 'thousands and thousands of Africans, whether Algerian, or in South Africa, Angola or Mozambique are treated worse than animals and there is not a single finger lifted in their defence by western powers including Canada'.[71] Such anger belied the idea of Canada as an exceptional country in its dealings with the Third World.

Another source of tension between Canada and the Afro-Asians centred around Diefenbaker's efforts to brand what he called Soviet colonialism. Partly motivated by an effort to appeal to voters of Eastern European ancestry and partly driven by his sense, as he told the General Assembly in 1960, that there 'can be no double standard in international affairs', Canada's prime minister sought a UN resolution condemning Moscow's denial of self-determination to peoples behind the iron curtain.[72] This effort tried to tap into Afro-Asian sentiment on self-determination by turning Third World delegates' attention towards Russia and away from the Western powers. The initiative was doomed to failure. Cautioning the prime minister, Green emphasized that garnering support would be exceedingly difficult given Afro-Asian reluctance to support a resolution on a distinctly '"cold war" issue'. More important was a disconnect in that for these countries, Soviet colonialism was 'not a reality' because their preoccupation was with 'white ascendancy over coloured peoples'.[73] Sure enough, there was a dearth of international support. Eventually relenting, the prime minister complained that the Afro-Asians 'were not particularly concerned about the domination of white over white'.[74] Diefenbaker was right to highlight the unequal treatment accorded to self-determination and to contrast waning Western colonialism with entrenched Soviet control of Eastern Europe. However, with its expansive interpretation of the right to self-determination, his initiative posed its own set of problems.

In raising Soviet colonialism, Diefenbaker unwittingly exposed Canada to potential criticism of its own human rights record. Soviet diplomats had indicated to their Canadian counterparts that they were preparing to launch a complaint through the UN Human Rights Commission highlighting racial discrimination faced by black Canadians, ethnic minorities, and indigenous peoples.[75] Potential criticism from Moscow exposed the problems faced by Canadian policymakers in positioning Canada as an exceptional country. Indeed, although UN anti-colonial initiatives in the early 1960s ignored indigenous people – unmentioned in Resolution 1514, the seminal declaration on self-determination – the situation soon changed. Aware of these inequalities, Diefenbaker made a conscientious attempt, however imperfect, at reform. In 1960, his government passed a Bill of Rights and gave the franchise to Status Indians. To Diefenbaker these developments had a global resonance for as he told radio and television listeners, the Bill of Rights would affirm 'the principle that every individual, whatever his colour, race or religion, shall be free from discrimination and will have guaranteed equality under the law. This is so important today, for wherever discrimination exists in the world there you have a seed-bed for Communism'.[76]

In addition, the Diefenbaker government removed racially discriminatory provisions from immigration laws, which had long undercut Canada's position with non-white countries. In introducing the new regulations, which came into effect in 1962, Ellen Fairclough, Diefenbaker's immigration minister, proclaimed that the 'newly-emerging nations of the world will be watching with interest to see how sincere we are in applying our new immigration policy and the reception the Canadian people give to the newcomers'. She added, referring to British prime minister Harold Macmillan's warning to the South Africans, that 'the winds of change are blowing'.[77] Like the Bill of Rights, immigration reform – though flawed, and replaced by a colour-blind system five years later – aimed to prove to the newly decolonized world that Canada was egalitarian, thereby deflecting charges of Canadian hypocrisy.

These charges were levelled at Canada following Diefenbaker's involvement in expelling apartheid South Africa from the Commonwealth. The South African situation was important to Diefenbaker as a civil libertarian, and there was a broad base of support for taking some action against South Africa among church groups, organized labour, the CCF, the Liberals, and even members of the prime minister's own party. By 1960, the issue was pressing because South Africa was poised to declare itself a republic, which opened the question of its continued Commonwealth membership. Prior to the May 1960 Commonwealth prime ministers' conference, Diefenbaker affirmed that he was dubious about the collected premiers serving as 'judge and jury' over individual members' domestic affairs. Even so, he was sharply critical of apartheid. After returning from the summit, he announced that this 'racial conflict' posed 'a fundamental problem for Commonwealth countries and, indeed, for the world community'. Diefenbaker's position worried Macmillan, who complained of the Canadian premier's ' "holier than thou" attitude, which may cause us infinite trouble. For if the "whites" take an anti-S. Africa line, how can we expect the Browns and Blacks to be more tolerant'.[78]

Matters came to a head in March 1961, when the Commonwealth leaders, in effect, withheld membership from South Africa. The decision had not been unanimous, but Diefenbaker had prevented a racial divide by siding with the non-white premiers in opposition to South Africa's readmission, the only white leader to take this stand. His decision is laudable and notable for its symbolism, earning him praise in the Indian press and provoking the ire of Hendrik Verwoerd, South Africa's repellent premier, who denounced the actions of the ' "Afro-Asian-Canadian" bloc'.[79] As with Suez, Canada's stance on South Africa was important because it signified Canadian policymakers' willingness to stand apart from like-minded powers. However, even though it burnished his reputation, Diefenbaker was not happy with South Africa's isolation, a development he regretted as the country was one of the old Dominions. Furthermore, his government did little to effect change within the apartheid state, opposing Afro-Asian efforts to impose arms and trade embargoes.[80] Since the 1930s, Canadian officials had long been hesitant about imposing sanctions, and Diefenbaker was no different, with his government trading with Cuba and China even though those states were committed cold war foes with dubious rights records.

Part of Diefenbaker's opposition to sanctioning South Africa stemmed from a belief in state sovereignty. He was aware, too, of Canada's own record, asking the Canadian Labour Congress in January 1960, 'what would be our reaction in Canada if some other part of the Commonwealth were to criticize us?'[81] Plenty of Canadians offered criticism, doing so by drawing international comparisons. Apartheid served as one reference point. Decrying the fact that after South Africa's departure Canadians 'wallowed in self-congratulation', one journalist highlighted Ottawa's treatment of indigenous peoples as worthy of 'kicking Canada out of the Commonwealth'. The following year, the *Globe and Mail* lamented that the 'effect of the Indian Act is to produce a real Apartheid'.[82] Racism in the United States was another point of comparison that loomed especially large in Canadians' moral imaginations. In 1962, readers of Canada's leading women's magazine were reminded that Canadians 'self-righteously denounce' racism elsewhere, 'yet we force some 200,000 Canadians – our Indians – to live in segregation'. The next year, journalist Peter Gzowski proclaimed that the decade's 'biggest story' was 'the showdown between the white and non-white people of the world'. Given the treatment of aboriginals, he was convinced that Canada was poorly positioned in this struggle. 'If Canada can afford to spend $70 million on foreign aid', Gzowski pleaded, 'and to admit that part of it is simply an attempt to buy good will, we can afford to spend a small fraction more to prevent giving to the West and to ourselves another list of Birminghams and Little Rocks'.[83] Such comments underline white Canadians' recognition that racial discrimination had an important and unnerving impact on Canada's international standing.

When the Liberals formed government in 1963, Prime Minister Pearson confronted many of the same colonial issues as his predecessor. The UN remained a forum for criticism of and growing activism towards Canadian allies. Within the Commonwealth, the colony of Southern Rhodesia's declaration of independence from Britain in 1965 outraged non-white members because the new state was ruled by the white minority, which imposed its own version of apartheid. Facing a split between non-white Commonwealth members and Britain over how to respond to the declaration of independence, an act of rebellion, Pearson brokered a compromise among members to impose sanctions against Rhodesia. The move, which led *The Times* to label Pearson 'an honorary Afro-Asian', kept the organization together even as it failed to satisfy either pro-Rhodesian sentiment in Britain and the white Dominions or African hardliners who sought the use of force to overthrow Rhodesia's government.[84] The Rhodesian situation represented in microcosm the growing distance between Canada and many Third World countries by the mid-1960s.

One Canadian who advocated the use of force against the Rhodesian rebels was diplomat Arnold Smith, who, as Commonwealth secretary general from 1965 to 1976, sought to make the organization into a 'post-colonial Commonwealth' more responsive to the demands of its Third World members, who formed the majority.[85] That a Canadian was chosen to lead the newly created Commonwealth Secretariat is a testament to Canada's special place between the old and new members. However, in trying to create a more formalized institution, Smith encountered considerable difficulties, not least of which was opposition from the British and the old white Dominions, which worried about yet another organization driven by perceived Third World grievances. Pearson's worry was with ballooning membership, which increasingly made international organizations cumbersome. As he had observed in 1963, 'the British Empire and Commonwealth, as it had previously existed, was in rapid dissolution by the emergence of colonial entities into independent states and that this advent of African Commonwealth states doomed the Commonwealth system', just as 'enlarged membership' of the UN posed immense problems in terms of creating a functional organization.[86] The Commonwealth's changing make-up was one small sign of decolonization's impact on global order. 'The Little group of white graduates from colonial status sitting around the fireplace at 10 Downing Street at periodic clubby meetings and listening to the old headmaster' had given way, Pearson once observed, so that 'As an old-school-tie bond, terms at Oxford or Cambridge have now had to yield precedence to a term in one of Her Majesty's penal institutions.'[87]

Due to this epidermal shift in the makeup of global affairs, in 1967, Pearson's government brought in a new immigration policy that improved upon the Diefenbaker-era changes. Among Pearson's initiatives was closer relations with the Commonwealth Caribbean, where local politicians were sharply critical of Canada's immigration controls. Visiting Jamaica in 1965, he vowed to remove restrictions 'in fact as well as in theory'.[88] The resulting changes ranked potential immigrants on a host of factors, but eliminated race as a category for selection. In addition, Canada's immigration department expanded its promotional efforts to encourage immigration outside Europe. New immigration offices were opened in Egypt (1963), in Japan, Trinidad, and Jamaica (1967), and in Lebanon, the Philippines, India, and Pakistan (1968). Immigration promotion and the availability of immigration offices remained a practical way in which Canada continued to restrict immigration, but the geographical spread of the offices that were opened led to considerable changes in the sources of Canadian immigration, a move that laid the groundwork for the emergence of a far more diverse Canada.

The change in Canadian immigration policy was a sign that until that point Canada was not as exceptional as some proponents of the honest broker role had suggested. In the immediate post-Second World War decades, Canadian exceptionalism was strong. Canada, as one journalist boasted in 1960, was a mediator because it was 'free, white, and untarnished by imperialism' and thus capable of dealing with all parties to a dispute.[89] The fact that Canada was free and white – that it was a part of the West – led Ottawa to champion Western interests, particularly as the Afro-Asian bloc countries grew more radical in their efforts to confront colonialism. That Canada took such a position should not be a surprise. As one Canadian diplomat noted in 1961, it was foolhardy to 'pose before Africans and Asians as an uncommitted nation' because 'we were not uncommitted, nor were we expected by African and Asian countries to behave as such'. 'So far as the Afro-Asians are concerned', wrote a leading strategic thinker at the time, 'Canadians are members of the well-fed white minority.'[90] Certainly, Ottawa was capable of a more forward-thinking course – witness Suez, Bandung, both Indian and South African membership in the Commonwealth, and Resolution 1514. However, Canadian officials were not neutral.

Nor was Canada free of its own failings. Throughout the 1960s, growing numbers of Québécois nationalists and indigenous people began to demand self-determination and challenge what they saw, respectively, as Anglo-Saxon imperialism and settler colonialism. 'We are definitely colonial people', affirmed one indigenous activist. 'The winds of change have been blowing through the ranks of the Indian people', added a Parliamentary report on Indian Affairs.[91] These winds were blowing among English Canadians as well, and before turning to examine calls for self-determination by minority groups, we will examine the post-war de-dominionization of Canada, for there was definite truth to Canadian claims of similarities with the Third World through 'the common experience of "colony to nation" '. However, there were concerns, too, that through its relationship with the United States, Canada had 'moved from colony to nation to colony'.[92] Anxieties over propinquity with the United States were common enough in Canada, but, in common with postcolonial people, many Canadians feared that the withdrawal of European colonial power left their country open to the penetration of American political, economic, and cultural power.

9

From colony to nation to colony?

Addressing Dartmouth College graduates in 1957, Canadian prime minister John Diefenbaker spoke in sentimental terms of the 'Anglo-Canadian-American Community', and described for his audience how this 'grand alliance for freedom' was held together by 'common tradition, a respect for the rights of man, [and] an unswerving dedication to freedom'. A year later, he told listeners in New York of the shared interests and mission of this 'great triangle of nations'.[1] As far as paeans for the North Atlantic Triangle went, Diefenbaker's effusions were boilerplate if increasingly out of date. In 1957, historian Frank Underhill noted that 'we survive as a distinct individual Canadian entity by the feat of balancing ourselves in a triangle of forces'. Given waning British influence and startling American power, maintaining this balance was increasingly difficult. Over the course of the first few decades of the twentieth century, Canada had grown closer to the United States even as it remained within the British World, but, as Underhill observed, during the Second World War Canadians 'passed from the British century of our history to the American century'.[2] Economic, military, and cultural ties to the Americans only deepened with the cold war, in turn generating resistance. Meanwhile, sentiment for Britain remained strong. Following a lecture tour of Canada in 1958, an Australian professor recorded that across the country, 'during the discussion period, someone in the audience would rise to make sure that I understood how deeply he "and a great many Canadians" deplore the weakening of Canada's unity with Britain over Suez'.[3] In his rise to power, Diefenbaker tapped into these pro-British sentiments, castigating Louis St Laurent and Lester Pearson for betraying Britain. The fiery Tory emphasized, too, that two decades of Liberal policy had transformed Canada into 'a virtual 49th economic state'.[4]

Clearly, by the 1950s, all was not well within the North Atlantic Triangle. The term itself fell into disuse, for as Canada emerged from Britain's shadow as a middle power it moved increasingly into the American orbit, and so there was less and less of a triangular relationship. This chapter's focus is upon Canada's shifting relations with Britain and the United States from the 1950s to the 1970s, years in which the Canadian process of decolonization reached its climax. At the same time the British sought entry into the European Community, raising the question: if Britain's postcolonial place was within Europe, was Canada's postcolonial future North American? The seemingly obvious answer – and what in fact had been occurring over the past half-century – filled growing numbers of politically active Canadians with dread. Once a testament to a positive internationalism, North Americanism became a danger. Without a British counterweight, English Canadians sensed that in the process of gaining independence from Britain, they had become overly dependent upon their southern neighbours. For Canadian nationalists it was evident that through cultural penetration, huge levels of investment, and close military ties Canada had become 'the foremost, biggest, and fattest colony in the current American Empire'.[5] This view, feeding off discontent with the cold war consensus, formed a key element of the so-called New Nationalism.[6] Emerging in the 1960s largely but not exclusively among youthful, left-wing English-Canadians, and drawing off of a centuries-old opposition to continentalism, the New Nationalist quest for independence took on an anti-colonial air and had an important and somewhat enduring influence on Canada's place in the world.

As the Second World War came to an end, Canadian-British ties were strong: Canada had come to Britain's aid militarily and economically; throughout the conflict half a million Canadians had served in the United Kingdom, bringing home with them some seventy thousand war brides and children; and King George VI remained ever present on money, stamps, and other ephemera. 'Canada is a British nation', one writer affirmed in 1945, 'and proposes to continue to be a British nation'.[7] Two decades later the situation was markedly different. Socialist politician Eugene Forsey, a lifelong monarchist, expressed a feeling that 'there is nothing ahead of me when I retire, but to walk down the hill to the British High Commission and ask for asylum because there will be no recognizable Canada left for me to live in'. 'I have become a Canadian like any other', conservative historian W. L. Morton likewise complained, 'a member of an ethnic minority'.[8] In the intervening decades, as the country's population became more diverse, English Canadian ethnic nationalism predicated around a British identity was, to some extent, supplanted with civic nationalism. The process involved more than the loosening of cultural bonds. What took place was the next stage of Canadian decolonization, or 'de-dominionization', a development afoot, too, in Australia and New Zealand.[9]

De-dominionization was largely a success in Canada. In 1993, literary critic Robert Fulford reflected, 'I grew up in a country of which my own children have seldom heard, a place nobody speaks about now, "the Dominion of Canada" '.[10] Part of the process was the unconscious development of a contested postcolonial identity. Partly, too, it involved efforts by Canadians, including federal government officials, to actively do away with the old imperial order. 'I think there has been progression', observed Louis St Laurent, 'and I can say at once that it is the policy of this government when statutes come up for review or consolidation to replace the word "Dominion" with the word "Canada".[11]

With the 1931 Statute of Westminster, any limitations on Canadian autonomy existed only so long as they were accepted by Ottawa. In Westminster's wake, independence came in dribs and drabs. The 1946 Canadian Citizenship Act established legal recognition of the term Canadian citizen, which supplanted British subject. Appeals to the Judicial Committee of the Privy Council in Britain ended in 1949, with the Supreme Court of Canada becoming the final appellate body. Three years later, Vincent Massey was named the first Canadian to serve as governor general, a development that some diehard traditionalists labelled 'a drab and melancholy milestone'.[12] There were further moves towards decolonization, most notably with Newfoundland, where residents voted to end their colonial status and join Canada as the tenth province in 1949. The narrow margin of victory for those favouring this move attests to lingering pro-empire sentiment on the island. As with Confederation in 1867, much of the impetus for Newfoundland's changed status came from London, which, in a period of economic depression and imperial retrenchment, had little interest in paying for the colony's upkeep.[13] Newfoundland's decolonization followed that of Palestine and India, and heralded the wider post-war end of empire.

Other signs of decolonization were subtler. Within Canada's Department of External Affairs, 'Foreign Office procedure' and British methods began to be phased out in the 1960s. A similar process occurred in the Canadian military, which, in its organization, doctrine, uniforms, training, and regulations, became less British. In 1968, as part of a cost-saving measure that unified the three branches of the Canadian military into a single whole, the Pearson government abolished the 'Royal' monikers of the Royal Canadian Navy and Royal Canadian Air Force, creating instead Maritime Command and Air Command (the Canadian Army, lacking a Royal title, became Land Force Command). Predictably, this move upset tradition-minded military personnel.[14]

De-dominionization occurred beyond government circles too. The 1960s saw educators and editors set down a distinct variety of English, generally using British spellings, but American words: colour not color and jail not gaol. 'In linguistics and rhetoric, as in most things', observed one poet, 'English Canadians are presumed by Americans to be rather British and are presumed by the British to be rather American.' Canadian English dictionaries, which outlined these spellings along with unique words – toque, chesterfield – were meant to differentiate Canadians from other English speakers.[15] In 1969, the Queen's visage was removed from most, though not all, paper money, and the Royal Mail become Canada Post. Over the course of the 1960s, annual 1 July celebrations on Parliament Hill, commemorating Confederation in 1867, evolved from displays of pomp and circumstance with parading red coated guardsmen to ceremonies celebrating the country's multi-ethnic, bilingual, and indigenous heritage complete with Ukrainian shumka dancers, Acadian chanteuses, and Inuit throat singers.[16] In 1982, in a vote that continues to outrage traditionalists, the House of Commons, although lacking quorum, approved changing Dominion Day to Canada Day. Two years earlier, 'O Canada', the country's de facto anthem, was officially adopted (though the author recalls that at elementary school in the early 1990s, he was required to sing 'God Save the Queen').

Most controversial proved to be the introduction of the new maple leaf flag, which supplanted the red ensign, viewed by Pearson as too British given that it bore the Union Flag. Such a move had been contemplated by various politicians over the preceding decades, but it was Pearson, who in a speech for which he was 'booed and hissed', told members of the Royal Canadian Legion that it was 'time now for Canadians to unfurl a flag that is truly distinctive and truly national in character'.[17] Legion members, having fought abroad under the existing flag, were irate, as were conservative politicians and other traditionalists. In February 1965, after a bruising months-long political slugfest, the distinctive maple leaf flag – a compromise of sorts – was raised on Parliament Hill. Conservative governments in Ontario and Manitoba responded by adopting provincial pennants modelled on the old flag. Still more controversial would have been abolishing the monarchy. There were Canadians who called for this step, one that would 'break our last colonial bond'. Although it came to nothing, Pearson did raise the monarchy's future with British officials and with Queen Elizabeth herself. Visiting Montreal in 1964, the Queen witnessed first-hand rioting Quebec separatists who objected to her presence, and she told Pearson that she did not wish that 'the monarchy, or any controversy over it', would damage Canadian unity.[18]

Promoting a unified Canada via civic nationalism was among Pearson's chief goals. At the 1967 Universal and International Exposition in Montreal, held during the centenary of Confederation and attended by fifty-three million visitors, his government showcased a new Canada. For many Canadians, Expo 67 and the Centennial celebrations were points of pride, showing, as Pearson boasted, that 'no longer is our national costume a union jacket worn with star striped trousers!'[19] His government's actions to define a new Canada had the effect of distancing Canadians from a British World that was shrinking in importance, influence, and reach. While Britain itself continued to attract attention among Canadians, especially tourists and international students, the rest of the Commonwealth largely faded from view. For many Canadians, Australia and New Zealand were distant places whose people had odd accents, played different sports, and produced the occasional Hollywood actor of note.

As had been true since 1867, signs of Canadian independence were matched by marks of continued sentiment. The half-million Canadians who had served in Britain during the Second World War created 'a network of affectionate transatlantic connections', that extended beyond wartime unions.[20] For a decade or so after the war, Britons constituted the largest post-war immigrant group, and no wonder given the dire economic straits in which the UK found itself. In all, over 430,000 British immigrants came to Canada between 1948 and 1957. Constituting the last major wave of immigration to Canada from the British Isles, these 'invisible immigrants' were welcomed, in the words of one Canadian official, because of how easily they could 'adapt themselves to Canadian life and to contribute to the development of the Canadian nation'.[21] In subsequent decades, even though their share of the total number of immigrants shrunk relative to other areas, enough British migrants continued to come to Canada that grocers found it feasible to stock British products of questionable palate – Marmite and Irn-Bru – and the Canadian Broadcasting Corporation judged daily airings of *Coronation Street* a worthy enterprise. Moreover, British pop music captivated Canadian youngsters. 'When the Beatles play', observed the normally humourless Young Socialists, 'even corpses will get on the dance floor.'[22] Every decades' iteration of British popular music has found avid listeners in Canada, though this development is less a sign of lingering ties to the old imperial metropole than it is to the global popularity of British performers.

The monarchy has remained another important, if intangible, link. Queen Elizabeth II's coronation led to a shortage of televisions, and her visits to Canada over the subsequent six decades elicited considerable interest and enthusiasm, at least outside of Quebec. During her 1959 Royal Tour, one Italian Canadian MP observed that 'the non-Anglo Saxons are more keen about the Queen than the Anglo Saxons', an indication that support for the monarchy was viewed as a means of assimilating into English Canadian society.[23] While monarchism waned and waxed, telegenic royals such as Princess Diana and her sons kept up a steady reserve of support, and republicanism in Canada was nowhere near as strong as in Australia. At an Ottawa ceremony in 1982, Elizabeth signed the Constitution Act, transferring control of Canada's constitution from the British Parliament to Canada's federal and provincial legislatures and completing the process of decolonization that had begun in 1848 with the grant of responsible government.

To return to the 1960s, Diefenbaker and other traditionally minded Canadians were upset by fraying British ties mixed with growing continentalism. Within weeks of becoming prime minister, Diefenbaker travelled to a Commonwealth summit, where he appealed for investment in Canada. High levels of American capital, he told his fellow premiers, posed a danger to Canada's 'independence', and he stated publicly his desire to shift fifteen per cent of Canadian trade from the US to Britain.[24] A bold idea, requiring Canadian businesses to focus away from a lucrative market just across the border, Diefenbaker's trade diversion scheme was a non-starter, one to which he devoted no new resources. Urging British officials not to take this initiative too seriously, one Canadian diplomat explained that the 'quest for the Holy Grail was well organised and far more hopeful in comparison'.[25] In response, Prime Minister Harold Macmillan suggested a Canada–UK free trade agreement. Like R. B. Bennett two decades earlier, Diefenbaker feared that such a pact would be of greater benefit to Britain and so he rejected the proposal. The failure to increase inter-Commonwealth trade was one of the reasons why Britain turned towards Europe, with Macmillan judging that his country's future prosperity lay not with the fading empire and fractious Commonwealth but with the Continent.

By laying bare Canadian antipathies about a postcolonial future in North America, Britain's effort to join the European Economic Community (EEC) created a terrific row between the three North Atlantic powers. Visiting Ottawa in April 1961, Macmillan extolled the benefits of EEC membership. Further, he assured Diefenbaker that he would seek to cushion blows to Canada and the rest of the Commonwealth that came from abandoning the tariff system favourable to Commonwealth trade.[26] Eliminating Commonwealth preferences threatened Canada's exports to Britain, raising the likelihood of further Canadian economic dependence on the United States. The British recognized Canada's precarious position. After consultations with Canadian ministers, Commonwealth Secretary Duncan Sandys reported on their anxiety over 'being sucked into the economic orbit of the United States'. Although 'all Western countries are now succumbing to the American way of life', High Commissioner Joe Garner explained, Canadians experienced Americanism most acutely for 'everything American – products, ideas, money, people – crosses the border without difficulty and with, in total, a massive impact', against which Canadians offered admirable resistance.[27] Sympathies aside, London forged ahead. The British outlined their proposal to enter the EEC at a 1961 Commonwealth conference at which Canadian ministers took turns savaging the plan; 'they're out for blood', remarked one British delegate.[28] Macmillan's domestic opponents – pro-empire Tories, including Canadian-born newspaper magnate Lord Beaverbrook – used Canadian objections to trash his plans to bring Britain into Europe, fuelling the British prime minister's disenchantment with Diefenbaker.

The divergence between London and Ottawa over Europe magnified the rocky relationship between Diefenbaker and US president John F. Kennedy, who famously loathed one another. With Washington supporting the British move to join the EEC, efforts by US diplomats to encourage this development were signs, in the Canadian prime minister's view, that Americans were 'interfering too much'.[29] Meeting with Macmillan in April 1962, Diefenbaker launched into a vigorous attack on his British counterpart's plan to join the EEC, but his comments showed anger with the United States, not Britain. Underlining that economic links to the UK were the means 'of staving off United States domination', he argued that the Americans were seeking 'to determine Canada's destiny', with Kennedy leading the charge.[30]

Diefenbaker's suspicions of the United States were a sign, in extreme form, of Canadian angst over the trans-Atlantic drift between Canada and Britain. Livingston Merchant, the US ambassador in Ottawa and one of the keenest American observers of Canadian affairs, saw the triangular dimension of the situation, explaining to President Kennedy that the Canadians were coming to realize that 'the power of Britain had declined' so that the United Kingdom 'no longer presented a refuge and a counter-poise to the power of the United States'.[31] Diefenbaker recognized as much, so at the September 1962 Commonwealth leaders' summit he launched into what Macmillan judged to be a 'broadside attack' and 'a false and vicious speech' against British membership in the EEC.[32] Brushing aside the Canadian prime minister's harangue, Macmillan pressed ahead. Happily for Diefenbaker, despite having wrong-footed Canada with its Anglo-American allies, French president Charles de Gaulle saved the day by vetoing Macmillan's bid. It was not until 1973 that Britain joined the European Community. By that point there was nothing of the Anglo-Canadian fuss of a decade earlier, for, as Lord Garner put it, the relationship between Canada and Britain was 'settling down to the comfortable one appropriate of an elderly couple'.[33] Likewise, in 1967, Charles Ritchie, the Canadian high commissioner in London and a staunch pro-British Tory, had characterized the Anglo-Canadian relationship as one between 'excellent friends who had known each other for a long time … There remained the bonds of the past, but our future was no longer any concern of theirs. If our preoccupations were with the United States, theirs was increasingly with Europe.'[34]

Beginning in the 1950s and just as the British connection began to wane in earnest, Canadian concern over American economic and cultural preponderance reached critical mass, in part due to the conclusions drawn by a series of royal commissions. In 1951, under chairperson Vincent Massey, the Royal Commission on National Development in the Arts, Letters and Sciences gave voice to concerns over the eclipse of Canadian culture, warning of 'a vast and disproportionate amount of material coming from a single alien source'. 'Hollywood', it added, 'refashions us in its own image.' As with the nationalist cultural panic of the 1920s and 1930s, the Massey commission led to a variety of state-funded cultural activities, from historical preservation efforts and investment in universities to the founding of the National Library of Canada and the Canada Council for the Arts, an artistic funding body.[35] Six years later, the Royal Commission on Canada's Economic Prospects – chaired by prominent businessperson Walter Gordon – outlined the vast extent of American ownership of Canadian resources and industry through subsidiaries and investment. While good for employment, this situation did little to foster an indigenous economy, for corporate profits went back to American shareholders, and US parent companies controlled the lucrative research and development process. Undergirding concerns with foreign ownership was 'the fear that continuing integration might lead to economic domination by the United States and eventually to the loss of our political independence'.[36] Four years later, the Royal Commission on Publications noted the global profusion of American culture and then highlighted Canada, which 'more than any other country is naked to that force, exposed unceasingly to a vast network of communications which reaches to every corner of our land; American words, images and print – the good, the bad, the indifferent – batter unrelentingly at our eyes and ears'.[37]

Against this growing consternation with the US connection, Diefenbaker's Progressive Conservatives swept into power. Despite his failure to boost Anglo-Canadian trade, the Tory leader remained committed to diversifying Canada's economic links, a goal adopted by all his successors. To this end, in 1958 he embarked on a Commonwealth tour that took him across South and Southeast Asia, and he visited Japan in 1960, the same year in which he travelled to Mexico, becoming the first Canadian prime minister to venture south of the Rio Grande. There were trade missions and ministerial visits across Asia, Europe, Latin America, and the Caribbean, and under Diefenbaker's watch Canada's overseas diplomatic presence expanded, brought on in part by the acceleration of decolonization – more than a dozen African countries gaining independence in 1960 alone. These efforts led to some increases in trade and they certainly succeeded in further broadening Canada's international reach, but they did little to affect the overall Canadian-US economic relationship.

Often, the desire for trade trumped other concerns. Despite his reputation as a fearsome cold warrior who denounced Soviet imperialism in Eastern Europe, Diefenbaker had few qualms about trading with communist regimes.

His government expanded links with the Soviet Union in cultural affairs, scientific exchanges, and sports competitions, and revived a trade pact that the St Laurent Liberals had suspended in 1956 after Soviet troops crushed the Hungarian Revolution. There were similar outreach efforts elsewhere behind the iron curtain. These links, Diefenbaker remarked, had the potential to encourage 'the development of more normal societies in the U.S.S.R. and Eastern Europe and gradually to bring them into more normal relationships with the West'.[38] The use of economic and cultural ties to break down barriers and promote long-term change infused – continues to infuse – Canadian trade policy towards morally reprehensible regimes, whether in Moscow or Pretoria. Plus, these contacts were good for business.

Although not recognizing the communist regime in Beijing, in the early 1960s Diefenbaker's government sold China hundreds of millions of dollars of wheat, needed by the Chinese to overcome the horrendous famine created by Mao Zedong's Great Leap Forward. Ottawa did so over Washington's objections. Since these wheat sales were a boon for Canadian farmers and cut down on a considerable Canadian trade deficit, Kennedy's national security advisor quipped that 'Diefenbaker will probably be re-elected by Mao'.[39] Throughout the 1960s there were other grain deals with the Soviet Union, a testament to the deficiencies of the communists' planned economy – the Soviet satirical magazine *Krokodil* once featured a cartoon showing Soviet grain being grown in Saskatchewan. Such lucrative trade aside, Canada refrained from recognizing Communist China's existence. 'Recognition would be interpreted as recognition of Communism', Diefenbaker declared, though one Canadian diplomat surmised that Canada's stance on China 'was due more to American influence than any other single factor'.[40] The cold war and the fact of alliance together placed limits on Canadian foreign policy, though nationalists came to see these limitations as signs of Canada's colonial or satellite status.

Cuba presented a similar situation to China. Of little economic importance to Canada, trade with the island took on immense political importance following the 1959 revolution and the American imposition of economic sanctions in 1960. Despite Washington's entreaties for support, Diefenbaker's government opposed instituting their own embargo, judging that the US effort to strangulate the Cuban economy was self-defeating and merely driving Cuba further into the communist bloc. This position became a point of nationalist pride. Facing criticism from US newspapers, members of Congress, and Kennedy administration spokespersons, Diefenbaker thundered that 'the decision as to the course Canada shall take should be made by Canada on the basis of policies which we believe are appropriate to Canada'.[41] Although some Canadian politicians and editors fretted over unduly upsetting Washington or abetting a communist revolution, there was broad support for the government's show of independence. Addressing an imaginary American, one poet wrote,

'When you've dined rather well / In your favourite hotel / And your gaiety's quite unassailable / You recall with a jar / A Havana cigar / Can't be smoked, for it isn't available / I conceive you may use / What invective you choose / But pray don't get your nerves in disorder / We've cigars on our shelves / For we roll them ourselves / We're conveniently north of your border.'[42]

Flaunting the American embargo was good politics, but had its limits. Diefenbaker's government cooperated with the Americans by limiting the export to Cuba of strategic goods, preventing smuggling of US products via Canada, restricting air travel to the island (Canadian tourism began in earnest only in the mid-1970s), and collecting and sharing intelligence gathered by diplomats in Havana. The latter operations ramped up during and after the Cuban missile crisis. Amid this nuclear showdown, Diefenbaker's initial response was famously ambivalent. Publicly he questioned Kennedy's brinksmanship and privately he equivocated over putting Canadian military forces on the same alert status as their American allies. Canada's military went on alert anyways, and Canadian diplomats denounced Soviet conduct and pressured the Cubans to stand down. Once the crisis abated, Soviet premier Nikita Khrushchev urged Ottawa to return to its 'sober and just' position towards Cuba.[43] The realities of the cold war placed limits on Canadian foreign policy, for when push came to shove the United States, not Cuba, was an ally.

The missile crisis threw Canadian defence policy into stark relief. In 1940, Canada and the United States had formed an arrangement to defend North America, and once the war ended, military cooperation continued. As the cold war ramped up, and with Canada occupying an important if unenviable position between the nuclear-armed superpowers, bilateral military links grew deeper. By the 1950s Canadian and US military planners' chief concern was a Soviet nuclear strike against North America; military strategy was predicated on protecting US nuclear weapons, thereby ensuring that the Americans could launch a retaliatory attack on the USSR, a threat that was intended to deter a Russian assault in the first place. To this end, the Canadians and Americans constructed lines of radar stations across Canada's vast north. Furthermore, to better coordinate the joint air defence of the continent, in 1957, Diefenbaker signed an agreement establishing the North American Air – later Aerospace – Defence Command (NORAD). Further integrating the Canadian and American militaries, the move was taken despite Diefenbaker's apprehension over Canada's economic links to the United States, a reminder that national security imperatives often trumped other concerns.

Equipping Canada's military became a source of intense controversy. To defend Canadian airspace, Ottawa considered a supersonic interceptor to shoot down incoming Soviet bombers. However, the aircraft, the AVRO Arrow, proved too expensive. To the great chagrin of Canada's aircraft industry and to Canadian nationalists, Diefenbaker cancelled the program, the prototypes were dumped into Lake Ontario and thousands of AVRO employees were laid off, gutting Canada's aerospace industry. Instead, his government opted to acquire less expensive, American-made jets as well as the BOMARC, an anti-aircraft missile of questionable utility. In addition, for its European-based forces, Canada procured Honest John rockets, to be used in battlefield situations. The BOMARCs, the Honest Johns, and the missiles to be fitted to the CF-104 jets all required tactical nuclear warheads, and it is a testament to the dire cold war situation of the late 1950s – the age of fallout shelters and duck and cover drills – that Canada moved to accept nuclear weapons. In announcing these acquisitions in the House of Commons, the prime minister made clear that the 'full potential of these defensive weapons is achieved only when they are armed with nuclear warheads'.[44] Despite this admission, no warheads were acquired from the Americans, only the weapons systems. Diefenbaker's hesitancy to go nuclear sprang from his concern with the political fallout, the result of mounting anti-nuclear sentiment.[45]

Prominent since the First World War, Canada's peace movement gained momentum thanks to the growing US-Canadian military ties and the looming threat of a nuclear conflagration. In parallel with developments in Britain and the United States, the late 1950s and early 1960s saw the formation of Canadian anti-nuclear groups, including the Combined Universities Campaign for Nuclear Disarmament, the Canadian Committee for the Control of Radiation Hazards, and the Voice of Women/La Voix des femmes (VOW), who joined established groups such as Women's International for Peace and Freedom (WILPF) and the communist-front Canadian Peace Congress. Anti-nuclear activists, explained a leading organizer, aimed 'to speak out against the tensions of the cold war and the imminent threat of nuclear conflict', and as part of its challenge to the cultural acceptance of war, VOW boycotted the sale of war toys.[46] Many of the apprehensions motivating peace activism were widely aired in *Peacemaker or Powdermonkey?*, the bestselling polemic by journalist James Minifie. Capturing the anxiety resulting from the apparent loss of Canadian independence, US belligerence, and Ottawa's support for American foreign policy, Minifie urged withdrawal from NATO and NORAD and the adoption of a neutralist foreign policy à la India. These moves, he emphasized, were necessary for maintaining Canada's 'leadership of the middle and emergent powers'.[47]

Minifie's position was very au courant: at the CCF's annual convention in 1960, the party narrowly approved a policy of withdrawing from NATO; the following year, when the CCF merged with the Canadian Labour Congress to form the New Democratic Party (NDP), there was a battle over neutralism, with opponents of this policy winning out. Young Liberals, too, embraced Minifie's idea, and at the party's National Rally in January 1961, they sought to pass a resolution to pull Canada out of both NATO and NORAD, an effort scuttled by party elders.[48] Within Diefenbaker's government, meanwhile, SSEA Howard

Green proved a staunch advocate of nuclear disarmament. His anti-nuclear activism extended to Canada's adoption of nuclear warheads, causing a rift in Cabinet with the pro-nuclear defence minister, and leading Diefenbaker to waffle over the atomic question. The issue dragged on interminably, with the prime minister offering his American counterparts the assurance that, when the political timing was right, he would acquire the warheads, but then failing to follow through on the acquisition itself.

The Cuban missile crisis put Canada's position on nuclear weapons to the forefront of events. Diefenbaker's slow response in backing the Americans became a point of criticism from the press, the public, and the Liberals, and attention turned to the weapons systems, which had been paid for and deployed, but had little utility without atomic tips. With the situation untenable, the Cabinet resolved to expedite negotiations with the Americans. High-level talks were carried out, but Green delayed any resolution as he looked for ways to back out. Diefenbaker, meanwhile, had come around to an anti-nuclear position, largely because in early January 1963 an American general visiting Ottawa had correctly noted that Canada's government was failing to meet its alliance commitments. A week later, sensing Diefenbaker's weakness on this file, Liberal leader Lester Pearson reversed party policy and advocated accepting nuclear warheads, citing the need to meet obligations. Diefenbaker could have pursued a bipartisan solution to the nuclear issue or informed the Kennedy administration that he wanted to back out of Canada's undertaking. Instead, viewing these incidents as evidence of collusion between the US military and the Liberals, he delivered a clarification of his nuclear policy that instead confused matters further. Irate at this double-dealing, the White House and the State Department issued a press release correcting the record and rebuking Diefenbaker.[49]

Denounced by the prime minister, the opposition parties, and newspaper editors as unwarranted interference in Canadian affairs, the US action helped precipitate a revolt by several cabinet members and the collapse of Canada's government in a non-confidence vote. The subsequent election was marred by Liberal charges that Diefenbaker had betrayed Canada's allies and Progressive Conservative accusations that Pearson was an American puppet. Diefenbaker would later allege election interference by the Kennedy administration as if Canada 'was an insignificant Banana Republic', but there is little evidence of intervention.[50] In the end, the Liberals won a minority government. Nuclear weapons was one of many issues in the campaign, and likely not a decisive one, as the Liberals had offered an attractive platform that included national health insurance and a policy to deal with growing Québécois nationalism. In May 1963, Pearson flew down to Kennedy's seaside mansion and made peace with the Americans. By August, his government had finalized an agreement to take possession of the warheads.

The nuclear decision was a blow to peace groups and it upset Canadians who believed that Pearson, a Nobel Peace Prize winner, personified Canada the benign middle power. Journalist Pierre Trudeau – Pearson's eventual successor – denounced him as the 'defrocked priest of peace'.[51] Allegations of Liberal collusion with the Americans found a ready audience among Canadians who expected the worst of Washington and who judged that the nuclear contretemps was a sign of Canada's limited independence. 'Because of the nature of the nuclear alliance system', wrote one long-time socialist, 'the United States is bound to take an ever more intimate interest in our politics just at the time when her indirect influence through mass-media and investment reaches almost the saturation point.' To preserve Canadian independence, he contended that in 'our domestic or foreign policies, Canadians will *have* to be anti-American'.[52] To philosopher George Grant, the return to Liberal rule in 1963 seemed to mark an embrace of pro-American policies that would only end in Canada's disappearance. In *Lament for a Nation*, a popular screed against the evils of the Liberal Party, the Americans, and modern life, he mourned 'the end of Canada as a sovereign state' in the face of economic and cultural absorption into the American 'empire'.[53] A staunch conservative who hailed from a long line of imperialists, Grant's views influenced a generation of youthful English Canadian nationalists who tended to identify as part of the global New Left. In an open letter to fellow leftist nationalists, one of the movement's leading members stressed the 'vital importance for Canadians and indeed, Americans, that there be an independent Canada, a Canada different from the U.S. in certain fundamental respects'.[54]

This New Nationalism reached a peak in the late 1960s and 1970s, though its influence continued to be felt over subsequent decades as baby boomers entered the Establishment. The movement focused primarily on American economic and cultural preponderance, and its members perceived an important connection between these two elements, for 'as long as the Canadian economy was dominated by the United States, Canadian culture will be submerged'.[55] The nationalist wave was more than a youth revolt – though young people were a key element – and had a base of support beyond the left. For instance, the Committee for an Independent Canada, founded in 1970, had a diverse leadership including prominent members of each of Canada's three major political parties and at its peak counted over one hundred thousand members. The Committee's goal, announced Mel Hurtig, the prominent nationalist publisher, was nothing less than 'Canadian survival', which could only be achieved through 'the preservation of Canadian economic and cultural sovereignty'.[56] For the New Nationalists, decades of North Americanization had gone too far.

Culturally, many of the developments linked to defining a new postcolonial identity separate from Britain were useful for the New Nationalists' anti-colonial efforts vis-à-vis the United States. Additionally, these efforts included Canadianizing university faculties and school curricula to ensure the teaching of Canadian history and literature and promoting Canadian values and knowledge through cultural products such as *Sesame Park*, a Canadian version of *Sesame Street*, a *Canadian Encyclopedia*, Canadian textbooks, Canadian superheroes, and Marjie, a wholesome, Canadian response to the 'sex kitten Barbie'.[57] New publishing houses championed Canadian authors and challenged American firms' control of Canada's literary scene, which, one of these nationalist publishers noted, had created 'a colonial and dependent state of mind and of intellectual life in Canada'.[58]

Cultural nationalism drove the federal government to implement Canadian content regulations requiring radio stations to play a certain percentage of Canadian music each hour, and Ottawa set up the Canadian Film Development Corporation (1967) and the Canadian Radio and Television Commission (1968) to provide government funding and oversight of the media.[59] Canadian universities developed Canadian Studies programs, an interdisciplinary field showcasing the vagaries of the Canadian experience. Abroad, Canadian Studies became central to Canada's cultural diplomacy efforts, with funding directed towards promoting the study of Canada at foreign universities. Inaugurating a Canadian Studies chair at the University of Edinburgh, SSEA Allan MacEachen outlined governmental efforts 'to project on the international scene the breadth, depth and creativity of Canadian cultural activities' and to expand cultural links to counteract 'the generally welcome but somewhat too pervasive influences from the United States'.[60] Like many nationalist cultural activities in Canada, Canadian Studies exemplified twin goals: to promote what was Canadian and, by doing so, to differentiate Canada from the United States.

In economic terms, there were a variety of measures directed towards restricting American investment and promoting Canadian ownership. In 1963, Walter Gordon, Liberal finance minister, implemented a short-lived tax on foreign investment; a stock market plunge forced its withdrawal. Gordon's inability to push nationalist economic policies led to his resignation, though after a brief interlude, during which he wrote and published *A Choice for Canada: Independence or Colonial Status*, he briefly returned to Cabinet, championing the formation of a Task Force on the Structure of Canadian Industry. Its report blamed foreign ownership for the 'widespread unease' over 'the continuing viability of Canada as an independent nation-state'. Other studies produced by various academics drew similar conclusions about the danger of foreign – but really, American – investment.[61]

The Trudeau government acted on this concern, particularly after the 1972 federal election, when the Liberals were reduced to minority status and held power with support from the NDP. There were several nationalist economic programs: the Canada Development Corporation (1971) promoted public/ private investment to purchase firms in danger of external control; the Foreign Investment Review Agency (1973) had the power to block or delay foreign takeovers of Canadian firms; and Petro-Canada (1975) was a state-owned oil company that sought a measure of control over a significant Canadian resource that was largely the preserve of US-owned companies. Trudeau adopted these measures because he was a politician, not a nationalist, but he too recognized the overwhelming presence of the United States. As he famously put it to a group of American reporters, 'Living next to you is in some ways like sleeping with an elephant. No matter how friendly and even tempered the beast, one is affected by every twitch and grunt.'[62]

Where the Trudeau government displayed its own initiative was in the launch of the Third Option, a ramping up of the Diefenbaker-era policy of seeking an economic counterweight to the United States with a goal of promoting political and cultural diversification as well. Its long-term goal was to 'lessen the vulnerability of the Canadian economy to external factors, including, in particular, the impact of the United States and, in the process, to strengthen our capacity to advance basic Canadian goals and develop a more confident sense of Canadian identity'.[63] Trudeau, his ministers, and Canadian diplomats and trade commissioners fanned out across the globe, seeking to drum up trade, sign cultural agreements, and promote Canada as a place for investment. These officials covered a lot of ground, but Mitchell Sharp, who as SSEA had articulated the policy but was no economic nationalist, later admitted ruefully that the Third Option 'was probably far too difficult an undertaking'.[64] Trade and cultural diversification remained both a goal for successive governments and a difficult task given the simple fact of geography.

Beyond cultural and economic sovereignty, much of the New Nationalism was about forging a Canadian identity, one that was un-American by necessity. Canadians had a long pedigree of finding distinctions between themselves and Americans, and in the era of the Vietnam War and the civil rights movement, naturally, for New Nationalists invested in portraying Canada as a 'peaceable kingdom', there was a tendency to point accusingly to two themes in Sixties American life: racism and Vietnam. In explaining 'Why I Am Anti-American', political economist John Warnock – an American by birth – pointed to Vietnam and 'the inability of the United States to offer any solution to poverty and racism'. 'The inability of American imperialism to manage its contradictions by liberal means, whether they be located in Harlem or in Vietnam, is more and more apparent', wrote Ian Lumsden in his appeal for Canadians to close the Canada–US border. In the most rousing articulation of this viewpoint, journalist Larry Zolf blared, 'Huzzah, we're not in Vietnam. Huzzah, we won't go there. Huzzah, we never will. Huzzah, we have no Watts-Newark-Detroit. Huzzah, we don't intend to build them.' And in

'American Woman', The Guess Who told their eponymous target: 'I don't need your war machines / I don't need your ghetto scenes'.[65] In protesting these issues, the New Nationalists were echoing young Americans, creating yet another issue for nationalists to lament. 'Even the Canadian Left is obsessed with American models', complained one journalist; by focusing on Vietnam and civil rights, political activist James Laxer groused that Canadians had failed 'to appreciate the seminal importance of the exploitation of Canadian society in general by the American empire'.[66] Such self-flagellation was warranted in that the counterculture of Haight-Ashbury and Greenwich Village appealed to Canadians, as did efforts to defend Vietnamese peasants and Mississippi freedom riders alike.

March 1965 saw nearly simultaneous protests in Canada against racist violence in Selma, Alabama, and the Lyndon Johnson administration's decision to expand American military involvement in Vietnam. 'The struggle for inalienable rights in the United States is our struggle here', Ontario MPP Stephen Lewis told a crowd of students, clergy, and labour and rights activists at a Toronto rally. Student Union for Peace Action, a New Left group, issued an open letter to MPs affirming that their interest in civil rights sprang from the fact that 'we share the North American continent with the United States'.[67] Vietnam revitalized the peace groups and anti-nuclear organizations whose fortunes had waned following the 1963 nuclear decision, and it generated a whole range of new activists. There were demonstrations at US consulate buildings in Canada's major cities and at the US embassy in Ottawa and sit-ins and teach-ins at Canada's universities. During protests on Parliament Hill and through petitions and letter-writing campaigns, Canadians urged government denunciation of US policy and an end to the sale of Canadian weaponry to the United States – Canada's 'quiet complicity' in the war. In a show of solidarity with the Vietnamese communists, some peace activists even travelled to North Vietnam. Additionally, there were efforts to support the tens of thousands of American war resisters, deserters, and draft dodgers who came to Canada just as Union deserters had come north during the American Civil War.[68]

For the New Nationalists, the Canadian government's unwillingness to take an independent course on Vietnam – that is, a position in line with what the nationalists themselves wanted – was a sign of the country's colonial status. Canadian foreign and defence policy, they noted, was suborned to 'the all-embracing and demanding continental demands of Imperial America', with Canada a 'satellite' of the 'American empire'. Clare Culhane, a leftist activist who worked on a humanitarian mission in South Vietnam before turning whistleblower on Canadian complicity in the war, complained that Canada's foreign policy was 'a mirror-image of our economic policy: in both cases the Americans are calling the shots.' Parroting *Peacemaker or Powdermonkey?*

the New Nationalists urged leaving NATO and NORAD and becoming a neutralist power. The choice to be made, in the view of political scientist Stephen Clarkson and other nationalists, was between independence and colonial status.[69] For Clarkson, a barometer of dependence was adherence to quiet diplomacy, Canadian officials' stance that Ottawa had a better chance of influencing Washington through diplomatic channels than through harangues in the House of Commons. This position was a sensible one, grounded in diplomatic practice, but it looked increasingly outdated in the maelstrom of the Sixties. Indeed, a joint study in 1965 by retired Canadian and US diplomats recommending such an approach was panned by the press and in academic and political circles. 'Today we are a mere echo of Washington's demanding voice', stated the NDP's David Lewis. 'We are disturbed by American escalation of the war in Vietnam, but our protest is mute.'[70]

Quiet diplomacy's critics had a point: having agreed to an alliance with the United States, Canada, like all alliance members, lacked a measure of independence in its foreign and defence policies. Whether Exxon Mobil's ownership of Imperial Oil or Big Bird's presence on Canadian television screens also affected Canada's international relations is a far more difficult matter to discern. Perhaps what counted most of all was that government policymakers perceived Canada as a Western country, sharing in the defence of Western interests. As SSEA Paul Martin remarked to US officials, 'Canada is the neighbor of the US and Canadians have a similar origin to Americans; if this were not the case, Canada would probably take a very strong stand against the US.'[71] This position did not preclude disagreement with the United States over policy, such as on Cuba, where Canadian officials refused to totally adhere to the US embargo partly because they judged that cutting trade ties would not effect change on the island and would harm the civilian population – the same position, incidentally, that Ottawa adopted towards apartheid South Africa. Yet, Canadian officials had little inclination to embrace Cuba so long as it was aligned with the Soviet Union. Even under Pierre Trudeau, who literally embraced Fidel Castro, Canadian policy displayed caution, particularly once thousands of Cuban soldiers began waging revolutionary warfare in Africa.[72] On China, too, dependence on the United States had its limits. Canadians responded to their American allies' wishes by refusing to recognize the regime in Beijing, even as they pursued trade with the communists. Once relations were established, links with China grew in fits and starts. Canadian foreign policy in these instances was driven by the dictates of the alliance system as well as by shared ideologies and interests on the part of policymakers in both Canada and the United States. On cold war fundamentals, Canadian officials perceived that it was in Canada's interests to back the Americans, a fact upsetting to the New Nationalists.

On Vietnam, Canada's government had little interest in seeing the regime in Saigon fall to communism. Canadian diplomats and military officers served on the International Control Commissions (ICC), set up via the 1954 Geneva Accords to police the borders of the new states of Laos, Cambodia, and North and South Vietnam. For some Canadians at the time and since, this role seemingly fell under the rubric of peacekeeping. Canada occupied the ICC's Western chair, alongside neutral India, and communist Poland, and while working to enforce the Geneva Accords the Canadians were not necessarily neutral observers. Moreover, many of the officials who did serve on the commission came away staunchly anti-communist, the result of their experiences dealing with the Polish and North Vietnamese and with the actions of communist guerrillas in the South. The Americans and their Southern allies were as guilty of violating the Geneva Accords as the North, and the situation in which Canadian foreign policymakers found themselves was unenviable. With the commissions in operation only for a matter of months, Pearson had already told US officials that Canada wanted 'any honourable way' to get out of this responsibility.[73]

Pearson recognized the unpleasant position occupied by both his country and the United States. Despite backing US goals in Vietnam, as he had done with Korea a decade and a half earlier, Pearson questioned American methods. In 1964, he told President Johnson that he 'fully understood the very difficult and important problems which the US faced in Southeast Asia. He agreed that the US could not simply pull out and that it must continue its support for governments which were not always very good at supporting themselves.' However, Pearson warned against a 'drastic escalation' in military involvement.[74] The dilemma here, one that Johnson and his own advisors wrestled with, was how to save South Vietnam without an undue commitment of US forces. In the end, the president judged that military might was needed, and he alone made the decision for war in early 1965, despite the warnings of Pearson and other foreign and domestic leaders.[75]

Having quietly warned the Americans against military escalation, in April 1965, Pearson spoke publicly on the matter. Against Paul Martin's advice and at the urging of Canada's senior professional diplomat, he used a speaking opportunity at Temple University in Philadelphia to urge Johnson to institute a bombing pause that would allow talks with Hanoi to proceed. Since the suggestion was made on US soil – a diplomatic faux pas – Johnson took it as a rebuke. Summoning Pearson, the president reamed him out for over an hour, famously shouting 'You don't come here and piss on my rug.' Former Secretary of State Dean Acheson soon denounced Canada – but really Pearson – as the 'Stern Daughter of the Voice of God', always hectoring the United States. American anger is worth noting, for Pearson had publicly offered only a mote of criticism and in his comments at Temple, he had been careful to state that his suggestion aside, he was not proposing 'compromise on points of principle, nor any weakening of resistance to aggression in South Vietnam

... resistance may require measured military strength to be used against the armed and attacking Communists.'[76]

Canada's position was characteristically in the middle. Supportive of American aims, Pearson and Martin also sought means of getting the United States out of an escalating situation. Between 1964 and 1966, Canadian diplomats secretly carried messages back and forth between Washington and Hanoi to lay the groundwork for negotiations to bring about a ceasefire. To this end, Martin travelled to Moscow, Warsaw, and Tokyo to promote peace talks. Ultimately, these efforts failed because neither warring side wanted them to succeed. As senior American officials later admitted, Canada's quiet initiatives were 'genuine efforts to get discussions going' and the Johnson administration was 'mistaken' in not taking them more seriously.[77]

Canadian quiet diplomacy failed to end the war – a tough feat for a middle power uninvolved directly in the conflict – but would loud denunciations have done any better? John Holmes, a former diplomat and a leading commentator on foreign policy raised another important aspect of the nationalist criticism of Pearson's government: 'By concentrating on the refusal of the Canadian government to denounce the United States for its policy on Vietnam, our independentists ignore the more significant fact that, contrary to expectation, the United States is at war we are not.' On this point, even George Grant agreed. 'However disgraceful has been our complicity in the Vietnam War', the nationalist philosopher wrote, 'however disgusting the wealth we have made from munitions for that war, one must still be glad that Canadian forces are not fighting there.' US officials were keenly aware of this fact as well. Having listened to Martin press him to put in place a truce for Christmas 1966, Dean Rusk responded by asking whether, if a ceasefire failed to produce peace, Canada would be willing to send troops to Vietnam. When Martin answered in the negative, Rusk asserted that 'in that case, Canada should let us make our own decision.'[78] For all the Pearson government's interest in seeing the United States succeed in Southeast Asia, it had no desire to fight in Vietnam and the war there was an American venture.

In reality, twelve thousand Canadians fought in Vietnam, doing so without Ottawa's sanction. Some of these men had been drafted while living in the United States; others had crossed the border to willingly fight communism. One Ottawa veteran recalled having been inspired to enlist by John F. Kennedy's 'commitment to support any friend and oppose any foe'. 'We saw in the United States and its constitution', added a Hamilton veteran, 'a thing we wanted to celebrate, to honor, to serve and protect'.[79] Like the Canadians who were drawn to fight fascism during the Spanish civil war, these men went to Vietnam to battle an ideological enemy in common cause with Americans, an important reminder that not all Canadian youth embraced the New Nationalist/New Left dogma. A conservative academic even lamented that because of the Pearson government's unwillingness to commit ground troops to Vietnam, 'it is regrettable that young Canadians are unable to bear arms against Communism under the flag of their own country.' As for quiet diplomacy, although a 1965 report by former Canadian and American diplomats calling for the practice had been trashed by editorial writers, polling two years later found that two-thirds of respondents opposed a vocal stance critical of the United States over Vietnam.[80] The youth revolt and the New Nationalism had their limits in Canada's position as a Western country.

The emergence of new Canadian national identities and nationalisms was part of a shift away from Britain, coupled with an effort to define what was Canadian and therefore un-American. The process had been afoot for decades, but accelerated in the post-war era. There were a variety of reasons for this development; one of them was that the English-speaking Canadian populace became less Anglo-Saxon. In his valedictory despatch in 1963 Britain's high commissioner in Ottawa had highlighted the growing number of Canadians who hailed from continental Europe, warning that 'the British connection naturally cannot mean so much to them'. Five years later, Canadian diplomats observed that with Pierre Trudeau's ascendancy 'we will no longer have as Prime Minister a man who, by training and by nature, was able to follow events in Britain and interpret them for himself'.[81] The British World was fading from view, along with many of the common reference points, shared cultural practices, and presumptions of collective interest in foreign policy matters. Assumptions of a cold war consensus between Canada and the United States were also subject to challenge, especially from Sixties youth.

The New Nationalism was an element of this generational change, for the sentiments fuelling it were strong among young people, for whom Canada's British heritage was a relic, its North American present a threat. For some members of this generation, shrinking pro-British sentiment tied to Sixties anti-Americanism led them to sneer at the notion of 'little Canada mediating between the United States and Britain in the interests of harmony for the Western Alliance, the Anglo-Saxon world, and the white race'. Similarly, a future Canadian foreign minister objected to the outmoded view of the 'old Canadian role of the lynch-pin between the United States and Great Britain'.[82] Fewer Canadians had an interest in the North Atlantic Triangle, though the concept was kept alive in some quarters. Formed in 1971 by prominent business and labour leaders, the British-North American Committee promoted the 'special relationship in world affairs between our three countries'. More frequently, however, the Triangle became a topic of historical study.[83] For many politically minded youth, 'Gaza, Da Nang, Newark' were 'on the signposts of the future', and it was these places of anti-imperialist struggle that captured their attention and sympathy, part of a growing awareness of and interest in the Third World. In Quebec too, there was a similar nationalist revolt. '*Le*

Vietnam aux Vietnamiens. Le Québec aux Québécois', was one battle cry.[84] Examining this Third World engagement is the subject we now turn towards, and in doing so, it is worth keeping in mind that the New Nationalism was an anti-colonial phenomenon and a means for youthful Canadians to imagine themselves as part of a global struggle.

10

Canada and the emerging global village

'**W**ho is my neighbour?' asked Prime Minister Pierre Trudeau while speaking on foreign aid. 'Is she the woman rummaging for food in the back streets of an Asian shanty town? Is he the man in South America in prison for leading a trade union? The people dying in Africa for lack of medical care, or clean water, are they my neighbour? What about those who are dying in the spirit in the villages of India for lack of a job, or an education, or hope? Are my neighbours the children running from the sound of gunfire in the streets of Beirut?'[1] Although rhetorical, Trudeau's line of questions encapsulated his interest in global inequalities and human rights, issues of increasing importance to Canadians in the 1960s and 1970s. Throughout these decades, activists, academics, and politicians took a more sustained interest in social, economic, and political conditions outside of their country. Movements for nuclear disarmament and peace in Vietnam were symptomatic of this attention, a result of the impacts of decolonization and the cold war, awareness of Western economic activities abroad, and important advances in air travel and electronic media. Information's ever more rapid movement was central to the emergence of what Canadian media theorist Marshall McLuhan labelled the global village, a term he coined in 1962 to characterize an increasingly interconnected world. A hallmark of what historians have referred to as the Global Sixties and Global Seventies – a precursor to the globalization of the 1980s – was the blurring of borders, mentally if not physically, so that many Canadians imagined themselves a part of various global struggles, whether against war, authoritarianism, or economic exploitation. In the global village, the distance between Canada and the Third World narrowed.

Emphasizing Canada's place in the global village is central to this chapter. While Pierre Trudeau's foreign policy has been ably analysed elsewhere, our interest here is with that policy's intersection with human rights and development, issues that became a focus of Canadian transnational activism.[2] Events in 'Chile, South Africa, and Guinea-Bissau', Canadian Labour Congress president Donald MacDonald noted, 'have at least brought these names into the everyday language of Canadians', while critics of Ottawa's stance towards national liberation movements in Southern Africa contended that 'progressive Canadians are participants in a world-wide struggle', which they characterized as an ' "unofficial" people's diplomacy'.[3] For the growing ranks of Canadian Third World activists, Canada's economic interactions with the Global South were a cause for protest as was the absence of human rights promotion in Canadian foreign policy. The authors of a report on Canada's role in Africa contended that Ottawa had 'placed a price tag on the basic social and political values which Canadians might expect that foreign policy to reflect'.[4] This outlook emanated out of a human rights revolution then unfolding at home, part of a 'breakthrough' for rights globally.[5] In a further sign of the consciousness emerging within the global village, many activists drew inspiration from abroad, connecting their own struggles to events in the Third World. Such was the case with Québécois separatists, who viewed Quebec as a colony of English Canada; with anti-corporate activists, who opposed the actions of Canadian multinational companies; and with indigenous people, who linked their fight for self-determination to the wider anti-colonial current. Bound up with Canadian foreign policy, and putting that policy in critical light, these ostensibly domestic issues highlight the internationalization of political issues in a globalizing world.

With long historical roots, notions of the Québécois as a colonized people reached critical mass as Europe's empires collapsed in the 1960s and as Quebec experienced a 'quiet revolution', the modernization and secularization of the province after the decades-long rule of the arch-conservative Union Nationale came to an end. This societal and economic transformation included a challenge to English-Canadian dominance both in Quebec and within the Canadian federation. Looking abroad, many Quebec francophones saw decolonization in India and Algeria and anti-imperialist struggles in Vietnam and across Latin America as 'exhilarating' examples of what they themselves could achieve.[6] Increasingly, instead of a pan-Canadian francophone identity, francophones in Quebec turned their backs on French Canadians in the rest of Canada, and Quebec and Québécois self-determination, assumed central importance.[7]

The Quebec-as-colony conception underscored the connection between local and global politics. Advocating for the development of an anti-colonial consciousness against 'Anglo-Saxon imperialism', in 1957 Raymond Barbeau, a Montreal professor, founded *Alliance laurentienne*, a short-lived political organization committed to creating an independent Quebec, or Laurentie. 'Quebec is still awaiting its turn', he stated in 1961, taking note of several dozen new UN member states.[8] Similarly, André d'Allemagne, one of the founders of *Rassemblement pour l'indépendance Nationale* (RIN), a nationalist political organization, pointed to Rhodesia, Congo, and Malaysia, other recently decolonized federations that he dismissed – like Canada – as 'artificial countries' in need of dissolution. In drawing comparisons, d'Allemagne carefully noted that the Québécois 'struggle of decolonization' should be peaceful rather than violent, for Quebec 'is neither Ireland, nor Algeria, nor Cuba', that is, it was not a place where the colonial elite ruled through force.[9] Surveying the nearly thirty colonies that had gained freedom since 1945, Marcel Chaput, another RIN co-founder, observed, with racist overtones, that while the Québécois remained colonized, abroad, 'people scarcely out of the Stone Age have obtained the independence they desired'.[10] For Québécois anti-colonialists, the power of comparison was important in framing their struggle. Important, too, to the developing Québécois consciousness were transnational links. Quebec's growing university student population drew upon real and imagined ties to other minority groups pressing for self-determination, from Cuban revolutionaries, to black nationalists, to Vietnamese peasants.[11] At protests such as *l'opération McGill français*, picketers shouting 'McGill aux Québécois!' bore signs with Che Guevara's stern visage.

For some Québécois nationalists, comparisons with Third World struggles went beyond identification, and while RIN sought to work within the existing political system, there were figures who advocated more radical solutions. '*Le Canada français, pays colonisé*' was socialist Raoul Roy's succinct judgement. Calling for a 'national liberation struggle', his journal, *La Revue Socialiste*, featured numerous articles playing up the connections between Quebec and violent decolonization struggles, for instance in Algeria, and it offered analysis of the relevance of Frantz Fanon's *The Wretched of the Earth* to the struggle against Anglophone imperialism.[12] Similarly, advocates of Quebec independence viewed the Québécois as a racial minority akin to black Americans. Writer Michèle Lalonde's poem 'Speak White', highlighted how the epithet hurled by Anglophones against French-speakers racialized Québécois, and Pierre Vallières characterized the Québécois as the *White Niggers of America*.[13] Whitewashing the profound and often violent oppression faced by African Americans not to mention black Canadians, it encapsulated, in extreme form, the way in which Sixties activists formed a global consciousness of dissent.

A leading militant nationalist, Vallières was involved with the *Front de libération du Québec* (FLQ), the terror group whose members drew inspiration from violent anti-colonial struggles in Latin America, Algeria, Palestine, and Ireland. In their April 1963 manifesto, the FLQ linked the Québécois to 'the various dominated peoples of the world' who had 'broken their chains in order to acquire the freedom to which they are entitled' and it appealed for a 'revolutionary war' for 'total liberation'.[14] FLQ cells engaged in a seven-year terror campaign of bank robberies and the bombing of federal government buildings as well as the Montreal Stock Exchange, murdering several bystanders in the process. Their efforts were ineffectual at fomenting revolution. However, authorities feared an insurrection when, in October 1970, the terrorists kidnapped a British diplomat and a Quebec government minister. Ottawa imposed martial law, deployed troops, and arrested hundreds of real and suspected FLQ sympathizers, actions that outraged civil libertarians. One of the hostages was murdered by his captors; the other was released following negotiations. As for Québécois nationalists, preferring the ballot box to bullets they rejected the FLQ. The group's terror campaign testifies to the potency and portability of Sixties anti-colonialism as well as to the global nature of left-wing national liberation violence. It was no coincidence that the FLQ hostage takers found refuge in Cuba.

Not all Québécois agreed with the colonial analysis, notably federalists who, while favouring more power for the province's French-speaking majority, wanted Quebec to remain within Canada. In a 1962 essay, leading federalist intellectual and soon-to-be-politician Pierre Trudeau mapped out his opposition to excessive nationalism and took issue with the practicalities of Québécois separatism by questioning the idea that the Quebec nation 'must necessarily be sovereign'. In Trudeau's view, Canada was a country in which multiple ethnic groups could live together and so, with a flash of Canadian exceptionalism, he posited that the country could 'serve as an example to all these new African and Asian states ... which should learn how to govern their multiethnic populations in justice and freedom'.[15] Gérard Pelletier, Trudeau's ally, contended that a problem with 'the separatists' colonial theory' was that Quebec enjoyed 'more freedom and a greater measure of political independence or self-determination than any other colonial country one can think of'.[16] Trudeau and Pelletier soon became federal MPs, encouraged by Lester Pearson who sought to give French Canadians a greater place within Canada and thereby combat growing separatism.

However one conceptualized the province, Quebec became tied up in Canadian international relations, principally because of France's meddling. Québécois' calls for self-determination resonated in Paris, where by 1963, French President Charles de Gaulle had concluded that just as France had granted self-determination to Algeria, Canada should do the same with Quebec.[17] For various reasons – loathing of Anglo-Saxons, hope of restoring French *gloire*, and genuine concern for the Québécois, who occupied a francophone outpost in an anglophone continent – de Gaulle actively supported Quebec's independence, doing so with the support of the 'Quebec lobby' of French politicians, bureaucrats, and journalists.[18] Even as it poisoned Franco-Canadian relations, French encouragement was a vital source of support for Québécois nationalists.

French officials met with separatist figures, tolerated the presence in Paris of an office of the *Comité internationale de l'indépendance de Quebec*, allowed Quebec to open a *Délégation générale* in the French capital in 1961, and signed a cultural accord with the province in 1965. Since the 1880s Canadian provinces had had overseas missions focused on promoting trade, culture, and immigration, but, in these cases, what proved galling was the delegation's quasi-diplomatic status, while the signing of the cultural accord tested Canada's federal model as Ottawa was constitutionally responsible for signing international agreements. Québécois nationalists justified these moves on the grounds that Quebec had its own 'international personality'. With the Canadian government maintaining that Canada had but 'one international personality', what ensued was what Claude Morin, a leading separatist, characterized as 'an arduous guerrilla war that spread over practically twenty years' as Ottawa tried to contain Quebec's international presence and Quebec City worked to expand it.[19] For federal officials, Quebec's baby steps towards international recognition looked all too reminiscent of Canada's own devolution from Britain. As Morin told federalist politician Jean Chrétien, 'we'll separate from Canada the same way that Canada separated from England: we'll cut the links one at a time, a concession here and a concession there, and eventually there'll be nothing left.'[20] Doubly worrisome for Ottawa was Paris's support for Quebec's quiet but deliberate emergence into the world.

Initially the Pearson government, especially Paul Martin, sought to placate the French, who were engaged in a running spat with the Americans and British over nuclear and NATO strategy. Martin pursued the role of mediator, a thankless task, that, in British and American eyes, made the Canadians appear too chummy with the French, who, in turn, took little interest in Canada's effort. In 1966, de Gaulle announced France's withdrawal from NATO's integrated military structure, ordered NATO headquarters removed from Paris, and expelled allied troops from French soil. 'So stupid', Pearson judged, 'and so shortsighted.'[21] Franco-Canadian relations were on a sour note, then, by 1967, a year of relative crisis. In April, in a fit of pique over not being consulted about Prince Phillip's invitation to the commemoration of the fiftieth anniversary of the Canadian victory at Vimy Ridge, Paris boycotted the ceremony.[22] In July, de Gaulle arrived in Quebec to tour the French pavilion at Expo 67 and visit Canada on its centenary. Purposefully and publicly, he threw his weight behind Quebec separatism. Addressing the throng from the balcony of Montreal's city hall, he likened the sense of excitement to the atmosphere surrounding the liberation of France from Nazi Germany and then, to huge cheers, he proclaimed, 'Vive le Québec! Vive le Québec libre!' 'Canadians do not need to be liberated', Pearson responded, but the damage was done.[23] Quebec nationalism continued to grow and in 1968 the province established its own immigration department, complete with representatives abroad to encourage francophone migration. Speaking at the opening of a constitutional conference that spring, just as he entered his final weeks as prime minister, Pearson explained that what was at stake was 'no less than Canada's survival as a nation'.[24]

In April 1968 Pierre Trudeau succeeded Pearson, and went on to win a Liberal victory in a June federal election. With a mandate in hand, he took a more combative stance towards Quebec separatism and French meddling. Domestically, he instituted a range of measures to make Canada more inclusive regarding its francophone population, including an official bilingualism policy within the federal government and, controversially, efforts to promote French language instruction in schools across the country.[25] Abroad, he sought to neuter Quebec's search for international recognition. In the closing months of the Pearson government the French had colluded with their former colony Gabon to invite Quebec representatives to an international cultural conference to plan the *Agence de coopération culturelle et technique*, precursor to *La Francophonie*. To outflank Quebec and ensure representation on a body of cultural importance to French Canadians, Ottawa solicited its own invitation, but its bid was rejected, leading Canada to suspend relations with Gabon. Eventually, a compromise was found: Quebec would be permitted to be a part of *La Francophonie*, participating under the Canadian umbrella; New Brunswick, home to the Acadian people, later joined via the same arrangement. As federal officials, such as SSEA Mitchell Sharp, emphasized, 'Québec does not speak for Canada or even French Canada on cultural affairs.'[26] Trudeau's international approach to Quebec separatism involved positive outreach to francophone Africa, including increased aid and development spending and expanded cultural contacts in former French colonies. Preserving the Canadian federation, he had stated in his first foreign policy speech as prime minister, meant 'reflecting in our foreign relations the cultural diversity and the bilingualism of Canada as faithfully as possible'.[27]

The international battle over separatism continued, especially once the separatist *Parti Québécois* (PQ) formed the provincial government in 1976. René Lévesque, the new premier, sought to further establish Quebec's international personality. In 1977, he visited Paris, receiving a lavish reception. Likewise, Claude Morin, the PQ intergovernmental affairs minister, travelled to Europe to drum up international support, both from governments and from business. Outside investment was a major concern for the separatist government: independence would be neither easy nor cheap. Two months after taking power, Lévesque assured New York's Economic Club that, despite the PQ's socialist bent, an independent Quebec would be a safe bet. Reassuring Americans was a goal he took seriously, both because he hoped for US recognition and because of his fondness for the country. 'I've never had any feeling of being Canadian', he once stated, 'but I've always had an incredibly strong sense of being North American. The place where I'm most at home outside Quebec is the United States.' Months before the PQ victory, he had defended Quebec independence in *Foreign Affairs*, promising – in a reversal of party policy – that an independent Quebec would participate in NATO and NORAD.[28]

Within Jimmy Carter's administration, there was divergence over how to respond to these developments. National Security Advisor Zbigniew Brzezinski, who grew up in Montreal as the son of a Polish diplomat in exile and who attended McGill before going off to the United States, believed – no doubt with a hopeful eye on Soviet subjugated Poland – that Quebec nationalism would win out. Other White House officials as well as the State Department took an opposing view, and so Trudeau was invited to Washington, where, in February 1977, he delivered a speech on Canadian unity to a joint session of Congress, a first for a Canadian prime minister. Privately, Trudeau emphasized to Carter that he was working hard to keep the country together, and publicly he told reporters that, for the United States, Canada's break-up would be 'more grave than the Cuban missile crisis'.[29] The US government indicated that the matter was one for Canadians to decide among themselves, but there were off-the-record comments stressing the administration's hopes for Canadian unity.

At home, the Quebec–Ottawa battle continued. While Trudeau opposed special deals for Quebec, especially in areas within federal jurisdiction, an exception was an agreement, concluded in 1978, allowing Quebec to set its own immigration policy, thereby ensuring that immigrants to the province spoke French. As for separatism, in 1980 Lévesque's government held a referendum on sovereignty-association, an ill-defined form of Quebec independence, winning 40 per cent of the vote. During the campaign, Trudeau promised far-reaching constitutional reforms. What ensued were nearly two years of lawsuits and constitutional wrangling among the federal and provincial governments as well as indigenous peoples, women's groups, and other stakeholders. The result, in 1982, was Canadian patriation of the British North America Act, transferring authority over Canada's constitution from Britain's Parliament to the federal and provincial legislatures. Several changes were made to the constitution, including an affirmation of indigenous rights, but because there were few special provisions for Quebec, Lévesque rejected the agreement and relations between the province and Ottawa remained tense. Nevertheless, at a rainswept signing ceremony on Parliament Hill in April 1982, Queen Elizabeth proclaimed the new Constitution Act, the penultimate step on the road to de-Dominionization – the British monarch remains Canada's head of state. Among its provisions was a Charter of Rights and Freedoms, a constitutionally entrenched bill of rights.

The Charter was the culmination of Trudeau's efforts to forge a 'Just Society' within Canada. It built on decades of effort by politicians, minority groups, and activists to see the federal, provincial, and municipal governments erect a human rights regime, one that eventually became among the most comprehensive in the world. However, for Canada's government, this rights revolution – part of a global development – largely stopped at the water's edge. Trudeau's foreign policy continued to prioritize traditional goals and interests and, above all, to respect state sovereignty. Given Quebec, the latter factor was important, because many of the international rights issues that dominated headlines in the Trudeau era involved self-determination movements. Mindful of Canada's own domestic situation, Ottawa was scrupulous in avoiding interference in other states' internal affairs.

The Nigerian civil war from 1967 to 1970, involving the Biafran attempt to secede from Nigeria, reflected growing Canadian interest in gross rights violations in the Third World. Activists, church groups, and opposition politicians urged the Trudeau government to intervene by negotiating a ceasefire, pressuring Nigeria's government to end the fighting, and disbursing humanitarian assistance.[30] Ottawa acted on the latter demand, sending supplies to starving Biafrans via military aircraft; individuals and the Canadian Red Cross and OXFAM Canada sent supplies, too. When it came to political involvement in the civil war, Trudeau was firm: 'we cannot intervene, short of committing an act of war against Nigeria and intervening in the affairs of that country.'[31] In laying out his reasoning for avoiding direct Canadian action, Trudeau stressed that Canada was 'distant' and that intervention would be 'an act of stupidity' alarming to African leaders who, with their history of colonialism, would bristle at Western meddling.[32] In response to a reporter's question, he asked, 'Where's Biafra?' As he later explained, 'To ask, "Where is Biafra?" is tantamount to asking "Where is Laurentia?" ' – neither country existed.[33] Nigeria was a federation like Canada, a fact noticed by Trudeau, by de Gaulle, who likened Biafra to Quebec, and by African diplomats, who asked Canada's UN ambassador, 'How would you like it if there were an armed uprising in Quebec and the United Nations decided to send a peacekeeping force to separate Quebec from the rest of Canada.'[34] Given French backing of Quebec separatism, Trudeau was wary of outside intervention in the internal affairs of other states.

Trudeau's stance on Biafra further reflected his position on Quebec in that he did not accept that 'groups of people within a country had the right of self-determination, and the rest of the world had the right to support them in seeking independence'.[35] He stuck to this position when it came to secessionist struggles between Indonesia and East Timor, between Pakistan and Bangladesh, and between the Soviet Union and its various Eastern European satellites.[36] Trudeau was consistent, meaning that Ottawa was silent in condemning human rights violations, including acts of genocide. Instead, as in the case of humanitarian aid shipments to Biafra, Canada's government provided practical assistance. Soon after Bangladesh won its independence, Canada established a high commission with the sole purpose of delivering aid to the war-shattered country.[37]

As was often the case on many emotionally charged issues, a quiet Canadian approach, one mindful of what Canada might accomplish and careful about intervention, was at odds with activists' demands for action and moral leadership. Asked why he did not take Jimmy Carter's vocal approach to rights promotion, Trudeau admitted that he was 'somewhat envious' of the president's ability to 'get results by speaking directly', but that for Canada, a small state with limited influence, loud statements were 'more rewarding in terms of self-satisfaction but not necessarily in terms of results'.[38] Quietly or otherwise, Trudeau showed little inclination to pursue bilateral human rights dialogues with repressive regimes, even those on the other side of the iron curtain, outraging Canadian anti-communists and nationalists among Canada's Eastern European population.

Among Trudeau's goals was the pursuit of détente with the communist powers, an issue that trumped human rights concerns. As he once explained, while he had briefly raised rights issues with Soviet leader Leonid Brezhnev in a quiet tête-à-tête during his 1971 visit to the USSR, rights violations 'shouldn't prevent talking' to communist apparatchiks.[39] Beyond expanding relations with the Soviet Union through trade and cultural agreements – the latter paving the way for the 1972 eight-game Summit Series of hockey, won by Team Canada – Trudeau became the first NATO leader to visit Cuba, spending several days with Fidel Castro that included philosophical debate and a snorkeling expedition.

More momentous was Trudeau's decision to recognize and establish diplomatic relations with Communist China. In 1969, Margaret Meagher, Canada's ambassador in Sweden, began negotiations with her Chinese counterpart, with the thorny issue proving to be the status of Taiwan, which claimed to be the legitimate government and which Beijing viewed as a part of China. By 1970, a formula had been worked out whereby Canada ended official relations with Taiwan, recognized the People's Republic as China's sole legal government, and simply took note of Beijing's claim to Taiwan.[40] Establishing relations with the world's most populous country and a nuclear-armed great power was an important development, though not as revolutionary a move as it might seem: most NATO members had taken the same step, and there was broad support for the move across Canada's political spectrum. Furthermore,

Washington – the reason Ottawa had not yet recognized Beijing – was kept abreast of Canadian moves and the Richard Nixon administration itself began normalizing Sino-American relations. Nixon's 1972 visit to China overshadowed a Canadian trade expo in Beijing. The following year, four beavers, a gift for the Beijing zoo, accompanied Trudeau on his own Chinese junket.

Neither China, nor Cuba, nor the USSR had a sterling human rights record, but that deterred Trudeau little from crossing the cold war divide. Virtually absent from his conversations with Brezhnev, Castro, or Zhou Enlai were meaningful discussions of human rights, evidence, concluded his sharpest anti-communist critic, of 'moral blindness' and of 'approval' of communist crimes.[41] Trudeau's quiescence on rights is a reminder of the limits of this early stage of the human rights revolution, for it contrasts with more contemporary Canadian foreign policy, where rights promotion forms a more politically significant portion of bilateral dialogue. Instead, Trudeau's stance rested on a long-term view of the importance of engaging rogue regimes. 'A China open to the world', he expounded, 'could be expected over time to adjust its political, economic, and social practices to bring them into harmony with international norms.'[42] Forming the basis of Canadian, indeed Western, engagement with China and Cuba, over the subsequent half century this policy bore little fruit in terms of prompting reform. It was good for business.

Where human rights saw greater acceptance in determining policy was with refugees. Here, Canadian policy could be generous but also displayed the limits of rights acceptance. On a positive note, in response to the crushing of the 1956 Hungarian revolution by Soviet forces, Canada launched a crash program that took in thirty-six thousand refugees within a matter of months; there was a similar program for twelve thousand Czechoslovakians fleeing Soviet terror after the Prague Spring in 1968. At the same time, only a trickle of Chinese and Tibetan refugees entered the country even though they too were fleeing communism, leading to charges of a racial double standard. Change began under Trudeau. In 1969, Canada ratified the 1951 Geneva Convention on Refugees, though it took until 1976 for Canadian immigration law to recognize asylum seekers.[43]

Despite the delay over the refugee convention, in response to international crises the Trudeau government launched ad hoc programs to take in refugees, including large numbers of non-white people. The special programs included several hundred Tibetans in 1971, over seven thousand Indians from Uganda in 1972–3, ten thousand refugees from Lebanon's civil war between 1975 and 1978, and nine thousand South Vietnamese refugees in 1975, as the Saigon regime collapsed. The boat people's exodus led Canada to take in an astonishing seventy-seven thousand Vietnamese between 1979 and 1981. Asylum seekers from South America's odious juntas were more problematic – Canadian authorities feared sheltering far left extremists whose numbers might have included the same sort of urban terrorists who had inspired the FLQ. Despite security fears and under considerable pressure from church and labour groups, opposition MPs, and activists, the Canadian government turned Canada into one of the largest receivers of Argentinian, Uruguayan, and Chilean refugees.[44] These programs marked an important change in Canadian policy given that Ottawa had historically barred refugees, such as Jews fleeing Nazi persecution. Indeed during deliberations on accepting the boat people, immigration officials had circulated copies of a recently published book on Canada's failure to help Europe's Jews.[45]

In saving and welcoming refugees, government actions were important, but so too were the thousands of Canadians who raised awareness, lobbied officials, and sponsored refugees and found them jobs, food, and shelter. In recognition of these efforts, in 1986, the UN High Commissioner for Refugees awarded the Nansen Medal to the people of Canada. However, the flow of refugees produced pushback. There were racist sentiments, fears of employment competition in the dire economic situation of the 1970s, and unease, as expressed by the *Toronto Star*, that refugees were jumping the immigration queue with the result that Canada's borders were akin to 'a collapsed seawall, over which flows flotsam and jetsam from all over the world'.[46] Acceptance of refugees remained a point of controversy, even as Canada increasingly became a place of refuge for people fleeing the world's hotspots.

Beyond asylum policy, the Trudeau era saw important rights activism through multilateral channels as opposed to bilateral ones. At the UN, the Canadian delegation backed a range of international instruments affirming, for instance, women's rights and religious freedom, and in 1976, the Trudeau government ratified the international human rights covenants. After considerable UN wrangling, in 1966 Canada had supported passage of the covenants, which sought to put the sentiments behind the Universal Declaration of Human Rights into practice, but securing provincial consent took a decade.[47] The covenants were legally binding, and so beyond necessitating action on Canada's part domestically, they provided international legal cover to criticize other signatories. As SSEA Mark MacGuigan explained, parties to the covenants and to the various UN rights agreements 'assume obligations both to their own citizens and to the international community'. Since these agreements opened Canada up to reciprocal scrutiny, Ottawa's 'first priority' was 'to ensure the health of our own society and institutions'. By advancing rights at home – and here he pointed to the Charter of Rights and Freedoms – Canada would become 'a creditable voice' for human rights abroad.[48] In short, by fulfilling its own multilateral rights commitments Canada would be positioned to criticize other states for failing to follow suit.

Another multilateral rights initiative came out of cold war Europe. In 1975, Canada signed the Helsinki Accords, agreed to by thirty-five states hoping to improve East-West relations and normalize Europe's post-war division. Negotiated over two years at the Conference on Security and Co-operation in Europe (CSCE), the agreement included language on human rights, which, combined with monitoring groups and follow-up meetings between its signatories, played an important role in fostering the rise of organized dissent within the Soviet empire. Canadian diplomats were enthusiastic about the CSCE negotiations, pushing the NATO allies towards a firm stand on the proposed agreement's human rights aspects.[49] Like the international covenants, the Helsinki Accords provided a legal means for Canadian officials to raise human rights concerns behind the iron curtain without infringing on Soviet sovereignty. Despite this multilateral cover, Trudeau remained hesitant. In weighing a response to the Polish regime's repression of the Solidarity protest movement, MacGuigan recalled that Trudeau asked 'how I could possibly justify Western meddling in the internal affairs of Poland. I replied that normal international law in this respect had been drastically altered' with the Helsinki Accords.[50]

South African apartheid was another situation where the Trudeau government balanced multilateral commitments with bilateral interests. John Diefenbaker had helped to expel South Africa from the Commonwealth in 1961, but otherwise his government and those of his successors had done little to meet anti-apartheid groups' demands. Isolating and sanctioning South Africa became a focal point for a growing transnational activist network and from Third World delegations at the UN. Within the Commonwealth, non-white members demanded sanctions, pitting them against the British government, which, largely because of economic interests and pro-Pretoria political pressure, was reluctant to break financial ties with South Africa. There was a showdown at the 1971 Commonwealth heads of government summit in Singapore, where Trudeau brokered a compromise statement requiring members to exercise their own judgement in imposing sanctions, a move credited by some observers with saving the Commonwealth.[51]

Canada's own position on sanctions evolved slowly. In 1970, Ottawa implemented an arms embargo; seven years later, under pressure from domestic groups and responding to UN sanctions, the Trudeau government announced an end to trade promotion efforts, the withdrawal of export credit insurance, and an ethics code for Canadian companies operating in South Africa. These steps failed to placate activists, who directed their opprobrium towards Canadian companies, such as Air Canada, which maintained links to the Pretorian pariahs.[52] Sport was another realm of activism. An international ban on South African involvement in sports competitions led twenty-two African states to boycott the 1976 Montreal Olympics, not because South Africa was present, but because New Zealand was participating and it had refused to cut sport ties. A similar fate awaited the 1978 Commonwealth

Games in Edmonton, although Canadian diplomats prevented a boycott.[53] Overall, the Canadian experience with South Africa during the Trudeau years encapsulates both the proliferation of human rights activism and interest in the Third World among Canadians, and government hesitation about making rights promotion a significant foreign policy plank.

Beyond détente, a centrepiece of Trudeau's foreign policy was the broadening of Canada's international links and trade diversification. There was an aggressive trade promotion campaign that included missions to Saudi Arabia, Iran, Indonesia, and various communist bloc countries, none of which had a sterling rights record.[54] Canadian government trade and finance officials supported expanded exports to and investment in Brazil, Chile, Argentina, and Uruguay, where military regimes attracted the attentions of human rights campaigners – labour unions, church groups, university students, and radicals of various stripes. A galvanizing force for protest was the 1973 Chilean coup, in which the military overthrew a democratically elected Marxist government. Just as there had been pressure on Ottawa to sanction Japan and Italy during the 1930s, Canadian rights activists urged Canada's government to denounce the Chilean junta, sanction Chile, and implement a refugee program. The Trudeau government relented on the latter point, but did little to interfere with the operations of Canadian banks and mining companies, and through the Paris Club of major creditor countries, Ottawa backed debt relief for Chile's government. Representing the Catholic Church and mainline Protestant denominations, the Canadian Council of Churches implored government ministers to prioritize 'the struggles of the Latin American peoples toward justice and liberty' over business interests.[55]

The Chilean solidarity movement's emergence was indicative of growing Canadian Third World activism, which included interest in Canadian economic actions abroad whether in Vietnam, South Africa, or the Caribbean. This interest led to the formation of a wide variety of protest groups, some of which, like GATT-fly (economic inequalities) and the Canadian Council for International Cooperation (development), focused on specific issues, while others – the Toronto Committee for the Liberation of Southern Africa, the Canada Asia Working Group, the Fair Play for Cuba Committee – concentrated on countries or regions. In terms of Latin America, first the Cuban revolution and then the political turbulence of the 1960s and 1970s brought the region into increasing focus for Canadians, for whom the area south of the Rio Grande had long been a blind spot.[56] Latin American solidarity groups in Canada protested US intervention across the hemisphere, mounted public education campaigns, promoted people-to-people contacts through exchanges and in-country visits, and lobbied Ottawa to punish repressive regimes – Cuba excepted.

Many solidarity activists drew comparisons between conflicts in Latin America and their own domestic struggles against capitalism and US imperialism. The Latin America Working Group contended that 'Canadians are exploited and share in exploitation', for while Canadian mining companies extracted Chile's wealth, Canada likewise faced 'external corporate domination'. New Leftist Philip Resnick took aim at multinational corporations whether 'engaged in exploiting Latin America or the Canadian hinterland'. Similarly, Québécois nationalists viewed the Chilean coup as an example of how Anglo-Saxon capitalists trampled upon Latin workers, both 'Chileans and Québécois'.[57] Links between Latin America and Quebec civil society were particularly strong thanks to long-standing networks established by Catholic missionaries. These religious networks were key to solidarity activism and served as a transmission point for liberation theology, the revolutionary doctrine developed in Latin America and embraced by some Québécois nationalists.[58]

The Chile–Canada comparison showed the attention being turned to Canadian economic involvement in the Global South, and the late 1960s and 1970s witnessed debate on the left about whether Canada could be both colony and colonizer. Toronto-based critics of Canadian backing of Portuguese colonialism in Angola and Mozambique chided Canadian neo-nationalists, who 'in their concern to emphasize Canada's dependent status vis-à-vis American imperialism', overlooked Canadian imperialism in the Third World. Journalists examining Canadian financial dealings with some of Latin America's loathsome military regimes saw investments in Brazil, Argentina, Chile, and Uruguay as evidence of Canadian 'sub-imperialism', for Canada benefitted from US hemispheric hegemony.[59] There were also charges of neocolonialism – a 1960s neologism – typifying Western economic interactions with the Third World.

For Canada, the Caribbean appeared as a neocolonial space. 'While Canada is not a country which seeks to build up imperial bases', Paul Martin affirmed in late 1963, 'I think Canada has recognized that there is a special relationship with Commonwealth countries in the Caribbean.'[60] Given economic links and the Commonwealth tie, Canadian–Caribbean relations did have an air of specialness for establishment figures like Martin, but relations were marred by Canadian immigration laws barring black migration, a barrier not demolished until 1967. A year earlier, Martin and Pearson had hosted their West Indian counterparts in Ottawa, a summit meant to strengthen ties and resolve economic sore spots.[61] *Maclean's* had called for Canada to take a major regional role and transform the Caribbean into a 'sphere of Canadian interest', and one reporter, reviewing the massive Canadian investment in West Indian banking and mining, had wondered: were these signs of 'a sort of mini-imperialism?'[62] In 1969–70, a Senate committee addressed this question. Under Liberal Senator John Aird, a director of the Bank of Nova Scotia, which had major interests in the region, the committee heard testimony from a variety of Canadian and West Indian officials, businesspeople, and civil society figures. Defending Canada's Caribbean role in the committee report, Aird carefully emphasized the 'essential imbalance' between Canada and Caribbean states. 'Accusations of "neo-colonialism"', Aird concluded, 'will continue to be made against Canada. Canadians can no longer expect to find in the area the uncritical and almost unlimited goodwill of former years.'[63] Casting Canada's presence abroad in a new light, this warning was at odds with the notion of a special Canada–Caribbean relationship let alone with the predominant post-war view of Canada as a benign middle power.

Charges of Canadian neocolonialism were not confined to Senate hearings, because protests had occurred against Canadian economic interests in Haiti (1967) and Jamaica (1968), and, beginning in March 1970, amid the hearings, large anti-Canadian demonstrations broke out in Trinidad. The immediate catalyst of the outcry was the Montreal trial of black West Indian students arrested for their part in the 1969 occupation of a building at Sir George Williams University in protest of a faculty member's racist actions. The trial, the leaders of the Trinidadian demonstrations contended, was 'only an extension of the oppression' exercised by Canada in the Caribbean.[64] Critics of Canada's economic presence looked, for instance, to the Aluminum Company of Canada's bauxite mining operations. The key ore used for aluminium, bauxite was extracted in the Caribbean, but the lucrative refining process was carried out at Alcan plants in Canada, leading to charges of exploitation. In 1971, Guyana nationalized Alcan holdings, though the company received compensation and moved its operations to Jamaica.[65] Other Canadian businesses came under similar scrutiny, with journalists characterizing Canada's economic role as differing little 'from colonial slavery in which the source of wealth is foreign and white, the source of labour local and Black'.[66] Covering a demonstration at the Royal Bank of Canada's main branch in Trinidad, reporters observed that the protests put Canadians 'in a startling new role ... that of the colonialist under siege'. 'We're not colonialists by intent', conceded a Canadian diplomat, 'but by circumstances we've taken on a neo-colonialist aura.'[67] These criticisms of Canadian corporations portrayed Canada not as victim of foreign capital but as exploiter.

However negatively they tarnished Canada's image abroad, the actions of Canadian businesses in the Caribbean, and throughout the Third World, were those of private enterprise. Ottawa had a more direct hand through Atomic Energy Canada Limited (AECL), a Crown corporation, and a subject of attention from anti-nuclear, environmental, and human rights campaigners. In 1956, AECL had begun looking for international buyers of its new CANDU reactor; by the early 1960s, contracts had been concluded with India and Pakistan. At the same time, Canada's government backed the creation of the International Atomic Energy Agency and a series of nuclear disarmament initiatives most notably the Nuclear Non-Proliferation Treaty (NPT). A problem, then, was that Canadian nuclear salesmanship did not require purchasers of CANDU reactors to adhere to the NPT and neither India nor Pakistan were signatories.

The explosive result was India's May 1974 detonation of a nuclear device utilizing plutonium from a Canadian reactor. In response Ottawa ended nuclear exports to India, souring Indo-Canadian relations for nearly four decades. Still, AECL continued to pursue foreign buyers in Romania, South Korea, and Argentina – despite the latter two countries having failed to ratify the NPT. Canadian activists turned their ire towards nuclear trade with the Argentinian junta, eventually pressuring Canada's government to require Buenos Aires to avow that it would not use Canadian technology or materials to build a nuclear bomb. Pakistan's unwillingness to sign a similar agreement led Ottawa to suspend Canadian nuclear exports and assistance to Islamabad. It was not until 1992 that Canada formally eliminated nuclear sales to countries that were not a party to the NPT.[68] Canadian nuclear exports encapsulated the problems involved in simultaneously promoting economic and political interests in the Global South.

This clash also played out in Canada's development programs. Ottawa had had a Third World aid program in place since 1951, with Canada's contributions to the Colombo Plan during its first two decades aimed principally at India, Pakistan, Ceylon, and Indonesia. After twenty years and an expenditure of $2 billion, aid specialist Keith Spicer observed that the program 'no longer excites among Ottawa's official philanthropists the sense of pioneering wonder' that inspired initial outlays during the middle power era.[69] Whatever pessimism existed over Colombo, Canadian aid and development spending had only increased throughout the 1960s, with new bilateral programs launched for Africa and the Commonwealth Caribbean and spending increases via multilateral channels such as the World Bank.

To signify development's importance the UN christened the 1960s as the decade of development – it did the same again for the 1970s – with the level and terms of spending an increasingly divisive factor in relations between donor and recipient countries. These divisions led World Bank President Robert McNamara to form a Commission on International Development, headed by recently retired Lester Pearson. After months of consultative meetings with officials from donor and recipient countries, the Pearson commission released *Partners in Development* (1969), which stressed, among other points, the need for developed countries to give more aid, setting a benchmark of 0.7 per cent of GNP. This figure continues to serve as a goal for many donor countries, but otherwise Pearson's report was panned, for it said little that was new and, by emphasising Western-style economic development, it failed to address a raft of issues that were increasingly important to aid specialists: poverty, the environment, and urbanization. In part, the commission report reflected a prevailing liberal economic outlook, but its limitations also stemmed from Pearson's sense of what was politically possible, for, as he recognized, many donor countries would not accept radical recommendations.[70] Like Spicer, Pearson was mindful of aid fatigue.

Pierre Trudeau was more hopeful. His government's 1970 foreign policy strategy was steeped in language reflecting a belief in social justice. 'We could not create a truly just society within Canada if we were not prepared to play our part in the creation of a more just world society', it affirmed. 'Thus our foreign policy in this field becomes a continuation of our domestic policy.'[71] His government boosted aid spending, launched new bilateral programs in Latin America, and coordinated it all through the Canadian International Development Agency (CIDA), a stand-alone department, while the International Development Research Centre was formed to study development issues. In 1978, Canadian aid reached a high of 0.54 per cent of GNP, a number never again matched despite repeated government pledges to attain Pearson's 0.7 per cent target.[72] Trudeau threw himself into debates over North-South issues, and he responded positively to the Third World effort, launched in 1974, to forge a New International Economic Order, chairing several high-profile conferences on the more equitable distribution of wealth. His efforts were hobbled by a poor economy, public fatigue with foreign aid, bureaucratic scepticism, opposition from conservative governments in the developed world, and the radicalism of certain countries in the Global South.[73]

Trudeau's enthusiasm for development was shared by thousands of Canadians, who supported government projects or the private efforts of NGOs, who volunteered to serve overseas building infrastructure, who passed along technical knowledge and training, or who hosted Third World academics, civil servants, and professionals at Canadian universities, hospitals, and technical colleges. While their motivations were diverse, these Canadians took part in a global effort to combat poverty and a host of associated issues, and many participants saw their efforts in a noble light. 'The missionary of yesterday has gradually been transformed into a development agent', boasted CIDA's president.[74] Several reports covering CIDA activities in Latin America exemplify this humanitarian impulse as well as the characteristic modernizing ethos behind efforts to turn 'backward' areas into productive ones. An analysis of Canadian agricultural training in Peru emphasized the 'miracle' of 'transforming the jungle into a field of wheat, corn or rice'. Mastery over nature and the use of advanced technology were putting Peruvian farmers on a path 'from machetes to mechanized farming', that is, on a path to modernity.[75] Similar grandiose expectations were expressed by CIDA staff writer Jack Redden, who foresaw Canadian efforts eventually transforming 'the vast and largely unused grasslands of South America' into grazing land for massive herds of cattle or perhaps into 'fields of rice stretching up the Americas'. Reflecting the then current preoccupation with malnutrition and starvation, but with little attention to environmental conservation, Redden mused about a 'solution to the current world-wide food shortage that is not in the realm of science fiction'.[76] These enthusiastic accounts highlight development specialists' hopes for what could be accomplished through the application of modern science.

At the same time as interest in development grew, there emerged various criticisms of Canadian aid programs and even a questioning of the very concept of development. The growing army of development specialists expressed concerns that spending was too low; that too much of Canada's aid was 'tied', meaning that it required aid recipients to spend the funds on Canadian goods; that a focus on economic growth models was mistaken and that development should prioritize human and environmental advancement; that Canadian programs failed both to adequately respond to local conditions and to promote mutual benefits; that debt relief should take priority; that development efforts were undermined by the actions of Canadian multinationals; and that Canadian programs promoted Western-style capitalist development wholly unsuited to promoting social justice in non-Western societies.[77]

Whatever the shortcomings of Canada's aid programs, attention to the plight of people in the Global South embodied the growing sense of interconnectedness. In *Our Beautiful, Solitary and Fragile Spaceship Home*, the World Federalists of Canada appealed for a realization that borders frequently had little meaning, for the pressing issues of pollution, population growth, and poverty were 'planetary in scope'. Founded in 1969 by American expatriates in Vancouver, Greenpeace began as a group protesting nuclear testing but expanded its interests and operations to include global environmental issues.[78] In this interconnected world, development advocates contended, Canadians, as a wealthy people, had a duty to contribute to alleviating problems elsewhere. 'We have to begin by recognizing that by any standard, we are a rich country', noted one proponent of greater aid spending. 'We have more telephones, cars, televisions, refrigerators, electric can-openers, single-detached homes, lawn-mowers, and motor boats than almost any other group of people in the world.'[79]

Not all Canadians had such a high standard of living, and a significant source of criticism of overseas development spending came from indigenous people and Canadians mindful of underdevelopment within Canada itself. In 1958, James Gladstone, the first indigenous senator, stated that if Canadians could 'freely grant aid, comfort and recognition to under-developed and distressed people all over the world', then they could assist aboriginal people. While praising Canadian aid abroad, members of an indigenous solidarity group contended that these efforts were 'rendered ridiculous by the fact that so little is being done about poverty, squalor and ignorance of our own native citizens'.[80]

Canada's government undertook several projects to develop indigenous communities, including an outlandish effort to bring Indian yaks to northern Quebec to encourage animal husbandry among the local Inuit. Additionally, there were development efforts by NGOS, such as Oxfam Canada, whose first project involved emergency relief in Northern Manitoba and the far north.[81] In 1973, the Canadian Council of International Cooperation, an organization focused on foreign aid, partnered with the Canadian Association in Support of the Native Peoples to highlight 'the Third World status characterizing underdeveloped peoples both at home and abroad', a call highlighting the connection between the global and the local.[82]

In a similar vein, as indigenous activism increased over the course of the 1960s and 1970s, there was growing anger that 'while Canadian urbanites have walked blisters on their feet and fat off their rumps to raise money for underdeveloped countries outside Canada' they did not 'give a damn' about indigenous people. Red Power theorist Howard Adams underscored resentment at the 'large sums of money being sent to other countries to glorify the Canadian government as a generous, kindly, and non-racist government at a time when Canadian natives are living in conditions of grim poverty that are sometimes worse than in the countries receiving foreign aid'.[83] These criticisms were harsh but fair and they emphasized that in focusing so much attention and money towards the Third World, Canadian do-gooders were ignoring what the Secwepemc (Shuswap) chief George Manuel had labelled the Fourth World.

In 1971, Manuel, the president of the National Indian Brotherhood, a leading lobby group, participated in a Canadian delegation that went to Australia and New Zealand to compare indigenous policy. Struck by the common experience of Maori, Australian aborigines, and indigenous Canadians, three years later, he and Michael Posluns conceptualized a Fourth World, essentially the space inhabited by indigenous peoples who were subjected to settler colonialism.[84] Their advocacy of global indigenous identity came during a period that saw growing attention in Canada to the treatment of the country's indigenous population, in part because of increased Canadian self-awareness but also because of mounting indigenous activism. Increasingly common were references to the 'colonial-like legal and administrative framework' imposed upon indigenous people. 'The Indian Act', one legal scholar observed, 'is only more subtle in form, but no less deadly in application, than the brutal means used to abridge the rights of the native peoples in countries such as South Africa and Rhodesia.' 'Why go to Europe or Africa?' asked a contributor to *Cité Libre*. 'We have colonialism at home.'[85] In a 1966 government commissioned report, anthropologist H. B. Hawthorn noted globally 'a dramatic change in the relations between the white and non-white peoples' that had 'increased the salience of race in international affairs, and as a byproduct have done the same for the domestic affairs of multi-racial states', thereby shining a light on Canada's indigenous policies.[86] In effect, the report concluded, it was becoming more common to examine Canadian treatment of indigenous peoples in a broader framework, and the comparisons being drawn were not kind.

Indigenous people themselves were highly cognizant of their colonial status and highly critical of it, and they too drew comparisons. 'Indians and Métis', wrote Howard Adams, 'will need to fight for independence and self-determination like other Third World peoples' and develop a social and political consciousness. Harold Cardinal, a prominent indigenous intellectual, also placed Canada's indigenous peoples within a Third World framework. Conditions of poverty and malnutrition existed not only in Asia and Africa, he pointed out, 'but here in Canada' in indigenous communities.[87] The solution to this situation, as in other instances of colonial domination, was self-determination, a term that emerged front and centre in indigenous activists' lexicon. In 1975, the Dene Nation declared their 'right to be regarded by ourselves and the world as a nation', adding that Africans and Asians 'have fought for and won the right to self-determination ... But in the New World the Native peoples have not fared so well.' Referring to the attention devoted to Quebec, the Native Council of Canada affirmed, 'No other minority in Canada can say that it has a greater right to self-determination than we.'[88]

One spur to increased activism was the Trudeau government's plan to abolish the Indian Act, eliminate Indian Status, and wash its hands of treaty commitments. The goal was to encourage indigenous peoples' 'full and equal participation in the cultural, social, economic and political life of Canada'.[89] The notion sprang from Trudeau's well-intentioned view that all people in Canada should be equal, a standpoint that drove his support for human rights legislation. 'It's inconceivable', he stated in 1969, 'that in any given society one section of the society have a treaty with another section of the society.' The following year, while visiting Australia, he decried the fact that 'we have set the Indians apart as a race'.[90] From the perspective of indigenous politicians, however, Trudeau's policy appeared as another means of assimilation, for although discriminatory, nonetheless Indian Status recognized aboriginals as distinct people. Worse, the plan to unilaterally abolish treaties was a violation of the commitments that Canada had made in those international agreements and carried with it the implication of nullifying indigenous sovereignty. Indigenous groups pushed back, most notably the Indian Chiefs of Alberta, who argued that aboriginals should be recognized as 'citizens plus', a notion coined in the Hawthorn report to denote indigenous people's right to special status as North America's original occupants.[91] Faced with this opposition, the Trudeau government withdrew its plan. 'We will not trust the government with our futures any longer', Cardinal concluded from the situation. 'Now they must listen to and learn from us.'[92]

Indigenous activism took many forms, from protesting stereotypical depictions of indigenous customs at government-sponsored cultural events, such as Expo 67, to the occupation of disputed territory. Often these protests were transnational in nature, a reminder that many indigenous groups did not recognize Canadian sovereignty or the Canada–US border. In 1968, Mohawk from the Akwesasne Reserve bordering Ontario and New York State, occupied the Seaway International Bridge spanning the St Lawrence River. The following year, indigenous activists from Canada took part in a two-year occupation of Alcatraz Island, and in 1974 members of the Ojibway Warrior Society and other groups protested land rights by occupying Anicinabe Park in Kenora, Ontario. That same year, the Native Peoples' Caravan traversed Canada to drum up awareness of indigenous rights and encourage protest on the part of aboriginal people across the country.[93] There were also efforts to forge wider transnational links, a goal for Manuel, who was a driving force behind the Arctic Peoples Conference in Copenhagen in 1973, and the 1977 International NGO Conference on Discrimination Against Indigenous Populations in the Americas in Geneva. The latter conference produced a declaration asserting that indigenous people were subjects of international law, leading indigenous activists to press for UN recognition of this fact.[94]

Activism led to clashes with the federal and provincial governments. In 1971, the Quebec government began a hydroelectric project in James Bay without consulting local Cree and Inuit communities, who then took the matter to court. Following court decisions, in 1975 the federal government and the James Bay Cree negotiated an agreement – the first treaty since the Numbered Treaties – under which land was exchanged for financial compensation, hunting and fishing rights, input into future land governance, and a measure of self-government. Soon concerned that the federal and Quebec governments were failing to live up to the agreement and upset too with other actions by Ottawa, the James Bay Cree lobbied international organizations such as the Organization of American States and the UN, and partnered with a transnational network of environmental and human rights advocates to fight for self-determination.[95] Similar protests were launched against the proposed Mackenzie Valley Pipeline, which would stretch across northern Canada. A 1975 inquiry into the project provided a forum for indigenous leaders to express their opposition not only to the pipeline but to policies that kept aboriginals under 'direct colonial rule'. 'One has to read about South Africa or Rhodesia', stated one northern resident, 'to get a clear picture of what is really happening in Northern Canada.'[96] Justice Thomas Berger, who oversaw the inquiry, ruled against the pipeline, citing environmental and social impacts of the project, and he recommended that the federal government settle land claims issues. Another victory was won by the Nisga'a, who had been forced off their traditional territories in BC without a treaty offering their consent. The Nisga'a had protested the issue for almost a century, and Chief Frank Calder took a complaint against land development to Canada's Supreme Court, which, in 1973 released its decision that indigenous land title existed in Canadian law. 'The fact is', Justice Wilfred Judson stated, 'that when the settlers came, the Indians were there, organized in societies and occupying land as their forefathers had done for centuries. This is what Indian title means.'[97]

Although Trudeau had once proclaimed, 'we won't recognize aboriginal rights', the Calder case led his government to begin negotiating comprehensive land settlement agreements.[98] Furthermore, the Constitution Act of 1982 affirmed indigenous and treaty rights as well as recognition of the Métis and Inuit peoples. Indigenous activists continued to press for Canada to respect these rights, to live up to treaty commitments, and to grant self-determination. Just as they had once gone to the League of Nations to press their case for sovereignty, indigenous people began appearing before the UN Human Rights Committee, creating an embarrassing situation for Canada's government, which was not used to receiving condemnations for human rights violations.[99] 'In terms of realpolitik', Trudeau had mused in 1968, 'French and English are equal in Canada because each of these linguistic groups has the power to break the country. And this power cannot yet be claimed by the Iroquois, the Eskimos, or the Ukrainians.'[100] That assessment changed, and rapidly so, the result of indigenous activism and the opening up of Canadian internal politics to global scrutiny. Moreover, separatists in Scotland, the Basque country, and Catalonia looked to Quebec's independence movement for inspiration.

The blurring of distinctions between local and global was one symptom of the global village. So was the shrinking distance between Canada and the rest of the world. It was the growing global consciousness that prompted Québécois nationalists to identify with Algerians or Chileans, university students to empathize with Vietnamese and Biafrans, and George Manuel to find common cause with other indigenous people around the globe. The sense of interconnectivity created a desire for action, whether promoting the civil rights of anti-apartheid activists in South African jails or pressuring Air Canada to suspend flights to Rhodesia. Through these activities and involvement in development and humanitarian projects, Canadians, such as the youth who took part in Miles for Millions Walkathon hunger marches, developed a 'global helpmate identity' and then projected it abroad.[101] The idea that they naturally had a role to play in making the world a better place formed an important element of the way in which many Canadians conceived of themselves and their country.

This same identity drove support for peacekeeping. During the 1960s and 1970s, Canadians in the peace movement and on the left embraced peacekeeping because it put Canada's military in the position of supporting the UN, as opposed to NATO or the United States. Moreover, peacekeeping provided a means of differentiating Canada from their southern neighbours. Whereas the Americans were napalming Vietnamese peasants, Canadians were keeping the peace in Cyprus, an action befitting 'the neutral, international Good Guy'.[102] This image of the peacekeeper and the wider issue of Canada's international identity came into question during the 1990s, as Canadians confronted a series of humanitarian crises, and then following the September 2001 terror attacks, events that underscored the interconnectedness of the global village.

11

War and peace in the new world order

'This was not a coup d'état', Bill Graham assured fellow MPs in March 2004. 'This was the Security Council of the United Nations acting with the highest authority of the charter to restore order in the area.' Canada's foreign minister was responding to just-deposed Haitian President Jean-Bertrand Aristide's accusations that an international coalition had forced him from office. 'I would like to remind the House', Graham added, 'of all that our country has already done for Haiti.'[1] A recipient of Canadian aid since the 1970s and a focus of Canada's human rights and democracy promotion efforts since the 1980s, Haiti occupies a small place in Canada's overall foreign policy. Canada, however, looms large in Haiti: beginning in the 1990s, the Canadian government was involved in Organization of American States (OAS) and UN efforts premised on bringing order to a country bearing the scars of international ostracism, outside intervention, and despotic rule. Between 1994 and 1997, Canadian soldiers participated in three short-lived UN missions to support Aristide's shaky government, and in February 2004, in the face of an anti-Aristide insurgency led by disaffected military officers, 500 Canadian troops returned to the island as part of the coalition that bundled Haiti's president out of the country and set up an interim government in his place. Aristide's departure under suspicious circumstances and at the hands of foreign powers led activist groups such as the Canada Haiti Action Network and members of the Haitian–Canadian community to charge Ottawa with complicity in a coup. Conservative foreign affairs critic Stockwell Day used a different term. 'This was clearly a regime change', he noted in March 2004. 'Whether we like to admit it or not, we took part.'[2]

Day's use of a phrase associated at that time with the American invasion of Iraq the previous March was embarrassing for the Liberal government. A point of pride for many Canadians was Prime Minister Jean Chrétien's refusal to join the Anglo-American coalition that brought regime change to Baghdad. Since the Iraq invasion lacked UN approval, the Chrétien government grounded its opposition in a defence of the rules-based international order. Yet Canada was no stranger to the use of force. Instead of sending troops to Iraq, Ottawa dispatched soldiers to Afghanistan on a UN-sanctioned, NATO-led nation-building mission cum counter-insurgency campaign. A few years earlier, the Canadian Forces had participated in a war in the Balkans meant to prevent ethnic cleansing, and military assets were deployed to Libya in 2011 and to Iraq beginning in 2014. From the Caribbean and Central Asia to Eastern Europe and North Africa, and for humanitarian and strategic reasons, the post-cold era saw Canadian troops committed almost continually to overseas operations. These missions, and even Canada's storied peacekeeping operations, recalled Canadian participation in British imperial wars in Sudan and South Africa, for they were small conflicts fought far from home to establish order and to demonstrate a commitment to the prevailing international system.

This chapter focuses on Canada's uneasy involvement in international conflict following the cold war. Renewed hopes that the multilateral system created in 1945 could set the world right were followed by a stark realization that traditional peacekeeping was inadequate to deal with the problems of a fractious world. Canada's turn away from peacekeeping alarmed Canadians who fancied their country an honest broker. However, in dispatching military forces to a variety of multilateral missions ranging from peacekeeping to warfighting, successive governments acted on the belief in Canada's responsibility to create order out of chaos. Underlying this sense of mission were the assumptions that failed states like Haiti or Afghanistan required Western assistance and that the international community had a right to intervene. Such thinking mimics the reasoning given by Victorian-era imperialists who professed to act for humanitarian reasons. Indeed, based on decades of experience in peacekeeping operations, Major General Lewis MacKenzie counselled that countries in the Global South saw 'a real danger of "UN colonialism"', and in advocating for US-led multilateral missions to fix failed states, liberal intellectual Michael Ignatieff acknowledged that nation-building required 'temporary imperialism – empire lite'.[3] In the renewed world order that arose after the cold war, Canadians were active promoters of humanitarian imperialism, and in doing so they wrestled with a difficult question that lays at the heart of this chapter: in an interconnected world, how should Canada respond to humanitarian crises and terrorist provocations?

In 1985, Brian Mulroney's Progressive Conservative government released a foreign policy strategy emphasizing growing interconnectedness, what was coming to be called globalization. The document affirmed that 'our security is everyone's security. Conditions abroad touch and change our lives. Tensions between Moscow and Washington, war in the Gulf, a refugee exodus from Indo-China, terrorist murders in London – or Ottawa – all diminish our security and demand our attention. There are few corners of the world which Canadians do not know or care about and few whose circumstances do not affect our welfare.'[4] Covering a range of issues and taking an expansive view of security, this statement was a call for a wide-ranging, global foreign policy, a reminder of how far Canada had come since Mackenzie King. Although many Canadians viewed Mulroney as excessively pro-American in outlook, he and his government backed Canadian involvement in multilateral fora, from the UN and the OAS, to Asia-Pacific Economic Cooperation (APEC) and the Conference on Security and Co-operation in Europe (CSCE). Outlining his approach in a speech to the UN General Assembly, Mulroney affirmed that 'the solitary pursuit of self-interest outside the framework of broader international cooperation is never enough to increase our freedom, safeguard our security, or improve our standard of living'.[5]

The Tory government's multilateralism was matched by support for the United States, the guarantor of the liberal international system, and whereas John Diefenbaker or Pierre Trudeau were circumspect in admitting this fact, Mulroney was not. Meeting with George H. W. Bush in Ottawa shortly after the president's inauguration, he stressed his government's 'loyalty and friendship', and praised Bush as the 'leader of the Alliance'. In a reference to contemporary speculation about the future of American power given rising Japanese economic clout, Mulroney added that he did not view 'the US as a "declining star" '.[6] Over the four-year Bush presidency, the two leaders forged a close relationship, with the American president using his Canadian counterpart as a sounding board and source of advice, particularly on winding up the cold war.[7]

For all the neutralist and nationalist sentiment among Canadians, Canada and the United States remained allies opposed to the Soviet Union. Still, Canadians largely supported détente with the Soviet bloc, including trade, cultural and sports ties, and confidence-building measures between government officials. To this end, in 1983 Ottawa hosted Mikhail Gorbachev, a relatively spry, up-and-coming Soviet official with an interest in Canadian technical programs. During this visit, Gorbachev met Soviet ambassador Aleksandr Yakovlev, an aging apparatchik who had been exiled to Ottawa for his criticism of Moscow's failed economic policies. Yakovlev soon returned to Moscow and became the intellectual force behind Gorbachev's reforms.[8]

Mulroney saw great promise in the developments taking place under Gorbachev. In 1986, his government renewed a Canada–USSR economic agreement that had been suspended with the Soviet invasion of Afghanistan in 1979. The revival of Canadian-Soviet economic contacts led McDonald's Canada, a subsidiary of the American parent company, to partner with the communist government in opening twenty eateries in Russia. Serving the Bolshoi Mac and employing nearly one thousand Russians, the fast food restaurants, in Mulroney's view, were a welcome sign of change behind the iron curtain, and he touted this development to his fellow G7 leaders as evidence that Gorbachev was serious about reform.[9] On a visit to Moscow in November 1989, Mulroney carried with him messages for Gorbachev from Bush. Afterwards, he urged the president to establish a close connection with the Soviet leader: 'If you take care, yet lend a hand, you and Gorbachev will walk together into the history books.'[10] To his enduring credit, Bush expertly managed the cold war's peaceful end in Europe. The Bolshoi Mac, meanwhile, encapsulated US economic and cultural power – the soft power that proved so important to the American victory over the Soviet system.

The Mulroney government took an interest in Europe's post-cold war fate. As the Soviet empire collapsed in Eastern Europe amid peaceful revolutions, Canada was quick to recognize the new governments that arose. Ottawa did the same with the various post-Soviet republics in the Baltics and the Caucasus; with more than one million Canadians tracing their ancestry to Ukraine, Canada was the first country to extend diplomatic relations to Kiev's new government, in December 1991. Ottawa worked to ensure Ukrainian adherence to the Nuclear NPT and the destruction of its nuclear stockpile.[11] Ukraine, the Baltics, and even Russia soon became recipients of Canadian aid programs and economic credits, part of a continuing commitment to ensure European stability alongside election monitoring and democracy promotion. On Germany, the cold war's European epicentre, Mulroney urged his American, Soviet, French, and British counterparts to support reunification and German entry into NATO. With Western European governments objecting to taking advice from a North American country, Mulroney explained to Bush that Canadians 'are not renting our seat in Europe. We paid for it. If people want to know how Canada paid for its seat in Europe, they should check out the graves in Belgium and France'.[12] By 1993, the Mulroney government judged that the European situation was stable enough to withdraw Canadian NATO forces in Germany, ending a four decade long deployment. In a sign of Canada's new priorities, the bulk of these troops were transferred to peacekeeping duties in Somalia and the former Yugoslavia. The latter mission provided a ready-made opportunity to show Canada's ongoing commitment to European security as well as its interest in a United Nations that seemed more relevant and necessary than it had in decades.

On 11 September 1990, before a joint session of Congress, George Bush made the case for the United States to lead an international response to Iraq's invasion of Kuwait. In doing so, the president was careful to note that since Iraq's act of aggression had violated the UN Charter, he would work through the United Nations. With the cold war thaw removing impediments towards the UN functioning as a collective security organization, Bush proclaimed the dawn of a 'new world order' where greater multilateral action was possible. The phrase was a fateful one, for despite its popularity with conspiracy theorists, it accurately described a sense of possibility. That very same day, the UK rock band Jesus Jones celebrated the cold war's end with their hit 'Right Here, Right Now'.[13]

The new world order faced its first test in the Persian Gulf. When Iraqi forces invaded Kuwait in August 1990, they laid siege to foreign embassies, including Canada's mission. After several months holed up in the building, Canadian diplomats surrendered and were paraded alongside other hostages before television cameras. Even without this outrage, Mulroney was invested in confronting Saddam Hussein, the Iraqi despot. The prime minister helped Bush to assemble a broad international coalition that included regional states – Mulroney lobbied Turkey, Egypt, and Jordan to support the US-led effort – and using Canada's non-permanent seat on the Security Council to help secure both international sanctions against Iraq and UN approval to liberate Kuwait should Hussein refuse to withdraw his forces. Furthermore, Mulroney pledged military support, sending three naval vessels, twenty-four aircraft, and a field hospital. Canada's small military contribution had greater political importance, for the prime minister and the president were agreed on the need to preserve 'the multinational aspect' of a mission to expel Iraqi forces.[14] This aspect was an important one in Canada given public wariness of joining an American-led war. Foreign minister Joe Clark vowed that Canada would not support unilateral American action, contending that the international community's response to Iraqi aggression served as 'a litmus test', to show 'that the world is now different'.[15] Here was Canadian affirmation of the new world order.

As the deadline for Iraqi withdrawal approached, the government introduced a motion authorizing the use of force, with Mulroney underscoring that Canada's 'most basic interest lies in the preservation of international law and order'. After several days of debate, the motion passed, with the NDP and a smattering of Liberals opposed to the mission despite UN approval. In words that might have surprised veterans of the Korean conflict and the Second World War, Liberal foreign affairs critic Lloyd Axworthy warned of a 'loss of innocence', for as a constituent had lamented to him, by participating in a military campaign 'it would no longer be possible for Canadians to see themselves in a world where, by wearing a little maple leaf on our lapel, that we would be seen as boy scouts'.[16]

Given the United States' role in the coalition, predictably there was pushback to Canadian involvement from peace groups, aging New Nationalists, and even the World Federalists of Canada. Sounding more like Mackenzie King than the representative of an organization championing multilateralism, the World Federalists' spokesperson explained that 'The problem with collective security is that you have to be prepared to start a war to stop a war … The time has come to recognize the practical limits of the [UN] Charter's collective security system.'[17] The military campaign to enforce collective security proved successful. Kuwait was liberated and, prudently, there was no intervention into Iraq to topple Hussein's regime. Subsequently, dozens of Canadian engineers took part in the years' long effort to douse Kuwaiti oil fields, ignited by retreating Iraqi soldiers. Mulroney welcomed the multinational coalition's victory, emphasizing to his fellow G7 leaders that the 'solidarity shown in the Gulf crisis was one of the finest moments in the UN's history'.[18] For the first time since 1950, the UN had shown itself to be an effective tool of collective security; the conflict had been Canada's first shooting war since Korea. Yet there were voices of caution, who contended that like the Korean War, the Gulf War was a US operation gussied up in multilateral garb and so just as they had been suckered into the cold war, Canadians were deluding themselves into supporting an American new world order.[19]

'Canada will continue as a peacekeeper', Joe Clark assured Canadians worried that the Gulf War marked a turn to militarism. Peacekeeping was one of the tasks performed by Canada's military but as a commentator complained, 'It is the only thing the public think the military are any good for."[20] Fears that the Gulf War marked a sea change were misplaced. Under Mulroney the tempo of Canadian peacekeeping operations swelled. In addition to existing deployments in Cyprus, Palestine, Sinai, the Golan Heights, Lebanon, and the India–Pakistan border, the Tories dispatched peacekeepers and diplomats to UN missions in Afghanistan (1988–9), the Iran–Iraq border (1988–91), Angola (1989–91), Namibia (1989–90), Central America (1989–92), El Salvador (1991–5), and Cambodia (1991–3). These operations occurred in areas destroyed by the cold war, with Canadians picking up after their American allies. In all, between 1988 and 1998 there were thirty-six new UN missions, all with Canadian participation, a peacekeeping renaissance that gave the UN new relevance but that led some observers to muse that the superpower struggle had provided a measure of stability. Barbara McDougall, Clark's successor, was not alone in lamenting the post-cold war world's 'rapid and widespread descent into instability', which required Canadians to be 'activists when it comes to peace and security, especially through the UN'.[21]

In recognition of peacekeeping's renewed importance in what wags dubbed the new world disorder, UN Secretary General Boutros Boutros-Ghali issued *Agenda for Peace,* a call for preventive diplomacy, peacekeeping, peacemaking, and peace enforcement. The latter was a muscular approach viewed as necessary to create conditions of peace in failed or fragile states – countries whose economic and political systems had fractured and that lacked a central government. Whether cobbled together by colonial powers or embroiled in cold war machinations, these states were coming undone leading to intervention by the international community – a perpetuation of outside interference.

Canada itself almost came apart in 1995. A referendum in Quebec on separation saw a razor-thin majority – 50.58 per cent – vote to remain within Canada. This development followed over a decade of constitutional wrangling between Quebec and Canada, and a longer process of heightened Québécois nationalism. It was that latter development that captured the attention of Michael Ignatieff, who was making a name for himself covering the increasing trend of ethnic nationalism and the often violent fracture of multi-ethnic states. In threatening to break up Canada, he postulated that Quebec separatists had much in common with Ukrainian, Kurdish, and Croatian nationalists.[22] At that point, in fact, Canadian peacekeepers were deployed in the former Yugoslavia, a multi-ethnic and multi-religious federation in the bloody process of devolution. 'I hope Quebec stays in Canada', a Canadian peacekeeper in Croatia told a reporter, 'but if they want to leave I hope we let them go … Not turn Canada into this.'[23]

As Yugoslavia collapsed into competing ethno-states intent on capturing territory and expelling opposing ethnic and religious groups, in April 1992 Canada became the first country to contribute to the UN Protection Force (UNPROFOR) in Croatia, mandated to ensure conditions for peace talks and monitor supposedly demilitarized zones. Mulroney dispatched 1,200 peacekeepers to the force. 'The situation is getting critical', he told President Bush. 'The cruelty unimaginable.' Appealing for US involvement in aid of the peacekeeping effort, the prime minister noted that 'we have begun – undercover of the UN – to come together again' as in the Gulf War.[24] Waging an unsuccessful re-election campaign, Bush had little time to devote to the issue. His successor, Bill Clinton, had no initial desire to send US troops to the Balkans, nor did isolationist members of Congress, particularly after a bungled American operation in Somalia. The new world order had its limits, and one American journalist would later deliver a stinging rebuke of US foreign policymakers' unwillingness to confront acts of genocide.[25]

In August 1992, Mulroney stepped up Canada's commitment in the Balkans, sending another 1,200 personnel to a second UNPROFOR in Bosnia. In the trite phrase used at the time, the peacekeepers found little peace to keep.

Instead, they were caught within a multisided war characterized by ethnic cleansing, the indiscriminate killing of civilians, and targeted attacks against the peacekeepers themselves. The peacekeeping force's unclear mandate and inability to defend itself – lacking UN authorization to do so – outraged many of the soldiers, though in September 1993, at Medak, Canadian peacekeepers fought Croat forces bent on massacring Serbian civilians, marking the Canadian Army's first pitched battle since the Korean War. In the face of a worsening situation, Canadian diplomats engaged the CSCE, the UN, and NATO to take a greater role in the war-torn region and confront acts of genocide.[26]

The tipping point was the mass slaughter of eight thousand civilians under UN guard at Srebrenica in 1995. Peace enforcement was judged to be in order and NATO airstrikes brought the warring sides to the peace table. To enforce the resulting accords, Canadian soldiers remained in Bosnia–Herzegovina until 2010, undertaking the frustrating but largely successful task of post-conflict reconstruction.[27] Overall, UN operations in the former Yugoslavia did little to inspire confidence in the UN or in peacekeeping. Cautioning against rash judgements, Major General Lewis MacKenzie, the senior Canadian UNPROFOR officer with decades of peacekeeping experience, pointed out that 'The UN is merely the sum of its parts: the best version we have of an international parliament.'[28]

At the same time as Canadian peacekeepers deployed to Bosnia, another contingent headed to Somalia as part of a UN mission meant to enforce a fragile UN-brokered ceasefire and to assist humanitarian relief efforts. The outbreak of a multisided civil war following the Somali central government's collapse led to a grave famine, with over one-third of the population at risk of starvation. 'We are losing an entire generation of children here', exhorted an aid worker. Other than contributing to the international pool of food aid and airlifting aid shipments, Ottawa had not envisioned a role in the country, but as Barbara McDougall admitted, the government was partly 'driven into Somalia because of the media coverage' and because there were critics in Canada and abroad who asked, 'If Sarajevo, Why Not Somalia?'[29] The implication of racism is ironic, because the mission in Somalia became synonymous with the racist actions of several Canadian soldiers who shot Somali thieves and tortured and murdered a Somali man while fellow soldiers stood by and allowed the crime to continue. An investigation showed that the soldiers' actions were part of a wider pattern of revolting conduct within their unit, the Airborne Regiment, which was disbanded amid a military cover-up and resulting investigations. The Somalia Affair discredited 'the peacekeeping tradition', complained one journalist, and damaged Canada's 'positive self-image to the world'.[30]

Quite apart from these soldiers' reprehensible actions, the experience in Somalia did little to credit peacekeeping. The ceasefire collapsed and with the humanitarian mission increasingly unable to function due to the violent situation, the UN Security Council approved the United States organizing its own force, United Task Force (UNITAF), to secure the relief efforts. Organizing UNITAF was one of President Bush's final acts and he urged Mulroney to devote troops to ensure 'that there be international contributions to make this a sound effort under United Nations auspices'. Mulroney's senior-most advisor agreed with this goal, for although Somalia was characterized by 'the absence of any significant bilateral interests', Canada's interest lay in ensuring a multilateral resolution to the country's security situation.[31] Fatefully, the Airborne Regiment was deployed to UNITAF, along with troops from twenty-three other countries. The American-led task force secured areas of the country and allowed the distribution of food aid, but the wider security situation outside of these areas remained fraught. In June 1993, Canadian forces withdrew, with Ottawa opting against participating in a new UN mission focused on peace enforcement. That mission descended into violent confrontations between Somali gangs and UN forces and, like the situation in the former Yugoslavia, became representative of peacekeeping's changed nature. A peacekeeping effort that Mulroney supported in the hopes that it would showcase multilateralism in action had the opposite effect.[32]

If Yugoslavia showed the failings of traditional peacekeeping and the need for peacemaking, and Somalia made clear peacemaking's limitations, then Rwanda was a swing back in the direction of the necessity of concerted international action. Between April and July 1994, over 800,000 members of the Tutsi group were massacred by Hutu militia, the result of long simmering ethnic tensions with their roots in the Belgian government's colonial policy of divide and rule. The slaughter was shocking, doubly so because a UN force was deployed in-country. Its commander, Canadian Lieutenant General Roméo Dallaire, had warned UN headquarters of the coming conflagration, but his calls were ignored. Although Dallaire's small force protected several thousand civilians, his belief was that with reinforcements and an expanded mandate, he might have been able to prevent the killings or at least reduce their extent. Many critics seized on the incident to show the UN's fecklessness, linking the failure in Rwanda to the ineffectual missions in the Balkans and Somalia. Critical of the organization's failures, Dallaire's true indictment was of the wider international community, 'of which the UN is only a symbol'. Humanity, he lamented, had 'failed to move beyond self-interest for the sake of Rwanda'.[33]

For Canada, what interests were at stake in these far-flung missions? Peacekeeping had always involved elements of danger and confrontation, but Yugoslavia, Somalia, and Rwanda demonstrated the difficulties of operating in multisided conflicts in failed states where peacekeepers were often acting against the wishes of some of the warring parties. The grim experience in these situations undermined Canadian confidence in peacekeeping. 'Canada faces an unpredictable and fragmented world, one in which conflict, repression and upheaval exist alongside peace, democracy and relative prosperity', Jean Chrétien's Liberal government observed in its 1994 defence White Paper. Chrétien saw peacekeeping's political appeal, remarking on his sense that the public felt that 'it is a nice way for Canadians to be present around the world'. 'We are always there, like the Boy Scouts', he added.[34]

It was under Chrétien's watch that Canada's participation in peacekeeping missions began to decline. The slowdown resulted from growing distaste with peacekeeping in failed states, where intervention seemed to be more trouble than it was worth. Furthermore, the military was constrained by the Liberals' austerity measures. Cuts to the defence budget even as troops remained on deployment, complained one senior officer, 'took the Canadian Forces to, and in some cases past, the breaking point'.[35] Among the military's defenders, there was increasing dislike for peacekeeping, a distraction from the military's core function, which was 'to fight wars'. However, this thinking had its own critics, who questioned the adherence to military policies that appeared outdated in a 'globalizing international system'. The Canada 21 Council, a group of leading intellectuals, advocated restructuring the Canadian Forces into a purely peacekeeping force.[36] In the post-cold war world, they wondered, did Canada require a traditional military? Indeed, Canada's tradition up to the cold war had been to keep a small peacetime military.

Enter Lloyd Axworthy, Chrétien's foreign minister from 1996 to 2000. From the Liberal Party's left-wing – he had quit the party briefly over the nuclear weapons issues in 1963 – Axworthy spoke of Canada's 'duty as a global citizen', and of the need to focus not on military matters but on 'peace-building operations', including 'preventive mediation and dialogue; human rights monitoring and investigation; media and police training; judicial reform; and demobilization'. Invoking the concept of 'soft power' – recently coined by Harvard's Joseph Nye – he outlined a foreign policy of negotiation and coalition-building to influence other countries through diplomatic tools, not force.[37] This approach included engaging the growing phalanx of international NGOs and making use of the increasingly interconnected global environment. Even before Axworthy came on board, the Department of Foreign Affairs and International Trade (DFAIT) had begun to work with international NGOs in fora such as the World Conference on Women in Beijing in 1995, the same year that DFAIT issued a White Paper calling for a broadened security policy that looked beyond a 'narrow orientation of managing state-to-state relationships', towards 'the importance of the individual and society for our shared security'.[38]

Axworthy's diplomacy focused on human security, the idea that an individual's security interests were as valid as those of a state. In his view, human security treated 'sustained economic development, human rights and fundamental freedoms, the rule of law, good governance, sustainable development and social equity' on par with 'arms control and disarmament', while also recognizing 'links between environmental degradation, population growth, ethnic conflicts, and migration'.[39] This expansive idea found a constituency in faculty lounges, among international journalists who had witnessed the horrors of Bosnia and Rwanda, with organizations such as environmental and women's groups whose activities had been peripheral in foreign policymaking, and with twelve other like-minded middle powers who joined Canada in forming the Human Security Network, a coalition committed to promoting the concept in multilateral bodies.

In advancing human security, Axworthy threw Ottawa's support behind the International Campaign to Ban Land Mines, an effort by hundreds of international NGOs, including Mines Action Canada, a coalition of forty-five groups, to ban the use of anti-personnel mines and to fund efforts to remove mines from former war zones. This disarmament initiative culminated in the 1997 Ottawa Treaty, shepherded by Axworthy and signed by an overwhelming majority of governments. Additionally, Axworthy played an important role in the negotiations over the Statute of Rome, which set up the International Criminal Court (ICC) to try international crimes of genocide, war crimes, and crimes against humanity. By punishing perpetrators of these horrors, he hoped that the ICC would make a world 'free from the Milosevics, the Idi Amins, the Pol Pots, the Suhartos, the Pinochets, the Hitlers, and all others who wield political power for the benefit of themselves and the destruction of others'.[40] To meet its commitment to the Statute of Rome, in 2000, Canada adopted universal jurisdiction for war crimes, genocide, and crimes against humanity – one of the few countries to do so – meaning that a person could be prosecuted even if they committed these crimes outside of Canada. In 2009, a Rwandan immigrant in Toronto was convicted for his part in the 1994 genocide, the first use of this legislation. Also, under Axworthy Canada devoted attention to the global trade in small arms and to the use of child soldiers.

On the merits alone, these welcome initiatives were a testament to coalition building and network diplomacy between states and NGOs that allowed Axworthy to act independent of Washington. Although members of the Clinton administration supported these developments in principle, in practice US policy was determined by strategic and military interests.[41] Here was a catch, then, for both the Ottawa Treaty and the Statute of Rome lacked the participation of the United States, Russia, and China, as well as a host of what were commonly viewed as 'rogue states' such as North Korea, Libya, and Iraq. The realities of hard power were one sign of human security's limits.

Human security abutted, too, with Canadian efforts to promote trade and investment. Chrétien's government undertook a major effort to expand economic ties beyond the United States, particularly to the Asia-Pacific region, where China and Indonesia – countries with terrible human rights records – loomed large. At the 1997 APEC summit in Vancouver, police cracked down on protestors angered by globalization and by the presence of Indonesia's president. While expanding economic links, the Chrétien government launched bilateral human rights dialogues – quiet diplomacy – with China and Indonesia as well as Cuba. In comments indicative of a long-standing Canadian position on such matters, Chrétien argued that isolating bad regimes was 'the worst recipe' for promoting rights, and Axworthy contended that trade and rights were 'not mutually exclusive, but mutually reinforcing'.[42] Certainly this approach was good for business. In terms of rights promotion, engagement proved less than fruitful.

The Canadian government's support of business interests, implicit or otherwise, was understandable, but it was at odds with the moralism of human security. For instance, the Canadian arms industry maintained a healthy export market that included several suspect regimes. Capturing much attention, though, was Calgary-based Talisman Energy's investment in an oil project in Sudan in 1998, a move denounced by human rights groups who pointed to the prevalence in that country of slavery and state-organized violence. Axworthy appointed a commission to study Sudan's human security situation. The report was unstinting – 'There are few other parts of the world where human security is so lacking' – but Canada's foreign minister turned a blind eye towards it: months after the report was issued, a diplomatic mission was opened in Khartoum. The reason for its existence, Canada's first envoy to the country admitted, 'was oil'.[43] Facing considerable public pressure, Talisman withdrew from Sudan and the incident became a reminder of the tension between Canadian economic interests and international human rights policy. Soon after, Sudan's Darfur region became the scene of genocidal acts carried out by government-supported militia against the non-Arab populace. Although Prime Minister Paul Martin pledged 'whatever is required' to intervene in Darfur, Canada and the international community, divided by the Iraq War, stood by in the face of the slaughter.[44]

Axworthy was not the only Canadian to push human security. The concept was embraced by human rights groups, such as Amnesty International, which were already engaged in promoting rights abroad. Canadian diplomat Robert Fowler helped engineer the Kimberley Process on blood diamonds, and General John de Chastelain, the Canadian military's former commander, co-chaired the peace process in Northern Ireland and oversaw the efforts to decommission the weapons held by Irish paramilitary groups. Jurists Louise Arbour and Jules Deschênes served at the International Criminal Tribunals for Yugoslavia and Rwanda, and from 2004 to 2008 Arbour was the UN High Commissioner for Human Rights. Roméo Dallaire devoted his post-military career to stopping the use of child soldiers, a focus, too, of the War Child charity, an international NGO founded by Canadian physician Samantha Nutt, whose medical career took her to Iraq, Afghanistan, Somalia, and other war-torn hotspots. Stephen Lewis, a former Canadian UN ambassador, battled the spread of HIV and AIDS in Africa, an issue that assumed major importance in the late 1990s and early 2000s.[45] These activities were just some of the ways in which Canadian individuals and organizations sought to act upon humanitarian principles and to engage internationally, through the state system, or transnationally, beyond it.

The Axworthy years saw a flurry of diplomatic activity either helping people in strife-torn countries or serving to right injustices, but did it advance Canadian national interests? One former diplomat chided the Chrétien government for wasting time on these initiatives, announcing that it was 'time we set aside our Pearsonian internationalism and took a crack at self-interest'. Among analysts concerned with hard power and state security, it became de rigueur to underline that human security did little to promote Canadian national interests at least as understood in terms of realpolitik. In the view of these figures, it was important that Canada embrace a more narrowly focused foreign policy lest it be 'cast as a Boy Scout imperialist, the busybody of international politics with a right to butt into everyone's business'.[46] Other academics dismissed Axworthy's positions as 'pulpit diplomacy', full of stirring but empty moralism, or as 'Pinchpenny Diplomacy', for under the Liberals not only was there a shrinking military capability but a slashed aid budget and cuts to the foreign service, actions that limited Canada's international presence.[47]

When necessary, Canada's approach to human security embraced airstrike diplomacy. Responding to ethnic cleansing in Kosovo, the restive Serbian province, the Chrétien government joined its NATO allies in fighting what diplomat Paul Heinbecker characterized as 'a war of values, a war for Human Security'.[48] As NATO's first war, undertaken not for collective security, but to end Serbian violence against the Kosovar Albanian populace, it marked a new role for the alliance. With the failure of diplomatic pressure, in March 1999 the air campaign began. Although there had been unanimous support in the House of Commons on the issue when the government had asked for political backing of its diplomatic initiatives and even military intervention, the NDP later retracted its support as the operation wore on; iconoclast NDP MP Svend Robinson even travelled to Belgrade to survey the warzone. Canada's eighteen CF-18 fighter-bombers flew 10 per cent of the combat sorties, a significant contribution to the 78-day bombing campaign whose utility in ending the ethnic cleansing remains a subject of debate. What seems to have forced a Serbian capitulation was a threatened NATO ground offensive, a development that Chrétien and British Prime Minister Tony Blair had spearheaded at the alliance's 50th anniversary conference in April 1999.[49] By June, with NATO troops massing on its borders, Belgrade sued for peace. 'It is a great success you got, that we got collectively', Chrétien told Clinton, 'to be able to remain together' during the alliance's first war.[50] As with Bosnia, in Kosovo Canada participated in post-conflict reconstruction – nation-building as it came to be called.

While steeped in moralism, the Kosovo war was fought under a cloud. NATO had acted without Security Council backing, with Russia supporting Serbia out of pan-Slavic solidarity, and the Chinese sceptical of human rights and dubious of a campaign challenging state sovereignty. Thus, intervention in Kosovo proceeded in violation of international law. Given the need to halt ethnic cleansing, Axworthy defended the allies' actions as justified under the circumstances. 'The policies that I espoused', he noted several years later, 'were founded on the premise of protecting people against violence and force. Yet it was those very principles that impelled me towards accepting the need for military action as a last resort. It was evident that 'hard power' might have to be used to protect against the abuses and atrocities that has become so endemic in the Balkans.'[51] Compared to the failings of UN peacekeeping in Somalia and Rwanda, military force had shown itself to be a more effective if extreme means of promoting human security. Over the next few years Western powers intervened to end brutal atrocities: Australia and New Zealand in East Timor (1999), and Britain in Sierra Leone (2000).

The question of whether the international community was justified in defending human rights even if it meant waging war was the focus of the International Commission on Intervention and State Sovereignty, formed by the Canadian government in partnership with UN Secretary General Kofi Annan. Made up of eminent human rights scholars and civil servants from a dozen countries – including Canadians Michael Ignatieff, Gisèle Côté-Harper, and Ramesh Thakur – the commission articulated the idea of Responsibility to Protest (R2P). The concept holds that humanitarian intervention is justified to prevent genocide, war crimes, ethnic cleansing, and crimes against humanity, and that state sovereignty provides no barrier to action by the international community. By challenging the fundamental principle of state sovereignty, R2P proved controversial, with countries in the Global South fearful that it gave the West carte blanche to meddle in their affairs. At the UN's September 2005 World Summit, held to honour the organization's sixtieth anniversary, Canadian lobbying secured R2P's unanimous acceptance, but only as a principle, not as an international law, with interventions to proceed only with Security Council approval.

International caution over R2P was parroted by domestic critics of peacekeeping and the human security agenda. Kosovo had outraged the usual suspects – peace groups and anti-US activists – as well as Serbian-Canadians and a smattering of establishment figures who objected to the war's illegal nature, including historian Michael Bliss, who professed that he was 'ashamed to be Canadian', and former diplomat James Bissett, who emerged later as an apologist for Serbian acts of genocide.[52] Canadian foreign policy had undergone quite a change over three decades. Outlining his opposition to Canadian involvement in international action against Nigeria over the Biafran war in the late 1960s, Pierre Trudeau had emphasized his respect for state sovereignty and his awareness of the colonial attitudes underpinning calls for intervention. With Kosovo, a change had occurred, in part because the moral universe had expanded since the 1960s as a human rights revolution transformed domestic politics in much of the West and with it, international relations. 'Human rights doctrine is now so powerful, but also so unthinkingly imperialist in its claim to universality, that it has exposed itself to serious intellectual attack', Ignatieff warned in 2001. Across the Global South there were doubts about the universality of human rights, which were viewed as 'just another cunning exercise in Western moral imperialism', a troubling development for rights advocates who emphasized the important adjective in the Universal Declaration of Human Rights.[53] Debate raged over whether the UN and the wider international community should stand aside in the face of crimes against humanity or whether intervention should proceed even if, as in the case of Somalia, there was no central authority with which to negotiate permission to distribute food aid to starving people, or in Liberia, where authority fell to warlords such as Charles Taylor and General Butt Naked. Realists, meanwhile, questioned whether it was in Canada's interest to spend blood and treasure on fixing problems in far-flung countries. Dismissing concerns along these lines regarding Canadian peacekeeping in the Balkans and Somalia, Barbara McDougall quipped that 'real life is not political science'.[54] Here was the dilemma for foreign policymakers.

While Kosovo had been an exercise in hard power and a demonstration of Canada's commitment to the Western alliance, among Canadians focused on traditional foreign policy concerns, the Chrétien years remained a period of deep retrenchment for Canada on the world stage. A group of eminent foreign policy analysts concluded that the Liberals' failure to invest in the military, aid, and diplomatic personnel and to devote attention away from human security towards major strategic issues meant that 'Canada has slipped badly in international influence'.[55] *Who Killed the Canadian Military?* asked the country's leading military historian in a bestselling polemic. Another bestseller carried the ominous title *While Canada Slept: How We Lost Our Place in the World*.[56] Even among liberal internationalists who championed Axworthy's policies there was a lament for the lack of investment in the infrastructure of Canadian foreign policy and in formulating a long-term strategy to shape the international environment in ways to benefit Canada. 'Either we make the choices that will allow us to thrive on the North American continent and contribute actively in creating a better world', wrote Jennifer Welsh, the Oxford academic and champion of a globally-engaged foreign policy, 'or we will cease to exist – in anything but name – as a sovereign country.'[57]

John Manley, Axworthy's successor, offered the trenchant observation that Canadians were 'still trading on a reputation that was built two generations and more ago – but that we haven't continued to live up to. You can't just sit at the G8 table and then, when the bill comes, go to the washroom.'[58] This remark came soon after the 11 September 2001 terrorist attack, an event that appeared to transform US foreign policy, heightening ongoing debates about Canada's position in the world.

For Americans, the terror attack was alarming, not simply because of the tremendous loss of life and damage to symbolic buildings, but because they demonstrated that even a country of unprecedented military and economic power was vulnerable to nineteen men armed with box-cutters. The American declaration of an open-ended global war on terror testified to the psychological shock. In March 2003, following Chrétien's announcement that Canada would not join the US-led invasion of Iraq, American Ambassador Paul Cellucci wrote of his doubts 'that the Canadian leadership and public understand, at a fundamental level, the implications of the 2001 terrorist attacks on America and the depth of US commitment to preventing a recurrence of such attacks'.[59] Certainly, Canadian officials, the press, and many average Canadians were alarmed by the George W. Bush administration's belligerence. Even before the attacks, a leading columnist had complained that Washington was full of 'military hawks and diplomatic unilateralists who reflect a mixture of Republican muscularity, American triumphalism and deep-seated US exceptionalism'.[60] The war on terror only magnified such views. Meeting with Bush at the White House two weeks after 9/11, Chrétien was alarmed when the president professed finding it difficult 'to manage the bloodlust of the American people'.[61] During his 2002 State of the Union speech, Bush proclaimed the need to confront the 'Axis of Evil' – coined by Canadian-American speechwriter David Frum – the improbable alliance of Iraq, Iran, and North Korea, and rhetoric that John Manley dismissed as 'bellicose'. Pre-emptive warfare became the centrepiece of the Bush's administration's 2002 *National Security Strategy.* 'The United States has a totally different perspective than we do on the world', Bill Graham, Manley's successor, had explained earlier in the year. 'They feel they can have their will.'[62] The question of pre-emptive war against Iraq assumed centre stage.

Over the autumn of 2002, the Americans began making the case that Saddam Hussein's regime, having stockpiled weapons of mass destruction (WMDs), represented a threat to world peace. Against such assertions, Graham struck a note of caution: Hussein was 'always a threat, but we have no evidence he is in possession of [WMDs] or that he would intend to use them at this time'.[63] The Americans continued pressing this notion as did the British government, and external and internal pressure mounted on the Chrétien government to support the White House. Chrétien responded by emphasizing the need for both multilateral action and evidence of a threat. Should the Security Council authorize force, he vowed in October 2002, then 'We will do our duty'.[64] One of the hallmarks of the Canada–US relationship is the intelligence sharing between security agencies, part of the wider Five Eyes network. Evidently, the available intelligence on Iraq's WMDs did little to convince Canadian policymakers of an imminent threat. Nor did Secretary of State Colin Powell's February 2003 presentation to the UN outlining the case against Hussein. 'I wouldn't have been able to convince a judge of the municipal court in Shawinigan with the evidence I was given', Chrétien later quipped.[65] With war clouds gathering, he used a speech at the Chicago Council on Foreign Relations to reaffirm that 'if it must come to war, I argue that the world should respond through the United Nations.' At the suggestion of Defence Minister John McCallum, Chrétien added that it was 'imperative to avoid the perception of a "clash of civilizations" ', a repudiation of some of the dangerous rhetoric then popular via Harvard academic Samuel Huntington's nativist screeds. Indeed, Bill Graham informed his British counterpart that 'an "Anglo-Saxon" coalition of the United States, Britain, Australia, and Canada was a political non-starter' among Canadians, a comment belying sentimental patter – voiced by neoconservatives on both sides of the Atlantic – about the essential unity of the English-speaking peoples in forging a new world order opposed to "evil".[66]

Chrétien's position was clear: Canada would go to war if Iraq could be shown to be violating its UN obligations regarding its weapons program and if there was UN authorization for the use of force. This stance was at odds with Canada's Anglo-American allies, though Ottawa left the door open to a Kosovo-style mission, but only if there was a clear threat from Iraq.[67] Unlike French President Jacques Chirac and German Chancellor Gerhard Schröder, who actively and vocally opposed Bush and Tony Blair, Chrétien was not malicious in his opposition. Not all Canadians were so polite. One Liberal MP dismissed the Americans as 'bastards' and a Chrétien aide called Bush a 'moron'. Americans took note. 'When even the Canadians, normally drearily polite, get colorfully steamed at us', a New York Times columnist observed, 'we know the rest of the world is apoplectic.'[68] Meanwhile, in February and March 2003 hundreds of thousands of Canadians took to the streets, part of a global wave of protests against the coming war. Addressing a crowd of two hundred thousand in Montreal, environmentalist David Suzuki announced, 'We are here as global citizens to show our firm opposition to the Bush administration's high handed policies of ignoring the dissenting opinions in the UN.' On 17 March, with the coalition set to invade Iraq, Chrétien offered his definitive statement on the matter, though it was a position that had been consistent for months. 'If military action proceeds without a new resolution in the Security Council', he told the House of Commons, 'Canada will not participate.' Opposition leader Stephen Harper, a staunch conservative, denounced Chrétien's stance as 'gutless – these guys are just reading the polls. We have historically as a country stood beside our best friends and allies ... that's where we should be now.'[69] On both counts, Harper was correct. Polls backed Chrétien's decision, and Canada's traditional allies – other than France and New Zealand – were committed to the war.[70] Although historical alliances are important, Canadian history is replete with instances – Chanak, Suez, Vietnam – where Canada broke with its allies because policymakers judged that there were interests at stake beyond solidarity.

Given the Kosovo war, the Americans had a reasonable expectation that Canada might have joined the coalition of the willing regardless of whether there was a UN stamp of approval. 'For those of us who worked so hard to persuade Canadians on the Iraq question', Ambassador Paul Cellucci reflected, 'it was a truly bitter disappointment.' With White House approval, Cellucci publicly rebuked Canada, stressing that the Bush administration was 'disappointed that Canada is not supporting us'.[71] Worried about the break with Washington, in the House of Commons Chrétien moved a motion in support of the US and British effort in Iraq and he urged Canadians to withhold criticism of their allies. But he doubled down on his position: 'We would have preferred to have been able to agree with our friends but we, as an independent country, make our own decisions based on our own principles, such as our longstanding belief in the value of a multilateral approach to global problems.'[72] A week later, in a further reprimand, Bush cancelled his planned visit to Ottawa, meeting, instead, with Australia's John Howard – an Iraq War backer – at his Texas ranch.

Chrétien's Iraq decision put him at odds with a sizeable chunk of Canadians who had advocated for Canada to join the effort to topple Hussein's regime, including the opposition conservative Canadian Alliance party, several provincial premiers, and even Wayne Gretzky, the expatriate hockey legend. Graham recalled that in airport business lounges he 'was set upon by every business executive in the room rushing over to scream at me for risking his exports to the United States or making his life uncomfortable in New York'. To allay American anger, Harper and Stockwell Day assured *Wall Street Journal* readers, 'Canadians Stand with You.'[73] Some of these figures supported the Bush administration's rationale for intervention; others backed Canadian involvement in the war less on the merits of the danger posed by Saddam Hussein than on the danger posed by vengeful Americans. Allan Gotlieb, a retired diplomat and among the most effective Canadian ambassadors to have served in Washington, complained that the Chrétien government was damaging Canada–US relations. 'We all want Canada to be sovereign and able to make its own policies in the world', stated historian J. L. Granatstein. 'But we also want to eat regularly.'[74] This reasoning for war was premised on the deep economic integration between the two countries, an important fact to be sure, and one that recalled New Nationalist criticisms over Vietnam, namely that Canadian dependence on the United States placed limits on Canada's foreign policy. Happily, fears of American economic retaliation were overblown, the North American economy continued to hum, and tens of thousands of travellers carried on their daily cross-border traffic albeit amid the heightened security measures of the post-9/11 era.

The demonstration of Canadian independence on Iraq had its limits. On the same day Chrétien announced that Canada would sit out the war, Canada's deputy foreign minister told the US and British envoys in Ottawa that although they would not join the military mission, Canadian personnel and units in the region would remain in place. The Canadians, the US embassy reported, were 'prepared to be as helpful as possible in the military margins'.[75] In February 2003 Canadian officers had assumed command of Task Force 151 in the Persian Gulf, a naval force connected to the Afghan war but on Iraq's periphery. In addition to the five Canadian warships devoted to the task force, thirty-one Canadian army officers were on exchange with US and British units involved in the Iraq operation. The Canadian government opted to continue the exchange program to keep defence ties with its allies intact. In the opinion of Department of National Defence legal advisors, these personnel implicated Canada as a belligerent. DFAIT officials and Chrétien countered that what mattered was that Canada had not declared war.[76] Given their rebukes of Canada's government, the Americans were clearly upset with the lack of political support, even as they recognized, as Cellucci did two days after publicly criticizing Chrétien, that 'ironically, Canada's indirect military contributions to the Gulf region' and its involvement in Afghanistan 'are far more significant than those of most of the coalition members'. Weeks later, Cellucci added that Canada had 'stepped up to the plate internationally in the war on terrorism'.[77] As with Canada's complicity or lack thereof in the Vietnam War, whether military involvement at the margins in Iraq overshadows Canada's public refusal to back the war and to formally commit troops no doubt depends on one's political outlook.

Cellucci had highlighted the connection between Iraq and Afghanistan, where the Canadian military was preparing to deploy. Operation Athena, based in Kabul, was Canada's contribution to the International Security Assistance Force (ISAF), the UN-authorized, NATO-led mission supporting the new Afghan government and the Western alliance's main contribution to the war on terror. Focused on providing security in the Afghan capital and its environs to allow the government and UN agencies to operate, Athena bore much in common with Canada's peacemaking and post-conflict nation-building efforts in the Balkans. The security aspect was vital because of the insurgency waged against the Afghan government and the international coalition by remnants of the Taliban, the medieval Islamist movement that had ruled much of Afghanistan and had harboured the terrorists responsible for the 9/11 attacks. Athena was Canada's second mission in the country. Operation Apollo (2001–3) had supported the Americans after they successfully toppled the Taliban regime and had involved a mix of military action to rout terrorists and efforts to assist Afghanistan's transitional government. In its deliberations over undertaking Operation Athena, the Liberal Cabinet had concluded that a military contribution to ISAF precluded involvement in the Iraq War, a point accepted by US Defense Secretary Donald Rumsfeld when it was put to him by his Canadian counterpart.[78]

The Kabul mission lasted until 2005, when Paul Martin's short-lived Liberal government opted to shift Athena to Kandahar province, the Taliban insurgency's epicentre. Taking seriously the idea that the Chrétien years were marked by Canadian retrenchment from the world, Martin pursued a foreign policy grounded in re-engaging multilateral institutions and reinvesting in both the military and the relationship with the United States. Kandahar was the price of entry. 'As members of NATO, which is after all a self-defence pact, we had a moral if not legal duty to support them', recounted Martin. 'We also had a self-interest in doing so.'[79] However, management of the war – for Athena's second phase in Kandahar was very much a combat situation – fell to Stephen Harper, who succeeded Martin in 2006. Having backed Canada's involvement in Afghanistan from the start, Harper, like Martin, sought a re-energized international presence. Harper's problem was that his Conservatives had a minority government and the opposition NDP and separatist Bloc Québécois opposed the war as did several Liberal MPs. Ahead of a close but successful 2008 vote on extending Athena until 2011, Harper arranged for former Liberal cabinet minister John Manley to study the commitment to Afghanistan. Manley recommended continued involvement in the country, citing Canada's 'obligations to the international community' and its record in the 'promotion and protection of human security in fragile states'.[80] The Afghan mission became the culmination of over a decade of Canadian foreign policy, a natural outgrowth of the frustrations over UN peacekeeping in Rwanda and Somalia and allied success in Kosovo.

Canadian involvement in Afghanistan was multisided. Ottawa planners envisioned a 'three-block war' or a 3D approach, mixing diplomacy, development, and defence. Diplomatic efforts included outreach to local communities and support for the Afghan government in establishing sovereignty. Afghanistan became a substantial recipient of Canadian official development assistance, with government and NGO development programs focused on public works, mine removal, teacher training, and microfinance projects, much of it geared to promoting women's engagement in society.[81] However, in Kabul but especially in Kandahar, Athena's primary focus was on defence. On the nature of Canada's counter-insurgency, campaign General Rick Hillier, the head of Canada's military, was blunt: 'We are the Canadian Forces, and our job is to be able to kill people.' Those people, Hillier explained, were 'detestable murderers and scumbags'.[82] This honesty was unsettling to the many Canadians who saw Canada's soldiers as peacekeepers. In a display of dishonesty, in their public comments federal politicians from all parties purposefully and consistently avoided the term 'war', instead using 'mission', an attempt to downplay the unpalatable military reality. This pusillanimity stemmed from political calculations about Canadian discomfort with the war, an assessment seen also in government aversion to casualties, a factor that commanders in the field kept in mind.[83]

Supporting the military benefitted the Conservatives politically, but the war did not. Public backing was never strong, and the Kandahar mission and the increased casualties that came with it, generated an uptick in opposition, though this sentiment was largely stable over the course of the conflict. For political and military reasons Harper had written off the war by March 2009, telling an interviewer that 'we're not ever going to defeat the insurgency'; that May he gave his last speech on the conflict even though Canadian troops remained in-country until 2011.[84] When Operation Athena was wrapped up, Harper spoke in glowing terms of a mission accomplished: 'The world came to Afghanistan because Afghanistan had become such a terrible and brutal place – it had become a threat to the entire world. Whatever the challenge and troubles that remain, Afghanistan is no longer a threat to the world.'[85] The insurgency continued, as did the international nation-building effort, and facing allied pressure for continued Canadian involvement, Harper agreed to a new commitment. 'Deep down my preference would be, would have been, to see a complete end to the military mission', the prime minister admitted as he announced that a small contingent of personnel would take part in training Afghan police and military forces.[86] The training mission concluded in March 2014, bringing an end to Canada's longest war.

Domestically, Afghanistan was a source of controversy, though thankfully the histrionics were nothing like the Great War divide. For the war's supporters, there was a vital need to ensure that Afghanistan would no longer harbour terrorists. 'This is not an American fight; it is ours', the Globe and Mail had declared in October 2001. There was recognition that Canada had a role to play in Afghanistan because the war was multilateral, authorized by the UN, and in fulfilment of alliance commitments to NATO and to the Americans. Recognizing the discomfort that some Canadians felt over the war, Michael Ignatieff pointed out that the war's opponents needed to confront the fact 'that the Afghan mission is multilateralism in action'.[87] To show their support for the troops, though not necessarily the war, Canadians displayed yellow ribbon decals on their cars and wore red clothing to work each Friday.[88] The war's opponents had their own cultural signifier, the white poppy, a long-standing symbol of peace that provoked paroxysms of hate from the Royal Canadian Legion. The opposition of peace groups, anti-globalization activists, and labour unions stemmed from the obvious fact that the Canadian Forces had abandoned peacekeeping and were committed to a war, one subsumed within the larger war on terror. Beyond knee-jerk anti-Americanism, many of the criticisms about the war involved important concerns about the long-term goals of Canadian and allied strategy in Afghanistan and about Canada's affiliation with a US approach to fighting terrorism that was open-ended in scope and scale. Beyond abetting American imperialism, critics seized upon statements by conservative politicians, outspoken soldiers, aging historians, and a blowhard former hockey coach to allege a conspiracy to transform Canadians into unthinking militarists and Canada into a 'warrior nation'.[89]

The military's defenders included figures pleased that Afghanistan marked 'a major step away from the "blue helmet" peacekeeping that Canadians in general seemed to believe was all their troops did'.[90] However, the turn away from traditional peacekeeping had begun nearly a decade earlier, in the killing fields of Rwanda and the Balkans. And it continued: in 2011, the same mix of humanitarian motivation and strategic support for multilateralism that drove the Chrétien government to commit to the air war over Kosovo led Harper to deploy Canadian forces to Libya, where Muammar Qaddafi's despotic regime was coming undone amid protests and a growing armed revolt connected to the wider Arab Spring. Qaddafi's indiscriminate killing of civilian protestors led the UN Security Council to invoke R2P. 'Far from protecting the Libyan people against peril', Harper stated in an invocation of the concept's basic premise, Gadhafi 'is the root cause of the dangers they face'.[91] NATO's seven-month campaign, under the operational command of Canadian Lieutenant General Charles Bouchard, enabled Gadhafi's fall from power. However, with no international engagement after the fact – a sharp difference from Kosovo – Libya descended into chaos.

Airstrike diplomacy was contemplated in autumn 2013, after the Syrian military employed poison gas against civilians, the latest outrage committed by government forces in Syria's brutal civil war. Western powers, Canada included, moved to the brink of war, until Britain's Parliament and the US Congress nixed the idea of intervention. Lloyd Axworthy was among intervention's Canadian advocates. Along with another Chrétien-era minister, he urged the invocation of R2P against 'the monstrous regime' in Damascus.[92] Without its allies, however, Canada's government was unwilling and unable to act alone, a reminder of the practical limits on Canadian military power. Syria, meanwhile, became a gaping wound in the heart of Eurasia, spawning a refugee crisis of significant geopolitical proportions. Whether concerted intervention would have helped the situation remains unknown, but international inaction proved disastrous. Indeed, in the 2015 Canadian federal election, the Conservatives' disregard for Syrian refugees – including the death of Alan Kurdi, a young boy photographed dead on a beach – contributed to their defeat at the polls, a stark reminder of global interconnectedness.

Canada's experiences with conflict during the post-cold war era reveals two important themes. First, successive governments shared a willingness to use Canada's military as a tool of statecraft, a fact as true about peacekeeping as it is about the military operations in Afghanistan, Libya, and Kosovo. Whether Canadian national interests were better advanced via peacekeeping missions or through war the point remains that Canadian soldiers were used to achieve specific goals including an overarching commitment to the US-led liberal international order signified by the UN and NATO. From Chanak to Iraq, Canadian officials had been careful about delimiting the extent of Canada's involvement in overseas campaigns. Yet, since 1885, when volunteers travelled west to crush the Métis and east to fight the Sudanese, Canadian policymakers have been no strangers to using military force for imperial purposes. While controversial, the use of Canada's military to bring order out of chaos has had its supporters. In 1932, two Canadian destroyers had helped to suppress a suspected communist uprising in El Salvador. 'Lucky for Salvador!' the Toronto *Globe* enthused, adding that 'at last from the mist of the sea, Canada emerges as a naval power . . . The Dominion's fleet is roaming the oceans in search of adventure; and finding it.' Eighty years later, the same newspaper praised involvement in Afghanistan, a war through which Canada 'at last shook off the myth of Canadian pacifism – of Canada almost solely as a peacekeeping nation, unable to shoot back – and reconnected with its past as a fighting force on the side of good, not shrinking from a challenge.'[93]

Second, while Canada's involvement in post-cold war conflicts has a long pedigree and came about from a mix of motives – commitments, variously, to the UN, NATO, the United States, human security – the overarching context was globalization. Growing interconnectivity, from ease of travel to the instantaneous transmission of information – whether images of humanitarian catastrophe or epistles from terrorist leaders to their adherents – created a new security environment predicated on the blurring of borders and the annihilation of distance. 'By taking the war on terrorism to [terrorists'] doorstep', Toronto's *National Post* stated in making the case for war in Afghanistan, 'it helps to keep them away from our own.' Similarly, in a defence of R2P, Louise Arbour, serving as UN High Commissioner for Human Rights, contended that in an interconnected world, states could no longer claim the status of 'impotent and powerless bystander.'[94] Nearly two decades earlier, as the new world order dawned, Lloyd Axworthy had questioned the continued relevance of state sovereignty, observing that this notion 'does not fit our growing interdependence'. Several weeks later, with Canadian officials weighing responses to the growing Yugoslav crisis, Brian Mulroney urged 're-thinking the limits of national sovereignty in a world where problems respect no borders'.[95] We turn now to other aspects of globalization and their impact upon Canada and the world.

12

Globalization redux

Between 1983 and 1985, following a decade of civil war, eight million Ethiopians became victims of a devastating famine, during which one million people died. 'I cannot remember in my entire adult life such scenes of such unendurable human desolation', Stephen Lewis, Canada's UN ambassador, stated after touring the country.[1] Canadians had responded to earlier humanitarian crises, for instance, in Belgium and Armenia during the First World War, but what was unprecedented about Ethiopia was the medium of television. Through a groundbreaking report from Ethiopia in November 1984, CBC reporter Brian Stewart brought scenes of the famine into Canadian living rooms. In the face of a growing outcry, Canada's government appealed to the public for help in collecting relief funds. 'One of the faults in past Canadian foreign policy', Prime Minister Brian Mulroney reflected, 'was that the Canadian people were shut out.'[2] Canadians donated tens of millions of dollars for food aid, all of it matched by Ottawa, and millions more were raised through campaigns by charities, and through celebrity appeals: British and Irish singers asked, 'Do They Know It's Christmas?'; Americans artists sang, 'We Are the World'; and Canadian musicians, including Anne Murray, Oscar Peterson, and Bryan Adams, contributed 'Tears Are Not Enough'.[3] In explaining Canadians' outpouring of interest in starving people half a world away, foreign minister Joe Clark stated that the constituents in his rural Alberta riding 'don't read [Food and Agriculture Organization] reports, but they do watch television'. Similarly, NDP MP Pauline Jewett attributed public support to television, which created a sense of there being a 'global village'.[4]

Canada's place in a globalized world is the focus of this, the final chapter. Globalization has been discussed previously, notably the global period that unfolded in the decades leading up to the First World War. As in that earlier era, globalization a century later was characterized by a blurring of borders and a conflation of global and local, the result of technological changes. The global village had emerged in the 1960s – the Sixties were a global event – but the developing sense of interconnection accelerated in the 1980s, generating great enthusiasm about the possibilities available to Canada through liberalized trade, a flow of people from around the world, and the spread of democracy, human rights, and other ideas. 'Canadians are on the road to global citizenship', enthused Lloyd Axworthy, foreign minister from 1996 to 2000; 'we win in a stable, equitable, cooperative world.'[5] Canadians were at globalization's epicentre. 'Based on the standard measure of information technology, finance, trade, travel, personal communications and international engagement', a Privy Council Office assessment put it, 'Canada is in fact considered to be one of the most globalized nations in the world.'[6] The process of globalization mirrored developments in Canada–US relations. 'Does the 49th Parallel Matter Any More?' asked two academics at the turn of the millennium.[7] But globalization had its discontents, who objected to growing economic and cultural integration, which often seemed akin to Americanization. Yet even its opponents used the spread of global communications to advance their causes and build transnational networks. In 2017, as they approached the 150th anniversary of Confederation, Canadians wrestled with their place within a shrinking world.

The New Nationalist fixation with the United States was not reciprocated. For the Americans, Canada was hardly a priority, and the issues that animated the diplomatic relationship were far from earth shattering. 'I hope you haven't come to talk to me about the sex life of the salmon', US Secretary of State Henry Kissinger once joked to Canada's ambassador.[8] Although New Nationalism grabbed headlines, the range of transborder issues confronting Canadian and American officials generated increasing intergovernmental contacts. Managing salmon stocks, tackling transborder criminal networks, and dealing with pollution became joint efforts as Canadian ministries established their own contacts and working relationships with the equivalent agencies or departments in the United States. Provincial and state governments built ties as well. 'I don't run an embassy here', Marcel Cadieux, Canada's ambassador in Washington in the early 1970s, complained of the constant flow of dignitaries and bureaucrats. 'I run a pissoir and a hot dog stand and no one comes near me unless they want to use one or the other.'[9] Bypassing traditional diplomatic channels, the day-to-day cooperation between government officials on a host of issues became a hallmark of Canada–US relations.

   The plethora of bilateral contacts, including civil society links – service clubs, academic societies, university exchange programs – formed the basis for what several American political scientists labelled 'transnational and transgovernmental relations'. One of these analysts, Joseph Nye, expanded upon this idea, and with colleague Robert Keohane he used the Canadian–American relationship as the basis of a concept, 'complex interdependence'. Like the North Americanists five decades earlier, Nye and Keohane applauded the range of contacts between the two neighbours, their avoidance of coercive diplomacy, and the Americans' willingness to deal with Canada largely on equal terms.[10] As political scientists are wont to do, they saw a wider relevance for their model, with globalization fostering greater interdependence. Other observers of Canada and the United States noticed a trend towards regionalization. In 1981, American journalist Joel Garreau published *The Nine Nations of North America*, a bestseller in which he divided the continent along cultural and economic lines. Among the regions Garreau identified were New England (the Northeast Atlantic coast), Quebec, the Foundry (the Great Lakes region), the Breadbasket (the prairies and the US Midwest), the Empty Quarter (the Rocky Mountains and the Arctic), and Ecotopia (the Pacific coast).[11] These somewhat arbitrary groupings had their basis in historical and contemporary fact – the Great Lakes Basin, for instance, was a centuries-old transnational region – but the recognition they received in Garreau's book signalled a growing willingness to look beyond national borders. This tendency gained popularity as academics and policymakers began to identify common regional problems, such as de-industrialization in the Rust Belt around the Great Lakes. Moreover, while Quebec separatism captured attention, a Cascadia Independence Movement emerged in the early 1990s with the goal of carving a new country out of BC, Washington, and Oregon.[12]

For all the *sturm und drang* of the New Nationalist era and despite Richard Nixon's mistaken view that Japan was his country's largest trading partner, the decades-long process of North American economic integration continued apace. The Auto Pact, a 1965 free trade agreement in auto parts, shored up Canada's automotive industry while recognizing that industry's ties to the United States, as the automakers – and even the auto unions – were American subsidiaries. As Canada's leading industry, automotive production was of immense importance to governments, workers, and consumers and served as a bellwether for economic and political changes that emerged in the 1970s: safety and environmental regulations, the continuing importance of but threats to unions, and the growth of overseas imports.[13] The Auto Pact appeared as an exception to rampant nationalism, a holdover from the 1950s rather than heralding further integration. But the trend line was towards deepening interdependence. 'Unless there is bungling on our part such as occurred in 1911', the US ambassador in Ottawa predicted in 1965, 'I believe closer US-Canadian trade ties will develop on an industry by industry free trade basis, possibly taking a more generalized form at some later date.' Speaking for many Canadians, Jean Chrétien, a Trudeau government minister and a native of Shawinigan, a Quebec town shaped by US investment, stated that there were 'a lot of places in Canada where people don't give a damn who owns what'.[14] Brian Mulroney, too, grew up in a US company town in Quebec and shared this outlook. In cultural terms, although the Trudeau government's investment in film and television and content restrictions meant that more Canadian content was available, Canadians continued to consume American media, thrilling in *The Godfather*, disco, and *M*A*S*H*. In a sign that, despite economic or diplomatic frustrations, US policymakers still prized Canada as an ally, in 1975, Gerald Ford brought Canada into the G5, the group of leading industrialized countries.

Canadian nationalism did strain Canada–US relations, particularly in the early 1980s, when Trudeau's twilight years coincided with Ronald Reagan's first term as president. Analysing potential flashpoints early on, one senior foreign policy official concluded, 'there are major differences in philosophy – we shouldn't kid ourselves about it. It is mainly in that Reagan has an ideology and we don't.'[15] Reagan's faith in unfettered free enterprise and hostility towards government intervention – neo-liberalism – certainly clashed both with Trudeau's policies, an amalgam of socialism and liberalism, and with Canadian nationalism. During the 1980 presidential campaign, Reagan had proposed a North American Accord, an ill-defined regional economic pact with Canada and Mexico out of step with the tenor of Canadian nationalism and quickly shelved. Indeed, in 1980, the Trudeau government implemented a National Energy Program (NEP), the latest economic nationalist step. Meant to spur greater Canadian ownership of natural resources, self-sufficiency, and lower prices for consumers, the NEP included caps on foreign – American – investment in the Canadian fossil fuel industry. Reagan recognized nationalism's public appeal, recalling for Trudeau in March 1981 that he recently saw 'on a truck a bumper sticker reading "Buy America", the only trouble was it was on a Toyota!'[16] Joking aside, the NEP exposed a fissure in Canada–US relations, with the *Wall Street Journal* labelling the program a 'xenophobic' policy stemming from the 'Canadian disease' of anti-Americanism. The move outraged many Canadian conservatives too, especially in oil-rich Alberta, which petroleum industry boosters had hoped to transform into 'a new and fantastic industrial empire of the vast northland.'[17] The NEP undercut this effort, creating considerable pushback in Western Canada, a reminder that the economic nationalism espoused in Ontario was not a universal force.

The cold war was another sore spot. Flashpoints in Central America, Afghanistan, and Africa; the deployment of new nuclear missiles; and Reagan's ramping up of military spending and confrontational rhetoric revived dormant fears. In Western countries, the peace movement experienced a renaissance, focusing attention on nuclear disarmament and cold war tension. A specific issue galvanizing Canadian peace activism was the Trudeau government's decision to allow the US military to test cruise missiles in Canada; in late 1983, this issue engaged more than five hundred groups, from the well-established Canadian Peace Congress to the newer Project Ploughshares.[18] The National Film Board produced the Oscar-winning documentary *If You Love This Planet* (1982), a call to arms for disarmament, and Canadian MPs participated in Parliamentarians for World Order's lobbying efforts in Moscow and Washington. One of those MPs, Progressive Conservative Douglas Roche, was a booster of the Twinning Movement, active since the 1940s but accelerating its efforts to twin cities throughout the world, what he called a form of 'global inter-personal relations'.[19] Trudeau addressed these public sentiments, and in 1983, with retirement approaching, he launched a reputation-burnishing effort to enhance the Non-Proliferation Treaty and bring about a Great Power détente. Quixotic and, ultimately, a failure, this Peace Initiative appeared to challenge Washington. Reagan, however, took it in stride: 'it isn't a sound idea but still we support his arousing interest in other nations.' Even as Ottawa's approval of cruise-missile testing showed the continuing ties of alliance and the balance inherent in Canada's foreign policy, a State Department official's dismissal of the prime minister's 'pot-induced behavior' encapsulated the gulf between Trudeau's Ottawa and Reagan's Washington. In 1984, one analyst declared the Canada–US relationship a 'forgotten partnership'.[20]

Brian Mulroney set out to renew that partnership. 'Good relations, super relations, with the US will be the cornerstone of our foreign policy', he assured the *Wall Street Journal*, a cardinal sin seized upon by Canadian nationalists who lambasted him as a 'Yankee Doodle Dandy' and 'A Star-Spangled Tory'.[21] Mulroney was pro-American, though like Lester Pearson and Louis St Laurent, he embraced multilateralism too. His government dismantled the NEP, sold off Petro-Canada, the state oil firm established by Trudeau's government, and transformed the Foreign Investment Review Agency, meant to control American ownership of Canadian industry, into Investment Canada, meant to encourage investors. Beyond improving bilateral relations, these moves stemmed from the Tories' embrace of the emerging neo-liberal mantra. Minister of Finance Michael Wilson led the way through privatization, deregulation, and tax reform meant to limit government, spur economic growth, and tackle ballooning debt. These economic polices bore much in common with Thatcherism and Reaganomics, but the North Atlantic Triangle of neo-liberalism had its limits in the streak of Red Toryism that ran through the Progressive Conservative Party. Describing Mulroney, Margaret Thatcher sniffed: 'As Leader of the Progressive Conservatives I thought he put too much emphasis on the adjective as opposed to the noun.'[22]

Mulroney's economic and foreign policy record became synonymous with the Canada–US Free Trade Agreement, concluded in 1988, after three years of tense negotiations. The impetus was growing Canadian concern at protectionist actions by the US Congress. To secure Congressional passage of the agreement and other legislation favourable to Canada, Ambassador Allan Gotlieb and other Washington embassy officials pioneered what they called the 'New Diplomacy', a mixture of public outreach, typical diplomacy channelled through the State Department, atypical diplomacy directed at other US departments and agencies, and an effective Congressional lobbying effort.[23] This strategy, which the Canadian foreign service would perfect over the following decades, was a success, and as in 1911 and 1948, it was Canada that proved to be the major hurdle in the way of free trade.

With its Parliamentary majority, the Mulroney government passed the trade treaty amid Opposition members' hoots and hollers.[24] However, the Liberal-controlled Senate held up final approval. His hand forced, Mulroney called an election, the third time in Canada's history that free trade with the Americans became the focal point of a federal vote. Unlike in 1891 and 1911, the Conservatives favoured reciprocity. 'The Mulroney trade agreement sells out Canada's sovereign control over its own economic, social, cultural, and regional policies', the Liberal opposition warned, taking a page from John A. Macdonald and Robert Borden. Popular polemics – *If You Love This Country*, *Canada Not for Sale*, and *On Guard for Thee* – emphasized the dangers of Americanization.[25] On election day, the nationalist appeal succeeded yet failed: the Liberals and NDP increased their seat totals and won more than 50 per cent of the popular vote; however, the Conservatives held on to their majority. The results showed, to one historian at least, that anti-Americanism in Canada was 'as dead as the dodo'.[26]

Quite apart from the trade agreement, over the course of the 1980s and 1990s, Canadians and Americans grew closer. Fed up with Canada's cold winters, 'snowbirds' began spending part of the year in Arizona and Florida. Through increasingly inexpensive air travel, Canadians travelled to the United States in ever greater numbers, attending trade shows and conventions or visiting Las Vegas and Disney World, dream palaces of American civilization come true. Fewer Americans came north, though the mountains of Banff and the fleshpot of Montreal attracted their share of thrill seekers. A 1995 Open Skies agreement between Ottawa and Washington vastly expanded the range of destinations available to North American air travellers as well as the frequency of direct flights between Canadian and American cities. Further, it paved the way for the establishment of US pre-clearance customs facilities at major Canadian airports, treating approved travellers from Canada as domestic American passengers. A prosperous American economy drew well-educated and well-heeled Canadians south, renewing concerns about a brain drain. By one journalist's count, in 2000 some six hundred thousand 'star-spangled Canadians' called the United States home.[27] Cross-border shopping's popularity fluctuated based upon exchange rates, and until the 2001 terror attacks, borderlands residents easily traversed the boundary line.

Culturally, American civilization loomed large. Though the trade agreement included cultural protections to appease Canada's nationalists, no amount of cultural protectionism could block the radio and television signals flowing across the border, with Canadians tuning in, as they had done for over half a century, to American programming. As in earlier eras, the extent to which Hollywood represented a foreign threat was overblown. After all, in 1983, Los Angeles ranked as the fourth largest 'Canadian' city by population thanks to the tens of thousands of Canadians drawn to show business.[28] Among them were Christopher Plummer and William Shatner, products of the Stratford Shakespearean Festival, and a generation of comedians who wrote, produced, directed, or starred in many of the definitive television shows and comedic films of the 1980s and 1990s. Furthermore, depending on the exchange rate, American film and television production occurred in Vancouver, Toronto, and Montreal, cities that fought over the title of 'Hollywood North'. Certainly, Hollywood studios' financial power was at play, but on the matter of Canadian films, the president of Canada's Odeon Theatres was blunt: they were 'no fucking good'.[29] The failure of Trudeau-era content regulations to beat back American culture led to further government intervention.

Recalling the tariff fight over magazines in the 1930s, the Liberal government that formed in 1993 waged a pitched battle against the Canadian versions of American periodicals such as *Time* and *Sports Illustrated*, which contained little Canadian content but sucked away advertising dollars from their Canadian competitors. The issue wound up before the World Trade Organization (WTO), where Canada lost. As a US embassy official later noted, the magazine question consumed 'an incredible amount of reporters' ink and diplomatic goodwill – although the commercial stakes were tiny'.[30] The economic stakes were important to Canadian publishers, who whipped up nationalist indignation. For nationalists, meanwhile, the issues was cultural and political for the WTO decision exemplified worries over globalization: if controls meant to protect culture could be deemed illegal under free trade regimes, were environmental protections or labour rights next? The leading nationalist combatant on the magazine front, Sheila Copps, Canada's heritage minister, blared the claxons over the 'Americanization of culture around the world'. In 1998, at a summit in Ottawa, she steered the creation of the International Network on Cultural Policy, a grouping of culture ministers committed to safeguarding cultural sovereignty and diversity. To this end, Copps barred US representatives from attending the Ottawa conference.[31] Other commentators were more ambivalent than hostile towards American culture. Kim Campbell, who succeeded Mulroney as Progressive Conservative prime minister for five months, observed that 'images of America are so pervasive in this global village that it is almost as if instead of the world immigrating to America, America has emigrated to the world, allowing people to aspire to be Americans even in distant countries'.[32]

To this line of thinking, one might add that the spread of American culture benefitted Canada, for globalization established English as a lingua franca, thereby helping to rocket performers such as Celine Dion, Shania Twain, and Justin Bieber to global superstardom.

From the perspective of two decades, what makes the cultural nationalist concerns of the 1990s seem quaint are the internet, which demolished cultural barriers, and the increasing globalization of Canada's population through immigration thereby bringing new cultural reference points into the mainstream. From the perspective of history, meanwhile, the cultural nationalism of the late twentieth century was merely rehashing decades-old arguments over whether American culture represented an alien threat polluting Canadian minds. Consumption of mass culture has provided Canadians and Americans with common reference points, but Canadians have adapted aspects of American culture to their own needs and discarded others. 'The more often I have visited this country', Welsh travel writer Jan Morris observed reassuringly in 1990, 'the more clearly I have come to realize that Canada is unique. It is pure nonsense to say that it might as well be part of the USA.'[33] Although defining it remains a perennial and contested task, Canadian identity has thrived despite, or indeed because of, the United States. The Canadian tendency to differentiate themselves from Americans reached its apogee in a 2000 commercial for *Molson Canadian*, in which a beer-swilling Canadian proudly declares: 'I have a prime minister, not a president. I speak English and French, not American. And I pronounce it "about", not "a-boot" I can proudly sew my country's flag on my backpack. I believe in peacekeeping, not policing; diversity, not assimilation, and that the beaver is a proud and noble animal.' Beaver-festooned clothing and an unpalatable brand of coffee joined beer and hockey as signifiers of genuine English-Canadian identity.[34] Lamentably, these products of consumer nationalism have likely had a more significant cultural impact than CBC programming.

In defining themselves in un-American terms, Canadians, particularly in central Canada, drew on a long tradition. Whereas many Canadians had once tended to emphasize their Britishness and conservatism – breaking with Britain through evolution not revolution, retaining the monarchy, pursuing peace, order, and good government rather than life, liberty, and the pursuit of happiness – as the new millennium dawned, they began to champion their more progressive values, building on the New Nationalist tendency to view Canada as a peaceable kingdom.[35] Importantly, Americans, too, took this view of Canada. On the right, there was full-blown anti-Canadianism, with commentators fearful of universal health insurance, marriage equality, and gun control. In the *Weekly Standard*, one writer described Canada as a 'mediocrity'. It was 'not a serious country anymore', declared another right-wing hack. 'It is a northern Puerto Rico with an EU sensibility.' To Pat Buchanan, the troglodytic-conservative, Canada was simply 'Soviet Canuckistan'.[36] On the left, Americans celebrated that Canadian public policy was driven largely by research rather than scripture; indeed, as Canadians became more secular, old hatreds, such as the Protestant anti-Catholicism of the Orange Order died away. The 2000s witnessed the phenomenon of liberal and progressive Americans declaring their intent to 'move to Canada' following the election of conservative officeholders. Journalists did find Americans fleeing north to escape homophobia or militarism, and a Californian immigrant in pursuit of medical marijuana described 'an exodus' of fellow stoners, adding that, 'Canada has a history of protecting American people from its own government, like during the Vietnam War and the Underground Railroad.' In early 2005, with President George W. Bush beginning his second term, one American journalist suggested a merger between Canada and the Democrat-leaning 'blue states' along the Pacific and Atlantic coasts.[37]

The sense of an imminent merger was a common theme in the late 1990s, with Mexico often thrown into the mix.[38] New Nationalists dusted themselves off and warned, as they had three decades earlier, that Canada was a 'Vanishing Country'. In the press, newer nationalist groups, such as the Council of Canadians – founded during the free trade fight – waged a battle over integration against the continentalist Canadian Council of Chief Executives.[39] If Canadian nationalists were opposed to integration, so were American conservatives. The terror attacks of 11 September 2001 were rightly seen as a turning point in North American relations. Yet over a year earlier, US lawmakers had called for greater border security, speculating that the 'porous border with Canada may be the place to start cleaning house'.[40] With the terror attacks, the border briefly shut, at a considerable economic cost. For Canadian authorities, businesspeople, and workers, the potential disruption of the easy flow of people and goods was dangerous. Officials and journalists spent considerable time correcting the fiction that the 9/11 terrorists had entered the United States through Canada, a lie repeated not only by fringe figures but by reputable sources such as New York Senator Hillary Clinton. There had been a cross-border terrorist incident, in December 1999, when Ahmed Rassam, an Algerian al-Qaeda operative living illegally in Montreal, was arrested while crossing into the United States on a mission to bomb Los Angeles International Airport. A repeat occurrence, or an actual attack stemming from Canada, in the words of a Canadian minister, was the government's 'worst nightmare'. Bluntly, American Ambassador Paul Cellucci warned, 'security will trump trade'.[41]

To allay US security concerns, Ottawa expanded its national security services, stepped up border protection and intelligence cooperation with US authorities, and implemented a tough anti-terror law. As was the case in much of the West, the war on terror veered into a war on civil liberties.

One senior Chrétien government minister later admitted that the 2001 Anti-Terrorism Act was 'certainly done in haste. In the heat of the crisis, when fear and anger ran high, there wasn't enough time or will for reflection.'[42] The expanding national security apparatus prevented several terror attacks, including a scheme to behead Prime Minister Stephen Harper. However, it ensnared innocent people, most notably the Syrian-born Canadian Maher Arar, who was detained by American authorities on suspicion of being a terrorist, and, with the knowledge of Canadian officials, deported to Syria, where he was tortured. More broadly, just as the Gouzenko revelations of a Soviet spy ring cast suspicion on Canadian leftists writ large, the actions of a few Islamist terrorists generated hatred towards the wider Muslim community and pockets of Islamophobia emerged among supposedly tolerant Canadians. As for the border, a series of bilateral agreements sought to balance security concerns with economic access. Having hitched themselves to the US economy and sharing a continent with the United States, the Canadian government moved to placate their American allies. Even Matthew Coon Come, the national chief of the Assembly of First Nations (AFN), met Cellucci to seek US collaboration with indigenous law enforcement on border security in indigenous territories that straddled or cut through the Canada–US boundary.[43] Rapidly, the undefended border became a fond memory.

Ottawa drew a line on security cooperation with ballistic missile defence. In 1985, Mulroney had opted out of participation in Reagan's planned missile defence system, designed to make the US impervious to a nuclear attack. Although the cold war ended, American politicians and military planners pursued the idea, which rose in prominence as rogue states such as Iran or North Korea began developing nuclear weapons. In the early 2000s the Bush administration invited Canada's government to join its missile defence program. Cellucci judged Canadian participation 'a no-brainer' and Paul Martin, prime minister from 2003 to 2006, agreed, noting that 'If somebody is going to be sending missiles over Canadian airspace, we want to be at the table.' Martin oversaw a minority government and faced a restive caucus, and after a Liberal convention at which opposition to missile defence was made clear, he opted out of involvement. 'We simply cannot understand why Canada would, in effect, give up its sovereignty – its seat at the table – to decide what to do about a missile that might be coming toward Canada', Cellucci told reporters.[44] However, opponents of Canada's participation in missile defence had themselves framed the issue in terms of sovereignty, that is, a need to safeguard against American control of Canadian defence policy. The move became a demonstration of Canada's independence, an affirmation, noted former foreign minister Lloyd Axworthy, of the 'times when truth must speak to power'.[45] Even Stephen Harper, whose pro-American government formed in 2006, avoided involvement in missile defence.

Beyond the American preoccupation with security and Canadian watchfulness over sovereignty, moves towards further North American integration were hobbled by protectionist sentiment in the United States, where 'Buy American' provisions continued creeping into legislation. There was also growing dysfunction in the US political system, symbolized by the fate of the Detroit–Windsor crossing. After much wrangling with the robber baron who owned the aging Ambassador Bridge, the sole means of crossing the Detroit River beyond an underground tunnel, in 2015 the Canadian government agreed to pay for a second bridge as well as related infrastructure on both sides of the crossing.[46] That Ottawa assumed the whole cost – to be recouped via tolls – indicated concern at keeping open vital trade and tourist links. That the American government was unwilling to pay costs associated with the project, including a customs facility to be built on US soil, revealed the level of gridlock and partisanship in Washington. Speaking with an American audience, Harper speculated that, 'the real barrier' to broader integration lay on the US side of the border.[47] Despite such frustrations, there remained advocates of further North American integration. In 2005, a Council on Foreign Relations task force of Mexican, Canadian, and US officials advocated for an EU-style customs union complete with common immigration controls, and in 2013 a journalist urged Canada and the United States to complete the 'merger of the century'. Reviving a century-old concept and giving it a new spin, in *The North American Idea*, retired American diplomat Robert Pastor recommended greater integration among United States, Mexico, and Canada.[48] While historians make terrible prophets, writing in 2019 amidst the Trumpian moment, such recommendations seem less like guideposts to the future than elegies for what might have been.

The North American Free Trade Agreement (NAFTA), which came into force in 1994, subsuming the Canada–US trade pact, marked Canadian recognition – one that continued to wax and wane – that Mexico was a part of North America rather than apart from it. 'Canada is not a big player in Mexico, but we hope to be', Brian Mulroney had confided to George H. W. Bush. Mulroney added, though, that NAFTA was 'especially important to counter the criticism that we're not doing enough for the developing countries. These countries don't want aid, they want access to our markets, and this is what they'll get.'[49] Breaking down protectionist barriers between the Global North and the Global South was at the heart of globalization. Whether that was a magnanimous policy on the part of developed countries was another matter. For Canadian policymakers, the issue was important because, having secured access to the US market, they looked to expand Canada's economic horizons.

Although Jean Chrétien had campaigned against NAFTA, once in power he reversed course. In trade terms, the Chrétien government followed Mulroney's script. Looking towards the Americas writ large, Chrétien backed the unsuccessful Free Trade Agreement of the Americas (FTAA). Although the FTAA process stalled, the Liberals secured bilateral deals with Chile and Costa Rica, and launched talks with other Latin American governments. Beyond trade, after decades of neglect, Latin America became a focus of Canada's foreign policy. The Mulroney government brought Canada into the Organization of American States (OAS) and made democracy promotion a major feature of its hemispheric approach, with Canada contributing election monitors, supporting peacekeeping missions in Central America, and advancing pro-democracy measures through the OAS. Collectively, these moves supported the region's nascent democracies, which were emerging from decades of state terrorism and US intervention. Chrétien continued this policy, championing the Inter-American Democratic Charter in 2001. Collectively, Canadian engagement in the Western hemisphere was belated recognition that Canada was an American country. In an address to the Mexican Senate, Chrétien noted that the Americas, Canada included, constituted '*una gran familia*'.[50]

NAFTA marked a Canadian turn towards free trade writ large. Rather than confining itself to North America and 'turning away from the world', Joe Clark had vowed that 'Canada's trade policy can only be global'. Roy MacLaren, Chrétien's trade minister, agreed, characterizing NAFTA as 'a nucleus for a more open, global trading endeavour'.[51] Canada's trade policy beyond North America was twofold: an emphasis on expanding the multilateral trade system centred around GATT; and the search for bilateral or regional trade deals. In terms of GATT, Canadian officials played an important part in the Uruguay round of talks that began in 1986 – just as Canada–US trade negotiations began in earnest – and ended in 1994 with agreement on a range of global trade issues and the formation of the WTO.[52]

In focusing on liberalizing trade, the WTO became one of globalization's driving forces, lumped in with the International Monetary Fund (IMF) and the World Bank as part of the neo-liberal 'Washington Consensus' favouring open markets and limited government. Using the lever of loans to countries in economic distress, the IMF and World Bank promoted structural adjustment, the privatization of public services, and removal of trade and investment barriers. Through these organizations, Ottawa backed structural adjustment, which was blamed for increases in poverty, political instability, and growing inequality between the Global North and Global South. Canada itself underwent structural adjustment as the Mulroney and Chrétien governments promoted neo-liberal reforms, the result of a grave financial situation. In 1995, the *Wall Street Journal* labelled Canada 'an honorary member of the Third World in the unmanageability of its debt problem'.[53] Under Finance Minister Paul Martin, the Chrétien government implemented austerity measures that put Canada's books back in the black. The Canadian Liberals' laissez-faire policies were reflected in the Bill Clinton–Tony Blair 'Third Way', the blend of economic policies that defined turn-of-the-millennium centrism.

Neo-liberalism was a sign of the influence and importance of multinational corporations and global investors who benefitted greatly from the unfettered spread of capital. In trade terms, the Canadian emphasis on globalization signified attention to new centres of economic power. 'Canada's geographic location gives it an important advantage as new poles of political and economic power emerge', declared the Chrétien government in its 1995 foreign policy strategy.[54] As in the late nineteenth century, Asia was a focus of Canada's trade efforts. In 1984, the Trudeau government created the Asia Pacific Foundation of Canada, a think tank promoting engagement with Asia, and in 1989, Mulroney brought Canada into the newly formed Asia-Pacific Economic Cooperation (APEC). The Chrétien government launched Team Canada missions, huge trade junkets that brought business leaders and politicians from all parties and all levels of government to China, Hong Kong, South Korea, Thailand, the Philippines, and Indonesia. Beyond drumming up trade and investment, Chrétien's goal, his diplomatic advisor noted, was to overcome 'generations of political neglect' and 'blast awareness of the world outside North America into the consciousness of Canadians, and to expose Asians to Canada'.[55] In terms of the diffusion of economic power, in 1999 Paul Martin teamed with US Treasury Secretary Larry Summers to found the G20, a forum for finance ministers and central bank governors from the world's richest countries; later Martin successfully pushed to expand these gatherings into summits of G20 leaders.[56]

Trade with Asian countries, and the wider phenomenon of globalization, raised a series of political concerns. Many of Canada's trade partners had poor environmental and labour standards, or denied civil liberties to their citizens. Such issues were largely brushed off by Canadian officials. At the 1995 Association of Southeast Asian Nations summit, Foreign Minister André Ouellet affirmed the government's desire to pursue trade and investment with countries 'irrespective of their human rights records'. The following year, the long-time president of the Canadian Exporters Association, admitted, 'I had always maintained that Canada, with a third of its income and employment coming from exports, should never adopt a policy of turning down customers for political reasons.'[57] This outlook was long-standing – during the 1930s, Canada had traded with Japan and Nazi Germany and throughout the cold war, Ottawa had sold foodstuffs to the Soviet Union and Red China. In the 1990s, with the instantaneous transmission of information, it became more difficult for countries and companies to hide poor human rights practices. As activists and reporters made deplorable working conditions a cause célèbre Western multinationals operating abroad faced mounting criticism for employing sweatshop workers. Defenders of the economic status quo responded that workers from impoverished countries were better off making a pittance than being unemployed, engendering a long-running debate about whether globalization had a net positive or negative impact in the Global South. Meanwhile, the outsourcing of jobs to countries with subsistence wages had a devastating effect on workers in Canada's manufacturing industries. Deindustrialization of Hamilton, Oshawa, Windsor and other industrial cities in Canada stands as a testament to globalizations' reciprocal nature.

Globalization generated a broad-based opposition movement of environmentalists, feminists, unions, indigenous groups, cultural nationalists, and anti-capitalists. 'Never has there been such a variety of initiatives and confrontations', wrote two long-time Canadian activists. 'Seldom has there been such a need for communication, dialogue and even new strategies between civil society actors.'[58] Anti-globalization was itself a global phenomenon, uniting concerned people from across the planet. As global elites held their various conclaves – WTO gatherings, G20 summits, World Economic Forum gabfests – parallel People's Summits were convened. One of the first confrontations occurred at the 1997 APEC summit in Vancouver. While a minority of protestors at these various conclaves grabbed headlines by clashing with police and smashing property, most demonstrators came to peaceably express their myriad reasons for opposing globalization. Central to that opposition was the sense that, particularly in its economic incarnation, globalization benefitted Western multinational corporations who plundered resources, supplanted culture with branding, and exploited cheap labour, whether on coffee plantations or in sweatshops. 'Anticorporatism is the brand of politics capturing the imagination of the next generation of troublemakers', wrote Canadian activist Naomi Klein, a leading light of the anti-globalization movement.[59] Adbusters, the Vancouver-based anti-globalization network known for their lively, eponymous magazine, was a driving force behind anti-corporate initiatives such as Buy Nothing Day, TV Turnoff Week, and, later, Occupy Wall Street. In contrast to free trade, anti-globalization activists promoted fair trade and criticized neo-liberals' market fundamentalism.

With Canada's government supporting its overarching structure, Canadian multinational corporations were engaged in globalization at the ground level. Banks, insurance companies, and mining firms had decades of experience operating abroad, and so the liberalization of markets removed impediments and made their operations easier. Given its inherently negative environmental impact, the often dangerous working conditions involved, and the extraction of mineral wealth from one country for the benefit of investors abroad, mining became a particular focus of attention. Mining, as magnate Peter Munk pointed out, was 'a very Canadian business, after fur trading, the second activity for which we are known' – though one might be tempted to add fossil fuel production into the mix.[60] Munk had little time for human rights concerns and his Barrick Gold was one of several Canadian firms – Alcan, Rio Tinto, IAMGOLD – dominating an industry where roughly half of the world's firms were listed on the Toronto Stock Exchange. While making a big show of upholding corporate social responsibility, many mining companies benefitted from operating in countries with dubious environmental and labour standards, and exploitation of non-white labour in Guatemala, Peru, Burkina Faso, and Ghana gave colonial overtones to Canadian mining operations.[61] Another move veering into colonial territory was the decision of Stephen Harper's Conservative government to partner with mining firms in the delivery of aid money, so that development spending, in the words of Canada's development minister, became 'investments'. Surveying this policy shift, a leading columnist warned that, 'Canada is no longer simply "doing business" or "providing aid" in Africa. What we're doing is something that bears a striking resemblance of the things Britain and France were doing in Canada two centuries ago.'[62]

The move to partner with mining companies preceded by a matter of weeks the Harper government's abolition of the Canadian International Development Agency (CIDA) as a stand-alone agency. CIDA was rolled up into the Department of Foreign Affairs and International Trade. As critics feared, much of Canada's shrinking development spending was then refocused towards countries with which Ottawa was pursuing trade and investment talks.[63] The Conservatives' move was not unprecedented in that Pierre Trudeau had merged Canada's trade and foreign affairs departments in 1982. CIDA's disappearance marked the retrenchment of Canadian development spending, a trend apparent since the late-1970s. Although the Mulroney government had increased aid to Africa in the wake of the Ethiopian famine – one analyst dubbed the period 1984–8 a 'veritable golden age' for African aid – austerity at home meant less aid abroad. The age of globalization saw demands for greater aid spending but CIDA had fewer resources, leading the Canadian Council for International Cooperation to decry Canada's 'tarnished image'.[64] Religious and secular NGOs filled the breach, many of them Canadian offshoots of international organizations: World Vision, CARE, Oxfam, and *Médecins Sans Frontières*.

Once Canada's fiscal situation improved in the early 2000s, aid spending had received a small boost, for as Chrétien readily admitted, poverty was 'the worst form of violence'.[65] Canadian aid was targeted towards issues that captured contemporary attention, including HIV/AIDS, debt forgiveness, and the UN's Millennium Development Goals. Hosting the 2002 G8 summit in Kananaskis, Chrétien made sub-Saharan Africa a focus, welcoming African leaders and establishing a G8 commitment to target poverty on the continent. Eight years later, Harper used his G8 chairmanship to champion maternal, newborn, and child health – though controversially Canadian funds towards the program ignored reproductive health. These targeted initiatives allowed

Canadian development specialists to make do with less funding, even as there were continual calls for Canada, a wealthy country, to make greater contributions. 'I believe the world needs more Canada', declared an Irish rock star interested in poverty alleviation.[66] Unfortunately for advocates of international development, Canada's aid spending plummeted, falling well below the 0.7 per cent of GNP goal set by Canada's Lester Pearson.

Like the Liberals, Stephen Harper's Conservative government made trade promotion a priority – to the point where critics questioned this seemingly singular focus and dismissed the prime minister as 'Free Trade Steve'. Characterizing Conservative foreign policy as a 'big break' from past governments, one columnist wrote, 'What was peacekeeping, foreign aid, collective security – you name it – became a relentless focus on trade agreements.'[67] Harper did not hide this emphasis. In 2014, in one of his only speeches to the UN General Assembly, he highlighted trade and aid delivery as 'the signatures of our Government's outreach in the world'. 'Trade', he emphasized, 'means jobs, growth and opportunities. It has made great nations out of small ones. The story of my own country, Canada, is a case in point.' This viewpoint stemmed from his recognition that decades of globalization had enmeshed Canada firmly within a global economy. Yet this development had pitfalls, as the near collapse of the global economic system in 2008–9 demonstrated. Canada, Harper stated in 2013, was 'a land of hope in a sea of uncertainty'.[68]

Like the Great Depression, the Great Recession showcased the external vulnerabilities confronting a trading nation such as Canada. Further, it underlined the importance of the Conservatives' trade promotion initiative, which, Harper noted, was an effort to 'broaden our trade beyond the US'.[69] Harper was not alone on this point. Bank of Canada Governor Mark Carney warned that Canada was 'overexposed to the United States and underexposed to faster-growing emerging markets', and the Canadian International Council recommended 'deepen[ing] our US connections while we broaden our economic portfolio away from reliance on a single market'.[70] Finding an economic counterweight to the United States was a long-standing Canadian goal, and globalization – the free market mantra, the rapid pace of transportation, and the ease of communication – provided a conducive environment. The Conservatives oversaw the conclusion of more bilateral trade deals than any previous government, signing pacts with Ukraine, South Korea, Honduras, Panama, Jordan, Colombia, Peru, and the European Free Trade Area. They updated existing agreements with Israel and Chile, and concluded two major regional deals: one with the European Union, the other, the Trans-Pacific Partnership with Asia-Pacific countries. Harper was realistic about what could be achieved by these diversification efforts. As he admitted, 'even with our best-case scenario of diversification, Canada's most important trading partner will always be the United States, by far'.[71] It remained to be seen whether the Third Option dream would become reality.

Asia loomed largest in Canada's trade diversification picture, a reflection of the long-term trajectory of waning American and Western economic power. Given the 'unprecedented shift of power and wealth away from the Western world' Harper mused about the diminishing 'ability of our most important allies, and most importantly the United States, to single-handedly shape outcomes and protect our interests'.[72] As a country on the Pacific Rim, with an economy based largely on resources, and with a diverse population including millions of people of Asian ancestry, Canada stood poised to benefit from this power shift, but doing so required considerable attention on the part of policymakers and civil society actors. 'We need a new kind of map', one analyst emphasized, one that 'will shrink oceans, especially the Pacific'.[73]

China dominated considerations of Asian engagement. After diplomatic relations were re-established in 1970, successive Canadian governments reached out to Beijing. Mulroney built on contacts established under Trudeau, hosting China's president in 1985 and paying a return visit in 1986. 'Much remains to be done in expanding the relationship', he reflected on the way back to Ottawa.[74] Growing Sino–Canadian contacts under Mulroney paralleled the accelerating ties between Canada and the Soviet Union, raising hopes of reform behind the bamboo curtain. Beijing's bloody crackdown on peaceful demonstrators at Tiananmen Square was an alarming turn of events. The Mulroney government temporarily recalled Canada's ambassador, supported G7 sanctions on strategic materials, and suspended high-level meetings and CIDA assistance; Chinese students in Canada were granted permanent residency. Disappointed that Beijing was taking a different path than Moscow, Mulroney remarked, 'It's a calamity for them and it's a calamity for the breath of fresh air that was a democratic impulse running through China.'[75] Canadian measures were temporary, and there was no suspension of a loan to Beijing. As Joe Clark made clear, although the massacre was a 'tragedy of global proportions', Ottawa would 'avoid measures that would push China towards isolation'. In a sign of what engagement could achieve, he reminded his listeners, 'We have seen elsewhere in the socialist world that the modernization of these societies can serve to advance political change.'[76]

China remained the great hope of trade enthusiasts, many of whom assumed that engagement would encourage political reform, and the country became the focal point for Chrétien's Asia-Pacific outreach. 'I'm sure that opening of the market, the opening of these countries to outsiders coming with our values and traditions will help a bit', Chrétien remarked in a defence of engaging China and Indonesia, two human rights pariahs.[77] Groups like the Canada China Business Council and the Canada-China Legislative Association promoted engaging Beijing economically and politically, and universities rushed to forge academic partnerships and court Chinese students. Taking note of these developments, Stanley Hartt, a former Mulroney advisor, praised the 'curative properties of trade and economic liberalism'.[78] Engagement embodied a liberal view that empowering China's middle class would lead to political change. As a retired diplomat observed, this standpoint was deeply rooted in a view that 'without human rights based on the individual, democracy, and the rule of law, China cannot modernize its society'.[79] Like the missionaries who set out for the Middle Kingdom a century earlier, advocates of engagement sought to save China from itself – all while making a profit.

Not all Canadians supported engaging China. Opponents of outreach emphasized that Beijing represented a geopolitical threat, that its human rights record was abysmal, and that engagement was failing to bring about political change. Many of these sceptics hailed from Canada's conservative movement, Harper among them. As prime minister, initially he took a tough stance towards China. 'I think Canadians want us to promote our trade relations worldwide, and we do that', he stated in 2006, 'but I don't think Canadians want us to sell out important Canadian values. They don't want us to sell that out to the almighty dollar.'[80] In addition to refusing to attend the 2008 Beijing Olympics, Harper hosted the Dalai Lama at his Parliamentary office. 'It's like our China policy is made in Tibet', complained David Emerson, Harper's first trade minister and a BC MP with an interest in Asia-Pacific trade.[81] The year 2009 saw a volte-face: Harper finally visited China and, as Ottawa began courting Chinese investment in its natural resource sector, rhetoric about China softened. The policy change stemmed from anger in the Chinese-Canadian community as well as recognition, with the Great Recession, of China's commercial importance. The positive trend continued in 2012, with Ottawa and Beijing concluding an agreement protecting investors, a concern for Canadians worried about working with Chinese state-run businesses. At the end of that year, Ottawa greenlit the takeover of a Canadian energy firm by China's state oil company, a move opposed by Tory backbenchers, who cited the communist government's failure 'to grant even the most basic of human freedoms to its citizens as they strip away their natural wealth to invest around the world'.[82]

Tension surrounding political and ideological differences remained a constant factor in Canada–China relations. Worrisome from a Canadian perspective was Beijing's use of hackers to target government computer systems, part of a wider pattern of Chinese economic espionage in Canada. 'Of all the countries that happily dance across the Canadian border to shoplift our technology,' observed two analysts, 'China is far and away the busiest and most aggressive.'[83] Although Canada's government has engaged in economic espionage – electronic eavesdropping on Brazil's natural resources ministry – fear of Chinese spying was magnified by its status as a great power and as an authoritarian regime engaging in horrific acts of repression. As an investigation by Canadian human rights activists revealed, Chinese authorities harvested the organs of jailed members of the Falun Gong religious movement, and in 2018 the UN identified more than one million members of the Uighur minority in 're-education' camps.[84] Whether these black marks would prevent further trade, academic exchanges, tourism and other forms of engagement was an issue facing Canada and other Western countries. And then there was the geopolitical rise of China, a threat to American hegemony in the Pacific and part of a wider diffusion of geopolitical power. China specialist Paul Evans counselled 'treating China for what it is and is becoming, irrespective of what we wish it to become', while David Mulroney, a former ambassador to Beijing, emphasized that as 'a globally engaged middle power, we need to understand that no country other than the United States is now more important to us than China'.[85] Overall, China loomed over considerations of Canada's Pacific future.

Engagement with China fits into a long-standing, economically self-interested Canadian pattern of dealing with countries no matter their ideological or political actions. Canada's foreign policymakers traditionally put little stock in sanctions, whether applied to imperial Japan, apartheid South Africa, or communist Cuba. With the human rights revolution of the 1970s, this position came under increasing attack as activists sought to prioritize rights over trade and investment, a struggle in which opposition to apartheid was a notable success. This transnational campaign engaged thousands of Canadians, individually and through labour unions, charities, and protest groups such as the Taskforce on Churches and Corporate Responsibility, the Inter-Church Coalition on Africa, and the South African Congress of Trade Unions Solidarity Committee. These NGOs lobbied government, named and shamed companies investing in South Africa, coordinated boycotts of South African goods and of businesses dealing with the apartheid regime, and arranged for speaking tours by opposition figures.[86] On campus, student anti-apartheid groups pressured university administrators to divest from South Africa and launched protests against pro-apartheid speakers.[87] Given this passionate and broad-based activism, when visiting Canada in 1990, Nelson Mandela, the black opposition leader, had good reason to praise Canadians as 'comrades in arms'.[88] Canadian actions were only a small part of the global effort to isolate South Africa, a struggle exemplifying increased attention to human rights, and Canadian solidarity with political movements in the Global South.

What made the anti-apartheid struggle in Canada more notable was the Mulroney government's involvement. John Diefenbaker had grudgingly helped to kick South Africa out of the Commonwealth, but he and his successors had done little else to combat apartheid or the South African police state that enforced it. Throughout the 1970s, and in response to multilateral sanctions, the Trudeau government imposed modest economic controls; nonetheless, Canadian corporations – Alcan, Falconbridge, Bata Shoes, Ford Canada, and Massey-Ferguson – entrenched themselves in South Africa.[89] However, domestically and in the UN and the Commonwealth, pressure built for a far-reaching boycott, and the Mulroney government responded accordingly, if cautiously, imposing a slate of sanctions. Although these measures allowed some trade to continue, they marked a tougher stance pitting Mulroney against British Prime Minister Margaret Thatcher. Pretoria had to be made to 'realize that effective reform can no longer be delayed', the Canadian leader informed his British counterpart, adding that 'change in South Africa could only be achieved by stepping up pressure from outside'.[90] Thatcher was not for turning. Beyond sanctions, Mulroney met with South African opposition figures such as Bishop Desmond Tutu and African National Congress President Oliver Tambo.[91] In 1987, in a show of solidarity, he visited the front-line states bordering South Africa, and three years later, Mulroney welcomed Mandela to the House of Commons to address gathered Parliamentarians.

One analyst judged that although a departure from the past, the Tory positon was less exceptional in comparison to other Western countries.[92] And yet, Canada differed from it closest allies, for Ronald Reagan shared Thatcher's opprobrium for the anti-apartheid movement. Moreover, Mulroney was at odds with members of his own party and other Canadian conservatives who either backed apartheid or questioned Mandela's left-wing views. Funded by South African business interests, the Canadian-South African Society lobbied against sanctions and sought to promote investment in South Africa and its spokesperson, who denounced Mulroney as a 'pipsqueak', drew the anti-apartheid movement's ire for declaring the need 'to round up business on our own for our people in South Africa'.[93] Rejecting this implied call for racial solidarity, the Mulroney government provided a measure of moral leadership, particularly in multilateral fora. Speaking at the UN in 1985, Mulroney harshly denounced the apartheid state. 'It was an extraordinary moment', recalled Stephen Lewis, the NDP politician who Mulroney had appointed Canada's UN ambassador. 'It was, for all the African delegations, a moment of hope.'[94]

As the Mulroney government was bringing pressure to bear on South Africa, several indigenous groups in Canada sought to call attention to their treatment by Canadian authorities. In 1987, Glenn Babb, South Africa's ambassador in Ottawa, helicoptered into the Peguis First Nation north of Winnipeg at the invitation of Nēhiyaw chief Louis Stevenson. Relishing the chance to embarrass Canada's government, Babb accepted an aid request and falsely struck a demur note, stating, 'Far be it from me to comment on the internal affairs of another country.' Stevenson had no such qualms, remarking to the reporters present that 'Canada's treatment of its aboriginal people makes a mockery of the image it portrays to the rest of the world.' Indigenous activists and concerned Canadians had been making this point in earnest since the 1960s, and the issue had renewed importance amid the human rights revolution.[95] Later that year, when Joe Clark visited South Africa on a fact-finding mission, his counterpart from the apartheid regime, hosting a group of Nēhiyaw elders, suggested that Canada should 'clean up its own backyard' before offering criticism.[96] Although most indigenous leaders condemned these moves, not wanting 'to go down in history as allies of racist fascism', Stevenson and the chiefs who went to South Africa raised uncomfortable questions about Canada's own record.[97] While this issue's exploitation by the apartheid state to excuse its crimes – something Nazi Germany had done to counter Canadian criticism over anti-Semitism – was reprehensible, Canada's treatment of indigenous people was hardly praiseworthy.

Despite rejecting cooperation with South African authorities, many indigenous leaders embraced the characterization of Canadian policy as apartheid. In August 1990, at the invitation of local elders, Archbishop Desmond Tutu spent two days on the Osnaburgh reserve in Northern Ontario. Drawing parallels between the Ojibwe and black South Africans, he promised to raise the situation with Mulroney. To emphasize the parallel, Georges Erasmus, national chief of the AFN, reminded Tutu that many of South Africa's apartheid laws had their basis in Canadian examples.[98] Concurrently, Mohawk warriors and their allies were engaged in a tense standoff with provincial police and federal forces at the Kanehsatà:ke territory near Oka, Quebec. The 78-day confrontation centred around Mohawk opposition to a local plan to build a golf course on their territory. Grand Chief Joseph Norton of the nearby Kahnawà:ke territory, spoke for over 150 other chiefs in urging that Canada be sanctioned 'because of the fact that they are dealing with natives in the same way as the South African white government is dealing with its black people'.[99] During a brief gunfight early on in the standoff, a provincial police officer was killed, but widespread violence was avoided. Through negotiation, the Mohawk removed their roadblocks and the crisis came to an end with the federal government promising to purchase the disputed land and transfer it to Kanehsatà:ke. Many Mohawk and the Haudenosaunee more widely, rejected Canadian and American citizenship, preferring to maintain independent governance and jurisdiction within their territories.[100] Enforcing their sovereign status created tensions with the Canadian government, raising questions about evolving indigenous-state relations and the nature and extent of decolonization within Canada, a goal for many aboriginal groups who opposed the ongoing imposition of the Indian Act.

The Oka standoff was the most prominent of a series of high profile confrontations between indigenous people and provincial and federal authorities, leading Ottawa to form a Royal Commission on Aboriginal Peoples. Among many recommendations, the commissioners suggested increased indigenous self-government, contending that 'through the nation – the traditional historical unit of self-governing power, recognized as such by imperial and later Canadian governments in the treaty-making process – and through nation-to-nation relationships, the Aboriginal people must recover and express their personal and collective autonomy'.[101] To this end, in 1993 Ottawa agreed to carve a new territory, Nunavut, out of the Northwest Territories, part of a land claims agreement. Six years later, when Nunavut was formally created, it marked a major development in indigenous-Canada relations as the territory's Inuit people assumed responsibility for governance, land, and resources. 'The Inuit agenda for the exercise of our right to self-determination is not to secede or separate from Canada', a member of Inuit Tapirisat, the group representing Inuit, had told a joint parliamentary committee reviewing Canadian foreign policy, 'but rather that we wish to share a common citizenship with other Canadians while maintaining our identity as a people, which means maintaining our identity as Inuit.'[102]

With globalization, the process of indigenous decolonization played out at an international level. Indigenous groups in Canada practiced their own brand of diplomacy, forging links with indigenous people from other areas of the world, such as the Chiapas in Mexico and various tribes and nations in the United States, and with other oppressed groups such as Palestinians. Globally, indigenous people held their own international gatherings. In 1992, in parallel with the Earth Summit in Rio de Janeiro, indigenous politicians and activists organized their own summit, which produced a declaration of indigenous rights. At the World Conference against Racism in Durban in 2001, Canadian and indigenous representatives clashed. Matthew Coon Come, AFN national chief, compared the Canadian 'racist and colonial syndrome of dispossession and discrimination' with South African apartheid. Demanding an apology, Indian Affairs Minister Bob Nault insisted that there was 'no proof of this in modern time that the Canadian government and the general population are racist towards aboriginal people'.[103] The standoff in Durban recalled Canada's opposition to Haudenosaunee petitions to the League of Nations in the 1920s. Indeed, while the 1960 UN Declaration on the Granting of Independence to Colonial Countries and Peoples had ignored indigenous populations, growing international interest and indigenous peoples' increasing clout in multilateral fora led to passage of the UN Declaration on the Rights of Indigenous Peoples (UNDRIP) in 2007, a development opposed only by Canada and other former British colonies of settlement.[104] It took until 2016 for Ottawa to support UNDRIP, and Canada's government then faced the task of enacting domestic legislation to fulfil this multilateral commitment.

Rarely has Canada found itself in the international community's bad books. Increasing attention to the poor standard of living on many reserves, indigenous life expectancy at levels lower than that of other Canadians, and high incarceration rates among indigenous people relative to their share of the overall population called into question Canada's image as a progressive, tolerant country. 'Canada's race problem?' noted one commentator. 'It's even worse than America's.'[105] A growing number of indigenous people, particularly a younger generation, sought to decolonize themselves rather than waiting for it to be granted by the federal government.[106] Idle No More, the aptly named protest movement, captured headlines in 2012 and 2013. In pursuing decolonization, indigenous activists encountered opposition from government and from within the body politic. Reflecting an important mainstream current, in 2013 the leading political affairs columnist for Canada's newspaper of record contended, 'To imagine that isolated communities of a thousand or so people can be vibrant and self-sustaining, capable of discharging the panoply of responsibilities of "sovereignty", is to live within the dream palace of memory.'[107] The indigenous search for self-determination and the evolving process of decolonization mark a rejection of the political boundaries imposed during the process of settlement. 'We shouldn't be classified as Canadian or American', a former Kutanei chief told a broadcaster. 'We are the same people; we're all Kootenays.'[108] Indigenous groups' status within Canada, and the extent to which they will be able to assert their sovereignty as nations within a state, was an issue of pressing importance as Canadians commemorated the 150th anniversary of Confederation in 2017.

In terms of its population, the Canada of 2017 was vastly different than the country of 1867. Canadians of British and French ancestry comprised sizeable minorities, sharing the country with people from across the globe. The change in immigration policy in 1967 led to an influx of people from the Global South and the creation of what many – though not all – Canadians celebrated as a more diverse population. Certainly, racism continues to work in subtle and unsubtle ways, with the differentiation between 'visible minorities' and those capable of blending into the general populace simply one sign of soft discrimination. More overt were acts of violence directed towards visible minorities. In the second decade of the twenty-first century, there was an increase in anti-Semitic hate crimes, part of a global uptick in Jew hatred in the wake of political and economic upheaval. Furthermore, since the 9/11 terror attacks, and as part of a wider trend in Western countries, Islamophobia had spread into Canada, fuelling nativist fantasies of a Muslim takeover and culminating in the murder of six Muslims at a Quebec City mosque in 2017. The murderer was one of a growing but small number of Canadians who embraced white supremacist hate spread via the internet, a reminder of one of the downsides of global interconnectivity. Unfortunately, several leading figures in the far right movement that gained prominence in the wake of Donald Trump's election hailed from Canada.

Yet in historical perspective, a country that once barred non-white immigration, whose leaders once worried over whether Ukrainians could be trusted, had come a long way. Moreover, a country that refused entry to Jews fleeing Nazism maintained among the most generous refugee systems in the world. The 2015 Canadian federal election was marked by the Harper government's slow response to the Syrian refugee crisis. Many voters judged the Conservatives' unwillingness to boost refugee numbers – 'It's not just enough to turn around and say, "Oh let's admit more refugees"', Harper told an interviewer – as callous.[109] When the Liberals formed government, the new prime minister, Justin Trudeau, announced a special refugee program for fifty thousand Syrians, who began arriving to homes and jobs provided by thousands of generous volunteers. The phrase is trite but true: Canada is a nation of immigrants. However, it is a fortunate country, bordered by three oceans and a neighbour that sends few illegal migrants north. No doubt the ability to control immigration kept nativism largely at bay. The head of the Institute for Canadian Citizenship, speculated that in terms of promoting social integration among a diverse populace 'Canada has had the history, philosophy and possibly the physical space to do some of that necessary thinking about how to build societies differently'. Indeed, in 2017 a leading columnist made the case for tripling Canada's population, a call at odds with the xenophobia and anti-immigrant hatred then becoming popular throughout much of the West.[110]

Whether due to fortune or a greater capacity for tolerance, the general and decades-long consensus among the leading political parties that high levels of annual immigration are a good thing – the primary reason for Canada's population growth given low birth rates – stands in marked contrast to other Western countries. As 'the most successful pluralist society on the face of our globe', the Aga Khan, leader of the world's Ismaili Muslims, characterized Canada as 'a model for the world'. 'Follow the moose', urged *The Economist*, citing Canada as 'a heartening exception' to the 'wall-builders, door-slammers and drawbridge-raisers' common in the West in the twenty-first century's second decade.[111] Multiculturalism did not go untested. Critics argued, variously, that it devalued Canada's British and French heritage, did little to promote a common identity, or confined minorities to 'social ghettos' through oversimplifying and stereotyping culture.[112] Even so, the idea of a diverse Canada had a potent hold for many Canadians, particularly in the metropolises of Toronto, Vancouver, and Montreal – cities tied to the globalized world through economic, transportation, and cultural networks. In 2015, Justin Trudeau went so far as to claim that Canada was the 'first postnational state'.

Lacking a 'core identity', he noted that, instead, Canadians were united by 'shared values – openness, respect, compassion, willingness to work hard, to be there for each other, to search for equality and justice'.[113] Whether these are indeed definitive values, Trudeau was not wrong in his other observation, for Canada had never been a homogenous nation-state. For all its faults, Canada was still a place where two foreign-born women, Adrienne Clarkson (Hong Kong) and Michaëlle Jean (Haiti), served as governor general, a remarkable development given the symbolism and history of the position and Canada's past immigration restrictions.

The country's multicultural makeup was seen to provide certain advantages. In introducing his government's 1995 foreign policy statement, Chrétien emphasized that 'Canada's cultural heritage gives it privileged access to the homelands of Canadians drawn from every part of the world who make up its multi-cultural personality'.[114] Businesses, universities, NGOS, and government departments benefitted from new Canadians' interpersonal links with their countries of birth. New Canadians brought diverse perspectives on international issues, a welcome development certainly in the small community of Canadian foreign policy specialists.[115]

The diasporic connection raised a variety of complications. One issue involved the Canadian government's responsibility for its citizens living abroad. During the 2006 war between Israel and Hezbollah, Canada's military scrambled to evacuate thousands of Canadian dual citizens in Lebanon. The rape, torture, and murder of Iranian-Canadian journalist Zahra Kazemi at the hands of Iranian secret police poisoned relations between Ottawa and Teheran, just as the Chinese government's jailing of Huseyin Celil, a Canadian citizen and human rights activist from the Uighur minority, fuelled the Harper government's hostility towards Beijing. Similarly, as Yugoslavia collapsed in the early 1990s, members of various ethnic and religious groups raised money for their respective sides in the war or left Canada to fight.[116] The Arab-Canadian Khadr family was notorious for their links to the al-Qaeda terror network through Egyptian-born Ahmed Said Khadr, who had migrated to Montreal in the 1970s. Jean Chrétien had intervened with Pakistan's government to free Ahmed, an al-Qaeda financier who went on to fight and die alongside other Islamist militants in Afghanistan during the US invasion. Two of his sons – both Canadian citizens – were captured by the Americans and imprisoned for a decade at Guantánamo Bay. The youngest, Omar, became the centre of a legal and political battle. Although he had killed an American soldier as an illegal combatant under international law, Omar was a child soldier and was tortured.[117] Quite apart from the merits of the case for or against him, Omar, and his family, symbolized the trouble Canadians could get up to in an interconnected world.

In 1998, Canadian Security Intelligence Service Director Ward Elcock had warned that other than the United States 'there are more international terrorist groups active here than any other country in the world', with their roots in 'virtually every significant regional, ethnic, and nationalist conflict'.[118] Fundraising in Canada had been carried out by Irish Republicans, Palestinians, Kurds, and, perhaps most prominently, the Liberation Tigers of Tamil Eelam, engaged in a decades-long civil war in Sri Lanka. Tamil Tiger fundraisers in Canada damaged Canadian-Sri Lankan relations and created embarrassing incidents for government ministers who appeared at these events. Since the Tamil community comprised an important source of votes, there was controversy over the extent to which Ottawa's interest in the Sri Lankan government's admittedly deplorable human rights record was driven by electoral concerns. As the civil war came to an end in 2009, tens of thousands of Canadian Tamils picketed in Toronto and Ottawa, urging Canada's government to impose sanctions. Further controversy came when Prime Minister Harper opted to skip the 2013 Commonwealth summit held in Sri Lanka. The move had all party support, but to Joe Clark, Harper had missed an opportunity to confront Sri Lankan officials.[119] As foreign minister Clark had cautioned against Canadian politicians involving themselves with members of the Khalistan independence movement, prominent among Canada's Sikh community. 'For elected Canadian officials to support the advocates of Khalistan today', he observed, 'would be the equivalent to endorsing the foreign interference in our affairs which Canadians found so objectionable only twenty-odd years ago.'[120] Beginning in the 1970s, as Canadian Sikhs began protesting Indian government repression of Sikhs, within the community, support grew for terror groups, and the pro-Khalistan World Sikh Organization operated an office in Canada. These connections received considerable attention after the 1985 Air India bombing, when members of a Sikh militant group blew up a Bombay-bound flight from Toronto, killing 329 people in the worst act of aviation terrorism until 2001.

In strict foreign policy terms, there stood the question of whether Canada would be drawn into situations abroad due to the interests of various ethnic groups. In 2005, a columnist discerned 'a subtle but profound shift in recent Canadian foreign policy priorities', in that 'the tsunami of last year, the chaos in Haiti, the exploding troubles in Sudan are not foreign-*aid* issues for Canada, they are foreign-*policy* priorities. They reflect our demographic transformation, from predominantly European to truly multinational. Problems in India and China and Haiti are *our* problems because India and China and Haiti *are* our motherlands.'[121] The issue is less of sea change than it might appear. Diasporic groups in Canada have always taken an interest in their ancestral lands, from French Canadian Zouaves who took up arms to defend the Pope in the 1860s and Irish Catholics and Protestants who battled on both sides of Ireland's war of independence to Eastern Europeans who protested Soviet colonialism and Jews who fought to defend Israel in the 1940s.[122] In a sense Canada's first century was marked by British diaspora politics, with tens of thousands of war graves in Europe a grim result.

Were Canadian national interests affected by incidents in these places? And did the national interests of an increasingly multicultural country change along with the makeup of its population? At the time of the Gulf War, the United Church's Reverend Tad Mitsui lamented that race was 'involved in judging who is an enemy and who is a friend'. Canadians, he contended, could view Arabs as enemies, but they 'will never think of America as an enemy, and neither can they think of British or the French as enemies'. In Mitsui's view, 'if Canada should exist as a multicultural, multiracial country, you cannot take sides with anybody.'[123] Taken to an extreme, would multiculturalism alter Canada's status as a Western country, a conception rooted in culture and race? If so, what impact would that have, say, on Canadian involvement in NATO operations? One commentator highlighted the difficulty that many Canadians would face in coming to terms with 'a world in which the United States and its Western allies are no longer the sole, or even dominant global power'.[124] For Indo-Canadians or Chinese-Canadians this diffusion of power may not come as much of a shock.

By way of a conclusion, at the time of writing, the liberal international order in which several generations of Canadian policymakers, academics, and journalists invested themselves seems in disarray. To quote Jennifer Welsh, the Oxford-trained, Saskatchewan-born academic and international civil servant, the world has witnessed 'The Return of History', and the end of the triumphalist hopes of progress that came with the collapse of the Soviet Union. Over a decade earlier, Welsh had offered a hopeful vision of a Canada 'At Home in the World'. In innumerable ways, Canadians are linked to a world filled with more tension, with historian Margaret Macmillan warning that 'ominous echoes' of the First World War are rumbling. As Canadian foreign minister under Justin Trudeau, Chrystia Freeland, a former journalist who examined the rise of the plutocratic elite dominating the globalized age, made saving the liberal international order against rising populism a prime focus of Canada's foreign policy.[125] One hopes that Canadians' diversity, security, and prosperity will be enough to weather the storm. Looming, too, is the catastrophic threat of climate change.

Global warming brought to the fore the importance of Canadian sovereignty in the Arctic and the question of whether or not the Northwest Passage, the long-desired trade route through arctic waters, now accessible thanks to melting ice, was an international waterway or lay in Canadian territorial waters.[126] While many Canadians can conceive of an issue such as melting arctic sea ice, many of the other effects of climate change are more abstract and so attract less concerted action from governments, which have sought to weigh economic concerns against environmental ones. Having contributed to climate change via fossil fuel production and consumption, Canadians, in common with people around the world, face an uncertain future, should scientists' dire predictions come true. Here, readers may sense the typical pessimism of the historian, for the failure to take meaningful action in tackling global warming has been the largest – and perhaps most consequential – public policy failure of the past two decades. The failure is a global one, and a reminder that Canada sits within the world.

Notes

Introduction: Canada and the world since 1867

1 'Every G20 Nation Wants to Be Canada, Insists PM', *Reuters*, 25 Sept. 2009; 'A Conversation with the Right Honorable Justin Trudeau, Prime Minister of Canada', 21 Apr. 2016. Available at: http://livestream.com/accounts/13327241/events/5231459. [accessed 11 March 2019].

2 'La Francophonie Gives Harper a Rare Foreign Policy Victory', *Toronto Star*, 1 Dec. 2014. Available at: https://www.thestar.com/opinion/editorials/2014/12/01/la_francophonie_gives_harper_a_rare_foreign_policy_victory_editorial.html. [accessed 11 March 2019].

3 Report, Sixteenth National Convention, 9–11 Aug. 1960, LAC, MG 28 IV 1 vol. 372, file National Council CCF; Lloyd Axworthy, 'Canada and the World Revolution', *Canadian Dimension*, Mar.–Apr. 1966.

4 Arnold Smith and Clyde Sanger, *Stitches in Time: The Commonwealth in World Politics* (Don Mills: General Publishing, 1981), 35.

5 Alexander Morris, *Nova Britannia: or, our New Canadian Dominion Foreshadowed. Being a Series of Lectures, Speeches and Addresses* (Toronto: Hunter, Rose, 1884), 88.

6 Daniel Drache, 'The Canadian Bourgeoisie and Its National Consciousness', in *Close the 49th Parallel*, ed. Ian Lumsden (Toronto: University of Toronto Press, 1970), 5.

7 Zara Steiner, 'On Writing International History: Chaps, Maps and Much More', *International Affairs* 73 (1997): 531. A recent, model work of Canadian international history by an old pro is Robert Bothwell, *Your Country, My Country: A Unified History of the United States and Canada* (New York: Oxford University Press, 2015).

8 Asa McKercher, 'Toward Canada and the World: Thoughts on the Future of Canadian Foreign Policy History', *International Journal* 72 (2017): 243–54.

9 Carl Bridge and Kent Fedorowich, eds, *The British World: Diaspora, Culture and Identity* (London: Frank Cass, 2003); Gary Magee and Andrew Thompson, *Empire and Globalisation: Networks of People, Goods, and Capital in the British World, c. 1850–1914* (Cambridge: Cambridge University Press, 2010).

10 Victoria De Grazia, *Irresistible Empire: America's Advance through Twentieth-Century Europe* (Cambridge: Harvard University Press, 2005); David Ellwood, *The Shock of America: Europe and the Challenge of the Century* (Oxford: Oxford University Press, 2012).

11 Charles Maier, *Among Empires: American Ascendancy and Its Predecessors* (Cambridge: Harvard University Press, 2007); A. G. Hopkins, *American Empire: A Global History* (Princeton, NJ: Princeton University Press, 2018).

12 Cole Harris and Jean Barman, 'Editorial', *BC Studies* 115/116 (1997/8): 4; Laura Ishiguro, 'Histories of Settler Colonialism: Considering New Currents', *BC Studies* 190 (2016): 5–13; Lorenzo Veracini, *Settler Colonialism: A Theoretical Overview* (Basingstoke: Palgrave, 2010).

13 Glenda Sluga and Patricia Clavin, *Internationalisms: A Twentieth-Century History* (Cambridge: Cambridge University Press, 2016).

14 Akira Iriye, Petra Goedde, and William I. Hitchcock, *The Human Rights Revolution: An International History* (Oxford: Oxford University Press, 2012); Donna Gabaccia, *Foreign Relations: American Immigration in Global Perspective* (Princeton, NJ: Princeton University Press, 2015); Marilyn Lake and Henry Reynolds, *Drawing the Global Colour Line: White Men's Countries and the International Challenge of Racial Equality* (Cambridge: Cambridge University Press, 2008).

1 Dominion-building and empire-building

1 A. L. Richardson, *Report of the Visit of the British Association to the Canadian North-West* (Winnipeg: McIntyre, 1884), 36; George Ham, *The New West: Extending from the Great Lakes across Plain and Mountain to the Golden Shores of the Pacific* (Winnipeg: Canadian Historical Publishing, 1888).

2 John Darwin, *The Empire Project: The Rise and Fall of the British World-System, 1830–1970* (Cambridge: Cambridge University Press, 2009), 148.

3 Stephen Leacock, *The Dawn of Canadian History* (Toronto: Glasgow, Brook, 1914), 44.

4 James Belich, *Replenishing the Earth: The Settler Revolution and the Rise of the Anglo-World, 1783–1939* (Oxford: Oxford University Press, 2009); John Weaver, *The Great Land Rush and the Making of the Modern World* (Montreal: McGill-Queen's University Press, 2003); Cecilia Morgan, *Building Better Britains: Settler Societies in the British World, 1783–1920* (Toronto: University of Toronto Press, 2017).

5 Patrick Wolfe, 'Settler Colonialism and the Elimination of the Native', *Journal of Genocide Research* 8 (2006): 387–409; Patrick Wolfe, 'Land, Labor, and Difference: Elementary Structures of Race', *American Historical Review* 106 (2001).

6 Andrew Woolford and Jeff Benvenuto, 'Canada and Colonial Genocide', *Journal of Genocide Research* 17 (2015); David Macdonald and Graham Hudson. 'The Genocide Question and Indian Residential Schools in Canada', *Canadian Journal of Political Science* 45 (2012): 427–49; Pamela Palmater, 'Genocide, Indian Policy and the Legislated Elimination of Indians in Canada', *Aboriginal Policy Studies* 3 (2014): 27–54.

7 Margaret Jacobs, 'Genocide or Ethnic Cleansing? Are These Our Only Choices?', *Western Historical Quarterly* 47 (2016): 448.

8 *Parliamentary Debates on the Subject of the Confederation of the British North American Provinces* (Quebec: Hunter, Rose, 1865), 85.

9 W. L. Morton, *The Critical Years: The Union of British North America, 1857–1873* (Toronto: McClelland & Stewart, 1964), 93.

10 John Boyko, *Blood and Daring: How Canada Fought the American Civil War and Forged a Nation* (Toronto: Knopf, 2013); Richard Reid, *African Canadians in Union Blue: Volunteering for the Cause in the Civil War* (Vancouver: UBC Press, 2014); Jacqueline Krikorian and David Cameron, 'The 1867 Union of the British North American Colonies: A View from the United States', in *Globalizing Confederation: Canada and the World in 1867*, ed. Jacqueline Krikorian, Marcel Martel and Adrian Shubert (Toronto: University of Toronto Press, 2017), 47–60.

11 Patrick Steward and Bryon McGovern, *The Fenians: Irish Rebellion in the North Atlantic World* (Knoxville: University of Tennessee Press, 2013).

12 Christopher Moore, *1867: How the Fathers Made a Deal* (Toronto: McClelland & Stewart, 1997), 43.

13 *Parliamentary Debates on the Subject of the Confederation of the British North American Provinces* (Quebec: Hunter, Rose, 1865), 86; 'The Great North West', *Globe*, 27 Feb. 1862.

14 Doug Owram, *Promise of Eden: The Canadian Expansionist Movement and the Idea of the West, 1856–1900* (Toronto: University of Toronto Press, 1980), 77; Edward Blake, *A National Sentiment! Speech of Hon. Edward Blake, MP at Aurora* (Ottawa: E.A. Perry, 1874), 8.

15 Macdonald to Bridges, 28 Jan. 1870 in *Correspondence of Sir John Macdonald*, ed., Joseph Pope (Toronto: Oxford University Press, 1921), 124; Joseph Pope, *Memoirs of the Right Honourable Sir John Alexander Macdonald* (Ottawa: J. Durie, 1894), 398.

16 'The Future of Canada', *Globe*, 10 July 1867; Richard Nuenherz, ' "Hemmed In": Reactions in British Columbia to the Purchase of Russian America', *Pacific Northwest Quarterly* 80 (1989): 101–11; David Shi, 'Seward's Attempt to Annex British Columbia, 1865–1869', *Pacific Historical Review* 47 (1978): 217–38.

17 Senate, *Debates*, 3 Apr. 1871, 152; H. B Gates, *The Dominion of Canada* (Montreal: n.p., 1872), 7.

18 John McMullen, *The History of Canada, from Discovery to the Present Time* (Brockville: McMullen, 1868), xxxi.

19 E. R. Young, 'The Indian Problem', *Canadian Methodist Magazine and Review*, June 1885, 468; E. R. Young, *Stories From the Indian Wigwams and Northern Campfires* (London: Charles Kelly, 1894), 233.

20 'Indignation Meeting', *Globe*, 7 Apr. 1870.

21 J. M. Bumsted, 'Louis Riel and the United States', *American Review of Canadian Studies* 29 (1999): 17–41.

22 House of Commons, *Debates*, 4 May 1870, 1353.

23 Tony Rees, *Arc of the Medicine Line: Mapping the World's Longest Undefended Border across the Western Plains* (Vancouver: Douglas & McIntyre, 2007).

24 Richard Gwyn, *Nation Maker: Sir John A. Macdonald: His Life, Our Times*, Vol. 2 (Toronto: Random House, 2011), 240.

25 Alexander Morris, *The Treaties of Canada, with the Indians of Manitoba and the North-West Territories* (Saskatoon: Fifth House, 1991 [1880]), 270; John McDougall, *Opening the Great West: Experiences of a Missionary* (Calgary: Glenbow-Alberta Institute, 1970), 15.

26 Morris, *The Treaties of Canada*, 249.

27 Amanda Nettelbeck, Russell Smandych, Louis A. Knafla, Robert Foster, *Fragile Settlements: Aboriginal Peoples, Law and Resistance in South-West Australia and Prairie Canada* (Vancouver: UBC Press, 2016), 70; Keith Smith, *Liberalism, Surveillance, and Resistance: Indigenous Communities in Western Canada, 1877–1927* (Edmonton: Athabaska University Press, 2009), 59.

28 Barry Gough, *Gunboat Frontier: British Maritime Authority and Northwest Coast Indians, 1846–90* (Vancouver: UBC Press, 1984), 210.

29 Michel Hogue, *Métis and the Medicine Line: Creating a Border and Dividing a People* (Chapel Hill: UNC Press, 2015).

30 Galen Roger Perras, 'The Greater Menace to the Peace of Nations? The 1877 Mills Mission and Direct Canadian-American Diplomatic Relations', *Diplomacy & Statecraft* 29 (2018): 143–66; Gary Pennanen, 'Sitting Bull: Indian Without a Country', *Canadian Historical Review* 51 (1970): 123–40.

31 Brian Hubner, 'Horse Stealing and the Borderline: The NWMP and the Control of Indian Movement, 1874–1900', *Prairie Forum* 20 (1995): 281–300; Lissa Wadewitz, *The Nature of Borders: Salmon, Boundaries, and Bandits on the Salish Sea* (Seattle: University of Washington, 2012).

32 Macdonald to Northcote, 1 May 1878 in *Correspondence of Sir John Macdonald*, 240.

33 J. R. Miller, *Compact, Contact, Covenant: Aboriginal Treaty-Making in Canada* (Toronto: University of Toronto Press, 2009); D. J. Hall, *From Treaties to Reserves: The Federal Government and Native Peoples in Territorial Alberta, 1870–1905* (Montreal: McGill-Queen's University Press, 2016).

34 Peter Erasmus, *Buffalo Days and Nights* (Calgary: Glenbow-Alberta Institute, 1976), 245; Morris, *The Treaties of Canada*, 62.

35 Maureen Lux, *Medicine that Walks: Disease, Medicine, and Canadian Plains Native Peoples 1880–1930* (Toronto: University of Toronto Press, 2001); Andrew Isenberg, *The Destruction of the Bison: An Environmental History, 1750–1920* (Cambridge: Cambridge University Press, 2000).

36 House of Commons, *Debates*, 27 Apr. 1882, 1186.

37 James Daschuk, *Clearing the Plains: Disease, Politics of Starvation, and the Loss of Aboriginal Life* (Winnipeg: University of Manitoba Press, 2013).

38 House of Commons, *Debates*, 5 May 1880, 1991.

39 Sarah Carter, 'Two Acres and a Cow: "Peasant" Farming for the Indians of the Northwest, 1889–97', *Canadian Historical Review* 70 (1989): 27; Sarah Carter, *Lost Harvests: Prairie Indian Reserve Farmers and Government Policy* (Montreal: McGill-Queen's University Press, 1990).

40 Smith, *Liberalism, Surveillance, and Resistance*, 60–73.

41 Douglas Cole and Ira Chaikin, *An Iron Hand Upon the People: The Law Against the Potlatch on the Northwest Coast* (Vancouver: Douglas & McIntyre, 1990); Katherine Pettipas, *Severing the Ties that Bind: Government Repression of Indigenous Religious Ceremonies on the Prairies* (Winnipeg: University of Manitoba Press, 1994).

42 House of Commons, *Debates*, 8 Feb. 1877, 3.

43 John McDougall, *Saddle, Sled, and Snowshoe* (Toronto: William Briggs, 1896), 252; John Hines, *The Red Indians of the Plains: Thirty Years' Missionary Experience in the Saskatchewan* (Toronto: McClelland and Stewart, 1916); J. R. Miller, *Skyscrapers Hide the Heavens: A History of Native-Newcomer Relations in Canada* (Toronto: University of Toronto Press, 2000), 314; Myra Rutherdale, *Women and the White Man's God: Gender and Race in the Canadian Mission Field* (Vancouver: UBC Press, 2003).

44 House of Commons, *Debates*, 9 May 1883, 1107–8.

45 Brian Titley, *The Frontier World of Edgar Dewdney* (Vancouver: UBC Press, 1999), 79.

46 J. R Miller, *Shingwauk's Vision: A History of Native Residential Schools* (Toronto: University of Toronto Press, 1996), 10; Brian Titley, *A Narrow Vision: Duncan Campbell Scott and the Administration of Indian Affairs in Canada* (Vancouver: UBC Press, 1986), 50; Andrew Woolford, *The Benevolent Experiment: Indigenous Boarding Schools, Genocide, and Redress in Canada and the United States* (Winnipeg: University of Manitoba Press, 2015); Ian Mosby, 'Administering Colonial Science: Nutrition Research and Human Biomedical Experimentation in Aboriginal Communities and Residential Schools, 1942–1952', *Histoire Sociale/Social History* 46 (2013).

47 Desmond Morton, 'Cavalry or Police: Keeping the Peace on Two Adjacent Frontiers, 1870–1900', *Journal of Canadian Studies* 12 (1977): 27; Rod Macleod, *The North-West Mounted Police and Law Enforcement* (Toronto: University of Toronto Press, 1976), 3.

48 House of Commons, *Debates*, 8 Feb. 1977, 3; 'The Indian War in the States', *Globe*, 15 Apr. 1873; Charles Acton Burrows, *North-Western Canada* (Winnipeg: n.p., 1880), 34; Jill St. Germain, *Indian Treaty-Making Policy in the United States and Canada, 1867–1877* (Lincoln: University of Nebraska Press, 2001).

49 Blair Stonechild and Bill Waiser, *Loyal Till Death: Indians and the North-West Rebellion* (Calgary: Fifth House Books, 1997); Titley, *The Frontier World of Edgar Dewdney*, 67–9.

50 House of Commons, *Debates*, 26 Mar. 1885, 745; Geoff Read and Todd Webb, '"The Catholic Mahdi of the North West": Louis Riel and the Metis

Resistance in Transatlantic and Imperial Context', *Canadian Historical Review* 93 (2012): 171–95.

51 Lewis Redman Ord, *Reminiscences of a Bungle, by One of the Bunglers*, ed. Rod Macleod (Edmonton: University of Alberta Press, 1983 [1887]).

52 Ian Radforth, 'Celebrating the Suppression of the North-West Rebellion of 1885: The Toronto Press and the Militia Volunteers', *Histoire Sociale/Social History* 47 (2014): 633.

53 House of Commons, *Debates*, 6 July 1885, 3119.

54 J. R. Miller, 'Macdonald as Minister of Indian Affairs: The Shaping of Canadian Indian Policy', in *Macdonald at 200: New Reflections and Legacies*, ed. Patrice Dutil and Roger Hall (Toronto: Dundurn, 2014), 332.

55 Gwyn, *Nation Maker*, 478.

56 Goldwin Smith, *Canada and the Canadian Question* (London: Macmillan, 1891), 197–9.

57 Dirk Hoerder, *Creating Societies: Immigrant Lives in Canada* (Montreal: McGill-Queen's University Press, 1999), 12.

58 Adam Shortt, 'Some Observations on the Great North-West', *QQ* 3 (1895): 14.

59 Ninette Kelley and Michael Trebilcock, *The Making of the Mosaic: A History of Canadian Immigration Policy*, Second Edition (Toronto: University of Toronto Press, 2010), 113.

60 Miller, *Skyscrapers Hide the Heavens*, 314.

61 George Parkin, *The Great Dominion: Studies of Canada* (London: Macmillan, 1895), 215; Shortt, 'Some Observations on the Great North-West'.

62 Pierre Berton, *The Promised Land: Settling the West, 1896–1914* (Toronto: Anchor, 2002), 67.

63 Basil Stewart, *The Land of the Maple Leaf* (London: Routledge, 1908), 151; Stephen Leacock, 'Canada and the Immigration Problem', *National Review* (Apr. 1911).

64 Donald Avery, *Reluctant Host: Canada's Response to Immigrant Workers, 1896–1994* (Toronto: McClelland and Stewart, 1995), 64.

65 House of Commons, *Debates*, 12 Apr. 1901, 2938; J. S. Woodsworth, *Strangers within Our Gates: Or Coming Canadians* (Toronto: University of Toronto Press, 1972 [1909]), 46.

66 Lucille Campey, *Ignored by Not Forgotten: Canada's English Immigrants* (Toronto: Dundurn, 2014), 224.

67 Sir Robert Falconer, 'The Unification of Canada', *University Magazine* 7 (1908): 4.

68 John Maclean, *The Indians of Canada: Their Manners and Customs* (Toronto: William Briggs, 1889), 339; Ishbel Maria Gordon, *Through Canada with a Kodak* (Edinburgh: W.H. White, 1893), 202–3.

69 William Butler, *The Great Lone Land* (London: Gilbert & Rivington, 1872), 242; George Grant, *Ocean to Ocean* (Toronto: Rose Belford, 1879), 48.

70 J. R. Seeley, *The Expansion of England* (London: Macmillan, 1884), 12, 13.

71 Owram, *Promise of Eden*, 126; Donald MacKay, *The Asian Dream: The Pacific Rim and Canada's National Railway* (Vancouver: Douglas & McIntyre, 1986), 29.

2 Canada and Greater Britain

1 'Canada at the Polls', *The Illustrated American*, 14 Mar. 1891, 167.

2 Duncan Bell, *The Idea of Greater Britain: Empire and the Future of World Order, 1860–1900* (Princeton, NJ: Princeton University Press, 2007).

3 Adam Hochschild, *To End All Wars: A Story of Loyalty and Rebellion, 1914–1918* (Boston, MA: Houghton Mifflin, 2011), 50.

4 Carl Berger, *The Sense of Power: Studies in the Ideas of Canadian Imperialism, 1867–1914* (Toronto: University of Toronto Press, 1970); Graeme Thompson, 'Ontario's Empire: Liberalism and Britannic Nationalism in Laurier's Canada, 1887–1919' (DPhil thesis, University of Oxford, 2017).

5 'Canada in Britain', *Globe*, 25 Sept. 1901.

6 *Parliamentary Debates on the Subject of the Confederation of the British North American Colonies* (Quebec: Hunter, Rose, 1865), 43–4.

7 Ben Gilding, 'The Silent Framers of British North American Union: The Colonial Office and Canadian Confederation, 1851–67', *Canadian Historical Review* 99 (2018).

8 Paul Stevens and John Saywell, eds, *Lord Minto's Canadian Papers*, vol. 1 (Toronto: Champlain Society, 1981), xxiv.

9 Barbara Messamore, *Canada's Governors General, 1847–1878: Biography and Constitutional Evolution* (Toronto: University of Toronto Press, 2006), 177–213.

10 Andrew Smith, *British Businessmen and Canadian Confederation: Constitution Making in an Age of Anglo-Globalization* (Montreal: McGill-Queen's University Press, 2008); Ged Martin, *Britain and the Origins of Canadian Confederation, 1837–67* (Vancouver: UBC Press, 1995).

11 Anthony Trollope, *Phineas Finn* (London: Virtue, 1869), 464.

12 George Stanley, *Canada's Soldiers: The Military History of an Unmilitary People* (Toronto: Macmillan, 1974), 240.

13 Joseph Pope, *Memoirs of the Right Honourable Sir John Alexander Macdonald* (Ottawa: J. Durie, 1894), 464.

14 Donald Creighton, *Dominion of the North* (Boston, MA: Houghton Mifflin, 1944), 349.

15 Richard Preston, *Canada and 'Imperial Defense': A Study of the Origins of the British Commonwealth's Defense Organization, 1867–1899* (Toronto: University of Toronto Press, 1967), 91–95.

16 C. P. Stacey, *Canada and the Age of Conflict, vol. I: 1867–1921* (Toronto: University of Toronto Press, 1984), 41.

17 C. P. Stacey, 'Canada and the Nile Expedition of 1884–85', *Canadian Historical Review* 33 (1952): 335–6.

18 Anthony Michel, 'To Represent the Country in Egypt: Aboriginality, Britishness, Anglophone Canadian Identities, and the Nile Voyageur Contingent, 1884–1885', *Histoire Sociale/Social History* 39 (2006): 45–77; Carl Benn, *Mohawks on the Nile* (Toronto: Dundurn, 2009).

19 House of Commons, *Debates*, 26 Mar. 1885, 745, 764; Read and Webb, 'The Catholic Mahdi of the North West'.

20 House of Commons, *Debates*, 21 Apr. 1882, 1078.

21 House of Commons, *Debates*, 29 Apr. 1880, 1859.

22 'Massacres deplored', *Globe*, 28 Nov 1905; House of Commons, *Debates*, 15 Mar. 1906, 229.

23 Bernard Pénisson, 'Le commissariat canadien à Paris (1882–1928)', *Revue d'histoire de l'Amérique française* 34 (1980): 357–76.

24 Stacey, *Canada and the Age of Conflict, I*, 47.

25 John Hilliker, *Canada's Department of External Affairs*, vol. 1 (Montreal: McGill-Queen's University Press, 1990); O. Mary Hill, *Canada's Salesman to the World: The Department of Trade and Commerce, 1892–1939* (Montreal: McGill-Queen's University Press, 1977).

26 George Johnson, *The All Red Line: The Annals and Aims of the Pacific Cable Project* (Ottawa: J. Hope & Sons, 1903), 7.

27 George Parkin, 'The Geographical Unity of the British Empire', *Geographical Journal* 4 (1894): 227.

28 David Torrance, 'Instructor to Empire: Canada and the Rhodes Scholarship, 1902–39', in *Canada and the British World: Culture, Migration, and Identity*, ed. Phillip Buckner and R. Douglas Francis (Vancouver: UBC Press, 2006); Tamson Pietsch, *Empire of Scholars: Universities, Networks and the British Academic World, 1850–1939* (Manchester: Manchester University Press, 2013).

29 George Parkin, *Imperial Federation: The Problem of National Unity* (London: Macmillan, 1892), 60.

30 George Grant, *Imperial Federation* (Winnipeg: Manitoba Free Press, 1890), 1.

31 Parkin, *Imperial Federation*, 27; Peter Price, 'Steppingstones to Imperial Unity? The British West Indies in the Late-Victorian Imperial Federation Movement', *Canadian Journal of History* 52 (2017): 240–63; John Kendle, *The Round Table Movement and Imperial Union* (Toronto: University of Toronto Press, 1975).

32 'The Ideal of Imperialism', *Globe*, 4 Jan. 1902.

33 House of Commons, *Debates*, 29 Mar. 1909, 3491.

34 Paula Hastings, 'Fellow British Subjects or Colonial "Others"? Race, Empire, and Ambivalence in Canadian Representations of India in the Early Twentieth Century', *American Review of Canadian Studies* 38 (2008): 3–26.

35 George Grant, 'Current Events', *Queen's Quarterly* 4 (1897): 236.

36 George Grant, *Advantages of Imperial Federation* (Toronto: C. Blackett Robinson, 1891), 18–19.

37 Roy MacLaren, ed. *African Exploits: The Diaries of William Stairs, 1887–1892* (Montreal: McGill-Queen's University Press, 1998), 61; A. H. M. Kirk-Greene, 'Canada in Africa: Sir Percy Girouard, Neglected Colonial Governor', *African Affairs* 83 (1984): 207–39.

38 H. V. Nelles, *The Art of Nation Building: Pageantry and Spectacle at Quebec's Tercentenary* (Toronto: University of Toronto Press, 1999), 27.

39 Henri Bourassa, *Les Canadiens-Français et L'Empire Britannique* (Québec: S.A. Demers, 1903), 10; Casey Murrow, *Henri Bourassa and French-Canadian Nationalism* (Montreal: Harvest House, 1968), 33.

40 André Siegfried, *The Race Question in Canada* (Toronto: McClelland and Stewart, 1966 [1907]), 138.

41 Bourassa, *Les Canadiens-Français*, 10; Arthur Silver, 'Quelques considerations sur les rapports du Canada français avec l'impérialisme britannique au XIX siècle', *Canadian Journal of African Studies* 15 (1981): 55–75; Réal Bélanger, 'L'Élite politique canadienne-française et l'Empire britannique: trois reflets représentatifs des perceptions canadiennes-françaises', in *Imperial Canada, 1867–1917*, ed. Colin Coates (Edinburgh: University of Edinburgh, 1997), 122–40; Serge Courville, *Rêves d'empire: le Québec et le rêve colonial* (Ottawa: University of Ottawa Press, 2000); Sylvie Lacombe, *La rencontre de deux peuple élus: Comparison des ambitions nationale et impérial au Canada entre 1896 et 1920* (Quebec: Les Presses de l'Université Laval, 2002)

42 Stanley Ryerson, *French Canada: A Study in Democracy* (Toronto: Progress Books, 1980), 99.

43 Charles Mair, 'The New Land', *Canadian Monthly and National Review* 8 (1875): 161.

44 House of Commons, *Debates*, 18 Feb. 1890, 832–3, 840, 848–9.

45 Alfred Milner, *The Nation and the Empire* (London: Constable and Company, 1913), xxxviii.

46 House of Commons, *Debates*, 14 Feb. 1902, 39.

47 John Buchan, *Lord Minto: A Memoir* (London: Thomas Nelson, 1924), 166.

48 Preston, *Canada and 'Imperial Defense'*, 240.

49 House of Commons, *Debates*, 5 Feb. 1900, 68.

50 Carman Miller, *Painting the Map Red: Canada and the South African War, 1899–1902* (Montreal: McGill-Queen's University Press, 1993), 41.

51 Gordon Heath, *A War with a Silver Lining: Canadian Protestant Churches and the War in South Africa* (Montreal: McGill-Queen's University Press, 2009).

52 Robert Page, *The Boer War and Canadian Imperialism* (Ottawa: Canadian Historical Association, 1987), 13.

53 E. B. Biggar, *The Boer War* (Toronto: Biggar, Samuel, 1900), 27; John Mitcham, *Race and Imperial Defence in the British World, 1870–1914* (Cambridge: Cambridge University Press, 2016), 72.

54 Carman Miller, *Canada's Little War: Fighting for the British Empire in Southern Africa, 1899–1902* (Toronto: James Lorimer, 2003), 58.

55 George Grant introduction in T. G. Marquis, *Canada's Sons on Kopje and Veldt* (Toronto: Canada's Sons, 1900), 4.

56 'The Canadian Contingent', *Globe*, 3 Oct. 1899; 'The Second Contingent', *Military Gazette*, 2 Jan. 1900.

57 Stanley McKeown Brown, *With the Royal Canadians* (Toronto: Publishers' Syndicate, 1900), 18.

58 House of Commons, *Debates*, 13 Mar. 1900, 1848; Ernest Chambers, *The Governor-General's Body Guard* (Toronto: E.L. Ruddy, 1902), 121.

59 Miller, *Painting the Map Red*, 436; Rudyard Kipling, 'The Islanders', in *The Collected Poems of Rudyard Kipling* (Ware: Woodsworth Editions, 2001), 313; Amy Shaw, 'The Boer War, Masculinity, and Citizenship in Canada, 1899–1902', in *Contesting Bodies and Nations in Canadian History*, ed. Jane Nichols and Patrizia Gentile (Toronto: University of Toronto Press, 2013), 97–114.

60 House of Commons, *Debates*, 1 Mar. 1902, 3951–61.

61 Miller, *Painting the Map Red*, 28; Carman Miller, 'English-Canadian Opposition to the South Africa War as seen through the Press', *Canadian Historical Review* 55 (1974): 422–38; Amy Shaw, 'Dissent in Canada against the Anglo-Boer War, 1899–1902', in *Worth Fighting For: Canada's Tradition of War Resistance from 1812 to the War on Terror*, ed. Lara Campbell, Michael Dawson and Catherine Gidney (Toronto: Between the Lines, 2015).

62 'Let Loose for a Day', *Globe*, 8 Mar. 1900; Miller, *Painting the Map Red*, 443.

63 W. Sanford Evans, *The Canadian Contingents* (Toronto: Publisher's Syndicate, 1901), 2.

64 Miller, *Painting the Map Red*, 33.

65 John S. Ewart, *The Kingdom of Canada* (Toronto: Morang, 1908), 6; Peter Price, 'Fashioning a Constitutional Narrative: John S. Ewart and the Development of a 'Canadian Constitution', *Canadian Historical Review* 93 (2012): 359–81.

66 Goldwin Smith, *In the Court of History: An Apology for Canadians Who Were Opposed to the Boer War* (Toronto: William Tyrrell, 1902), 63.

67 Grant, *Advantages of Imperial Federation*, 13; 'Canada and the Empire', *Globe*, 7 Apr. 1899; Stephen Leacock, 'Greater Canada: An Appeal', *University Magazine* 6 (1907): 139.

68 House of Commons, *Debates*, 23 Oct. 1903, 14785.

69 House of Commons, *Debates*, 23 Oct. 1903, 14817; O. D. Skelton, *Life and Letters of Sir Wilfrid Laurier*, vol. II (Toronto: McClelland and Stewart, 1965), 298.

70 John Foster Fraser, *Canada as It Is* (London, 1905), 42.

71 Lisa Chilton, *Agents of Empire: British Female Migration to Canada and Australia, 1860s-1930* (Toronto: University of Toronto Press, 2007).

72 Gary Magee and Andrew Thompson, ' "Migrapounds": Remittance Flows Within the British World, c. 1875–1913', in *Britishness Abroad: Transnational Movements and Imperial Cultures*, ed. Kate Darian-Smith, Patricia Grimshaw, and Stuart MacIntyre (Melbourne: Melbourne University Press, 2008); Andrew Diller, *Finance, Politics, and Imperialism: Australia, Canada, and the City of London, c. 1896–1914* (Basingstoke: Palgrave, 2012).

73 Katie Pickles, *Female Imperialism and National Identity: Imperial Order Daughters of the Empire* (Manchester: Manchester University Press, 2002).

74 Sarah Glassford, *Mobilizing Mercy: A History of the Canadian Red Cross* (Montreal: McGill-Queen's University Press, 2017); E. Maud Graham, *A Canadian Girl in South Africa: A Teacher's Experiences in the South African War, 1899–1902*, ed. Michael Dawson, Catherine Gidney and Susanne Klausen (Edmonton: University of Alberta Press, 2015).

75 Marcel Martel, Allison Ward, Joel Belliveau and Brittney Anne Bos, 'Promoting a "Sound Patriotic Feeling" in Canada through Empire Day, 1899–1957', in *Celebrating Canada Vol. I: Holidays, National Days, and the Crafting of Identities*, ed. Matthew Hayday and Raymond Blake (Toronto: University of Toronto Press, 2017); Agnes Christina Laut, *Canada, The Empire of the North: Being the Romantic Story of the New Dominion's Growth from Colony to Kingdom* (Toronto: Briggs, 1909).

76 Robert Baden Powell, *The Canadian Boy Scout* (Toronto, 1911), 279; Patricia Dirks, 'Canada's Boys – An Imperial or National Asset? Responses to Baden-Powell's Boy Scout Movement in Pre-War Canada', in *Canada and the British World*, ed. Phillip Buckner and R. Douglas Francis (Vancouver: UBC Press, 2011).

77 John Herd Thompson, *Harvests of War: The Prairie West, 1914–1918* (Toronto: McClelland and Stewart, 1978), 19.

78 James Hughes, 'National and Ethical Value of Cadet Training', in *The Empire Club of Canada Speeches, 1911–1912* (Toronto: Empire Club of Canada, 1913), 111.

79 Fraser, *Canada as It Is*, 52.

80 House of Commons, *Debates*, 12 May 1902, 4726.

81 James Wood, *Militia Myths: Ideas of the Canadian Citizen Soldier, 1896–1921* (Vancouver: UBC Press, 2010), 67.

82 Stephen Harris, *Canadian Brass: The Making of a Professional Army, 1860–1939* (Toronto: University of Toronto Press, 1988), 73.

83 Samuel Wells Jr., 'British Strategic Withdrawal from the Western Hemisphere', *Canadian Historical Review* 49 (1968): 348; Christopher Bell, 'Sentiment vs. Strategy: British Naval Policy, Imperial Defence, and the Development of Dominion Navies, 1911–1914', *International History Review* 37 (2015): 1–20.

84 Clive Phillipps-Wolley, *The Canadian Naval Question* (Toronto: William Briggs, 1910), 36; Robert Borden, *The Naval Question* (Ottawa: n.p., 1910), 2.

85 W. M. Baker, 'A Case Study of Anti-Americanism in English-Speaking Canada; The Election Campaign of 1911', *Canadian Historical Review* 51 (1970): 435.

86 Martin Thornton, *Churchill, Borden and Anglo-Canadian Naval Relations, 1911–14* (Basingstoke: Palgrave, 2013).

87 Minutes of 113th Meeting, Committee of Imperial Defence, 30 May 1911, The National Archives, Kew [hereafter TNA], CAB 2/2.

3 Canada and the first age of globalization

1 'Marching On', *Halifax Daily Reporter and Times*, 1 Apr. 1871.

2 George Grant, 'Response on Behalf of Canada to Address of Welcome, at the World's Parliament of Religions', *Queen's Quarterly* 1 (1893): 158.

3 George Parkin, 'Canada and the Pacific', in *The Empire and the Century*, ed., Charles Sydney Goldman (London: John Murray, 1905), 411.

4 Goldwin Smith, *Canada and the Canadian Question* (London: Macmillan, 1891), 62.

5 W. T. Stead, *The Americanization of the World* (New York: Garland, 1972 [1902]); Samuel Moffett, *The Americanization of Canada* (Toronto: University of Toronto Press, 1972 [1907]).

6 Lake and Reynolds, *Drawing the Global Colour Line*; David Atkinson, *The Burden of White Supremacy: Containing Asia Migration in the British Empire and the United States* (Chapel Hill: UNC Press, 2016).

7 *Mission to England to Confer with the British Authorities on the Subject of Immigration from the Orient and Immigration from India in Particular* (Ottawa: King's Printer, 1908); Woodsworth, *Strangers within Our Gates*, 232; Kornel Chang, *Pacific Community: The Making of the U.S.-Canadian Borderlands* (Berkeley: University of California Press, 2012).

8 Moffett, *The Americanization of Canada*, 114.

9 MacKay, *Asian Dream*, 29.

10 David Davies, 'The Pre-1917 Roots of Canadian-Soviet Relations', *Canadian Historical Review* 70 (1989): 180–205.

11 Anne Sannon, *Finding Japan: Early Canadian Encounters with Asia* (Victoria: Heritage House, 2012), 106.

12 Andrew Smith and Kirsten Greer, 'Monarchism, an Emerging Canadian Identity, and the 1866 British North American Trade Mission to the West Indies and Brazil', *Journal of Imperial and Commonwealth History* 44 (2016): 214–40.

13 House of Commons, *Debates*, 5 Apr. 1893, 3105.

14 Christopher Armstrong and H. V. Nelles, *Southern Exposure: Canadian Promoters in Latin America and the Caribbean, 1896–1930* (Toronto: University of Toronto Press, 1988), 38–9.

15 Gregory Marchildon, *Profits and Politics: Beaverbrook and the Gilded Age of Canadian Finance* (Toronto: University of Toronto Press, 1996); B. J. C. McKercher and S. Enjamio, ' "Brighter Futures, Better Times": Britain, the Empire, and Anglo-American Economic Competition in Cuba,

1898–1920', *Diplomacy & Statecraft* 18 (2007): 663–87.; Peter McFarlane, *Northern Shadows: Canadians and Central America* (Toronto: Between the Lines, 1989).

16 Paula Hastings, 'Dreams of a Tropical Canada: Race, Nation, and Canadian Aspirations in the Caribbean Basin, 1883–1919' (PhD Dissertation, Duke University, 2010), 1.

17 Andrew Smith, 'Thomas Bassett Macaulay and the Bahamas: Racism, Business and Canadian Sub-imperialism', *Journal of Imperial and Commonwealth History* 37 (2009): 34; Paula Hastings, 'Rounding Off the Confederation: Geopolitics, Tropicality and Canada's 'Destiny' in the West Indies in the Early Twentieth Century', *Journal of Colonialism and Colonial History* 14 (2013).

18 Borden to Perley, 3 June 1916, *Documents on Canadian External Relations*, vol. 1, 715.

19 Joseph Pope, *Confidential Memorandum upon the Subject of the Annexation of the West India Islands to the Dominion of Canada* (Ottawa: Dominion of Canada, 1917).

20 Borden to Keefer, 1 Jan. 1919, *Documents on Canadian External Relations*, vol. 3, 758; Paula Hastings, 'Territorial Spoils, Transnational Black Resistance, and Canada's Evolving Autonomy during the First World War', *Histoire Sociale/Social History* 47 (2014): 443–70.

21 Jacques Langlais, *Les Jésuites du Québec en Chine* (Quebec: Les presses de l'université Laval, 1979); Alvyn Austin, *Saving China: Canadian Missionaries in the Middle Kingdom, 1888–1959* (Toronto: University of Toronto Press, 1986); Hamish Ion, *The Cross and the Rising Sun: The Canadian Protestant Missionary Movement in the Japanese Empire, 1872–1931* (Waterloo: Wilfrid Laurier University Press, 1990); Richard Leclerc, *Des Lys à l'Ombre du Mont Fuji: Histoire de la présence de l'Amérique française au Japon* (Sillery: Éditions du Bois-du-Coulonge, 1995); Serge Granger, 'Les Lotbinière au Cachemire avant la Première Guerre mondiale', *Synergies Inde* 3 (2008): 129–40.

22 Rosemary Gagan, *A Sensitive Independence: Canadian Methodist Women Missionaries in Canada and the Orient, 1881–1925* (Montreal: McGill-Queen's University Press, 1992); Margaret Prang, *A Heart at Leisure from Itself: Caroline Macdonald of Japan* (Vancouver: UBC Press, 1995).

23 Mark Noll, *A History of Christianity in the United States and Canada* (Grand Rapids, MI: William Eerdmans, 1992), 533.

24 'The Expansive Nature of Christianity', *Globe*, 25 Mar. 1899.

25 Graeme Mount, 'The Canadian Presbyterian Mission to Trinidad, 1868–1912', *Revista/Review Interamericana* 7 (1977): 73–86; Ruth Compton Brouwer, *New Women for God: Canadian Presbyterian Women and India Missions, 1876–1914* (Toronto: University of Toronto Press, 1990), 80; Alvyn Austin and Jamie Scott, *Canadian Missionaries, Indigenous Peoples: Representing Religion at Home and Abroad* (Toronto: University of Toronto Press, 2005).

26 'The Unity of the Empire', *Globe*, 15 May 1901.

27 Austin, *Saving China*, 9.

28 Margaret Brown, *MacGillivray of Shanghai: The Life of Donald MacGillivray* (Toronto: Ryerson Press, 1968).

29 Ruth Compton Brouwer, 'A Disgrace to "Christian Canada": Protestant Foreign Missionary Concerns about the Treatment of South Asians in Canada, 1907–1940', in *A Nation of Immigrants: Women, Workers, and Communities in Canadian History, 1840s-1960s*, ed. Franca Iacovetta, Paula Draper, Robert Ventresca (Toronto: University of Toronto Press, 1998), 361–84.

30 George Woodcock, *British Columbia: A History of the Province* (Vancouver: Douglas & McIntyre, 1990), 100.

31 J. F. Bosher, *Vancouver Island in the Empire* (Tamarac, FL: Llumina Press, 2012); Terry Reksten, *More English than the English: A Very Social History of Victoria* (Victoria: Orca, 1986).

32 Chang, *Pacific Community*, 93; Patricia Roy, *A White Man's Province: British Columbia Politicians and Chinese and Japanese Immigrants, 1858–1914* (Vancouver: UBC Press, 1989).

33 House of Commons, *Debates*, 1907–8, 728–30.

34 Elliot Young, *Alien Nation: Chinese Migration in the Americas from the Coolie Era through World War II* (Chapel Hill: UNC Press, 2014); Chang, *Pacific Community*, 24–33.

35 House of Commons, *Debates*, 12 May 1882, 1477.

36 House of Commons, *Debates*, 4 May 1885, 1582, 1589.

37 Carl Berger, *The Sense of Power: Studies in the Ideas of Canadian Imperialism, 1867–1914* (Toronto: University of Toronto Press, 1970), 57.

38 Roy, *A White Man's Province*, 230; David Goutor, 'Constructing the "Great Menace": Canadian Labour Opposition to Asian Migration, 1880–1914', *Canadian Historical Review* 88 (2007): 549–76.

39 Ninette Kelley and Michael Trebilcock, *The Making of the Mosaic: A History of Canadian Immigration Policy*, Second Edition (Toronto: University of Toronto Press, 2010), 141.

40 A. W. Currie, *The Grand Trunk Railway of Canada* (Toronto: University of Toronto Press, 1957), 409.

41 House of Commons, *Debates,* 24 Mar. 1898, 2441–2.

42 Roy, *A White Man's Province*, 189.

43 Atkinson, *The Burden of White Supremacy*, 85.

44 Lake and Reynolds, *Drawing the Global Colour Line*, 184–5.

45 House of Commons, *Debates*, 21 Jan. 1908, 1614 and 28 Jan 1908, 2140.

46 Kirk Niergarth, '"This Continent must belong to the White Races": William Lyon Mackenzie King, Canadian Diplomacy and Immigration Law, 1908', *International History Review* 32 (2010): 599–617; Julie Gilmour, *Trouble on Main Street: Mackenzie King, Reason, Race and the 1907 Vancouver Riots* (Toronto: Penguin, 2014).

47 J. A. Cooper, 'Editorial Comments', *Canadian Magazine* 14 (Dec. 1899).

48 'Current Events', *Queen's Quarterly* 6 (1898); Edward Kohn, *This Kindred People: Canadian-American Relations in the Anglo-Saxon Idea, 1895–1903* (Montreal: McGill-Queen's University Press, 2005), 118.

49 Carman Cumming, 'The Toronto *Daily Mail*, Edward Farrer, and the Question of Canadian-American Union', *Journal of Canadian Studies* 24 (1989): 121–39.

50 Hugh Johnson, *The East Indians in Canada* (Ottawa: Canadian Historical Association, 1984), 7.

51 J. B. Harkin, *The East Indians in British Columbia: A Report Regarding the Proposal to Provide Work in British Honduras for the Indigent Unemployed Among Them* (Ottawa: Department of the Interior, 1908).

52 Reg Whitaker, Gregory Kealey and Andrew Parnaby, *Secret Service: Political Policing in Canada from the Fenians to Fortress America* (Toronto: University of Toronto Press, 2012), 48.

53 Seema Sohi, *Echoes of Mutiny: Race, Surveillance, and Indian Anticolonialism in North America* (New York: Oxford University Press, 2014).

54 'Hindu Invaders Now in the City Harbour', *Vancouver Sun*, 23 May 1914.

55 Hugh Johnston, *The Voyage of the Komagata Maru: The Sikh Challenge to Canada's Colour Bar* (Toronto: Oxford University Press, 1979), 37–8.

56 Daniel Gorman, *Imperial Citizenship: Empire and the Question of Belonging* (Manchester: Manchester University Press, 2006).

57 O. D. Skelton, 'Current Events', *Queen's Quarterly* 15 (1907).

58 Barrington Walker, *The African Canadian Legal Odyssey: Historical Essays* (Toronto: University of Toronto Press, 2012), 45. John Schultz, 'White Man's Country: Canada and the West Indian Immigrant, 1900–1965', in *Canada and the Commonwealth Caribbean*, ed. Brian Douglas Tennyson (Lanham: University Press of America, 1988), 257–77; Bruce Shepard, 'Diplomatic Racism: Canadian Government and Black Migration from Oklahoma, 1905–1912', *Great Plains Quarterly* 3 (1983): 5–16.

59 J. A. Macdonald, *Democracy and the Nations: A Canadian View* (Toronto: S.B. Gundy, 1915), 81; George Parkin, 'The Relations of Canada and the United States', *Empire Club Speeches* (1907–8), 160; Woodsworth, *Strangers within Our Gates*, 190.

60 Goldwin Smith, *Canada and the Canadian Question* (London: Macmillan, 1891), 278–9.

61 Bothwell, *Your Country, My Country*, 121–2.

62 Leon Truesdell, *The Canadian Born in the United States* (New Haven, CT: Yale University Press, 1943), 10; Gerald Brault, *The French-Canadian Heritage in New England* (Montreal: McGill-Queen's University Press, 1986), 86; Randy William Widdis, *With Scarcely a Ripple: Anglo-Canadian Migration into the United States and Western Canada, 1880–1920* (Montreal: McGill-Queen's University Press, 1998); Bruno Ramirez, *Crossing the 49th Parallel: Migration from Canada to the United States, 1900–1930* (Ithaca, NY: Cornell, 2001).

63 James Cappon, 'Current Events', *Queen's Quarterly* 9 (1902).

64 Beth LaDow, *The Medicine Line: Life and Death on a North American Borderland* (New York: Routledge, 2001), 76.

65 A. D. Gilbert, '"On The Road To New York": The Protective Impulse and the English-Canadian Cultural Identity, 1896–1914', *Dalhousie Review* 58 (1978): 410.

66 Pelham Edgar, 'A Fresh View of Canadian Literature', *University Magazine* (October 1912); J. W. L. Forster, 'Art and Artists in Ontario', in *Canada: An Encyclopaedia of the Country IV*, ed. J. Castell Hopkins (Toronto: Linscott Publishing, 1900), 352.

67 George Wrong, 'Canadian Nationalism and the Imperial Tie', *University Monthly* (February 1910), 175.

68 J. Castell Hopkins, *Continental Influence in Canadian Development* (Toronto: W. Briggs, 1908)

69 Siegfried, *The Race Question in Canada*, 95; André Siegfried, *Deux Mois en l'Amérique du Nord à la Veille de la Guerre* (Paris: Armand Colin, 1916).

70 Ramsay Cook, *The Regenerators: Social Criticism in Late Victorian English Canada* (Toronto: University of Toronto Press, 1985); Daniel Rodgers, *Atlantic Crossings: Social Politics in a Progressive Age* (Cambridge: Harvard University Press, 1998); Ian McKay, *Reasoning Otherwise: Leftists and the People's Enlightenment in Canada, 1890–1920* (Toronto: Between the Lines, 2008).

71 Robert H. Babcock, *Gompers in Canada: A Study in American Continentalism before the First World War* (Toronto: University of Toronto Press, 1974), 36; Bryan Palmer, *Working-Class Experience: The Rise and Reconstruction of Canadian Labour, 1800–1980* (Toronto: University of Toronto Press, 1983), 169.

72 P. B. Waite, *Canada 1874–1896: Arduous Destiny* (Toronto: McClelland and Stewart, 1971), 91; J. H. Dales, '"National Policy" Myths, Past and Present', *Journal of Canadian Studies* 14 (1979); Robert Craig Brown, 'The Nationalism of the National Policy', in *Nationalism in Canada*, ed. Peter Russell (Toronto: McGraw-Hill, 1966), 155–63.

73 Stephen Scheinberg, 'Invitation to Empire: Tariffs and American Economic Expansion in Canada', *Business History Review* 47 (1973): 218–38.

74 Stead, *Americanization of the World*, 44.

75 W. R Graham, 'Sir Richard Cartwright, Wilfrid Laurier and Liberal Party Trade Policy, 1887', *Canadian Historical Review* 33 (1952): 1–18; Christopher Pennington, *The Destiny of Canada: Macdonald, Laurier, and the Election of 1891* (Toronto: Penguin, 2011).

76 *Congressional Record*, 14 Feb. 1911, 2520; House of Commons, *Debates*, 14 Feb. 1911, 3560.

77 Robert Borden, *Robert Laird Borden: His Memoirs*, vol. I (Montreal: McGill-Queen's University Press, 1969), 327.

78 Paul Stevens, *The 1911 General Election: A Study in Canada Politics* (Toronto: Copp Clark, 1970), 2.

79 Baker, 'A Case Study of Anti-Americanism in English-Speaking Canada', 435, 438.

80 Henri Bourassa, *The Reciprocity Agreement and Its Consequences as Viewed from the Nationalist Standpoint* (Montreal: Le Devoir, 1911), 28; O. D Skelton, 'Current Events', *Queen's Quarterly* 18 (1911): 332.

81 Patrice Dutil and David MacKenzie, *Canada 1911: The Decisive Election That Shaped the Country* (Toronto: Dundurn, 2011).

82 R. E. Hannigan, 'Reciprocity 1911: Continentalism and American Weltpolitik', *Diplomatic History* 4 (1980): 16.

83 C. P. Stacey, *Canada and the Age of Conflict, vol. 1: 1867–1921* (Toronto: University of Toronto Press, 1984), 151.

84 Kurkpatrick Dorsey, *The Dawn of Conservation Diplomacy: US-Canadian Wildlife Protection Treaties in the Progressive Era* (Seattle: University of Washington Press, 1998).

85 Robert Spencer, John Kirton and Kim Richard Nossal, *The International Joint Commission Seventy Years On* (Toronto: University of Toronto Press, 1981).

86 Alvin Gluek Jr., 'Programmed Diplomacy: The Settlement of the North Atlantic Fisheries Question, 1907–1912', *Acadiensis* 6 (1976): 43–70.

87 Tony McCulloch, 'Theodore Roosevelt and Canada: Alaska, the "Big Stick" and the North Atlantic Triangle, 1901–1909', in *A Companion to Theodore Roosevelt*, ed. Serge Ricard (Malden: Wiley-Blackwell, 2011), 293–313.

88 King Diary, 16 Sept. 1912.

89 J. A. Macdonald, *Addresses Delivered Before the Canadian Club of Toronto, Season of 1913–1914* (Toronto: Canadian Club, 1914), 119.

90 W. P. Ward, *White Canada Forever: Popular Attitudes and Public Policy Towards Orientals in British Columbia* (Montreal: McGill-Queen's University Press, 1978), xii.

91 Frank Underhill, 'Laurier and Blake, 1891–2', *Canadian Historical Review* 24 (1943): 135–55.

92 'First Annual Banquet', 18 Jan. 1904, *Addresses Delivered Before the Canadian Club of Ottawa, 1903–1909* (Ottawa: Mortimer Press, 1910), 15.

93 'Canada's Excuse for Existence', *Busy Man's Magazine* (August 1907).

94 Jeremy Adelman, *Frontier Development: Land, Labour, and Capital on the Wheatlands of Argentina and Canada, 1890–1914* (Oxford: Oxford University Press, 1994); Carl Solberg, *The Prairies and Pampas: Agrarian Policy in Canada and Argentina, 1880–1930* (Stanford: Stanford University Press, 1987); Mary Schaeffer Conroy, *Peter Arka'evich Stolypin: Practical Politics in Late Tsarist Russia* (Boulder: Westview Press, 1976), 47.

95 Trygve Ugland, *Jean Monnet and Canada: Early Travels and European Unity* (Toronto: University of Toronto Press, 2011).

4 Canada's Great War

1 Tim Cook, *At the Sharp End: Canadians Fighting the Great War, 1914–1915* (Toronto: Viking, 2007), 211; 'Enthusiasm Sweeps Canada', Vancouver *Daily News Advertiser*, 5 Aug. 1914; Ian Miller, *Our Glory and Our Grief: Torontonians and the Great War* (Toronto: University of Toronto Press, 2002), 16.

2 Robert Craig Brown and Ramsay Cook, *Canada 1896–1921: A Nation Transformed* (Toronto: McClelland and Stewart, 1974), 303.

3 Imperial War Cabinet, 26, 23 July 1918, TNA, CAB 23/43.

4 Robert Borden, *Robert Laird Borden: His Memoirs*, vol. II (Montreal: McGill-Queen's University Press, 1969), 157.

5 George Wrong, *The War Spirit of Germany* (Toronto: Oxford University Press, 1915), 26–7; House of Commons, *Debates*, 19 Aug. 1914, 17.

6 Wood, *Militia Myths*, 53.

7 House of Commons, *Debates*, 19 Aug. 1914, 10; Skelton, *Life and Letters of Sir Wilfrid Laurier*, II, 163–4.

8 Keith Neilson, 'R.H. Brand, the Empire and Munitions from Canada', *English Historical Review* 126 (2011):1430–55.

9 Avner Offer, *The First World War: An Agrarian Interpretation* (Oxford: Oxford University Press, 1989), 403.

10 Max Aitken, *Canada in Flanders*, vol. 1 (London: Hodder & Stoughton, 1916), 182.

11 Douglas Delaney, *The Imperial Army Project: Britain and the Land Forces of the Dominions and India, 1902–1945* (Oxford: Oxford University Press, 2018), 95–164.

12 Miller, *Our Glory and Our Grief*, 143; R. M. Bray, 'The English-Canadian Patriotic Response to the Great War', *Canadian Historical Review* 61 (1980): 149; 'Canada's Birthplace as a Nation', *Canadian Courier* (Toronto), 7 Aug. 1915.

13 Borden to Perley, 4 Jan. 1916, *Documents on Canadian External Relations*, vol. 1, 104.

14 J. L. Granatstein, *Canada's Army: Waging War and Keeping the Peace*, Second Edition (Toronto: University of Toronto Press, 2011), 72–3; Thomas White, *The Story of Canada's War Finances* (Montreal: n.p., 1921), 31.

15 Borden to Perley.

16 Nic Clarke, *Unwanted Warriors: Rejected Volunteers of the Canadian Expeditionary Force* (Vancouver: UBC Press, 2015).

17 Linda Quiney, *This Small Army of Women: Canadian Volunteer Nurses and the First World War* (Vancouver: UBC Press, 2018); Cynthia Toman, *Sister Soldiers of the Great War: The Nurses of the Canadian Army Medical Corps* (Vancouver: UBC Press, 2016); Steve Marti, 'For Kin and Country: Scale, Identity, and English-Canadian Voluntary Societies, 1914–1918', *Histoire Sociale/Social History* 47 (2014): 333–51.

18 Glassford, *Mobilizing Mercy*.

19 Stacey, *Canada and the Age of Conflict,* II, 213; R. Craig Brown and Robert Bothwell, 'The Canadian Resolution', in *Policy by Other Means: Essays in Honour of C.P. Stacey*, ed. Michael Cross and Robert Bothwell (Toronto: Clarke, Irwin, 1972), 163–77.

20 Lita-Rose Betcherman, *Ernest Lapointe: Mackenzie King's Great Quebec Lieutenant* (Toronto: University of Toronto Press, 2002), 274.

21 Skelton, *The Life and Letters of Sir Wilfrid Laurier*, II, 510.

22 John Prescott, *In Flanders Fields: The Story of John McCrae* (Erin, ON: Boston Mills Press, 1985), 125.

23 Tarah Brookfield, 'Divided by the Ballot Box: The Montreal Council of Women and the 1917 Election', *Canadian Historical Review* 89 (2008): 475.

24 Patrice Dutil and David MacKenzie, *Embattled Nation: Canada's Wartime Election of 1917* (Toronto: Dundurn, 2017).

25 Martin Auger, 'On the Brink of Civil War: The Canadian Government and the Suppression of the 1918 Quebec Easter Riots', *Canadian Historical Review* 89 (2008): 503–40; Serge Marc Durflinger, 'Vimy's Consequence: The Montreal Anti-Conscription Disturbances, May to December 1917', in *Turning Point 1917: The British Empire at War*, ed. Douglas Delaney and Nikolas Gardner (Vancouver: UBC Press, 2017), 160–87.

26 'Joy and Grief', *Globe*, 12 Nov. 1918.

27 Patricia Roy, *The Oriental Question: Consolidating a White Man's Province, 1914–41* (Vancouver: UBC Press, 2003), 14; Gaddis Smith, 'Canadian External Affairs During World War I', in *The Growth of Canadian Policies in External Affairs* (Durham, NC: Duke University Press, 1960), 36.

28 House of Commons, *Debates*, 8 June 1917, 2145.

29 Xu Guoqi, *Strangers on the Western Front: Chinese Workers in the Great War* (Cambridge: Harvard University Press, 2011), 56–9.

30 A. W. Crawford, 'The Fear of Russia', *Canadian Magazine* (June 1915).

31 William Rodney, 'Broken Journey: Trotsky in Canada, 1917', *Queen's Quarterly* 74 (1967): 649–65.

32 Raymond Massey, *When I Was Young* (Halifax: Formac, 1983), 200.

33 Stacey, *Canada and the Age of Conflict*, I, 278, 281; Benjamin Isitt, *From Victoria to Vladivostok: Canada's Siberian Expedition, 1917–19* (Vancouver: UBC Press, 2010).

34 Hugh Keenleyside, *Canada and the United States* (New York: Knopf, 1929), 372.

35 Michael Hadley and Roger Sarty, *Tin-Pots and Pirate Ships: Canadian Naval Forces and German Sea Raiders, 1880–1918* (Montreal: McGill-Queen's University Press, 1991), 133–78; Brandon Dimmel, *Engaging the Line: How the Great War Shaped the Canada-US Border* (Vancouver: UBC Press, 2016).

36 Margaret MacMillan, 'Canada and the Peace Settlements', in *Canada and the First World War: Essays in Honour of Robert Craig Brown*, ed. David MacKenzie (Toronto: University of Toronto Press, 2005), 384.

37 Ibid., 381.

38 W. Stewart Wallace, *The Memoirs of the Rt. Hon. Sir George Foster* (Toronto: Macmillan, 1933), 194.

39 Francine McKenzie, 'Race, Empire, and World Order: Robert Borden and Racial Equality at the Paris Peace Conference of 1919', in *Dominion of Race: Rethinking Canada's International History*, ed. Laura Madokoro, Francine McKenzie and David Meren (Vancouver: UBC Press, 2017), 82–6.

40 Ibid., 85.

41 'Shall *these* be the arbiters of Canada's future?' *Halifax Herald*, 18 Feb. 1920; James Gibson, 'Sir Robert Borden', in *Our Living Tradition: Second and Third Series*, ed. Robert McDougall (Toronto: University of Toronto Press, 1959), 110–111.

42 MacMillan, 'Canada and the Peace Settlements', 394.

43 J. W. Dafoe, 'Canada and the Peace Conference of 1919', *Canadian Historical Review* 24 (1923): 235; 'General Currie and Peace', *Globe*, 12 June 1919.

44 Gwendolen Carter, *The British Commonwealth and International Security: The Role of the Dominions, 1919–1939* (Toronto: Ryerson, 1947), 77.

45 George Wrong, 'Canada and the Imperial War Cabinet', *Canadian Historical Review* 1 (1920): 25; Sir Robert Falconer, *Idealism in National Character* (London: Hodder & Stoughton, 1920), 137.

46 House of Commons, *Debates*, 18 May 1917, 1539.

47 Margaret Macmillan, 'Sibling Rivalry: Australia and Canada from the Boer War to the Great War', in *Parties Long Estranged: Canada and Australia in the Twentieth Century*, ed. Margaret Macmillan and Francine McKenzie (Vancouver: UBC Press, 2003), 20; Smith, 'Canadian External Affairs During World War I', 57.

48 Charles Yale Harrison, *Generals Die in Bed* (1930); Fred Varley quoted in Charles C. Hill, *The Group of Seven: Art for a Nation* (Toronto: McClelland and Stewart, 1995), 65.

49 Tim Cook, *Shock Troops: Canadians Fighting The Great War, 1917–1918* (Toronto: Viking, 2008), 115–6; Jeff Keshen, 'The Great War Soldier as Nation Builder in Canada and Australia', in *Canada and the Great War*, ed. Briton Busch (Montreal: McGill-Queen's University Press, 2003), 3–26; Geoffrey Hayes, Andrew Iarocci and Mike Bechthold, eds, *Vimy Ridge: A Canadian Reassessment* (Waterloo: Wilfrid Laurier University Press, 2007); Tim Cook, *Vimy: The Battle and the Legend* (Toronto: Penguin, 2017); Ian McKay and Jamie Swift, *The Vimy Trap* (Toronto: Between the Lines, 2016).

50 Alfred Gordon, 'Vimy Ridge', in *'Vimy Ridge' and New Poems* (Toronto: J. M. Dent and Sons, 1918), 5; J. W. Dafoe, *Over the Canadian Battlefields* (Toronto: Thomas Allen, 1919), 13, 23.

51 James Shotwell, *The Heritage of Freedom: The United States and Canada in the Community of Nations* (New York: Charles Scribner's Sons, 1934), 123.

52 Jonathan Vance, *Death so Noble: Memory, Meaning, and the First World War* (Vancouver: UBC Press, 1996).

53 Frank Underhill, 'The Canadian Forces in the War', in *The Empire at War*, ed. Sir Charles Lucas (Toronto: Oxford University Press, 1923), 286; Bray, 'The English-Canadian Patriotic Response to the Great War', 97–122.

54 R. B. Fleming, *The Wartime Letters of Leslie and Cecil Frost, 1915–1919* (Waterloo: Wilfrid Laurier University Press, 2007), 93.

55 Editorial, 'English-Speaking Solidarity', *University Magazine* 16 (Apr. 1917): 154; McKenzie, 'Race, Empire, and World Order', 81.

56 Address, 25 Sept. 1919, in *The Papers of Woodrow Wilson*, ed., Arthur Link (Princeton, NJ: Princeton University Press, 1990), 505; George Egerton, 'Ideology, Diplomacy, and International Organisation: Wilsonianism and the League of Nations in Anglo-American Relations, 1918–1920', in *Anglo-American Relations in the 1920s*, ed. B. J. C. McKercher (London: Macmillan, 1991).

57 Joseph Schull, *Laurier: The First Canadian* (Toronto: Macmillan, 1966), 590.

58 Mark McGowan, *The Imperial Irish: Canada's Irish Catholics Fight the Great War, 1914–1918* (Montreal: McGill-Queen's University Press, 2017).

59 Robert Lawson, 'Joachim von Ribbentrop in Canada, 1910–1914: A Note', *International History Review* 29 (2007): 821–32; Martin Kitchen, 'The German Invasion of Canada in the First World War', *International History Review* 7 (1985): 245–60.

60 Bohdan Kordan, *Enemy Aliens, Prisoners of War: Internment in Canada During the Great War* (Montreal: McGill-Queen's University Press, 2002).

61 James W. St.G. Walker, 'Race or Recruitment in World War I: Enlistment of Visible Minorities in the Canadian Expeditionary Force', *Canadian Historical Review* 70 (1989*)*: 5; Melissa N. Shaw, '"Most Anxious to Serve their King and Country": Black Canadians' Fight to Enlist in WWI and Emerging Race Consciousness in Ontario, 1914-1919', *Histoire Sociale/Social History* 49 (2016): 543–80.

62 Roy, *The Oriental Question*, 16.

63 Timothy Winegard, *For King and Kanata: Canadian Indians and the First World War* (Winnipeg: University of Manitoba Press, 2012), 8; Eric Story, '"The Awakening Has Come": Canadian First Nations in the Great War Era, 1914–1932', *Canadian Military History* 24 (2015): 11–35; John Moses, 'The Return of the Native: Six Nations Veterans and Political Change at the Grand River Reserve, 1917–1924', in *Aboriginal Peoples and the Canadian Military: Historical Perspectives*, ed. P. Whitney Lackenbauer and Craig Leslie Mantle (Kingston: Canadian Defence Academy Press, 2007), 117–28.

64 Keith Smith, *Strange Visitors: Documents in Indigenous-Settler Relations in Canada from 1876* (Toronto: University of Toronto Press, 2014), 130.

65 Peter Kulchyski, 'A Considerable Unrest: F.O. Loft and the League of Indians', *Native Studies Review* 4 (1988): 95–117.

66 Duncan Campbell Scott, 'The Canadian Indians and the Great War', in *Canada and the Great War*, Vol. III (Toronto: United Publishing, 1919), 19.

67 Craig Heron, ed., *The Workers' Revolt in Canada, 1917–1925* (Toronto: University of Toronto Press, 1998).

68 McKay, *Reasoning Otherwise*, 431.

69 Borden, *Robert Laird Borden*, 192.

70 'Bolshevism in Canada', *Globe*, 15 Apr. 1919.

71 Tom Mitchell, '"Legal Gentlemen Appointed by the Federal Government": The Canadian State, the Citizen's Committee of 1000, and Winnipeg's Seditious Conspiracy Trials of 1919–1920', *Labour/Le Travail* 53 (2004): 24; David Bercuson, *Confrontation at Winnipeg: Labour, Industrial*

Relations and the General Strike (Montreal: McGill-Queen's University Press, 1974), 136.

72 Whitaker, Kealey and Parnaby, *Secret Service*, 74–5, 81.

73 Laurel Sefton MacDowell and Ian Radforth, *Canadian Working-class History: Selected Readings*, Third Edition (Toronto: Canadian Scholars Press, 2006), 227.

74 Michel Beaulieu, *Labour at the Lakehead: Ethnicity, Socialism, and Politics, 1900–34* (Vancouver: UBC Press, 2011); Barbara Roberts, *From Whence They Came: Deportation from Canada, 1900–1935* (Ottawa: University of Ottawa Press, 1988).

75 Gerry van Houten, *Canada's Party of Socialism: History of the Communist Party of Canada, 1921–1976* (Toronto: Progress Books, 1982), 16–18; J. L. Black, *Canada in the Soviet Mirror: Ideology and Perception in Soviet Foreign Affairs, 1917–1991* (Ottawa: Carleton University Press, 1998), 57.

76 House of Commons, *Debates*, 23 Jan. 1919, 140; W. G. Smith, *A Study in Canadian Immigration* (Toronto: Ryerson Press, 1920), 146; Gerald Tulchinsky, *Canada's Jews: A People's Journey* (Toronto: University of Toronto Press, 2008), 126.

77 Thomas Fraser, 'Is Bolshevism Brewing in Canada?' *Maclean's*, Jan. 1919.

78 Ian Dowbiggan, *Keeping America Sane: Psychiatry and Eugenics in the United States and Canada, 1880–1940* (Ithaca, NY: Cornell University Press, 1997); Angus McLaren, *Our Own Master Race: Eugenics in Canada, 1885–1945* (Toronto: McClelland and Stewart, 1990); Erika Dyck, *Facing the History of Eugenics: Reproduction, Sterilization and the Politics of Choice in 20th Century Alberta* (Toronto: University of Toronto Press, 2013).

79 Kent Fedorowich, 'Restocking the British World: Empire Migration and Anglo-Canadian Relations, 1919–30', *Britain and the World* 9 (2016): 236–69.

80 Lothrop Stoddard, *The Rising Tide of Colour: Against White World Supremacy* (New York: Charles Scribner's Sons, 1923), 281.

81 Lianbi Zhu and Timothy Baycroft, 'A Chinese Counterpart to Dominion Day: Chinese Humiliation Day in Interwar Canada', in *Celebrating Canada, Volume I: Holidays, National Days, and the Crafting of Identities,* ed. Matthew Hayday and Raymond B. Blake (Toronto: University of Toronto Press, 2016).

82 Christopher Moore, 'Before the Fall', in *Canada's Great War Album: Our Memories of the World War*, ed. Mark Colin Reid (Toronto: HarperCollins, 2015), 11.

83 O. D. Skelton, 'Current Events', *Queen's Quarterly* (July–Sept. 1919): 127.

84 'The "Balance of Power" ', *Globe*, 13 Nov. 1918; 'The Problem of World Peace', *Globe*, 28 Feb. 1919.

5 North Americanism and the search for peace

1 Newton Rowell, *The British Empire and World Peace* (Toronto: Oxford University Press, 1922), 1, 3.

2 Ibid., 207; Margaret Prang, *N.W. Rowell: Ontario Nationalist* (Toronto: University of Toronto Press: 1975), 361.

3 Daniel Laqua, *Internationalism Reconfigured: Transnational Ideas and Movements Between the World Wars* (New York: Palgrave Macmillan, 2011); Cecelia Lynch, *Beyond Appeasement: Interpreting Interwar Peace Movements in World Politics* (Ithaca, NY: Cornell University Press, 1999); Norman Hillmer, 'O.D. Skelton and the North American Mind', *International Journal* 60 (2004–5): 93–110.

4 Donald Page, 'Canada as the Exponent of North American Idealism', *American Review of Canadian Studies* 3 (1973): 36; Brandon Dimmel, 'Children of a Common Mother: The Rise and Fall of the Anglo-American Peace Centenary', in *Celebrating Canada Vol. II: Commemorations, Anniversaries, and National Symbols*, ed. Raymond Blake and Matthew Hayday (Toronto: University of Toronto Press, 2018).

5 J. A. Macdonald, *The North American Idea* (Toronto: McClelland, Goodchild & Stewart, 1917), 185; Macdonald, *Democracy and the Nations*, 128.

6 Murray Donnelly, *Dafoe of the Free Press* (Toronto: Macmillan, 1968), 99; Richard Veatch, *Canada and the League of Nations* (Toronto: University of Toronto Press, 1975), 51; Sir Robert Falconer, *The United States as a Neighbour* (Cambridge: Cambridge University Press, 1925), 242.

7 Page, 'Canada as the Exponent of North American Idealism', 37.

8 Roger Swanson, *Canadian-American Summit Diplomacy, 1923–1973* (Toronto: McClelland and Stewart, 1975), 312.

9 House of Commons, *Debates*, 11 Sept. 1919, 230.

10 Thomas Socknat, *Witness against War: Pacifism in Canada, 1900–1945* (Toronto: University of Toronto Press, 1987), 4.

11 Barbara Roberts, *'Why Do Women Do Nothing to End the War?' Canadian Feminist-Pacifists and the Great War* (Ottawa: Canadian Research Institute for the Advancement of Women, 1985).

12 Doris Pennington, *Agnes Macphail: Reformer* (Toronto: Simon and Pierre, 1989), 99.

13 House of Commons, *Debates*, 25 Apr. 1922, 1854.

14 Priscilla Roberts, 'Tweaking the Lion's Tail: Edgar J. Tarr, the Canadian Institute of International Affairs, and the British Empire, 1931–1950', *Diplomact & Statecraft* 23 (2012): 636–59; Lawrence Woods, 'Canada and the Institute of Pacific Relations', *Canadian Foreign Policy Journal* 6 (1999): 119–38.

15 Donald Page, 'The Institute's "Popular Arm": The League of Nations Society in Canada', *International Journal* 33 (1977/78): 49.

16 Veatch, *Canada and the League of Nations*, 72–81.

17 House of Commons, *Debates*, 15 June 1923, 4001.

18 House of Commons, *Debates*, 1 Feb. 1923, 33.

19 'Canada Offers to Take Mandate for Armenia', *New York Times*, 23 Apr. 1920; Henry Angus, 'Next for Duty', *University Magazine*, Feb. 1920; *Globe*, 24

Apr. 1920; Meighen to Perley, 1 Dec. 1920, *Documents on Canadian External Relations*, vol. 3, 74.

20 'The Call from Armenia', *Globe*, 9 Jan. 1920; 'Turks Slay 14,800 in One Massacre', *Globe*, 26 Aug. 1915; 'L'extermination des Arméniens', *L'Action Catholique*, 20 Oct. 1915; 'Graduate of Knox on Turkish horrors', *Globe* 12 Oct. 1915; 'Whole Race in Peril', *Globe*, 1 Apr. 1918.

21 'The Bestial Turk', *Globe*, 26 Jan. 1918.

22 Keith David Watenpaugh, 'The League of Nations' Rescue of Armenian Genocide Survivors and the Making of Modern Humanitarianism, 1920–1927', *American Historical Review* 115 (2010): 1315–39.

23 Isabel Kaprielian-Churchill, *Like Our Mountains: A History of Armenians in Canada* (Montreal: McGill-Queen's University Press, 2005), 155.

24 House of Commons, *Debates*, 23 Apr. 1918, 1049.

25 Yale Belanger, 'The Six Nations of Grand River Territory's Attempts at Renewing International Political Relationships, 1921–1924', *Canadian Foreign Policy Journal* 13 (2007): 37.

26 Six Nations, *The Redman's Appeal for Justice* (Brantford: D. Wilson Moore, 1924); Emery Kelen, *Peace in Their Time: Men Who Led Us In and Out of War, 1914–1945* (New York: Knopf, 1963), 148.

27 'Brantford Learns, but via Detroit, of Indian Defiance', *Globe*, 2 July 1928.

28 Lapointe to Skelton, 5 July 1927, *Documents on Canadian External Relations,* vol. 4, 623; House of Commons, *Debates*, 12 Apr. 1928, 1960; Lorna Lloyd, ' "Another National Milestone": Canada's 1927 Election to the Council of the League of Nations', *Diplomacy & Statecraft* 21 (2010): 650–68; John MacFarlane, *Ernest Lapointe and Quebec's Influence on Canadian Foreign Policy* (Toronto: University of Toronto Press, 1999).

29 Daniel Gorman, *The Emergence of International Society in the 1920s* (Cambridge: Cambridge University Press, 2012), 44.

30 Norman Hillmer, *O.D. Skelton: A Portrait of Canadian Ambition* (Toronto: University of Toronto Press, 2015), 122.

31 House of Commons, *Debates*, 19 Feb. 1929, 240–41.

32 Skelton, 'The Locarno Treaties/Proposed Imperial Conference, 1 Jan. 1926', in *O.D Skelton: The Work of the World, 1923–1941*, ed. Norman Hillmer (Montreal: McGill-Queen's University Press, 2013), 139–40.

33 Imperial War Cabinet Minutes 47, 30 Dec. 1918, TNA, CAB 23/43.

34 Governor General to Colonial Secretary, 15 Feb. 1921, *Documents on Canadian External Relations*, vol. 3 1919-1925 (Ottawa: DEA, 1970), 163.

35 Henry Angus, 'Canada and Naval Rivalry in the Pacific', *Pacific Affairs* 8 (1935); Michael Fry, *Illusions of Security: North Atlantic Diplomacy, 1918–1922* (Toronto: University of Toronto Press, 1972).

36 J. B. Brebner, 'Canada, the Anglo-Japanese Alliance and the Washington Conference', *Political Science Quarterly* 50 (1935).

37 J. B. Brebner, 'Canadian and North American History', *Canadian Historical Association Annual Report* 41 (1931).

38 King Diary, 22 May 1928.

39 Carl Berger, 'Comments on the Carnegie Series on the Relations of Canada and the United States', in *The Influence of the U.S. on Canadian Development*, ed. R. A. Preston (Durham, NC: Duke University Press, 1972), 32–50.

40 Jeffrey Brison, *Rockefeller, Carnegie and Canada: American Philanthropy and the Arts and Letters in Canada* (Montreal: McGill-Queen's University Press, 2005).

41 James Shotwell, *The Heritage of Freedom: The United States and Canada in the Community of Nations* (New York: Charles Scribner's Sons, 1934), 128.

42 Robert Bothwell, 'Canadian Representation at Washington: A Study in Colonial Responsibility', *Canadian Historical Review* 53 (1972):125–48.

43 Armour to Hull, 17 Oct. 1935, US National Archives and Records Administration, RG 59, Decimal File 1930–1939, box 3182.

44 Esme Howard, *Theatre of Life*, vol. II (London: Hodder and Stoughton, 1936), 516–17; Massey, *What's Past Is Prologue*, 164.

45 John Wirth, *Smelter Smoke in North America: The Politics of Transborder Pollution* (Lawrence: University Press of Kansas, 2000).

46 Ernest Hemingway, 'Canuck Whiskey Pouring into US', *Toronto Star Weekly*, 5 June 1920; 'Wage the War to Beat Huns', *Globe*, 1 Mar. 1918.

47 John Herd Thompson with Allen Seager, *Canada 1922–1939: Decades of Discord* (Toronto: McClelland and Stewart, 1985), 67.

48 Stephen Moore, *Bootleggers and Borders: The Paradox of Prohibition on a Canada-U.S. Borderland* (Lincoln: University of Nebraska Press, 2014), 50; Massey, *What's Past is Prologue*, 155.

49 James Cowan, 'Prosperity's Leap from the Bush', *Maclean's*, 15 Oct. 1928.

50 David Massell, *Amassing Power: J.B. Duke and the Saguenay River, 1897–1927* (Montreal: McGill-Queen's University Press, 2000).

51 House of Commons, *Debates*, 20 Feb. 1928, 637.

52 Yves Roby, *Les Québécois et les investissements américains, 1918–1929* (Québec: Les presses de l'Université Laval, 1976), 141; Peter Kresl, 'Before the Deluge: Canadians on Foreign Ownership, 1920–1955', *American Review of Canadian Studies* 6 (1976): 86–125.

53 W. A. Irwin, 'Can We Stem the Exodus?' *Maclean's*, 15 May 1927.

54 Archibald MacMechan, 'Canada as a Vassal State', *Canadian Historical Review* 1 (1920): 347; Robert Ayre, 'The American Empire', *Canadian Forum*, Jan. 1927.

55 Damien-Claude Bélanger, *Prejudice and Pride: Canadian Intellectuals Confront the United States, 1891–1945* (Toronto: University of Toronto Press, 2011), 81.

56 Mary Vipond, 'Canadian Nationalism and the Plight of Canadian Magazines in the 1920s', *Canadian Historical Review* 58 (1977): 53.

57 John Schultz, 'Whose News: The Struggle for Wire Service Distribution, 1900–1920', *American Review of Canadian Studies* 10 (1980): 27–35.

58 Elton Johnson, 'Canada's Radio Consciousness', *Maclean's*, 15 Oct. 1924.

59 George Drew, 'Have British Films a Chance?' *Maclean's*, 15 Oct. 1931; Ian Jarvie, *Hollywood's Overseas Campaign: The North Atlantic Movie Trade, 1920–1950* (Cambridge: Harvard University Press, 1992), 25–42.

60 Peter Morris, *Embattled Shadows: A History of Canadian Cinema, 1895–1939* (Montreal: McGill-Queen's University Press, 1978), 232.

61 Paul Morton, 'Starring Canada', *Maclean's*, 15 June 1934.

62 Sarah-Jane Mathieu, *North of the Color Line: Migration and Black Resistance in Canada, 1870–1955* (Chapel Hill: UNC Press, 2010), 140; Carla Marano, '"Rise Strongly and Rapidly": The Universal Negro Improvement Association in Canada, 1919–1940', *Canadian Historical Review* 91 (2010): 233–59.

63 'Canadian Province Turns to the Klan', *New York Times*, 8 July 1928; James Pitsula, *Keeping Canada British: The Ku Klux Klan in 1920s Saskatchewan* (Vancouver: UBC Press, 2013), 5; Allan Bartley, 'A Public Nuisance: The Ku Klux Klan in Ontario 1923–27', *Journal of Canadian Studies* 30 (1995): 156–74.

64 William Phillips, *Ventures in Diplomacy* (London, 1955), 70.

65 Mary Vipond, *Listening In: The First Decade of Canadian Broadcasting, 1922–1932* (Montreal: McGill-Queen's University Press, 1992).

66 Margaret Prang, 'The Origins of Public Broadcasting in Canada', *Canadian Historical Review* 46 (1965): 9–31.

67 House of Commons, *Debates*, 18 May 1932, 3035.

68 Simon Potter, *Broadcasting Empire: The BBC and the British World, 1922–1970* (Oxford: Oxford University Press, 2012), 52.

69 Ross King, *Defiant Spirits: The Modernist Revolution of the Group of Seven* (Vancouver: Douglas & McIntyre, 2011), 309; F. B. Housser, *A Canadian Art Movement: The Story of the Group of Seven* (Toronto: Macmillan, 1926), 13.

70 J. Marjorie Van derHoek, 'The Penetration of American Capital in Canada', *Canadian Forum*, Aug. 1926.

71 'Canadian Prosperity and the United States', *Round Table* 15 (1925): 572; F. R. Scott, *Canada Today* (Toronto: Oxford University Press, 1938), 103.

72 King Diary, 17 Sept. 1922.

73 King Diary, 4 Oct. 1922.

74 Power to Lapointe, 19 Nov. 1925, Queen's University Archives [hereafter QUA], Charles Power Papers, box 6.

75 King Diary, 15 Aug. 1929 and 10 June 1939.

76 King Diary, 26 Aug. 1928.

77 King Diary, 8 Apr. 1922.

78 King Diary, 27 Sept. 1920.

79 J. L. Granatstein, *Canada's Army: Waging War and Keeping the Peace*, Second Edition (Toronto: University of Toronto Press, 2011), 158.

80 Leo Amery, *My Political Life*, vol. II (London: Hutchinson, 1953), 276.

81 Gorman, *The Emergence of International Society in the 1920s*, 29; Katherine Moor, '"The Warmth of Comradeship": The First British Empire Games and Imperial Solidarity', *International Journal of the History of Sport* 6 (1989): 242–51.

82 James Eayrs, *In Defence of Canada: From the Great War to the Great Depression* (Toronto: University of Toronto Press, 1965), 79.

83 Hillmer, *O.D. Skelton*, 105.

84 Amery, *My Political Life*, 335.

85 Anne Clendinning, 'Exhibiting a Nation: Canada at the British Empire Exhibition, 1924–1925', *Histoire Sociale/Social History* 39 (2006): 79–107.

86 Michel Lacroix, 'Faire connaître "nouveau": Philippe Roy et la diplomatie culturelle du Canada à Paris, 1911–1938', in *Mission Paris: Les ambassadeurs du Canada en France at le triangle Ottawa-Quebec-Paris*, ed. Greg Donaghy and Stéphane Roussel (Montreal: Éditions Hurtubise, 2012); John Meehan, *The Dominion and the Rising Sun: Canada Encounters Japan, 1929–41* (Vancouver: UBC Press, 2004).

87 Douglas Anglin, 'United States Opposition to Canadian Membership in the Pan American Union: A Canadian View', *International Organization* 15 (1961): 1–20.

88 King Diary, 25 May 1927.

89 House of Commons, *Debates*, 6 Feb. 1928, 223.

90 'Empire Wares', *Globe*, 2 Nov. 1929; 'Let Uncle Sam Go His Own Way – Our Way is With John Bull', *Globe*, 14 July 1930.

91 House of Commons, *Debates*, 6 May 1930, 1826.

92 P. B. Waite, *In Search of R.B. Bennett* (Montreal: McGill-Queen's University Press, 2012), 98; 'Americans Warned that Empire Trade is Goal of Canada', *Globe*, 19 May 1932.

93 'City Bows in Prayer for Success of Imperial', *Globe*, 25 July 1932; Hector Charlesworth, *I'm Telling You: Being Further Candid Chronicles of Hector Charlesworth* (Toronto: Macmillan, 1937), 152.

94 Keith Feiling, *The Life of Neville Chamberlain* (London: Macmillan, 1946), 215.

95 David Jacks, 'Defying Gravity: The Imperial Economic Conference and the Reorientation of Canadian Trade', *Explorations in Economic History* 53 (2014): 19–39.

96 Ben Borsack, 'The Workers Hold a Conference', *Canadian Forum*, Sept. 1932.

97 R. B. Bennett, 'Democracy on Trial', in *Canadian Problems as Seen by Twenty Outstanding Men of Canada* (Toronto: Oxford University Press, 1933), 21–22.

98 IODE, *Canada within the Empire* (Toronto: IODE, 1939).

6 Canada and the descent to war

1 Escott Reid, 'Canada and the Threat of War', *University of Toronto Quarterly* 6 (1937): 242.

2 Pearson to Skelton, 4 Nov. 1938, Library and Archives Canada [hereafter LAC], RG 25, vol. 54, file 319-2.

3 King Diary, 8 Sept. 1936.

4 J. L. Granatstein, *Canada's War: The Politics of the Mackenzie King Government, 1939–1945*, 2nd Edition (Oakville: Rock's Mills, 2016), 420.

5 John Manley, '"Starve, Be Damned!" Communists and Canada's Urban Unemployed, 1929–1939', *Canadian Historical Review* 79 (1998): 489.

6 Douglas Irwin, *Peddling Protectionism: Smoot-Hawley and the Great Depression* (Princeton: Princeton University Press, 2011), 154; Richard Kottman, 'Herbert Hoover and the Smoot-Hawley Tariff: Canada, a Case Study', *Journal of American History* 62 (1975): 609–35.

7 Richard Kottman, 'Herbert Hoover and the St Lawrence Seaway Treaty of 1932', *New York History* 56 (1975): 314–46.

8 King Diary, 30 Oct. 1935.

9 Donald Forster and Colin Read, 'The Politics of Opportunism: The New Deal Broadcasts', *Canadian Historical Review* 60 (1979): 324–49; Larry Glassford, *Reaction and Reform: The Politics of the Conservative Party under R.B. Bennett, 1927–38* (Toronto: University of Toronto Press, 1992).

10 Doug Owram, 'Economic Thought in the 1930s: The Prelude to Keynesianism', *Canadian Historical Review* 66 (1985): 344–77.

11 Desmond Morton, *The New Democrats, 1961–1986* (Toronto: Copp Clark Pitman, 1986), 12; David Lewis, *The Good Fight: Political Memoirs, 1909–1958* (Toronto: Macmillan, 1981), 81.

12 Alvin Finkel, *The Social Credit Phenomenon in Alberta* (Toronto: University of Toronto Press, 1989); Janine Stingel, *Social Discredit: Anti-Semitism, Social Credit, and the Jewish Response* (Montreal: McGill-Queen's University Press, 2000).

13 Manley, '"Starve or Be Damned"'; John Manley, '"Communists Love Canada!": The Communist Party of Canada, the "People" and the Popular Front, 1933–1939', *Journal of Canadian Studies* 36 (2001–2): 59–86.

14 Michael Petrou, *Renegades: Canadians in the Spanish Civil War* (Vancouver: UBC Press, 2008), 22, 175; Roderick Stewart and Jesús Majada, *Bethune in Spain* (Montreal: McGill–Queen's University Press, 2014).

15 House of Commons, *Debates*, 15 Feb. 1937, 910; Louis-Philippe Roy, 'Franco ou le Comité?', *L'Action catholique*, 27 July 1937; Caroline Désy, *Si loin, si proche: La guerre civile espagnole et le Québec des années trente* (Québec: Les Presses de l'Uinversité Laval, 2003).

16 'Parable of Talents Is Cited by Bennett as Economic Truth', *Globe*, 10 Nov. 1932.

17 Robert Comeau and Bernard Dionne, *Le droit de se taire: Histoire des communistes au Québec, de la Première Guerre mondiale à la Révolution tranquille* (Montréal: VLB Éditeur, 1989), 15; Gregory Baum, *Catholics and Canadian Socialism: Political Thought in the Thirties and Forties* (Toronto: Lorimer, 1980), 189–211.

18 'A Lesson for Communists', *Montreal Gazette*, 14 Nov. 1931.

19 Lita-Rose Betchernan, *The Little Band: The Clashes between the Communists and the Political and Legal Establishment in Canada, 1928–32* (Ottawa: Deneau, 1982); Dennis Molinaro, *An Exceptional Law: Section 98 and the Emergency State, 1919–1936* (Toronto: University of Toronto Press, 2017).

20 Bill Waiser, *All Hell Can't Stop Us: The On-to-Ottawa Trek and the Regina Riot* (Calgary: Fifth House, 2003), 47.

21 House of Commons, *Debates*, 28 May 1928, 3477.

22 House of Commons, *Debates*, 1 Apr. 1935, 2290.

23 Hillmer, *O.D. Skelton*, 215, 216.

24 F. R. Scott, 'Impressions of a Tour in the USSR', *Canadian Forum* (Dec. 1935); Terry Crowley, *Agnes Macphail and the Politics of Equality* (Toronto: James Lorimer, 1990), 148.

25 Alexey Golubev and Irinia Takala, eds, *The Search for a Socialist El Dorado: Finnish Immigration to Soviet Karelia from the United States and Canada in the 1930s* (Winnipeg: University of Manitoba Press, 2014).

26 House of Commons, *Debates*, 13 May 1939, 4039.

27 '"Nefarious Power" of Jewry Attacked', *Montreal Gazette*, 21 Apr. 1933; Gerald Tulchinsky, *Branching Out: The Transformation of the Canadian Jewish Community* (Toronto: Stoddart, 1998), 180; Esther Delisle, *The Traitor and the Jew: Anti-Semitism and the Delirium of Extremist Right-Wing Nationalism in French Canada from 1929 to 1939* (Toronto: Robert Davies, 1993), 148.

28 Robert Comeau, 'Le tentation fasciste du nationalisme canadien-français avant la guerre, 1936–1939', *Bulletin d'Histoire Politique* 3 (1995): 159–67.

29 HughesThéorêt, *The Blue Shirts: Adrien Arcand and Fascist Anti-Semitism in Canada* (Ottawa: University of Ottawa Press, 2017).

30 Cyril Levitt and William Shaffir, *The Christie Pits Riot* (Toronto: Lester & Orpen Denys, 1987).

31 Théorêt, *The Blue Shirts*, 157.

32 Bruno Ramirez, *The Italians in Canada* (Ottawa: Canadian Historical Association, 1989), 18–19.

33 Paul-André Linteau, *Histoire de Montréal depuis la Confédération* (Montreal: Boréal, 1991), 332; Whitaker, Kealey, and Parnaby, *Secret Service*, 160; Luigi Pennacchio, 'Exporting Fascism to Canada: Toronto's Little Italy', in *Enemies Within: Italian and Other Internees in Canada and Abroad*, ed. Franca Iacovetta, Roberto Perin, and Angelo Principe (Toronto: University of Toronto Press, 2000).

34 Jonathan Wagner, *Brothers Beyond the Sea: National Socialism in Canada* (Waterloo: Wilfrid Laurier University Press, 1981).

35 Dandurand to the editor, *Le Devoir*, 25 Apr. 1933; 'Protest by Germany to Ottawa possible over Croft Remarks', *Globe & Mail*, 30 June 1938.

36 Richard Menkis and Harold Troper, *More Than Just Games: Canada and the 1938 Olympics* (Toronto: University of Toronto Press, 2015).

37 Dana Wilgress, *Memoirs* (Toronto: Ryerson, 1967), 105; 'Nazis Want Trade Treaty with Canada', *Globe*, 7 Aug. 1936.

38 'A Frenzy of Persecution', *Toronto Star*, 16 Nov. 1938; 'Canada's Silent Voice', *Globe & Mail*, 18 Nov. 1938; Amanda Grzyb, 'From Kristallnacht to the *MS St Louis* Tragedy: Canadian Press Coverage of Nazi Persecution of the Jews and the Jewish Refugee Crisis, September 1938 to August 1939', in *Nazi Germany, Canadian Responses: Confronting Antisemitism in the Shadow of War*, ed. L. Ruth Klein (Montreal: McGill-Queen's University Press, 2012).

39 'Leading Citizens Assail Pogrom before 4,500 at Meeting House', *Montreal Gazette*, 21 Nov. 1938; 'Big Canadian Meetings Urge Aid to Refugees', *Ottawa Citizen*, 21 Nov. 1938.

40 'Hitler Paper Sees "Atrocities" among Canadian Indians', *Globe & Mail*, 21 Nov. 1938.

41 Irving Abella and Harold Troper, *None Is Too Many: Canada and the Jews of Europe, 1933–1948* (Toronto: University of Toronto Press, 1983), 46.

42 King Diary, 29 Mar. 1938.

43 King Diary, 12 Nov. 1938.

44 Valerie Knowles, *First Person: A Biography of Cairine Wilson* (Toronto: Dundurn, 1988), 213.

45 Abella and Troper, *None Is Too Many*, xix.

46 A. R. M. Lower, 'Foreign Policy and the Empire: A Canadian View', *The Nineteenth Century and After* 114 (1933): 263–64.

47 'Think Internationally', *Saturday Night*, 2 Dec. 1933; 'Why Disarmament Conferences Fail', *Saturday Night*, 22 Oct. 1932.

48 'Women Will Not Countenance Another War!' *Vancouver Sun*, 4 Feb. 1933; 'Veterans are for Peace', *Saturday Night*, 1 June 1934; 'The World's Demand for Disarmament', *Manitoba Free Press*, 12 Dec. 1931; George Drew, 'Salesmen of Death', *Maclean's*, 1. Aug. 1931; Arthur Meighen, 'To Get Rid of War', *Maclean's*, 15 Jan. 1931.

49 Page, 'The Institute's "Popular Arm" ', 55.

50 Socknat, *Witness against War*, 167.

51 CYC, *Youth's Peace Policy* (Toronto: Canadian Youth Congress, 1936).

52 Massey, *What's Past Is Prologue*, 234.

53 Lester Pearson, *Mike: The Memoirs of the Right Honourable Lester B. Pearson*, vol. I (Toronto: University of Toronto Press, 1972), 92; Hillmer, *O.D. Skelton*, 189, 260.

54 Meehan, *The Dominion and the Rising Sun*.

55 Fraser Hunter, 'Realities of the Manchurian Muddle', *Saturday Night*, 16 Jan. 1932; 'Japan Represents Order', *Saturday Night*, 28 Nov. 1931.

56 Bennett to Cahan, 2 Dec. 1932, *Documents on Canadian External Relations*, vol. 5, 314; D. C. Story, 'Canada, the League of Nations and the Far East, 1931–33: The Cahan Incident', *International History Review* 3 (1981): 236–55.

57 House of Commons, *Debates*, 25 May 1932, 3437; Hillmer, *O.D. Skelton*, 208.

58 'The Silent League', *Vancouver Sun*, 23 Nov. 1931; 'The League's Weakness', *Globe*, 29 Sept. 1931.

59 F. J. Savage, 'Has White Control of World Affairs Ended?' *Saturday Night*, 12 Aug. 1933; C. E. Hope and W. K. Earle, 'The Oriental Threat', *Maclean's*, 1 May 1933; Herbert Johnston, 'How Japan Got in Wrong with the West', *Saturday Night*, 25 Mar. 1933.

60 Henry Angus, 'A Contribution to International Ill-Will', *Dalhousie Review*, Apr. 1933; House of Commons, *Debates*, 22 June 1934, 4206.

61 N. A. M. MacKenzie, 'Canada and the Changing Balance of Power in the Pacific', *Canada: The Empire and the League* (Toronto: Thomas Nelson, 1936), 61; A. R. M. Lower, *Canada and the Far East-1940* (New York: Institute of Pacific Relations, 1940), 89; Roy, *The Oriental Question*, 166–230.

62 Hillmer, *O.D. Skelton*, 219.

63 Brock Millman, 'Canada, Sanctions, and the Abyssinian Crisis of 1935', *Historical Journal* 40 (1997): 149.

64 W. A. Riddell, *World Security by Conference* (Toronto: Ryerson, 1947), 115.

65 Frank Underhill, 'Canada and Post-League Europe', *Canadian Forum*, Oct. 1936; Frank Underhill, 'Canadian Foreign Policy in the 1920s', in *Canada and the Organization of Peace* (Toronto: Canadian Institute of International Affairs, 1935), 64.

66 King Diary, 15 Dec. 1936.

67 'Teachers, Veterans Push Sanctions Move', *Globe & Mail*, 18 Oct. 1937; Meehan, *Dominion and the Rising Sun*, 157–60, 175; John Meehan, 'Steering Clear of Great Britain: Canada's Debate over Collective Security in the Far Eastern Crisis of 1937', *International History Review* 25 (2003): 276.

68 Doris Pennington, *Agnes Macphail: Reformer* (Toronto: Simon and Pierre, 1989), 188.

69 House of Commons, *Debates*, 11 Feb. 1938; 'Chinese Consul Warns against Helping Japan', *Ottawa Citizen*, 6 Jan. 1938; Meehan, 'Steering Clear of Great Britain', 270.

70 King Diary, 19 and 28 Oct. 1937.

71 King Diary, 11 Feb. 1937.

72 Hankey, 'Impressions of Canada, December 1934', TNA, CAB 63/81.

73 Norman Hillmer, 'Defence and Ideology: The Anglo-Canadian Military "Alliance" in the 1930s', *International Journal* 33 (1978): 595; Delaney, *The Imperial Army Project*, 201–29.

74 Gordon Beadle, 'Canada and the Abdication of Edward VIII', *Journal of Canadian Studies* 4 (1969): 33–46; Tony McCulloch, 'Roosevelt, Mackenzie King and the British Royal Visit to the USA in 1939', *London Journal of Canadian Studies* 23 (2007/8): 81–104; Simon Potter, 'The BBC, the CBC, and the 1939 Royal Tour of Canada', *Cultural and Social History* 3 (2006): 424–44.

75 'Le seul parlement français de l'empire britannique rend des hommages officiels à son roi', *La Presse*, 17 May 1939; 'Grâce et sagesse', *Le Devoir*, 19 May 1939.

76 *The Legionary*, June 1939.

77 Imperial Conference, 3rd Meeting, 21 May 1937, TNA, CAB 32/128.

78 King, 'Memorandum on a Talk with German Leaders Held 29 June 1937, TNA, PREM 1/344.

79 King Diary, 29 June 1937; Orme Sargent Minute, 25 July 1937, TNA, FO 371/20750.

80 Hillmer, *O.D. Skelton*, 239.

81 H. Blair Neatby, *William Lyon Mackenzie King, 1932–1939: The Prism of Unity* (Toronto: University of Toronto Press, 1976). 293; 'Thinks Civilization Saved by Chamberlain Settlement' *and* 'May Link Chamberlain with Ottawa Memorial', *Ottawa Citizen*, 4 Oct. 1938; 'Ottawa Baby Is Christened with Honor to Chamberlain' *and* 'Peace, Liberty Symbols Placed on War Memorial', *Ottawa Citizen*, 1 Oct. 1938.

82 'What's the Cheering For?' *Winnipeg Free Press*, 30 Sept. 1938; James Gray, *The Winter Years: The Depression on the Prairies* (Toronto: Macmillan, 1966), 17.

83 *The Legionary*, Jan. 1938.

84 King Diary, 13 Sept. 1938; J. L. Granatstein and Robert Bothwell, ' "A Self-Evident National Duty": Canadian Foreign Policy, 1935–1939', *Journal of Imperial and Commonwealth History* 3 (1975): 212–33.

85 King Diary, 31 Aug. and 12 Sept. 1938.

86 King Diary, 14 Nov. 1938.

87 Wilgress, *Memoirs*, 109; King to Chamberlain, 10 Oct. 1938, TNA, FO 371/21506; Ian Drummond and Norman Hillmer, *Negotiating Freer Trade: The United Kingdom, the United States, Canada and the Trade Agreements of 1938* (Waterloo: Wilfrid Laurier University Press, 1989).

88 King Diary, 7 Jan. 1939.

89 House of Commons, *Debates*, 30 Mar. 1939, 2419, 2422 and 20 Mar. 1939, 2043.

90 House of Commons, *Debates*, 31 Mar. 1939, 2469.

91 Campbell to DO, no. 258, 25 Aug. 1939, TNA, FO 371/23966.

92 Ian Miller, 'Toronto's Response to the Outbreak of War, 1939', *Canadian Military History* 11 (2002): 8.

93 King Diary, 9 Sept. 1939.

94 Skelton, 'Canada and the Polish War, A Personal Note', 25 Aug. 1939, *Documents on Canadian External Relations*, vol. 6, 1247–9; André Laurendeau, *La crise de la conscription, 1942* (Montreal: Les Editions du Jour, 1962), 37.

95 Campbell to DO, no. 283, 20 Sept. 1939, TNA, DO 114/98.

96 Watson Kirkconnell, *Canada, Europe and Hitler* (Toronto: Oxford University Press, 1939), v; 'War against Nazis Crusade to Save Christian Civilization', *Ottawa Journal*, 28 Oct. 1939.

97 Margaret Stewart and Doris French, *Ask No Quarter: A Biography of Agnes Macphail* (Toronto: Longman's, 1959), 248.

7 The North Atlantic Triangle from world war to cold war

1 J. B. Brebner, *North Atlantic Triangle: The Interplay of Canada, the United States and Great Britain* (New Haven: Yale University Press, 1945), xi, 328, vii; Srdjan Vucetic, *The Anglosphere: A Genealogy of a Racialized Identity in International Relations* (Palo Alto, CA: Stanford University Press, 2011).

2 King Diary, 8 Nov. 1945; R. R. James, *Winston Churchill: His Complete Speeches, 1897–1963*, VII (London: Chelsea House, 1974), 7289.

3 J. B. Brebner, 'A Changing North Atlantic Triangle', *International Journal* 3 (1948): 314.

4 Delaney, *The Imperial Army Project*, 230; Iain Johnston-White, *The British Commonwealth and Victory in the Second World War* (London: Palgrave, 2016); John A. English, 'Not an Equilateral Triangle: Canada's Strategic Relationships with the United States and Britain, 1939–1945', in *The North Atlantic Triangle in a Changing World*, ed. B. J. C. McKercher and Larry Aronsen (Toronto: University of Toronto Press, 1996).

5 Minister Designate in Switzerland to SSEA, 25 Apr. 1947, *Documents on Canadian External Relations*, vol. 13, 365.

6 King Diary, 30 May 1940.

7 King Diary, 23 May 1940.

8 Olivier Courteaux, *Canada between Vichy and Free France, 1940–1945* (Toronto: University of Toronto Press, 2013); Éric Amyot, *Le Québec entre Pétain et de Gaulle: Vichy, La France Libre, et les Canadiens Français, 1940–1945* (Montreal: Éditions Fides, 1999).

9 John MacCormac, *Canada: America's Problem* (New York: Viking, 1940), 13.

10 C. P. Stacey, *Arms, Men and Governments: The War Policies of Canada, 1939–1945* (Ottawa: Information Canada, 1970), 339.

11 King to Pearson, 13 Mar. 1946, LAC, MG 26 N1, vol. 7, file King W. L. Mackenzie 1942–1950; Galen Roger Perras, *Franklin Roosevelt and the Origins of the Canadian-American Security Alliance, 1933–1945* (Westport: Praeger, 1998).

12 Stacey, *Canada and the Age of Conflict, II*, 226; FDR to Tweedsmuir, 31 Aug. 1938, QUA, Buchan Papers, box 10, file Correspondence July–August 1938.

13 King Diary, 18 Aug. 1938.

14 King Diary, 27 Jan. 1939 and 14 Nov. 1938; Galen Roger Perras, 'The Myth of Obsequious Rex: Mackenzie King, Franklin D. Roosevelt, and Canada-US Security, 1935–1940', in *Transnationalism: Canada-United States History into the Twenty-first Century*, ed. Michael Behiels and Reginald Stuart (Montreal: McGill-Queen's University Press, 2010).

15 King Diary, 25 Mar. 1948.

16 Francine McKenzie, 'In the National Interest: Dominions' Support for Britain and the Commonwealth after the Second World War', *Journal of Imperial and Commonwealth History* 34 (2006): 553–76.

17 Desmond Morton, *A Military History of Canada*, Fifth Edition (Toronto: McClelland and Stewart, 2007), 192; King Diary, 24 Mar. 1943.

18 Granatstein, *Canada's War*; Robert Bothwell and William Kilbourn, *C.D. Howe: A Biography* (Toronto: McClelland and Stewart, 1979).

19 Randall Hansen, *Fire and Fury: The Allied Bombing of Germany, 1942–1945* (Toronto: Penguin, 2009).

20 Tim Cook, *The Necessary War: Canadians Fighting the Second World War*, vol. I (Toronto: Penguin, 2017); Tim Cook, *Fighting to the Finish: Canadians Fighting the Second World War*, vol. II (Toronto: Penguin, 2017); Roy MacLaren, *Canadians Behind Enemy Lines, 1939–1945* (Vancouver: UBC Press, 2004).

21 King Diary, 15 June 1942.

22 King Diary, 4 and 6 Aug. 1945.

23 'Atomic Bomb Rocks Japan', *Globe & Mail*, 7 Aug. 1945; 'Pre-eminence of the Anglo-Saxon', *Canadian Forum*, Sept. 1945.

24 'Genies out of the Bottle', *Saturday Night*, 11 Aug. 1945.

25 Brian Buckley, *Canada's Early Nuclear Policy: Fate, Chance, and Character* (Montreal: McGill-Queen's University Press, 2000).

26 Nancy Harvison Hacker, *The Moffat Papers: Selections from the Diplomatic Journals of Jay Pierrepont Moffat, 1919–1943* (Cambridge: Harvard University Press, 1956), 342.

27 King Diary, 7 Aug. 1941.

28 Cabinet War Committee Minutes, 29 Dec. 1941, LAC, RG 2, vol. 810; Lord Moran, *Churchill: Taken from the Diaries of Lord Moran* (Boston, MA: Houghton Mifflin, 1966), 117, note 3.

29 Minutes of a Joint meeting of War Cabinet of the United Kingdom and the War Committee of the Canadian Cabinet, 11 Aug. 1943, LAC, RG 2, vol. 5679.

30 Pearson, *Mike* I, 170–1.

31 Massey, *What's Past Is Prologue*, 353.

32 Pope, *Soldiers and Politicians*, 209.

33 Wrong to Robertson, 20 Jan. 1942, LAC, RG 25, file 3265-A-40.

34 King Diary, 29 Sept. 1944; Memorandum from Minister-Counsellor, Legation in the United States, to Minister in the United States, 'Certain Developments in Canada-United States Relations', 18 Mar. 1943, *Documents on Canadian External Relations*, vol. 9, 1142.

35 Kenneth Coates and William Morrison, *The Alaska Highway in World War II: The US Army of Occupation in Canada's Northwest* (Toronto: University of Toronto Press, 1992), 3.

36 King Diary, 21 Mar. 1942.

37 Shelagh Grant, *Sovereignty or Security: Government Policy in the Canadian North, 1936–1950* (Vancouver: UBC Press, 1988), 71.

38 King Diary, 25 Jan. 1944; Adam Chapnick, 'Testing the Bonds of Commonwealth with Viscount Halifax: Canada in the Post-War International System, 1942–1944', *International History Review* 31 (2009): 24–44.

39 Amery to Cranborne, 4 Feb. 1944, TNA, DO35/1485.

40 Kim Richard Nossal, Stéphane Roussel and Stéphane Paquin, *The Politics of Canadian Foreign Policy*, Fourth Edition (Montreal: McGill-Queen's University Press, 2015), 61.

41 King Diary, 6 Sept. 1944.

42 J. W. Pickersgill, *The Mackenzie King Record I, 1939–1944* (Toronto: University of Toronto Press, 1960), 678–9.

43 Final Report of Advisory Committee on Post-Hostilities Problems, Jan./Feb. 1945, *Documents on Canadian External Relations*, vol. 11, 1567–73.

44 Adam Chapnick, *The Middle Power Project: Canada and the Founding of the United Nations* (Vancouver: UBC Press, 2005).

45 King Diary, 4 Oct. 1945.

46 Memorandum, 9 Oct. 1945, *Documents on Canadian External Relations*, vol. 11, 1991; Reg Whitaker, 'Cold War Alchemy: How America, Britain and Canada Transformed Espionage into Subversion', *Intelligence & National Security* 15 (2000); Hector Mackenzie, 'Canada's International Relations in the Early Cold War: The Impact and Implications of the Gouzenko Affair', in *The Gouzenko Affair: Canada and the Beginnings of Cold War Counter-Espionage*, ed. J. L. Black and Martin Rudner (Manotick: Penumbra Press, 2006), 15–37.

47 King Diary, 5 Mar. 1946.

48 Ambassador in United States to Secretary of State for External Affairs, 11 Mar. 1946, *Documents on Canadian External Relations*, vol. 12, 2043–4; 'Vodka honeymoons, 21 Mar. 1946, No. 110', document CDT00013, *Canada Declassified*.

49 Memorandum from Under-Secretary of State for External Affairs to Prime Minister, 'Defence Discussions', 12 Nov. 1946, *Documents on Canadian External Relations*, vol. 12, 1670–72.

50 King Diary, 15 Dec. 1947.

51 House of Commons, *Debates*, 29 Apr. 1948, 3448.

52 King Diary, 10 Mar. 1948; Prime Minister to Prime Minister of United Kingdom, 11 Mar. 1948, *Documents on Canadian External Relations*, vol. 14, 422.

53 Hector Mackenzie, 'Canada, the Cold War and the Negotiation of the North Atlantic Treaty', in *Diplomatic Documents and Their Users*, ed. John Hilliker and Mary Halloran (Ottawa: Department of Foreign Affairs and International Trade, 1995), 145–73; Hector Mackenzie, 'The North Atlantic Triangle and North Atlantic Treaty: A Canadian Perspective on the ABC Security Conversations of March-April 1948', *London Journal of Canadian Studies* 20 (2004/5): 89–116.

54 DEA, *Statements & Speeches* 52/6, 26 Jan. 1952.

55 Pearson to Wrong, 21 May 1948, *Documents on Canadian External Relations*, vol. 14, 1794–5.

56 'The Atlantic Pact', *Canadian Forum*, Apr. 1949; 'Isolationism in Its Grave', *Maclean's*, 1 May 1949.

57 'Hands across the Sea', *Time*, 8 Nov. 1948.

58 Bruce Hutchinson, 'Last Ottawa Memo', 1949, QUL, Grant Dexter Papers, TC5, file 35.

59 Memorandum from SSEA to Cabinet, 'North Atlantic Treaty', 4 Oct. 1948, *Documents on Canadian External Relations*, vol. 14, 610; John Milloy, *The North Atlantic Treaty Organization, 1948–1957: Community or Alliance?* (Montreal: McGill-Queen's University Press, 2006).

60 Memorandum from USSEA to Prime Minister, 'Proposed Pact of Mutual Assistance', 14 Mar. 1948, *Documents on Canadian External Relations*, vol. 14, 432; 'The Peace Council Men', *Saturday Night*, 29 Mar. 1949.

61 Briefing Note, '"Western Union" and an Atlantic Pact: A Survey of Recent Developments', 11 Sept. 1948, LAC, RG 2, vol. 107, file U-10–11; DEA, *Statements & Speeches* 51/11, 19 Mar. 1951.

62 B. K. Sandwell, 'The Clash of Ideologies in the Post-War World and Its Implications for North America', *Canada in a New World*, ed. Eugene Forsey (Toronto: Ryerson, 1947), 1; DEA, *Statements & Speeches* 47/16, 7 Oct. 1947.

63 Andrew Brewin, 'Canadian Economic Assistance to Under-Developed Areas', *International Journal* 5 (1950–1): 304.

64 Dennis Molinaro, '"In the Field of Espionage, There's No Such Thing as Peacetime": The Official Secrets Act and the PICNIC Wiretapping Program', *Canadian Historical Review* 98 (2017); Steve Hewitt, *Spying 101: The RCMP's Secret Activities at Canadian Universities, 1917–1997* (Toronto: University of Toronto Press, 2002); Christabelle Sethna and Steve Hewitt, *Just Watch Us: RCMP Surveillance of the Women's Liberation Movement in Cold War Canada* (Montreal: McGill-Queen's University Press, 2018); J. L. Granatstein and David Stafford, *Spy Wars: Espionage and Canada from Gouzenko to Glasnost* (Toronto: Key Porter, 1990).

65 Richard Cavell, ed., *Love, Hate, and Fear: Canada in the Cold War* (Toronto: University of Toronto Press, 2004); Gary Kinsman and Patrizia Gentile, *The Canadian War on Queers: National Security as Sexual Regulation* (Vancouver: UBC Press, 2009); Adam Chapnick, *Canada's Voice: The Public Life of John Wendell Holmes* (Vancouver: UBC Press, 2009).

66 Benjamin Isitt, 'Confronting the Cold War: The 1950 Vancouver Convention of the Co-operative Commonwealth Federation', *Canadian Historical Review* 9 (2010): 465–501.

67 Jennifer Anderson, *Propaganda and Persuasion: The Cold War and the Canadian-Soviet Friendship Society* (Winnipeg: University of Manitoba Press, 2017).

68 Stephen Endicott, *James G. Endicott: Rebel Out of China* (Toronto: University of Toronto Press, 1980), 185, 247.

69 Victor Huard, "The Canadian Peace Congress and the Challenge to the Postwar Consensus, 1948–1953', *Peace and Change* 19 (1994): 25–49.

70 Kurt Jensen, *Cautious Beginnings: Canadian Foreign Intelligence, 1939–51* (Vancouver: UBC Press, 2008).

71 House of Commons, *Debates*, 24 June 1948, 5779.

72 Claxton and Pearson, 'The International Situation', 28 Dec. 1950, *Documents on Canadian External Relations*, vol. 16, 1159–62.

73 DEA, *Statements & Speeches* 51/17, 20 Apr. 1951.

74 King Diary, 18 and 6 Dec. 1947; John Price, 'The "Cat's Paw": Canada and the United Nations Temporary Commission on Korea', *Canadian Historical Review* 85 (2004): 297–324.

75 Cabinet Conclusions, 27 June 1950, LAC, RG 2; House of Commons, *Debates*, 28 June 1950, 4251; The Secretary of State to All Diplomatic Missions and Certain Consular Offices, 29 June 1950, *Foreign Relations of the United States* 1950, vol. VII, 232.

76 Extract from Memorandum from SSEA to Prime Minister, 27 June 1950, *Documents on Canadian External Relations*, vol. 16, 49–50.

77 Pearson to St Laurent, 3 Aug. 1950, LAC, MG 26 N1, vol. 35; George Egerton, 'Lester B. Pearson and the Korean War: Dilemmas of Collective Security and International Enforcement in Canadian Foreign Policy, 1950–1953', *International Peacekeeping* 4 (1997): 51–74.

78 Pearson, 'Korea and the Atomic Bomb', 3 Dec. 1950, *Documents on Canadian External Relations*, vol. 16, 254–5.

79 'Briefing on Canada for General Ridgway', 1952, NARA, RG 84, Entry UD2195C, Classified General Records, box 6, folder 310.

80 Greg Donaghy, 'Pacific Diplomacy: Canadian Statecraft and the Korean War, 1950–53', in *Canada and Korea: Perspectives 2000*, ed. Rick Guisso and Yong-Sik Yoo (Toronto: University of Toronto Press, 2002), 81–100; Denis Stairs, *The Diplomacy of Constraint: Canada, the Korean War, and the United States* (Toronto: University of Toronto Press, 1974).

81 Pearson to Wrong, 1 Feb. 1951, LAC, RG 25, vol. 4742, file 50069-A-40.

82 DEA, *Statements & Speeches* 51/13, 31 Mar. 1951; DEA, *Statements & Speeches* 51/14, 10 Apr. 1951.

83 Evelyn Shuckburgh, *Descent to Suez: Foreign Office Diaries, 1951–1956* (New York: Norton, 1987), 54; Greg Donaghy, 'Blessed are the Peacemakers: Canada, the United Nations, and the Search for a Korean Armistice, 1952–53', *War & Society* 30 (2011): 134–46.

84 Heeney to Pearson, 18 July 1950, *Documents on Canadian External Relations*, vol. 16, 67–8; Pearson to Wrong, 3 Mar. 1950, LAC, MG 26 N, vol. 17, file HH Wrong, 1948–1953; Foulkes to Wilgress, 10 Mar. 1953, LAC, RG 25, file 50273-40.

85 'Death of the Veto', *Globe & Mail*, 30 June 1950; 'The UN Proves Its Worth with the Blue Chips Down', *Maclean's,* 1 Aug. 1950.

86 Wrong to Pearson, 7 Mar. 1951, LAC, MG 26 N1, vol. 17.

87 Davis to Pearson, 5 Dec. 1948, LAC, RG 25, file 50055-40-pt. 3.

88 Arnold Heeney, 'Policy Toward Communist China', 4 Nov. 1949, LAC, RG 25, file 50055-B-40-pt. 3.

89 Meehan, *Chasing the Dragon in Shanghai*, 176; Serge Granger, *Le Lys et le Lotus: les relations du Québec avec la Chine de 1850 à 1950* (Montréal: VLB Éditeur, 2005), 119.

90 Jacques Hébert and Pierre Trudeau, *Two Innocents in Red China* (Toronto: Oxford University Press, 1968), 2.

91 Norman Vorano, 'Inuit Art: Canada's Soft Power Resource to Fight Communism', *Journal of Curatorial Studies* 5 (2016); Kailey Hansson, 'Dancing into Hearts and Minds: Canadian Ballet Exchanges with the Communist World, 1956–76', in *Undiplomatic History: The New Study of Canada and the World*, ed. Asa McKercher and Phil van Huizen (Montreal: McGill-Queen's University Press, 2019); Graham Carr, ' "No Political Significance of Any Kind": Glenn Gould's Tour of the Soviet Union and the Culture of the Cold War', *Canadian Historical Review* 95 (2014).

92 Memorandum of a Conversation with Mr. John Foster Dulles, 16 Mar. 1954, LAC, MG 26 N1, vol. 65; Timothy Andrews Sayle, 'A Cold Warrior? Pearson and the Soviet Bloc', in *Mike's World: Lester B. Pearson and Canadian External Affairs*, ed. Asa McKercher and Galen Roger Perras (Vancouver: UBC Press, 2017).

93 DEA, *Statements & Speeches* 50/26, 14 July 1950.

94 John Lewis Gaddis, *We Now Know: Rethinking Cold War History* (Oxford: Oxford University Press, 1997); Geir Lundestad, 'Empire by Invitation? The United States and Western Europe, 1945–1952', *Journal of Peace Research* 23 (1986).

95 King Diary, 30 Mar. 1948; Harrington to Snow, 12 Aug. 1949, NARA, RG 84, Entry UD2195C, Classified General Records, box 6, folder 320.

96 DEA, *Statements & Speeches* 51/14, 10 Apr. 1951; Pearson to Wrong, 16 Apr. 1951, LAC, MG 26 N1, vol. 35, file Korea: Canadian Policy 1950–1951.

8 The middle power and the end of empire

1 Lester Pearson, 'The Nature of the Crisis', in *Crisis '58: Report of the 27th Annual Couchiching Conference* (Toronto: Canadian Institute of Public Affairs, 1958), 2.

2 I. Norman Smith, 'Pearson, people, and press', *International Journal* 29 (1973–4): 18.

3 DEA, *Statements & Speeches* 56/9, 21 Mar. 1956.

4 Vijay Prashad, *The Darker Nations: A People's History of the Third World* (New York: The New Press, 2007).

5 Blair Fraser, 'Canada's New "Bad-boy" role', *Maclean's*, 19 Dec. 1959.

6 John Holmes, 'The Relationship in Alliance and in World Affairs', in *The United States and Canada: The American Assembly* (Englewood Cliffs, NJ: Prentice Hall, 1964), 114–5.

7 Odd Arne Westad, *The Global Cold War* (Cambridge: Cambridge University Press, 2005).

8   'A foreign idea?', *The Economist*, 29 May 1943.

9   Lionel Gelber, 'Canada's New Stature', *Foreign Affairs* 24 (1946): 277.

10 Brooke Claxton, 'The Place of Canada in Post-War Organization', *Canadian Journal of Economics and Political Science* 10 (1944): 421; Grant Dexter, *Canada and the Building of Peace* (Toronto: Canadian Institute of International Affairs, 1944), 18; Adam Chapnick, 'The Canadian Middle Power Myth', *International Journal* 55 (2000).

11 Louis St Laurent, *The Foundations of Canadian Policy in World Affairs* (Toronto: University of Toronto Press, 1947), 33; Hector Mackenzie, 'Shades of Gray? "The Foundations of Canadian Policy in World Affairs" in Context', *American Review of Canadian Studies* 37 (2007): 459–73.

12 J. L. Granatstein, *The Ottawa Men: The Civil Service Mandarins, 1935–1957* (Toronto: Oxford University Press, 1982); John W. Holmes, *The Shaping of Peace: Canada and the Search for World Order*, vol. I (Toronto: University of Toronto Press, 1979), 25.

13 David Webster, 'Modern Missionaries: Canadian Postwar Technical Assistance Advisors in Southeast Asia', *Journal of Canadian Historical Association* 20 (2009): 86–111; John Farley, *Brock Chisholm, The World Health Organization, and the Cold War* (Vancouver: UBC Press, 2009).

14 Susan Armstrong-Reid and David Murray, *Arms for Peace: Canada and the UNRRA Years* (Toronto: University of Toronto Press, 2008); David Mackenzie, *ICAO: A History of the International Civil Aviation Organization* (Toronto: University of Toronto Press, 2010).

15 C. D. Howe, 'Employment and Income with Special Reference to the Initial Period of Reconstruction', in *Canadian Foreign Policy, 1945–1954*, ed. R. A. MacKay (Toronto: University of Toronto Press, 1971), 52–3; Francine McKenzie, 'Preparing for Peace: Canada and the Reconstruction of Postwar Trade, 1943–1945', in *Uncertain Horizons: Canadians and Their World in 1945*, ed. Greg Donaghy (Ottawa: Canadian Committee for the History of the Second World War, 1996), 135–64; Bruce Muirhead, *Against the Odds: The Public Life and Times of Louis Rasminksy* (Toronto: University of Toronto Press, 1999).

16 Tarah Brookfield, 'Save the Children/Save the World: Canadian Women Embrace the United Nations, 1940s-1970s', in *Canada and the United Nations: Legacies, Limits, Prospects*, ed. Colin McCullough and Robert Teigrob (Montreal: McGill-Queen's University Press, 2016), 105; Tarah Brookfield, 'Modeling the UN's Mission in Semi-Formal Wear: Edmonton's Miss United Nations Pageants of the 1960s', in *Contesting Bodies and Nations in Canadian History*.

17 John Humphrey, 'The Magna Carta of Mankind', in *Human Rights*, ed. Peter Davies (London: Routledge, 1988), 31–9.

18 DEA to UN Delegation, tel. 117, 8 Oct. 1948 and UN Delegation to DEA, tel. 461, 23 Nov. 1948, LAC, RG 25, file 5475-DP-40-pt. 1; Michael Behiels, 'Canada and the Implementation of International Instruments of Human Rights: A Federalist Conundrum, 1919–1982', in *Framing Canadian*

Federalism: Historical Essays in Honour of John T. Saywell, ed. Dimitry Anastakis and P.E. Bryden (Toronto: University of Toronto Press, 2009), 151–84.

19 Dominique Marshall, 'The Cold War, Canada, and the United Nations Declaration of the Rights of the Child', in *Canada and the Early Cold War, 1943–1957*, ed. Greg Donaghy (Ottawa: Department of Foreign Affairs and International Trade, 1998), 183–212.

20 Howard Margolian, *Conduct Unbecoming: The Story of the Murder of Canadian Prisoners of War in Normandy* (Toronto: University of Toronto Press, 1998); Howard Margolian, *Unauthorized Entry: The Truth about Nazi War Criminals in Canada, 1946–1956* (Toronto: University of Toronto Press, 2000); Marc Bergère, *Vichy au Canada: L'exil québécois de collaborateurs français* (Montreal: Les Presses de l'Université de Montréal, 2016).

21 Pope, *Soldiers and Politicians*, 177.

22 Stephanie Bangarth, *Voices Raised in Protest: Defending North American Citizens of Japanese Ancestry, 1942–49* (Vancouver: UBC Press, 2008), 32.

23 'Civil Liberties – 1942', *Canadian Forum* (June 1942); Ross Lambertson, *Repression and Resistance: Canadian Human Rights Activists, 1930–1960* (Toronto: University of Toronto Press, 2005).

24 Pai to St Laurent, 4 Dec. 1946, LAC, RG 25, file 5550-40; John Hilliker, 'The British Columbia Franchise and Canadian Relations with India in Wartime, 1939–1945', *BC Studies* 46 (1980): 40–60; A. E. Davis and Vineet Thakur, 'Walking the Thin Line: India's Antiracist Diplomatic Practice in South Africa, Canada, and Australia, 1946–55', *International History Review* 38 (2016): 880–99.

25 Nehru to St Laurent, 17 Apr. 1947, LAC, RG 25, file 5550-40.

26 King Diary, 13 Feb. 1947; F. J. McEvoy, ' "A Symbol of Racial Discrimination": The Chinese Immigration Act and Canada's Relations with China, 1942–1947', *Canadian Ethnic Studies* 14 (1982): 24–42; Stephanie Bangarth, ' "We Are Not Asking You to Open Wide the Gates for Chinese Immigration": The Committee for the Repeal of the Chinese Immigration Act and Early Human Rights Activism in Canada', *Canadian Historical Review* 84 (2003): 395–422; Patricia Roy, *The Triumph of Citizenship: The Japanese and Chinese in Canada, 1941–67* (Vancouver: UBC Press, 2008).

27 House of Commons, *Debates*, 1 May 1947, 2644–5; Laura Madokoro, *Elusive Refuge: Chinese Migrants in the Cold War* (Cambridge: Harvard University Press, 2016).

28 Reid to Pearson, 10 Mar. 1949, LAC, RG 25, file 50017-40-pt. 1.

29 Pearson to Harris, 11 Sept. 1950, LAC RG 25, file 232-AH-40-pt. 1.1.

30 Cabinet Conclusions, 20 Dec. 1951, LAC, RG 2, vol. 2649.

31 Cabinet Conclusions, 17 Mar. 1949, LAC, RG 2, vol. 2643; Hector Mackenzie, 'An Old Dominion and the New Commonwealth: Canadian Policy on the Question of India's Membership, 1947–49', *Journal of Imperial and Commonwealth History* 27 (1999): 82–112.

32 DEA, *Statements & Speeches*, 51/14, 10 Apr. 1951; Ryan Touhey, *Conflicting Visions: Canada and India in the Cold War World, 1946–76* (Vancouver: UBC Press, 2015).

33 Ford to Reid, 16 Mar. 1949, LAC, RG 25, file 50054-40-pt. 10.

34 Holmes to Pearson, 22 Dec. 1949, LAC, RG 25, file 5475-N-40-pt. 4.1.

35 David Webster, *Fire and the Full Moon: Canada and Indonesia in a Decolonizing World* (Vancouver: UBC Press, 2009), 61–5.

36 Brewin, 'Canadian Economic Assistance to Under-Developed Areas', 306.

37 Pearson to Abbott, 3 June 1950, LAC, RG 25, file 10170-C-40-pt. 2.1; R. G. Cavell, 'Canada and the Colombo Plan', 4 Dec. 1952, in *The Empire Club of Canada Addresses* (Toronto: Empire Club of Canada, 1953); Pearson to St Laurent, 27 Nov. 1950, LAC, RG 25, file 11038–40; Jill Campbell-Miller, 'Encounter and Apprenticeship: The Colombo Plan and Canadian Aid in India, 1950–1960', in *A Samaritan State Revisited: Historical Perspectives on Canadian Foreign Aid*, ed. Greg Donaghy and David Webster (Calgary: University of Calgary Press, 2019).

38 *Canada's External Aid Programmes 1965–66* (Ottawa: External Aid Office, 1966); Douglas LePan, *Bright Glass of Memory: A Set of Four Memoirs* (Toronto: McGraw-Hill, 1979), 223.

39 A. F. W. Plumptre, 'Perspective on Our Aid to Others', *International Journal* 22 (1967): 487.

40 DEA, *Statements & Speeches* 51/38, 5 Oct. 1951.

41 DEA, *Statements & Speeches* 52/59, 9 Dec. 1952; DEA, *Statements & Speeches* 53/4, 4 Feb. 1953; Robin Gendron, *Towards a Francophone Community: Canada's Relations with France and French Africa, 1945–1968* (Montreal: McGill-Queen's University Press, 2006), 6–25.

42 A. R. M. Lower, *Colony to Nation: A History of Canada* (Toronto: Longmans, Green, 1947).

43 DEA, *Statements & Speeches* 53/22, 19 May 1953.

44 DEA, *Statements & Speeches* 54/14, 23 Feb. 1954; 'Canada's Part', Halifax *Chronicle Herald*, 7 June 1956.

45 Permanent Representative, UN to DEA, NL-811, 10 Sept. 1954, LAC, RG 25, file 5475-DW-33–40.

46 Paul Martin, *A Very Public Life*, Vol. II (Toronto: Deneau, 1985), 178–217.

47 DEA, Circular Document B.43/55, 27 July 1955, LAC, RG 25, file 12173-40-pt. 3.2; Adam Clayton Powell, 'My Mission to Bandung', *The Nation*, 28 May 1955.

48 Léger to Pearson, 7 Nov. 1956, LAC, RG 25, file 5475-DW-45-40-pt. 2.2.

49 DEA to Paris, tel. S-43, 24 Apr. 1956, LAC, RG 25, file 50115-J-40-pt. 8.

50 Cabinet Conclusions, 7 Aug. 1956, LAC, RG 2, vol. 5775.

51 House of Commons, *Debates*, 27 Nov. 1956, 51, 55; Michael Carroll, *Pearson's Peacekeepers: Canada and the United Nations Emergency Force, 1956–67* (Vancouver: UBC Press, 2009), 39; Antony Anderson, *The Diplomat: Lester Pearson and the Suez Crisis* (Fredericton: Goose Lane Editions, 2015).

52 'A Well-Earned Peace Prize', *New York Times*, 15 Oct. 1957; Pearson, *Mike*, II, 213.

53 Hassan Husseini, 'A "Middle Power" in Action: Canada and the Partition of Palestine', *Arab Studies Quarterly* 30 (2008): 41–55; David Bercuson, *Canada and the Birth of Israel: A Case Study in Canadian Foreign Policy* (Toronto: University of Toronto Press, 1985).

54 Holmes to European Division, 'The Charge against Israel in the Security Council', 10 Nov. 1953, LAC, RG 25, file 50134–40 pt. 5.2; Léger to LBP, 'The Middle East', 21 Mar. 1956, LAC, MG 26 N1, vol. 66; Michael Oren, 'Canada, the Great Powers, and the Middle Eastern Arms Race, 1950–1956', *International History Review* 12 (1990): 280–300; David Taras and David Goldberg, *The Domestic Battleground: Canada and the Arab-Israeli Conflict* (Montreal: McGill-Queen's University Press, 1989).

55 Cairo to DEA, tel. 277, 9 Dec. 1956, LAC, RG 25, file 50134–40 pt. 27.1; Pearson, *Mike* II, 262–3.

56 Lloyd to Macmillan, 19 July 1958, TNA, PREM 11/2407; Janice Cavell, 'Suez and after: Canada and British Policy in the Middle East, 1956–1960', *Journal of Canadian Historical Association* 18 (2007): 157–78.

57 House of Commons, *Debates*, 26 Nov. 1956, 20.

58 E. L. M. Burns, *Between Arab and Israeli* (Toronto: Clarke, Irwin, 1962), 8.

59 Robertson to Green, 13 July 1960, LAC, RG 25, file 6386-C-40-pt. 6; Kevin Spooner, 'Just West of Neutral: Canadian "Objectivity"; and Peacekeeping during the Congo Crisis, 1960–61', *Canadian Journal of African Studies* 43 (2009): 303–36; Kevin Spooner, *Canada, the Congo Crisis, and UN Peacekeeping, 1960–1964* (Vancouver: UBC Press, 2009).

60 J. L. Granatstein and David Bercuson, *War and Peacekeeping: From South Africa to the Gulf – Canada's Limited Wars* (Toronto: Key Porter, 1991), 199; John Macfarlane, 'Sovereignty and Standby: The 1964 Conference on UN Peacekeeping Forces', *International Peacekeeping* 14 (2007): 599–612.

61 Colin McCullough, *Creating Canada's Peacekeeping Past* (Vancouver: UBC Press, 2016).

62 House of Commons, *Debates*, 27 Nov. 1956, 51.

63 Canada: High Commissioner's Valedictory Despatch, 8 Oct. 1963, TNA, DO 182/85.

64 DEA, *Statements & Speeches* 60/32, 26 Sept. 1960; DEA, *Statements & Speeches* 59/13, 28 Nov. 1958.

65 DEA, *Statements & Speeches* 62/10, 31 Aug. 1962.

66 Christopher Kilford, *The Other Cold War: Canada's Military Assistance to the Developing World 1945–1975* (Kingston: Canadian Defence Academy Press, 2010); Ruth Compton Brouwer, '"Canada's Peace Corps"? CUSO's Evolving Relationship with its US Cousin, 1961–1971', *International Journal* 70 (2015): 137–46; Ruth Compton Brouwer, *Canada's Global Villagers: CUSO in Development, 1961–86* (Vancouver: UBC Press, 2013).

67 Ruth Compton Brouwer, 'When Missions Became Development: Ironies of "NGO-ization" in Mainstream Canadian Churches in the 1960s', *Canadian Historical Review* 91 (2010): 661–93.

68 Will Langford, 'International Development and the State in Question: Liberal Internationalism, the New Left, and Canadian University Service Overseas in Tanzania, 1963–1977', in *Undiplomatic History: The New Study of Canada and the World*, ed. Asa McKercher and Philip Van Huizen (Montreal: McGill-Queen's University Press, 2019).

69 Holmes to Robertson, 27 Jan. 1959, LAC, RG 25, file 5475-DW-58-D-40-pt. 1; Robin Gendron, 'Tempered Sympathy: Canada's Reaction to the Independence Movement in Algeria, 1954–1962', *Journal of Canadian Historical Association* 9 (1998): 225–41.

70 DEA to Can. Del. New York, 15 Nov. 1960, LAC, RG 25, file 12858-40-pt. 1.1; Asa McKercher, 'The Centre Cannot Hold: Canada, Colonialism, and the "Afro-Asian Bloc" at the United Nations, 1960–1962', *Journal of Imperial and Commonwealth History* 42 (2014).

71 DEA, *Statements & Speeches* 61/16, 14 Nov. 1961.

72 DEA, *Statements & Speeches* 60/32, 26 Sept. 1960.

73 Green to Diefenbaker, 14 Feb. 1962, LAC, RG 25, file 11389-A-40-pt. 1.1.

74 Asa McKercher, 'The Trouble with Self-Determination: Canada, Soviet Colonialism and the United Nations, 1960–1963', *International Journal of Human Rights* 20 (2015): 355.

75 Ibid., 356.

76 Asa McKercher, 'Sound and Fury: Diefenbaker, Human Rights, and Canadian Foreign Policy', *Canadian Historical Review* 97 (2016): 173.

77 David Corbett, 'Canada's Immigration Policy, 1957–1962', *International Journal* 18 (1963): 179–80.

78 Cabinet Conclusions, 11 Apr. 1960, LAC, RG 2, vol. 2746; DEA, *Statements & Speeches* 60/19, 16 May 1960; Diary, 16 Nov. 1960, Bodleian Library, Oxford, Harold Macmillan Papers, dep. c. 21/1. Extract from the Macmillan archive used with the kind permission of the Trustees of the Harold Macmillan Book Trust.

79 Delhi to DEA, tel. 214, 17 Mar. 1961, LAC, RG 25, file 5475-GU-40-pt. 1; Harold Evans, *Downing Street Diary: The Macmillan Years 1957–63* (London: Hodder & Stoughton, 1981), 141.

80 McKercher, 'Sound and Fury', 180–1.

81 Douglas Anglin, 'Canada and *Apartheid*', *International Journal* 15 (1960): 126.

82 Kildare Dobbs, 'The Case for Kicking Canada out of the Commonwealth', *Maclean's*, 6 May 1961; 'The Lowering of the Color Bar', *Globe & Mail*, 31 Jan. 1962.

83 Frances McNab, 'The Forgotten Canadians', *Chatelaine*, June 1962; Peter Gzowski, 'Last Chance to Head Off a Showdown with the Canadian Indian', *Maclean's*, 6 July 1963.

84 'How Everyone Was Won', *The Sunday Times*, 18 Sept. 1966; Carl Watts, 'Britain, the Old Commonwealth and the Problem of Rhodesian Independence, 1964–65', *Journal of Imperial and Commonwealth History* 26 (2008): 75–99.

85 W. David McIntyre, 'Canada and the Creation of the Commonwealth Secretariat, 1965', *International Journal* 53 (1998): 777.

86 Memorandum of conversation, 23 May 1963, *FRUS, 1961–1963*, vol. XIII, 1206.

87 DEA, *Statements & Speeches* 65/3, 10 Feb. 1965.

88 Prime Minister's Press Conference, 30 Nov. 1965, LAC, RG 76, file 552-1-577.

89 Peter Stursberg, 'Canada, Colonialism and Color', *Saturday Night*, 26 Nov. 1960.

90 Record of First Meeting of Departmental Panel on Africa, 6 June 1961, LAC, RG 25, file 12858-40; R.J. Sutherland, 'Canada's Long Term Strategic Situation', *International Journal* 17 (1962): 205.

91 Harold Cardinal, *The Unjust Society: The Tragedy of Canada's Indians* (Edmonton: Hurtig, 1969), 1; *Summary of Findings and Recommendations, Joint Committee of House of Commons and Senate on Indian Affairs, 1959–1961* (Ottawa: Government of Canada, 1961).

92 Geoffrey Pearson, 'Canadian Attitudes toward Peacekeeping', in *Peacekeeping: Appraisals and Proposals*, ed. Henry Wiseman (New York: Pergamon, 1983), 121; Harold Innis, *Changing Concepts of Time* (Lanham: Rowman and Littlefield, 2004 [1952]), 115.

9 From colony to nation to colony?

1 DEA, *Statements & Speeches* 57/30, 28 Oct. 1957; DEA, *Statements & Speeches* 58/43, 28 Oct. 1958.

2 Frank Underhill, *In Search of Canadian Liberalism* (Toronto: Macmillan, 1961), 256.

3 Fred Alexander, *Canadians and Foreign Policy* (Toronto: University of Toronto Press, 1960), 138.

4 James Eayrs, *Canada in World Affairs, 1955–57* (Toronto: Oxford University Press, 1959), 125.

5 Rick Salutin, 'Oh! Canada! The Eruption of a Revolution', *Harper's*, July 1971.

6 Abraham Rotstein, 'Canada: The New Nationalism', *Foreign Affairs* 55 (1976): 97–118; Stephen Azzi, 'The Nationalist Moment in English Canada', in *Debating Dissent: Canada and the Sixties*, ed. Lara Campbell et al. (Toronto: University of Toronto Press, 2012), 213–28.

7 David Harkness, *This Nation Called Canada* (Toronto: Elliott Press, 1945), 56.

8 Eugene Forsey, 'Concepts of Federalism: Some Canadian Aspects', in *Concepts of Federalism*, ed. Gordon Hawkins (Toronto: Canadian Institute of Public Affairs, 1965), 22; Brain McKillop, *Contexts of Canada's Past: Selected Essays of W.L. Morton* (Toronto: Macmillan, 1980), 259.

9 José. Igartua, *The Other Quiet Revolution: National Identity in English Canada, 1945–1971* (Vancouver: UBC Press, 2005), 1; A. G. Hopkins, 'Rethinking Decolonization', *Past and Present* 200 (2008); Stuart Ward, 'The "New Nationalism" in Australia, Canada and New Zealand: Civic Culture in the Wake of the British World', in *Britishness Abroad: Transnational*

Movements and Imperial Cultures, ed. Kate Darian-Smith et al. (Melbourne: Melbourne University Press, 2007).

10 Robert Fulford, 'A Post-Modern Dominion', in *Belonging: The Meaning and Future of Canadian Citizenship*, ed., William Kaplan (Montreal: McGill-Queen's University Press, 1993), 117.

11 House of Commons, *Debates*, 8 Nov. 1951, 851.

12 'The Shadow of the Crown', *Calgary Herald*, 26 Jan. 1952.

13 David MacKenzie, *Inside the Atlantic Triangle: Canada and the Entrance of Newfoundland into Confederation, 1939–1949* (Toronto: University of Toronto Press, 1986).

14 Arthur Andrew, *The Rise and Fall of a Middle Power* (Toronto: James Lorimer, 1993), 55; Peter Kasurak, *A National Force: The Evolution of Canada's Army, 1950–2000* (Vancouver: UBC Press, 2013); Marc Milner, 'More Royal than Canadian? The Royal Canadian Navy's Search for Identity, 1910–68', in *Canada and the End of Empire*, 272–84.

15 Doug Fetherling, 'Speak American or Speak English: A Choice of Imperialisms', *Saturday Night*, Sept. 1970; Steven High, 'The "Narcissism of Small Differences": The Invention of Canadian English', in *Creating Postwar Canada: Community, Diversity, and Dissent, 1945–75*, ed. Magda Fahrni and Robert Rutherdale (Vancouver: UBC Press, 2007).

16 Matthew Hayday, 'Fireworks, Folk-dancing, and Fostering a National Identity: The Politics of Canada Day', *Canadian Historical Review* 91 (2010): 287–314.

17 'Pearson Booed and Hissed Over Maple Leaf Flag', *Globe & Mail*, 18 May 1964; Lester Pearson, *Words and Occasions* (Toronto: University of Toronto Press, 1970), 228–32; Gregory Johnson, 'The Last Gasp of Empire: The 1964 Flag Debate Revisited', in *Canada and the End of Empire*, 232–50.

18 Arnold Edinborough, 'Canada and the Queen of England', *Saturday Night*, July 1967; James to Garner, 24 Nov. 1967, TNA, FCO 49/108; Pearson, *Mike* 3: 301.

19 Pearson, *Words and Occasions*, 275; Helen Davies, 'Canada's Centennial Experience', in *Celebrating Canada Vol. II*.

20 C. P. Stacey and Barbara Wilson, *The Half-Million: The Canadians in Britain, 1939–1946* (Toronto: University of Toronto Press, 1987), 174.

21 Jean Bruce, *After the War* (Don Mills: Fitzhenry & Whiteside, 1982), 91; Marilyn Barber and Murray Watson, *Invisible Immigrants: The English in Canada since 1945* (Winnipeg: University of Manitoba Press, 2015).

22 'British Beatles Send Canadian Youth', *Young Socialist Forum*, Dec. 1963.

23 Paul Rutherford, *When Television Was Young: Primetime Canada, 1952–1967* (Toronto: University of Toronto Press, 1990), 50; Phillip Buckner, 'The Last Great Royal Tour: Queen Elizabeth's 1959 Tour to Canada', in *Canada and the End of Empire*, 88.

24 London to DEA, tel. 1688, 5 July 1957, LAC, RG 25, file 50085-G-40.

25 Note of a discussion with Mr. Bryce and Mr. Kenneth Taylor, 10 Sept. 1957, TNA, DO 35/8731; Tim Rooth, 'Britain, Europe, and Diefenbaker's Trade Diversion Proposals, 1957–58', in *Canada and the End of Empire*, 117–32.

26 Meeting between Prime Minister Macmillan and Prime Minister Diefenbaker, 10 Apr. 1961, LAC, RG 25, file 50412–40; Andrea Benvenuti and Stuart Ward, 'Britain, Europe, and the "Other Quiet Revolution" in Canada', in *Canada and the End of Empire*, 165–82.

27 Sandys, 'Europe: Talks with the New Zealand, Australian and Canadian Governments', 21 July 1961, TNA, CAB 129/106; Garner, Valedictory Despatch, 17 July 1961, TNA, DO 182/84.

28 'Must Pick Commonwealth or Inner 6, Hees Tells U.K.', *Globe & Mail*, 14 Sept. 1961.

29 Robinson to Stoner, 18 Apr. 1962, LAC, MG 31 E83, vol. 6, file 1.

30 Meeting between Prime Minister Macmillan and Prime Minister Diefenbaker, 30 Apr. 1962, LAC, RG 25, file 50412-40-pt. 4.

31 Asa McKercher, *Camelot and Canada: Canadian-American Relations in the Kennedy Era* (Oxford: Oxford University Press, 2016).

32 Peter Catterall, *The Macmillan Diaries: Prime Minister and After, 1957–66* (London: Macmillan, 2011), 496.

33 Lord Garner, 'Britain and Canada in the 1940 and 1950s', in *Britain and Canada: Survey of a Changing Relationship*, ed. Peter Lyon (London: Frank Cass, 1976), 102.

34 Charles Ritchie, *Storm Signals: More Undiplomatic Diaries* (Toronto: Macmillan, 1983), 90.

35 Royal Commission on National Development in the Arts, Letters, and Sciences, *Report* (Ottawa: King's Printer, 1951), 18, 50; Paul Litt, *The Muses, the Masses, and the Massey Commission* (Toronto: University of Toronto Press, 1992).

36 Royal Commission on Canada's Economic Prospects, *Report* (Ottawa: Queen's Printer, 1957), 390; Stephen Azzi, 'Foreign Investment and the Paradox of Economic Nationalism', in *Canadas of the Mind: The Making and Unmaking of Canadian Nationalisms in the Twentieth Century*, ed. Norman Hillmer and Adam Chapnick (Montreal: McGill-Queen's University Press, 2007).

37 Royal Commission on Publications, *Report* (Ottawa: Queen's Printer, 1961), 5–6.

38 DEA, *Statements & Speeches* 59/41, 14 Nov. 1959.

39 Bundy-Ball Telcon, 7 May 1962, John F. Kennedy Library, George Ball Papers, box 2, folder Canada, 4/26/61-11/8/63; Greg Donaghy and Michael Stevenson, 'The Limits of Alliance: Cold War Solidarity and Canadian Wheat Exports to China, 1950–1963', *Agricultural History* 83 (2009): 29–50.

40 House of Commons, *Debates*, 1 Nov. 1957, 654; Chester Ronning, *A Memoir of China in Revolution: From the Boxer Rebellion to the People's Republic* (New York: Pantheon, 1974), 178; Greg Donaghy, 'Red China Blues: Paul Martin, Lester B. Pearson, and the China Conundrum, 1963–1967', *Journal of American-East Asian Relations* 20 (2013): 190–202.

41 House of Commons, *Debates*, 2 Feb. 1962, 479–80.

42 'Hand Across the 49th: A Poem', *Saturday Night*, 7 July 1962.

43 Asa McKercher, 'A "Half-hearted Response"?: Canada and the Cuban Missile Crisis, 1962', *International History Review* 33 (2011): 333.

44 House of Commons, *Debates*, 20 Feb. 1959, 1223; Andrew Burtch, *Give Me Shelter: The Failure of Canada's Cold War Civil Defence* (Vancouver: UBC Press, 2012).

45 Patricia McMahon, *Essence of Indecision: Diefenbaker's Nuclear Policy, 1957–1963* (Montreal: McGill-Queen's University Press, 2009).

46 Thérèse Casgrain, *A Woman in a Man's World* (Toronto: McClelland and Stewart, 1972), 157; Tarah Brookfield, *Cold War Comforts: Canadian Women, Child Safety, and Global Insecurity* (Waterloo: Wilfrid Laurier University Press, 2012); Braden Hutchinson, 'Fighting the War at Home: Voice of Women and War Toy Activism in Postwar Canada', in *Worth Fighting For.*

47 James Minifie, *Peacemaker or Powdermonkey?: Canada's Role in a Revolutionary World* (Toronto: McClelland and Stewart, 1960), 4–5.

48 'CCF Wants Canada to Leave NATO Pact', *Globe & Mail*, 12 Aug. 1960; 'New Party's Foreign Policy Facing Test', *Globe & Mail*, 31 Mar. 1961; Liberal Resolutions at the National Rally, 9–11 Jan. 1961, LAC, MG 32 B44, vol. 13, folder 15.

49 McKercher, *Camelot and Canada*; Michael Stevenson, ' "Tossing a Match into Dry Hay": Nuclear Weapons and the Crisis in U.S.-Canadian Relations, 1962–1963', *Journal of Cold War Studies* 16 (2014): 5–34.

50 John Diefenbaker, 'Across the Border', in *The Star-Spangled Beaver*, ed. John H. Redekop (Toronto: Peter Martin, 1971), 44.

51 Pierre Trudeau, 'Pearson ou l'Abdication de l'Espirit', *Cite Libre*, Apr. 1963.

52 Kenneth McNaught, 'Uncle Sam Again', *Canadian Forum*, May 1963.

53 George Grant, *Lament for a Nation: The Defeat of Canadian Nationalism* (Montreal: McGill-Queen's University Press, 2000 [1965]), 24, 97.

54 C. W. Gonick, 'An Open Letter', *Canadian Dimension*, July-Aug. 1964; Ian Milligan, *Rebel Youth: 1960s Labour Unrest, Young Workers, and New Leftists in English Canada* (Vancouver: UBC Press, 2015).

55 Gail Dexter, 'Yes, Cultural Imperialism too!' *Close the 49th Parallel*, 161.

56 'Canadian "Nationalism": Independence for What?' *The Independencer*, Sept. 1973; Robert Wright, 'From Liberalism to Nationalism: Peter C. Newman's Discovery of Canada', in *Creating Postwar Canada: Community, Diversity, and Dissent, 1945–75*, ed. Magda Fahrni and Robert Rutherdale (Vancouver: UBC Press, 2007).

57 Kendall Garton, ' "Apocalypse at the Doll Counter": Barbie, Marjie, and the North American Toy Industry, 1959–67' (PhD thesis, Queen's University, 2017); Jeffrey Cormier, *The Canadianization Movement: Emergence, Survival, and Success* (Toronto: University of Toronto Press, 2004); Ryan Edwardson, 'The Many Lives of Captain Canuck: Nationalism, Culture, and the Creation of a Canadian Comic Book Superhero', *Journal of Popular Culture* 37 (2003): 184–201; Matthew Hayday, 'Brought to You by the Letters C, R, T, and C: *Sesame Street* and Canadian Nationalism', *Journal of Canadian Historical Association* 27 (2016): 95–137.

58 James Lorimer, 'The Political Economy of Canadian Publishing', *This Magazine*, July–Aug. 1975.

59 Ryan Edwardson, *Canadian Content: Culture and the Quest for Nationhood* (Toronto: University of Toronto Press, 2008).

60 DEA, *Statements & Speeches* 75/31, 21 Oct. 1975.

61 Task Force on the Structure of Canadian Industry, *Report* (Ottawa: Queen's Printer, 1968), 21; Kari Levitt, *Silent Surrender: The Multinational Corporation in Canada* (Toronto: Macmillan, 1970), xix; Stephen Azzi, *Walter Gordon & the Rise of Canadian Nationalism* (Montreal: McGill-Queen's University Press, 1999); Bruce Muirhead, *Dancing Around the Elephant: Creating a Prosperous Canada in an Era of American Dominance, 1957–1973* (Toronto: University of Toronto Press, 2007).

62 Pierre Trudeau, *Conversations with Canadians* (Toronto: University of Toronto Press, 1972), 174.

63 Mitchell Sharp, 'Canada-US Relations: Options for the Future', *International Perspectives* (Autumn 1972): 17.

64 Mitchell Sharp, *Which Reminds Me…A Memoir* (Toronto: University of Toronto Press, 1994), 180.

65 John Warnock, 'Why I Am Anti-American', *Canadian Dimension*, Nov.–Dec. 1967; Ian Lumsden, *Close the 49th Parallel, etc.*, 324; Larry Zolf, 'Boil Me No Melting Pot, Dream Me No Dream', in *The New Romans: Candid Canadian Opinions of the U.S.*, ed. Al Purdy (Edmonton: Hurtig, 1968), 123; Ryan Edwardson, ' "Of War Machines and Ghetto Scenes": English-Canadian Nationalism and The Guess Who's "American Woman" ', *American Review of Canadian Studies* 33 (2003): 339–56.

66 Salutin, 'Oh! Canada!'; James Laxer, 'The Americanization of the Student Movement', in *Close the 49th Parallel*, 280.

67 '2000 Student Pickets to March on Ottawa', *Globe & Mail*, 13 Mar. 1965; Open letter to the Parliament and Government of Canada, 15 Feb. 1966, LAC, MG 28 I218, vol. 5, file SUPA.

68 Victor Levant, *Quiet Complicity: Canadian Involvement in the Vietnam War* (Toronto: Between the Lines, 1986); John Hagan, *Northern Passage: American Vietnam War Resisters in Canada* (Cambridge: Harvard University Press, 2001); Frances Early, 'Re-imaging War: The Voice of Women, the Canadian Aid for Vietnam Civilians, and the Knitting Project for Vietnamese Children, 1966–1976', *Peace & Change* 34 (2009): 148–63; Jessica Squires, *Building Sanctuary: The Movement to Support Vietnam War Resisters in Canada, 1965–73* (Vancouver: UBC Press, 2014); David Churchill, 'An Ambiguous Welcome: Vietnam Draft Resistance, the Canadian State, and Cold War Containment', *Histoire Sociale/Social History* 37 (2004): 1–26.

69 Lewis Hartzman, 'Foreign Policy Review and the National Debate', in *Alliance and Illusions: Canada and the NATO-NORAD Question*, ed. Lewis Hartzman, John Warnock, and Thomas Hockin (Edmonton: Hurtig, 1969), 3; John Warnock, *Partner to Behemoth: The Military Policy of a Satellite Canada* (Toronto: New Press, 1970); Philip Resnick, 'Canadian Defence Policy and the American Empire', in *Close the 49th Parallel*, 94; Clare Culhane, 'Why are

Canadians in Vietnam?' *This Magazine* (May/June 1973); Stephen Clarkson, 'The Choice to Be Made', in *An Independent Foreign Policy for Canada?* (Toronto: McClelland and Stewart, 1968), 253–69.

70 David Lewis, 'We Are an Echo of Washington', *Maclean's*, Jan. 1967.

71 Secretary's Conversation with Canadian Foreign Minister Martin: US-Canadian Relations and Over-all Policies, 25 Nov. 1966, NARA, RG 59, Bureau of European Affairs, Country Director for Canada, Records Relating to Political Matters, 1957-1966, box 8, folder Visit of Paul Martin; Greg Donaghy, *Tolerant Allies: Canada and the United States, 1963–1968* (Montreal: McGill-Queen's University Press, 2002).

72 Greg Donaghy and Mary Halloran, '*Viva el pueblo Cubano*: Pierre Trudeau's Distant Cuba, 1968–78', in *Our Place in the Sun: Canada and Cuba in the Castro Era*, ed. Robert Wright and Lana Wylie (Toronto: University of Toronto Press, 2009).

73 Pearson to St Laurent, 'Second Conversation with Mr. Dulles', 19 Mar. 1955, LAC, MG 26 N1, vol. 65; Robert Bothwell, 'The Further Shore: Canada and Vietnam', *International Journal* 56 (2000/1): 89–114; Brendan Kelly, '"Six mois à Hanoi": Marcel Cadieux, Canada, and the International Commission for Supervision and Control in Vietnam, 1954–5', *Canadian Historical Review* 99 (2018): 394–427.

74 Memorandum for the Record of a Conversation Between President Johnson and Prime Minister Pearson, 28 May 1964, *FRUS*, 1964–1968, Vol. I, 395.

75 Fredrik Logevall, *Choosing War: The Lost Chance for Peace and the Escalation of War in Vietnam* (Berkeley: University of California Press, 1999).

76 Brendan Kelly, 'Lester B. Pearson's Temple University Speech Revisited: The Origins and Evolution of the Proposal for a Bombing Pause', *American Review of Canadian Studies* 47 (2017): 372–84; John English, *The Worldly Years: The Life of Lester Pearson, 1949–1972* (Toronto: Knopf, 1992), 364; Dean Acheson, 'Canada: "Stern Daughter of the Voice of God"', in *Neighbors Taken for Granted: Canada & the United States*, ed. Livingston Merchant (New York: Praeger, 1966); Pearson, *Mike*, III, 148.

77 George Ball Interview, Oral History Collection, LBJ Library; Robert McNamara, *In Retrospect: The Tragedy and Lessons of Vietnam* (New York: Random House, 1995), 248; Andrew Preston, 'Missions Impossible: Canadian Secret Diplomacy and the Quest for Peace in Vietnam', in *The Search for Peace in Vietnam, 1964–1968*, ed. Lloyd Gardner and Ted Gittinger (College Station: Texas A&M University Press, 2004), 117–43.

78 John Holmes, 'Canada and the Pax Americana', in *Empire and Nations: Essays in Honour of Frederic H. Soward* (Toronto: University of Toronto Press, 1969). 81; George Grant, *Technology and Empire: Perspectives on North America* (Toronto: Anansi, 1969), 77; Memorandum of conversation, 'Secretary's Conversation with Canadian Foreign Minister Martin: Vietnam', 25 Nov. 1966, RG 59, Bureau of European Affairs, Country Director for Canada, Records Relating to Political Matters, 1957-1966, box 8, folder Visit of Paul Martin.

79 Fred Gaffen, *Unknown Warriors: Canadians in the Vietnam War* (Toronto: Dundurn, 1990), 36; Mark Kennedy, 'Our Forgotten Veterans', *Ottawa Citizen*, 18 June 1983.

80 Kenneth Hilborn, 'The War's Real Meaning', *Canada Month*, Nov. 1966; Asa McKercher, 'Principles and Partnership: Merchant, Heeney, and the Craft of Canada-US Relations', *American Review of Canadian Studies* 42 (2012): 67–83; Liberal Federation, 'National Political Issues in Canada, Summer-Fall 1967', n.d., LAC, MG 32 B33 vol. 55, file L. B. Pearson: Liberal Federation of Canada.

81 Canada: High Commissioner's Valedictory Despatch, 8 Oct. 1963, TNA, DO 182/85; Commonwealth Division to African and Middle Eastern Division, 4 Mar. 1968, LAC, RG 25, 20-1-2-BRIT.

82 Terry Morley, *Canadian Nationalism and Canadian-American Relations* (Toronto: Student Union for Peace Action, 1966); Axworthy, 'Canada and the World Revolution'.

83 British-North American Committee, *Purposes and Projects: A Policy Statement by the British-North American Committee* (London: British-North American Committee, 1971).

84 Barry Lord, 'A Visit to Expo '67', *Canadian Dimension*, Sept.–Oct. 1967; Robert Chodos and Eric Hamovitch, *Quebec and the American Dream* (Toronto: Between the Lines, 1991), 156.

10 Canada and the emerging global village

1 House of Commons, *Debates*, 15 June 1981, 10593.

2 J. L. Granatstein and Robert Bothwell, *Pirouette: Pierre Trudeau and Canadian Foreign Policy* (Toronto: University of Toronto Press, 1990).

3 Donald MacDonald, 'The continuing struggle for freedom', *Canadian Labour*, Mar. 1974; Toronto Committee for the Liberation of Southern Africa (TCLSA), *Words and Deeds: Canada, Portugal, and Africa* (Toronto: TCLSA, 1976), 94.

4 Cranford Pratt et al., *The Black Paper: An Alternative Policy for Canada towards South Africa* (Ottawa: Canadian Council for International Cooperation, 1970), 1.

5 Dominique Clément, *Canada's Rights Revolution: Social Movements and Social Change, 1937–82* (Vancouver: UBC Press, 2008); Jan Eckel and Samuel Moyn, *The Breakthrough: Human Rights in the 1970s* (Philadelphia, PA: University of Pennsylvania Press, 2014).

6 Pierre Beaudet, *On a raison de se révolter: Chronologie des années 70* (Montreal: Écosociété, 2008), 239; Sean Mills, *The Empire Within: Postcolonial Thought and Political Activism in Sixties Montreal* (Montreal: McGill-Queen's University Press, 2010), 4; David Meren, 'An Atmosphere of *Libération*: The Role of Decolonization in the France-Quebec Rapprochement of the 1960s', *Canadian Historical Review* 92 (2011); Serge Granger, 'L'Inde et la décolonisation au Canada français', *MENS: Revue* *d'histoire intellectuelle et culturelle* 13 (2012): 55–79; Magali Deleuze, *L'une et l'autre indépendance 1954–1964: Les medias au Québec et la Guerre d'Algérie* (Montreal: Éditions Point de fuite, 2001).

7 Marcel Martel, *French Canada: An Account of Its Creation and Break-Up, 1850–1967* (Ottawa: Canadian Historical Association, 1998).

8 Raymond Barbeau, *J'ai choisi l'indépendance* (Montreal: Éditions de l'Homme, 1961), 17, 27.

9 André d'Allemagne, *Le Colonialisme au Québec* (Montreal: Éditions R-B, 1966), 13, 146, 189.

10 Marcel Chaput, *Pourquoi je suis séparatiste* (Montreal: Éditions du Jour, 1961), 1, 70.

11 Jean Lamarre, *Le mouvement étudiant québécois des années 1960 et ses relations avec le mouvement international* (Quebec: Septentrion, 2017); Jean-Phillipe Warren, 'L'opération McGill français. Une Page inconnue de l'histoire de la gauche nationaliste', *Bulletin d'histoire politique* 16 (2008): 97–116.

12 Raoul Roy, 'Le France et notre independence', *Revue Socialiste*, 1963–1964; Raoul Roy, 'Quebec est une colonie! Sus au colonialism!', *Revue Socialiste*, Autumn 1962; 'Algerie et Quebec', *Revue Socialiste*, Autumn 1959; André Major, 'Les damnés de la terre et nou's'' *Revue Socialiste*, Autumn 1962.

13 David Austin, *Fear of a Black Nation: Race, Sex, and Security in Sixties Montreal* (Toronto: Between the Lines, 2013), 51; Pierre Vallières, *White Niggers of America: The Precocious Autobiography of a Quebec 'Terrorist'* (Toronto: McClelland and Stewart, 1971 [1968]), 21.

14 Robert Comeau, *FLQ: Un Projet Révolutionnaire Lettres et Écrits Felquistes 1963–1968* (Montreal: VLB Éditeur, 1990), 13, 18, 206.

15 Pierre Trudeau, 'La nouvelle trahison des clercs', *Cité Libre*, Apr. 1962.

16 Gérard Pelletier, 'The Trouble with Quebec', *Atlantic Monthly*, Nov. 1964.

17 Alain Peyrefitte, *De Gaulle et le Québec* (Montreal: Stanké, 2000), 17; Robin Gendron, 'The Two Faces of Charles de Gaulle, France, and Decolonization in Quebec and New Caledonia', *International Journal* 69 (2014): 94–109.

18 Paul André Comeau and Jean-Pierre Fournier, *Le Lobby du Quebec à Paris: Les précurseurs du général de Gaulle* (Montreal: Québec-Amérique, 2002).

19 Paul Martin, *Federalism and International Politics* (Ottawa: Queen's Printer, 1968), 23; Claude Morin, *Les choses commes ells étaient: une autobiographie politique* (Montreal: Boréal, 1994), 191–2; Brendan Kelly, 'Pearson, France, and Quebec's International Personality', in *Mike's World*.

20 Ron Graham, *One-Eyed Kings: Promise and Illusion in Canadian Politics* (Toronto: HarperCollins, 1986), 66.

21 Pearson to Martin, 20 Apr. 1966, LAC, MG 26 N6, vol. 9, file NATO.

22 Serge Durflinger, 'Marring the Memory: The 1967 Vimy Ridge Commemorations and Canada-France Relations', *International History Review* 41 (2018).

23 Robert Bothwell, Ian Drummond, and John English, *Canada since 1945: Power, Politics, and Provincialism* (Toronto: University of Toronto Press, 1981), 285.

24 DEA, *Statements & Speeches* 68/4, 5 Feb. 1968.

25 Matthew Hayday, *So They Want Us to Learn French: Promoting and Opposing Bilingualism in English-Speaking Canada* (Vancouver: UBC Press, 2015).

26 J. L. Granatstein, 'External Affairs and Defence', *Canadian Annual Review, 1970* (Toronto: University of Toronto Press, 1971), 319; Robin Gendron, 'Advancing the National Interest: Marcel Cadieux, Jules Léger, and Canadian Participation in the Francophone Community, 1964–1972', in *In the National Interest: Canadian Foreign Policy and the Department of Foreign Affairs and International Trade, 1909–2009*, ed. Greg Donaghy and Michael Carroll (Calgary: University of Calgary Press, 2011); David Meren, *With Friends Like These: Entangled Nationalisms and the Canada-Quebec-France Triangle* (Vancouver: UBC Press, 2012), 174–81

27 DEA, *Statements & Speeches* 68/17, 29 May 1968.

28 Jacques Guay, 'Comment René Lévesque est devenu indépendentiste', *Le Magazine Maclean*, Feb. 1969; René Lévesque, 'For an Independent Quebec', *Foreign Affairs* 54 (1976).

29 DEA to Washington, GWP-17, 25 Feb. 1977, LAC, RG25, file 20-CDA-9-TRUDEAU-USA-pt. 5; 'Separation worse than Cuba crisis: PM', *Montreal Gazette*, 24 Feb. 1977.

30 Stephanie Bangarth, 'The Politics of African Intervention: Canada and Biafra, 1967–70', in *From Kinshasa to Kandahar: Canada and Fragile States in Historical Perspective*, ed. Michael Carroll and Greg Donaghy (Calgary: University of Calgary Press, 2016), 53–72.

31 House of Commons, *Debates*, 27 Sept. 1968, 535.

32 DEA, *Statements & Speeches* 69/22, 27 Nov. 1969.

33 Peter Newman, *Here Be Dragons: Telling Tales of People, Passion and Power* (Toronto: McClelland and Stewart, 2004), 342.

34 'Biafra Backed by De Gaulle, Canada Cited', *Globe & Mail*, 19 Sept. 1968; George Ignatieff, *The Making of a Peacemonger: The Memoirs of George Ignatieff* (Toronto: University of Toronto Press, 1985), 238.

35 'Trudeau Defends Stand against Outside Interference in Nigerian Civil War', *Globe & Mail*, 28 Oct. 1968.

36 'MP Slams PM On Ukrainian Issue', *Ottawa Journal*, 1 June 1971; David Webster, 'Self-fulfilling Prophecies and Human Rights in Canada's Foreign Policy: Lessons from East Timor', *International Journal* 65 (2010): 739–50; Richard Pilkington, 'In the National Interest? Canada and the East Pakistan Crisis of 1971', *Journal of Genocide Research* 13 (2011): 451–74.

37 James Bartleman, *On Six Continents: A Life in Canada's Foreign Service, 1966–2002* (Toronto: McClelland and Stewart, 2004), 60.

38 House of Commons, *Debates*, 2 Mar. 1977, 3574.

39 J. L. Granatstein and Robert Bothwell, 'Pierre Trudeau on his Foreign Policy: A Conversation in 1988', *International Journal* 66 (2010–11): 177; Leigh Sarty, 'A Handshake Across the Pole: Canadian-Soviet Relations During the Era of Détente', in *Canada and the Soviet Experiment*, ed. David Davies (Toronto: Canadian Scholars Press, 1992), 117–35.

40 Robert Edmonds, 'Canada's Recognition of the People's Republic of China: The Stockholm Negotiations, 1968–1970', *Canadian Foreign Policy Journal* 5 (1998): 201–17.

41 Lubor Zink, *Viva Chairman Pierre* (Toronto: Griffin House, 1977), 83; Lubor Zink, *Trudeaucracy* (Toronto: Sun Publishing, 1972), 91.

42 Ivan Head and Pierre Trudeau, *The Canadian Way: Shaping Canada's Foreign Policy, 1968–1984* (Toronto: McClelland and Stewart, 1995), 227.

43 Laura Madokoro, '"Belated Signing": Race-Thinking and Canada's Approach to the 1951 Convention Relating to the Status of Refugees', in *Dominion of Race*.

44 Laura Madokoro, 'Good Material: Canada and the Prague Spring Refugees', *Refuge* 26 (2009): 161–71; Jan Raska, 'Humanitarian Gesture: Canada and the Tibetan Resettlement Program, 1971–75', *Canadian Historical Review* 97 (2016): 546–75; John Hilliker, Mary Halloran, and Greg Donaghy, *Canada's Department of External Affairs, Volume 3: Innovation and Adaptation, 1968–1984* (Toronto: University of Toronto Press, 2017), 137; Michael Molloy, Peter Duschinsky, Kurt Jensen, and Robert Shalka, *Running on Empty: Canada and the Indochinese Refugees, 1975–1980* (Montreal: McGill-Queen's University Press, 2017); Francis Peddie, *Young, Well-Educated and Adaptable: Chilean Exiles in Ontario and Quebec, 1973–2010* (Winnipeg: University of Manitoba Press, 2014); José del Pozo, *Les Chiliens au Québec: Immigrants et réfugiés, de 1955 à nos jours* (Montreal: Boréal, 2009).

45 Madokoro, *Elusive Refuge*, 200–1.

46 'Canada's Integrity is Being Violated', *Toronto Star*, 24 Oct. 1972.

47 Jennifer Tunnicliffe, 'A Limited Vision: Canadian Participation in the Adoption of the International Covenants on Human Rights', in *Taking Liberties: A History of Human Rights in Canada*, ed. David Goutor and Stephen Heathorn (Oxford: Oxford University Press, 2013), 166–89.

48 DEA, *Statements & Speeches* 82/23, 31 Aug. 1982.

49 Michael Cotey Morgan, 'North America, Atlanticism, and the Making of the Helsinki Final Act', in *Origins of the European Security System: The Helsinki Process Revisited, 1965–75*, ed. Andreas Wenger, Vojtech Mastny, and Christian Nuenlist (London: Routledge, 2008), 37.

50 P. Whitney Lackenbauer, ed., *An Inside Look at External Affairs during the Trudeau Years: The Memoirs of Mark MacGuigan* (Calgary: University of Calgary Press, 2002), 55, 56–57.

51 Smith, *Stitches in Time*, 219.

52 Stephanie Bangarth, '"Vocal but not Particularly Strong?": Air Canada's Ill-fated Vacation Package to Rhodesia and South Africa and the Anti-Apartheid Movement in Canada', *International Journal* 71 (2016): 488–97.

53 Donald Macintosh, Donna Greenhorn, and David Black, 'Canadian Diplomacy and the 1978 Edmonton Commonwealth Games', *Journal of Sport History* 19 (1992).

54 Alastair Gillespie with Irene Sage, *Made in Canada: A Businessman's Adventures in Politics* (Toronto: Robin Brass, 2009), 161.

55 Canadian Council of Churches, 'Canadian Policy Toward Chile', 9 Oct. 1974, LAC, MG 28 I103, vol. 495, file 18.

56 David Sheinin, 'Cuba's Long Shadow: The Progressive Church Movement and Canadian-Latin American Relations, 1970–1987' and Cynthia Wright, 'Between Nation and Empire: The Fair Play for Cuba Committees and the Making of Canada-Cuba Solidarity in the 1960s', in *Our Place in the Sun*.

57 Latin America Working Group (LAWG), *Chile versus the Corporations. A Call for Canadian Support* (Toronto: LAWG, Jan. 1973); Philip Resnick, 'The New Left in Ontario', *The New Left in Canada* (Montreal: Black Rose Books, 1970), 96; Serge Mongeau, 'lecons a retenir au Quebec', *Chili-Quebec Informations*, Jan. 1974.

58 Maurice Demers, 'Promoting a Different Type of North-South Interactions: Québécois Cultural and Religious Paradiplomacy with Latin America', *American Review of Canadian Studies* 46 (2016): 196–216; Catherine LeGrand, 'Les réseaux missionaries et l'action sociale des Québécois en Amérique latine, 1945–1980', *Études d'histoire religieuse* 79 (2013): 93–116.

59 TCLPAC, 'Larceny by Proxy: Gulf Oil (Canada) Ltd. and Angola', *This Magazine*, Jan. 1974; Tim Draimin and Jamie Swift, 'What's Canada Doing in Brazil', *This Magazine*, Jan. 1975.

60 Standing Committee on External Affairs, *Minutes and Proceedings* (3 Dec. 1963), 23.

61 Cabinet Memorandum, 'Commonwealth Caribbean-Canada Conference', 24 June 1966, LAC, RG 25, file 20-4-CCCC-1-pt. 2.

62 'Sphere of Influence in the Sun', and Nicholas Steed, 'The Caribbean: Our New Frontier', *Maclean's*, Feb. 1967.

63 Standing Committee on Foreign Affairs of the Senate of Canada on Canada-Caribbean Relations, *Report* (Ottawa: Queen's Printer, 1970).

64 'Trinidad Rebels Vow They'll End Our 'Control', *Toronto Star*, 9 Mar. 1970; Peter James Hudson, 'Imperial Designs: The Royal Bank of Canada in the Caribbean', *Race & Class* 52 (2010): 33–48.

65 Robin Gendron, 'Canada and the Nationalization of Alcan's Bauxite Operations in Guinea and Guyana', in *Aluminum Ore: The Political Economy of the Global Bauxite Industry* (Vancouver: UBC Press, 2014).

66 'The Caribbean: The People Revolt against Canadian Control', *Last Post*, Apr. 1970.

67 'O Canada, He Stands On Guard For Thee', *Maclean's*, July 1970.

68 Ron Finch, *Exporting Danger* (Montreal: Black Rose Books, 1986); Duane Bratt, *The Politics of CANDU Exports* (Toronto: University of Toronto Press, 2006).

69 Keith Spicer 'Clubsmanship Upstaged: Canada's Twenty Years in the Colombo Plan', *International Journal* 25 (1970): 23.

70 Kevin Brushett, 'Partners in Development? Robert McNamara, Lester Pearson, and the Commission on International Development, 1967–1973', *Diplomacy & Statecraft* 26 (2015): 84–102.

71 Canada, *Foreign Policy for Canadians: International Development* (Ottawa: Queen's Printer, 1970), 9.

72 Head and Trudeau, *Canadian Way*, 161.

73 Greg Donaghy, 'A Wasted Opportunity: Canada and the New International Economic Order, 1974–82', in *Canada and the United Nations*, 183–207.

74 Paul Gérin-Lajoie, *Plan of Action for Cooperation between Canada and Latin America: New Forms of Cooperation for Middle-Income Countries* (Ottawa: Government of Canada, 1976), 7.

75 'From machetes to mechanized farming: the Andes', *Cooperation Canada*, Nov.-Dec. 1972.

76 Jack Redden, 'South America: The New Food Bowl', *Cooperation Canada*, Sept.-Oct. 1975.

77 Keith Spicer, *A Samaritan State? External Aid in Canada's Foreign Policy* (Toronto: University of Toronto Press, 1966); Clyde Sanger, *Half a Loaf: Canada's Semi-Role Among Developing Countries* (Toronto: Ryerson, 1969); Robert Carty and Virginia Smith, *Perpetuating Poverty: The Political Economy of Canadian Foreign Aid* (Toronto: Between the Lines, 1981).

78 World Federalists of Canada, *Our Beautiful, Solitary and Fragile Spaceship Home*, n.d., LAC, MG 28 I327, vol. 185; Frank Zelko, *Make It a Green Peace! The Rise of Countercultural Environmentalism* (Oxford: Oxford University Press, 2013).

79 Douglas Roche, *Justice not Charity* (Toronto: McClelland and Stewart, 1976), 6.

80 Canada, Senate, *Debates*, 13 Aug. 1958, 518; Indian Eskimo Association, *Annual Report*, 21 Nov. 1964.

81 David Meren, '"Commend me the Yak": The Colombo Plan, the Inuit of Ungava and "Developing" Canada's North', *Histoire Sociale/Social History* 102 (2017); Hugh Shewell, '"Bitterness behind Every Smiling Face": Community Development and Canada's First Nations, 1954–1968', *Canadian Historical Review* 83 (2002); Dominique Marshall and Julia Sterparn, 'Oxfam Aid to Canada's First Nations, 1962–1975: Eating Lynx, Starving for Jobs, and Flying a Talking Bird', *Journal of Canadian Historical Association* 23 (2012).

82 Joanna Hoople and J. W. E. Newberry, *And What About Canada's Native Peoples?* (Ottawa: Canadian Council of International Cooperation, 1973), 26.

83 Cardinal, *The Unjust Society*, 3; Howard Adams, *Prison of Grass: Canada from the Native Point of View* (Toronto: New Press, 1975), 150–1.

84 George Manuel and Michael Posluns, *The Fourth World: An Indian Reality* (Don Mills: Collier-Macmillan, 1974).

85 Peter Cumming, 'The State and the Individual (Indian Affairs) – The New Policy: Panacea or Put-On?', *Harrison Liberal Conference Series* (Ottawa, 1970), 2, 3; Pierre Vennat, "Serions-nous des colonistes," *Cité libre*, May 1961.

86 H. B. Hawthorn, *A Survey of the Contemporary Indians of Canada* (Ottawa: Department of Indian Affairs and Northern Development, 1966).

87 Adams, *Prison of Grass*, x, 195; Cardinal, *The Unjust Society*, 3.

88 Mel Watkins, ed., *Dene Nation: The Colony Within* (Toronto: University of Toronto Press, 1977), 3; Native Council of Canada (NCC), 'Towards Co-equality: Integration and Assimilation', in *We are the New Nation: The Métis and National Native Policy* (Ottawa: NCC, 1979), 48.

89 Department of Indian Affairs and Northern Development, *Statement of the Government of Canada on Indian Policy* (Ottawa: Queen's Printer, 1969).

90 Keith Smith, *Strange Visitors: Documents in Indigenous-Settler Relations in Canada from 1876* (Toronto: University of Toronto Press, 2014), 340; Trudeau, 'Canadians Like All Other Canadians', in *The Indian: Assimilation, Integration, or Separation?*, ed. R. P. Bowles et. al. (Scarborough: Prentice-Hall, 1972), 3.

91 Indian Chiefs of Alberta, *Citizens Plus* (Edmonton: Indian Association of Alberta, 1970), 37.

92 Cardinal, *The Unjust Society*, 17.

93 Myra Rutherdale and Jim Miller, '"It's Our Country": First Nations' Participation in the Indian Pavilion at Expo 67', *Journal of Canadian Historical Association* 17 (2006): 148–73; Scott Rutherford, 'Canada's Other Red Scare: Indigenous anti-colonialism and the Anicinabe Park Occupation', in *The Hidden 1970s: Histories of Radicalism*, ed. Dan Berger (New Brunswick: Rutgers University Press, 2010); Vern Harper, *Following the Red Path: The Native People's Caravan, 1974* (Toronto: NC Press, 1979).

94 James (Sa'ke'j) Youngblood Henderson, *Indigenous Diplomacy and the Rights of Peoples: Achieving UN Recognition* (Saskatoon: Purich Publishing, 2008).

95 Jane Jenson and Martin Papillon, 'Challenging the Citizenship Regime: The James Bay Cree and Transnational Action', *Politics & Society* 28 (2000): 255.

96 Thomas Berger, *The Mackenzie Valley Pipeline, Proceedings at Community Hearing*, vol. 12 (Vancouver: Allwest Reporting, 2003), 1077.

97 Michael Asch, '*Calder* and the Representation of Indigenous Society in Canadian Jurisprudence', in *Let Right Be Done: Aboriginal Title, the Calder Case, and the Future of Indigenous Rights*, ed. Hamar Foster et al. (Vancouver: UBC Press, 2007), 103.

98 Michael Asch, *Home and Native Land: Aboriginal Rights and the Canadian Constitution* (Toronto: Methuen, 1984), 9.

99 Andrew Thompson, *On the Side of the Angels: Canada and the United Nations Commission on Human Rights* (Vancouver: UBC Press, 2017).

100 Sally Weaver, *Making Canadian Indian Policy: The Hidden Agenda, 1968–70* (Toronto: University of Toronto Press, 1981), 55.

101 Tamara Myers, 'Local Action and Global Imagining: Youth, International Development, and the Walkathon Phenomenon in Sixties' and Seventies' Canada', *Diplomatic History* 3 (2014): 282–93.

102 Thomas Hockin, 'Federalist Style in International Politics', in *An Independent Foreign Policy For Canada?*, 126.

11 War and peace in the new world order

1 House of Commons, *Debates*, 10 Mar. 2004.

2 House of Commons, *Debates*, 10 Mar. 2004; Andrew Thompson, 'Entangled: Canadian Engagement in Haiti, 1968–2010', in *From Kinshasa to Kandahar*, 97–119; Yves Engler and Anthony Fenton, *Canada in Haiti: Waging War on the Poor Majority* (Halifax: Fernwood, 2004).

3 Lewis MacKenzie, *Peacekeeper: The Road to Sarajevo* (Vancouver: Douglas & McIntyre, 1993), xvi; Michael Ignatieff, *Empire Lite: Nation-Building in Bosnia, Kosovo and Afghanistan* (Toronto: Penguin, 2003), vii.

4 Canada, *Competitiveness and Security: Directions for Canada's International Relations* (Ottawa: Minister of Supply and Services, 1985): 17.

5 DEA, *Statements & Speeches* 85/14, 23 Oct. 1985.

6 Memcon, Bush-Mulroney, 10 Feb. 1989, George H. W. Bush Library, Memcons & Telcons; Paul Kennedy, *The Rise and Fall of the Great Powers: Economic Change and Military Conflict from 1500 to 2000* (London: Unwin Hyman, 1988).

7 George Bush and Brent Scowcroft, *A World Transformed* (New York: Knopf, 1998), 160.

8 Christopher Shulgin, *The Soviet Ambassador: The Making of the Radical Behind Perestroika* (Toronto: McClelland and Stewart, 2008).

9 McDonald's in Moscow', *New York Times*, 30 Apr. 1988; Group of 7 Plenary Session, 10 July 1990, George H. W. Bush Library, Memcons & Telcons.

10 Telcon, Bush-Mulroney, 27 Nov. 1989 and Memcon, Bush-Mulroney, 29 Nov. 1989, George H. W. Bush Library, Memcons & Telcons.

11 Bohdan Kordan, *Strategic Friends: Canada-Ukraine Relations from Independence to the Euromaidan* (Montreal: McGill-Queen's University Press, 2018).

12 Telcon, Bush-Mulroney, 24 Feb. 1990, George H. W. Bush Library, Memcons & Telcons; Paul Heinbecker, *Getting Back in the Game: A Foreign Policy Playbook for Canada* (Toronto: Key Porter, 2010), 80.

13 Bruce Russett and James Sutterlin, 'The UN in a New World Order', *Foreign Affairs* 70 (1991).

14 Telcon, Bush-Mulroney, 9 Aug. 1990, George H. W. Bush Library, Memcons & Telcons.

15 'Canada urging No Unilateral Move', *Globe & Mail*, 27 Sept. 1990.

16 House of Commons, *Debates*, 15 Jan. 1991, 17025–7.

17 Hugh Winsor, 'War's Foes and Friends Claim Pearson's Legacy', *Globe & Mail*, 11 Feb. 1991.

18 Group of Seven Plenary Session, 15 July 1991, George H. W. Bush Library, Memcons & Telcons.

19 Reg Whitaker, 'Prisoners of the American Dream: Canada, the Gulf, and the New World Order', *Studies in Political Economy* 35 (1991): 13–27.

20 DEA, *Statements & Speeches* 91/05 24 Jan. 1991; Desmond Morton, 'Defence Policy for a Nice Country', *Peace and Security* (1990): 5.

21 DEA, *Statements & Speeches* 93/7, 8 Feb. 1993; John Mearsheimer, 'Why We Will Soon Miss the Cold War', *Atlantic Monthly*, Aug. 1990.

22 Michael Ignatieff, *Blood and Belonging: Journeys into the New Nationalism* (Toronto: Penguin, 1993).

23 'Canadians Try to Defuse Minefields of Hate', *Vancouver Sun*, 18 Apr. 1992.

24 Telcon, Bush-Mulroney, 27 June 1992, George H. W. Bush Library, Memcons & Telcons.

25 Samantha Power, *A Problem from Hell: America and the Age of Genocide* (New York: Basic Books, 2002).

26 Carol Off, *The Ghosts of Medak Pocket: The Story of Canada's Secret War* (Toronto: Random House, 2004); Misha Boutilier, 'The Mulroney Government and Humanitarian Intervention in the Former Yugoslavia', *International Journal* 73 (2018): 49–67.

27 Norman Hillmer and Dean Oliver, 'The NATO-United Nations Link: Canada and the Balkans, 1991–1995', in *A History of NATO: The First Fifty Years*, ed. Gustav Schmidt (London: Palgrave, 2001); Nicholas Gammer, *From Peacekeeping to Peacemaking: Canada's Response to the Yugoslav Crisis* (Montreal: McGill-Queen's University Press, 2001); Duane Bratt, 'Bosnia: From Failed State to Functioning State', in *From Kinshasa to Kandahar*, 143–64.

28 MacKenzie, *Peacekeeper*, xvi.

29 'Smell of Death Haunts Desolate Somalian City', *Ottawa Citizen*, 7 Aug. 1992; 'A Few Parting Shots', *Maclean's*, 5 July 1993; 'If Sarajevo, Why Not Somalia?' *Globe & Mail*, 22 July 1992.

30 Robert Lewis, 'Canada's Shame', *Maclean's*, 28 Mar. 1994; Sherene Razack, *Dark Threats and White Knights: The Somalia Affair, Peacekeeping and the New Imperialism* (Toronto: University of Toronto Press, 2004).

31 Bush to Mulroney, 3 Dec. 1992 and Shortliffe to Mulroney, 8 Dec. 1992, LAC, RG 25, file 21-14-6-UNOSOM.

32 Grant Dawson, *'Here is Hell': Canada's Engagement in Somalia* (Vancouver: UBC Press, 2007), 5.

33 Roméo Dallaire with Brent Beardsley, *Shake Hands with the Devil: The Failure of Humanity in Rwanda* (Toronto: Viking, 2004), 516.

34 DND, *Defence White Paper* (Ottawa: Minister of Supply and Services, 1994), 3; 'Peacekeepers: Military Budget Puts Constraints on Canadians', *Washington Post*, 26 Sept. 1999.

35 Kevin Spooner, 'Legacies and Realities: UN Peacekeeping and Canada, Past and Present', in *Canada and the United Nations*, 208–20; Michael Carroll, 'Canada and Peacekeeping: Past, but not Present and Future?' *International Journal* 71 (2016): 167–76; Rick Hillier, *A Soldier First: Bullets, Bureaucrats and the Politics of War* (Toronto: HarperCollins, 2009), 115.

36 David Bercuson, *Significant Incident: Canada's Army, the Airborne, and the Murder in Somalia* (Toronto: McClelland and Stewart, 1996), 60; Janice Gross Stein, 'Ideas, Even Good Ideas, Are Not Enough: Changing Canada's Foreign and Defence Policies', *International Journal* 50 (1994–5): 40; Canada 21 Council, *Canada and Common Security in the Twenty-First Century* (Toronto: Centre for International Studies, 1994)

37 Lloyd Axworthy, *Navigating a New World: Canada's Global Future* (Toronto: Knopf, 2003), 7; DEA, *Statements & Speeches* 96/46, 30 Oct. 1996; Axworthy, 'Why "Soft Power" Is the Right Policy for Canada', *Ottawa Citizen*, 25 Apr. 1998.

38 Elizabeth Riddell-Dixon, *Canada and the Beijing Conference on Women: Government Politics and NGO Participation* (Vancouver: UBC Press, 2001); Canada, *Canada in the World* (Ottawa: Department of Foreign Affairs and International Trade, 1995).

39 Lloyd Axworthy, 'Canada and Human Security: The Need for Leadership', *International Journal* 52 (1997): 184.

40 Lloyd Axworthy, 'Human Security: An Opening for UN Reform', in *The United Nations and Global Security*, ed. Richard Price and Mark Zacher (New York: Palgrave, 2004), 252.

41 Greg Donaghy, 'All God's Children: Lloyd Axworthy, Human Security, and Canadian Foreign Policy, 1996–2000," *Canadian Foreign Policy Journal* 10 (2003): 39–58.

42 David Webster, 'Canada and Bilateral Human Rights Dialogues', *Canadian Foreign Policy Journal* 16 (2010): 46.

43 John Harker, *Human Security in Sudan: The Report of a Canadian Assessment Mission* (Ottawa: Department of Foreign Affairs and International Trade, 2000), 1; Nick Coghlan, *Far in the Waste Sudan: On Assignment in Africa* (Montreal: McGill-Queen's University Press, 2005), 25.

44 'Martin vows to ease Darfur's suffering', *Globe & Mail*, 23 Feb. 2005; Peter Pigott, *Canada in Sudan: War without Borders* (Toronto: Dundurn Press, 2009).

45 Roméo Dallaire, *They Fight Like Soldiers, They Die Like Children: The Global Quest to Eradicate the Use of Child Soldiers* (Toronto: Random House, 2010); Samantha Nutt, *Damned Nations: Greed, Guns, Armies and Aid* (Toronto: McClelland and Stewart, 2011); Stephen Lewis, *Race Against Time* (Toronto: Anansi, 2005).

46 Rudyard Griffiths, 'The Day of Pearson Internationalism is Past', *Globe & Mail*, 12 Apr. 1997; Robin Hay, 'Present at the Creation? Human Security and Canadian Foreign Policy in the Twenty-first Century', in *Canada among Nations 1999*, ed. Fen Osler Hampson, Michael Hart, and Martin Rudner (Don Mills: Oxford University Press, 1999), 228.

47 Dean Oliver and Fen Hampson, 'Pulpit Diplomacy: A Critical Assessment of the Axworthy Doctrine', *International Journal* 53 (1997–8): 379–406; Kim Richard Nossal, 'Pinchpenny Diplomacy: The Decline of "Good International Citizenship" in Canadian Foreign Policy', *International Journal* 54 (1998–9): 88–105.

48 Paul Heinbecker, 'Human Security', *Canadian Foreign Policy Journal* 7 (1999): 21.

49 Michael Manulak, 'Canada and the Kosovo Crisis', *International Journal* 64 (2009): 576.

50 Memorandum of Telephone Conversation, 10 June 1999, National Security Council and Records Management Office, 'Declassified Documents Concerning Tony Blair', William J. Clinton Digital Library.

51 Axworthy, *Navigating a New World*, 183.

52 Michael Bliss, 'Ashamed to Be a Canadian', *Peace Research* 31 (1999): 57; James Bissett, 'The Tragic Blunder in Kosovo', *Globe & Mail*, 10 Jan. 2000.

53 Michael Ignatieff, 'The Attack on Human Rights', *Foreign Affairs* 80 (2001).

54 House of Commons, Standing Committee on External Affairs and International Trade, 17 Feb. 1993.

55 Denis Stairs et al., *In the National Interest: Canadian Foreign Policy in an Insecure World* (Calgary: Canadian Defence and Foreign Affairs Institute, 2003), viii.

56 J. L. Granatstein, *Who Killed the Canadian Military?* (Toronto: HarperCollins, 2004) Andrew Cohen, *While Canada Slept: How We Lost Our Place in the World* (Toronto: McClelland and Stewart, 2003).

57 Jennifer Welsh, *At Home in the World: Canada's Global Vision for the 21st Century* (Toronto: HarperCollins, 2014), 21.

58 Paul Wells, 'We Don't Pull Our Weight: Manley', *National Post*, 5 Oct. 2001.

59 Ottawa to State, tel. 917, 28 Mar. 2003, Wikileaks.

60 Jeffrey Simpson, 'When the US Won't Listen to Its Friends', *Globe & Mail*, 31 July 2001.

61 Eddie Goldenberg, *The Way It Works: Inside Ottawa* (Toronto: McClelland and Stewart, 2006), 280.

62 'Deputy PM Calls "Axis of Evil" Remark Too Harsh as Canada Discusses Joint Defence Plan', *Ottawa Citizen*, 9 Feb. 2002; 'Canada to Chart Own Course, Graham Vows', *Toronto State*, 22 Jan. 2002.

63 'Graham Critical of US Stance', *Calgary Herald*, 7 Aug. 2002.

64 Eddie Goldenberg, *The Way It Works: Inside Ottawa* (Toronto: McClelland and Stewart, 2006), 289; 'Canada Will Go to War if UN OKs It: PM', *National Post*, 11 Oct. 2002.

65 Jean Chrétien, *My Years as Prime Minister* (Toronto: Viking, 2008), 312; Timothy Andrews Sayle, 'Taking the Off-Ramp: Canadian Diplomacy, Intelligence, and Decision-Making before the Iraq War', in *Australia, Canada, and Iraq: Perspectives on an Invasion*, ed. Ramesh Thakur and Jack Cunningham (Toronto: Dundurn, 2015).

66 Jean Chrétien, 'Don't Act Alone', *Globe & Mail*, 14 Feb. 2003; Goldenberg, *The Way It Works*, 295; Bill Graham, *The Call of the World: A Political Memoir* (Vancouver: UBC Press, 2016), 289; David Frum and Richard Perle, *An End to Evil: How to Win the War on Terror* (New York: Random House, 2003); Andrew Roberts, *A History of the English-Speaking Peoples since 1900* (London: Weidenfeld & Nicolson, 2006); Walter Russell Mead, *God and Gold: Britain, America, and the Making of the Modern World* (New York: Knopf, 2007).

67 Graham, *The Call of the World*, 274.

68 'Canada to Stay Out of Iraq War', *Maclean's*, 31 Mar. 2003; Nicholas Kristoff, 'Losses before Bullets', *New York Times*, 7 Mar. 2003.

69 'Antiwar Protests Held Worldwide', *Globe & Mail*, 16 Mar. 2003; House of Commons, *Debates*, 17 Mar. 2003, 4245; 'War Isn't Justified, PM Says', *Globe & Mail*, 19 Mar. 2003.

70 'Canadians Back Chretien on War, Poll Finds', *Toronto Star*, 22 Mar. 2003.

71 Paul Cellucci, *Unquiet Diplomacy* (Toronto: Key Porter, 2007), 141; 'US Rebukes Canada', *Globe & Mail*, 26 Mar. 2003.

72 House of Commons, *Debates*, 8 Apr. 2003.

73 'Bush a Great Leader, Gretzky Feels', *Globe & Mail*, 25 Mar. 2003; Graham, *The Call of the World*, 312; Stephen Harper and Stockwell Day, 'Canadians Stand with You', *Wall Street Journal*, 28 Mar. 2003.

74 Allan Gotlieb, 'Ottawa Let Down Two Nations', *National Post*, 26 Mar. 2003; J. L. Granatstein, 'The Empire Strikes Back', *National Post*, 26 Mar. 2003.

75 Ottawa to State, tel. 747, 17 Mar. 2003, Wikileaks.

76 Graham, *The Call of the World*, 306.

77 Ottawa to State, tel. 917, 28 Mar. 2003 and Ottawa to State, tel. 1123, 22 Apr. 2003, Wikileaks.

78 Janice Gross Stein and Eugene Lang, *The Unexpected War: Canada in Kandahar* (Toronto: Viking, 2007), 67–9.

79 Paul Martin, *Hell or High Water: My Life In and Out of Politics* (Toronto: McClelland and Stewart, 2008), 391.

80 Independent Panel on Canada's Future Role in Afghanistan, *Final Report* (Ottawa: Government of Canada, 2008), 32.

81 Stephen Saideman, 'Six Years in Kandahar: Understanding Canada's Multidimensional Effort to Build a Sustainable Afghan State', in *From Kinshasa to Kandahar*, 165–84.

82 'Canada's Military: Hockey Sticks and Helicopters', *The Economist*, 24 July 2008; 'General Hillier Explains the Afghan Mission', *Globe & Mail*, 16 July 2005.

83 Jean-Christophe Boucher and Kim Richard Nossal, *The Politics of War: Canada's Afghanistan Mission, 2001–14* (Vancouver: UBC Press, 2017); David Fraser with Brian Hanington, *Operation Medusa: The Furious Battle That Saved Afghanistan from the Taliban* (Toronto: McClelland and Stewart, 2018).

84 Boucher and Nossal, *The Politics of War*, 79.

85 Tim Harper, 'Afghan Mission a "Great Success", Harper Tells Troops in Kandahar', *Toronto Star*, 30 May 2011.

86 'Harper's Turnaround: PM Says He Felt He had to Extend Afghan Mission', *Globe & Mail*, 11 Nov. 2010.

87 *Globe & Mail*, 10 Oct. 2001; Michael Ignatieff, 'Canada and the Waning of US Primacy', in *American Power: Potential and Limits in the 21st Century*, ed., Patrick Luciani and Rudyard Griffiths (Toronto: Key Porter, 2007), 60.

88 'A Sea of Red Washes over Hill', *Ottawa Citizen*, 23 Sept. 2006.

89 George Melnyk, *Canada and the New American Empire* (Calgary: University of Calgary Press, 2004); Lucia Kowaluk and Steven Staples, *Afghanistan and Canada: Is There an Alternative to War?* (Montreal: Black Rose Books, 2009); Jerome Klassen and Greg Albo, *Empire's Ally: Canada the War in Afghanistan* (Toronto: University of Toronto Press, 2013); Ian McKay and Jamie Swift. *Warrior Nation: Rebranding Canada in an Age of Anxiety* (Toronto: Between the Lines, 2012).

90 David Bercuson and J. L.Granatstein, *Lessons Learned? What Canada Should Learn from Afghanistan* (Calgary: Canadian Defence and Foreign Affairs Institute, 2011), 21.

91 'Canada Imposes Wide Range of Sanctions against Libya', *Globe & Mail*, 27 Feb. 2011.

92 Lloyd Axworthy and Allan Rock, 'Syrians Suffer "our" Collective Failure', *Globe & Mail*, 10 Sept. 2013.

93 Harvey Levenstein, 'Canada and the Suppression of the Salvadoran Revolution of 1932', *Canadian Historical Review* 62 (1981); 'Lucky for Salvador!' *Globe*, 26 Jan. 1932; 'Leaving with Our Heads Held High', *Globe & Mail*, 23 May 2012.

94 'We Belong in Afghanistan', *National Post*, 15 Dec. 2005; Louise Arbour, 'The Responsibility to Protect as a Duty of Care in International Law and Practice', *Review of International Studies* 34 (2008): 445.

95 Lloyd Axworthy, 'Perfect Chance to Repair the UN Charter', *Globe & Mail*, 14 Aug. 1991; 'Mulroney on Canadian, US roles in New World Order', Stanford News Service, 29 Sept. 1991.

12 Globalization redux

1 'Lewis Supports African Aid Plan', *Globe & Mail*, 8 Nov. 1984.

2 Brian Mulroney, *Memoirs, 1939–93* (Toronto: McClelland and Stewart, 2007), 331–2.

3 'The Northern Lights Sparkle for Fans and Famine Victims', *Globe & Mail*, 11 Feb. 1985.

4 'Clark Satisfied Food Getting Through', *Globe & Mail*, 6 Nov. 1984; House of Commons, *Debates*, 16 Nov. 1984, 307; Nassisse Soloman, ' "Tears are not Enough": Canadian Political and Social Mobilization for Famine Relief in Ethiopia, 1984–88', in *A Samaritan State Revisited*.

5 Axworthy, *Navigating a New World*, 1.

6 Privy Council Office (PCO), *Toward an International Policy Framework for the 21st Century* (Ottawa: PCO, 2003), 14.

7 Fen Osler Hampson and Maureen Appel Molot, 'Does the 49th Parallel Matter Any More', in *Canada Among Nations 2000*, ed. Maureen Appel Molot and Fen Osler Hampson (Don Mills: Oxford University Press, 2000).

8 Robert Bothwell, 'Thanks for the Fish: Nixon, Kissinger, and Canada', in *Nixon in the World: American Foreigh Relations, 1969–1977*, ed. Fredrik Logevall and Andrew Preston (New York: Oxford University Press, 2008), 309.

9 Arthur Andrew, *The Rise and Fall of a Middle Power* (Toronto: James Lorimer, 1993), 122.

10 Annette Baker Fox, Alfred Hero, and Joseph Nye, *Canada and the United States: Transnational and Trangovernmental Relations* (New York: Columbia University Press, 1976); Robert Keohane and Joseph Nye, *Transnational Relations in World Politics* (Cambridge: Harvard University Press, 1971); Robert Keohane and Joseph Nye, *Power and Interdependence: World Politics in Transition* (Boston: Little Brown, 1977).

11 Joel Garreau, *The Nine Nations of North America* (Boston, MA: Houghton Mifflin, 1981).

12 Randy William Widdis, *Permeable Border: The Great Lakes Basin as Transnational Region, 1650–1990* (Calgary: University of Calgary Press, 2005); Steven High, *Industrial Sunset: The Making of North America's Rust. Belt, 1969–1984* (Toronto: University of Toronto Press, 2003); Tracy Neumann, *Remaking the Rust Belt: The Postindustrial Transformation of North America* (Philadelphia: University of Pennsylvania Press, 2016); 'Welcome to Cascadia', *The Economist*, 21 May 1994.

13 Dimitry Anastakis, *Auto Pact: Creating a Borderless North American Auto Industry, 1960–1971* (Toronto: University of Toronto Press, 2005); Dimitry Anastakis, *Autonomous State: The Struggle for a Canadian Car Industry from OPEC to Free Trade* (Toronto: University of Toronto Press, 2012).

14 Butterworth to Schaetzel, 4 Mar. 1965, NARA, RG 59, Bureau of European Affairs, Country Director for Canada, Records Relating to Economic Matters, 1957-1966, box 4, folder Policy/Plans/Programs; Ian Urquhart, 'The Welcome Wagon', *Maclean's*, 1 Nov. 1976.

15 Kinsman, 'Reagan Visit – Strategy', 12 Feb. 1981, LAC, RG 25, file 20-USA-9-Reagan R.

16 Douglas Brinkley, *The Reagan Diaries* (Toronto: HarperCollins, 2007), 7; DEA to Washington, EGL-0057, 11 Mar. 1981, LAC, RG 25, vol. 16815, file 20-1-2-USA.

17 'Welcoming Mr. Trudeau', *Wall Street Journal*, 9 July 1981; 'The Canadian Disease', *Wall Street Journal*, 9 Mar. 1981; David Breen, 'The Making of Modern Alberta', in *Alberta Formed, Alberta Transformed*, vol. 2, ed. Michael Payne, Donald Wetherell, and Catherine Cavanaugh (Edmonton: University of Alberta Press, 2006), 558.

18 Susan Colbourn, 'The Elephant in the Room: Rethinking Cruise Missile Testing and Pierre Trudeau's Peace Mission', in *Undiplomatic History*.

19 Douglas Roche, *Politicians for Peace: A New Global Network of Legislators Looking for Human Survival* (Toronto: NC Press, 1983); Douglas Roche, *Canada and the Pursuit of Peace* (Ottawa: External Affairs, 1985), 38.

20 Brinkley, *Reagan Diaries*, 205; 'Top US Official Quoted as Ridiculing Trudeau', *New York Times*, 23 Dec. 1983; Charles Doran, *Forgotten Partnership: U.S.-Canada Relations Today* (Baltimore: Johns Hopkins University Press, 1984); Luc-André Brunet, 'Unhelpful Fixer? The Euromissile Crisis and Trudeau's Peace Initiative, 1983–1984', *International History Review* 40 (2018); Susan Colbourn, 'Cruising towards Nuclear Danger: Canadian Anti-Nuclear Activism, Pierre Trudeau's Peace Mission, and the Transatlantic Partnership', *Cold War History* 18 (2018): 19–36.

21 John Urquhart, 'An Outspoken US Friend in Ottawa', *Wall Street Journal*, 24 Sept. 1984; Marci McDonald, *Yankee Doodle Dandy: Brian Mulroney and the American Agenda* (Toronto: Stoddart, 1995); Lawrence Martin, *Pledge of Allegiance: The Americanization of Canada in the Mulroney Years* (Toronto: McClelland and Stewart, 1993), 11.

22 Margaret Thatcher, *The Downing Street Years, 1979–1990* (Toronto: HarperCollins, 1993), 321.

23 Allan Gotlieb, '*I'll Be with You in a Minute, Mr. Ambassador': The Education of a Canadian Diplomat in Washington* (Toronto: University of Toronto Press, 1991).

24 'Tories Pass Trade Bill over Chorus of Opposition', *Montreal Gazette*, 1 Sept. 1988.

25 'Liberal Blueprint for Canada', *Toronto Star*, 29 Sept. 1988; Laurier LaPierre, ed., *If You Love This Country* (Toronto: McClelland and Stewart, 1987); Marjorie Bowker, *On Guard for Thee: An Independent Review of the Free Trade Agreement* (Hull: Voyageur, 1987); Keith Davey, *Canada Not For Sale: The Case Against Free Trade* (Toronto: General Paperbacks, 1987).

26 J. L. Granatstein, *Yankee Go Home? Canadians and Anti-Americanism* (Toronto: HarperCollins, 1996), ix.

27 Jeffrey Simpson, *Star-Spangled Canadians: Canadians Living the American Dream* (Toronto: HarperCollins, 2000).

28 Ron Graham, 'Born Again in Babylon', *Saturday Night*, June 1983.

29 Manjunath Pendakur, *Canadian Dreams and American Control: The Political Economy of the Canadian Film Industry* (Toronto: Garamond, 1990), 155.

30 John Stewart, 'Magazines, Ministers and "Monoculture": The Canada–United States Dispute Over "Split Run" Magazines in the 1990s', *Canadian Foreign Policy Journal* 16 (2010): 35–48.

31 Canada, House of Commons, Standing Committee on Canadian Heritage, Proceedings, 17 Nov. 1998; John Demont, 'Copps Defends Canadian Culture', *Maclean's*, 24 Feb. 1997.

32 C. Christopher Baughn and Mark Buchanan, 'Cultural Protectionism', *Business Horizons* 44 (2001): 6.

33 Jan Morris, *City to City: Canada through the Eyes of the Greatest Travel Writer of Our Day* (Toronto: Macfarlane Walter & Ross, 1990), xiii.

34 Robert Seiler, 'Selling Patriotism / Selling Beer: The Case of the "I am Canadian!" Commercial', *American Review of Canadian Studies* 32 (2002): 45–66; Catherine Carstairs, 'Roots Nationalism: Branding English Canada Cool In The 1980s and 1990s', *Histoire Sociale/Social History* 39 (2006): 235–55; Patricia Cormack and James Cosgrave, *Desiring Canada: CBC Contests, Hockey Violence, and Other Stately Pleasures* (Toronto: University of Toronto Press, 2013).

35 Michael Adams, *Fire and Ice: The United States, Canada and the Myth of Converging Values* (Toronto: Penguin, 2003).

36 Matt Labash, 'Welcome to Canada: The Great White Waste of Time', *Weekly Standard*, 21 Mar. 2005; Jonah Goldberg, 'Bomb Canada: The Case for War', *National Review*, 25 Nov. 2002; Colin Freeze, 'Head to the bunkers, the Yanks are coming', *Globe & Mail*, 9 Nov. 2002; Richard Baker, '"Catnip for Cranks": Depictions of Canadian Threat in US Conservative News Commentary', *American Review of Canadian Studies* 43 (2013).

37 'Ill Americans Seek Marijuana's Relief in Canada', *New York Times*, 8 Sept. 2002; 'Dispirited US Gays Choosing Canada', *Globe & Mail*, 10 Nov. 2004; 'More Americans Heading North', *Toronto Star*, 6 Aug. 2007; Jeremy Rifkin, 'Continentalism of a Different Stripe', *The Walrus*, Mar. 2005.

38 'Say It Ain't So – Canadian Sovereignty' *Maclean's*, 15 July 1999; Anthony DePalma, *Here: A Biography of the New North American Continent* (New York: PublicAffairs, 2001); Ronald Inglehart, Neil Nevitte, and Miguel Basañez, *The North American Trajectory: Cultural, Economic, and Political Ties among the United States, Canada, and Mexico* (New York: Aldine De Gruyter, 1996).

39 Mel Hurtig, *The Vanishing Country: Is It Too Late to Save Canada?* (Toronto: McClelland and Stewart, 2002); Stephen Clarkson, *Uncle Sam and Us: Globalization, Neoconservatism and the Canadian State* (Toronto: University of Toronto Press, 2002).

40 Lamar Smith, 'Plugging our porous border', *National Post*, 24 Jan. 2000.

41 'Dispelling Myth about Canada as Terrorist Portal', *Globe & Mail*, 4 Dec. 2001; Graham Allison, 'Is Nuclear Terrorism a Threat to Canada's National Security?' *International Journal* 60 (2005): 717; 'Trade Concerns as Canada Sits Out War', *New York Times*, 1 Apr. 2003.

42 Graham, *The Call of the World*, 223.

43 Ottawa to State, tel. 123, 13 Jan. 2003, Wikileaks.

44 Ottawa to State, tel. 1123, 22 Apr. 2003, Wikileaks; 'Ottawa to Move on Missile Defence', *Globe & Mail*, 30 May 2003; 'Missile Defence Flip-Flop Compounds Mr. Dithers Tag', *Halifax Herald*, 26 Feb. 2005.

45 Lloyd Axworthy, 'Missile Counter-Attack', *Winnipeg Free Press*, 3 Mar. 2005.

46 Luiza Ch. Savage, 'Land of the Freeloaders: The Battle for a New Cross-border Bridge', *Maclean's*, 21 May 2015.

47 Robert Rubin, 'A Conversation with Stephen Harper', Council on Foreign Relations, 16 May 2013.

48 CFR, *Building a North American Community* (New York: Council on Foreign Relations, 2005); Diane Francis, *Merger of the Century: Why Canada and America Should Become One Country* (Toronto: HarperCollins, 2013); Robert Pastor, *The North American Idea: A Vision of a Continental Future* (Oxford: Oxford University Press, 2011).

49 Telcon, Bush-Mulroney, 12 Aug. 1992, George H. W. Bush Library, Memcon & Telcons.

50 Excerpts from Prime Minister Jean Chrétien's speech to the Senate of the United Mexican States, 9 Apr. 1999, *Canada World View* 4 (1999), 13.

51 DEA, *Statements & Speeches* 89/14, 19 Apr. 1989; DEA, *Statements & Speeches* 94/23, 24 May 1994.

52 Michael Hart, *Fifty Years of Canadian Tradecraft: Canada at the GATT 1947–1997* (Ottawa: Centre for Trade Policy and Law, 1998), 190–1.

53 'Bankrupt Canada?' *Wall Street Journal*, 12 Jan. 1995.

54 Canada, *Canada in the World*.

55 James Bartleman, *Rollercoaster: My Hectic Years as Jean Chrétien's Diplomatic Advisor, 1994–1998* (Toronto: McClelland and Stewart, 2005), 200.

56 Paul Martin, 'A Global Answer to Global Problems', *Foreign Affairs* (2005).

57 'Unusual Alliances', *Maclean's*, 22 May 1995; Frank Petrie, *As Far As Ever the Puffin Flew* (Toronto: Vintage, 1997), 304.

58 John W. Foster and Anita Anand, *Whose World Is It Anyway?* (Ottawa: UN Association of Canada, 1999), 133.

59 Naomi Klein, *No Logo* (Toronto: Knopf, 2000), xvii.

60 'An Interview with Peter Munk', *The Economist*, 29 Apr. 2014.

61 Timothy David Clark and Viviana Patroni, *Community Rights and Corporate Responsibility: Canadian Mining and Oil Companies in Latin America* (Toronto: Between the Lines, 2006); Paula Butler, *Colonial Extractions: Race and Canadian Mining in Contemporary Africa* (Toronto: University of Toronto Press, 2015).

62 'Fantino Defends CIDA's Corporate Shift', *Globe & Mail*, 4 Dec. 2012; Doug Saunders, 'Canada's African Adventure Takes a Colonial Turn', *Globe & Mail*, 2 Feb. 2013.

63 'Ottawa Stresses Trade Prospects in Foreign Aid Decisions', *Globe & Mail*, 8 Jan. 2014.

64 Stephen Brown, 'Canadian Aid to Africa', in *Canada-Africa Relations: Looking Back, Looking Ahead*, ed. Rohinton Medhora and Yigadeesen Samy (Waterloo: Centre for International Governance Innovation, 2013), 181–2; 'Canada Far below Average among World's Top Aid Donors', *Toronto Star*, 17 Oct. 1997.

65 'Rock Steady', *Canada World View* 16 (2002).

66 'Bono Endorses Martin, Canada in Helping Third World', *Globe & Mail*, 16 Nov. 2003.

67 'Free Trade Steve – A Polarizing Force', *Embassy* 22 Apr. 2009, 6; John Ibbitson, *The Big Break: The Conservative Transformation of Canada's Foreign Policy* (Waterloo: Centre for International Governance Innovation, 2014), 5.

68 PMO, 'Statement by the Prime Minister of Canada in New York', 25 Sept. 2014; PMO, 'PM Delivers Remarks on Canada Day', 1 July 2013.

69 Janice McGregor, 'Stephen Harper Confident as Final EU Trade Deal Released', *CBC News*, 26 Sept. 2014.

70 Mark Carney, 'Globalisation, Financial Stability, and Employment', speech to the Canadian Autoworkers, 22 Aug. 2012; Edward Greenspon, *Open Canada: A Global Positioning Strategy for a Networked Age* (Toronto: Canadian International Council, 2010), 20.

71 'Evidence Still Points to Growth in Canada', *Wall Street Journal*, 26 Aug. 2011.

72 Rubin, 'A Conversation with Stephen Harper'; Kenneth Whyte, 'In Conversation: Stephen Harper', *Maclean's*, 5 July 2011.

73 Paul Evans, 'Canada, Meet Global China', *International Journal* 61 (2006): 283.

74 Mulroney, *Memoirs*, 444–5.

75 Ibid., 666.

76 House of Commons, *Debates*, 5 June 1989; 'China Loan Will Assist in Reforms Clark Insists', *Toronto Star*, 5 Aug. 1989.

77 'PM Confident Asia Tour Will Help Human Rights', *Toronto Star*, 18 Nov. 1994.

78 Stanley Hartt, 'Must We Choose between Trade and Human Rights', *Globe & Mail*, 20 Jan. 2005.

79 Brian Evans, *Pursuing China: Memoir of a Beaver Liaison Officer* (Edmonton: University of Alberta Press, 2012), 257.

80 'Won't "sell out" on Rights Despite China Snub: PM', *CBC News*, 15 Nov. 2006.

81 Lawrence Martin, *Harperland: The Politics of Control* (Toronto: Viking, 2010), 83.

82 Kim Richard Nossal and Leah Sarson, 'About Face: Explaining Changes in Canada's China Policy, 2006–2012', *Canadian Foreign Policy Journal* 20 (2014); 'Tory MP Slams CNOOC Takeover Bid for Nexen', *National Post*, 7 Nov. 2012.

83 'China's Government Hacked Computers, Ottawa Says', *Globe & Mail*, 29 July 2014; Fabrice de Pierrebourg and Michel Juneau-Katsuya, *Nest of Spies* (Toronto: HarperCollins, 2009), 147.

84 'Five Highlights from the Canada-Brazil Spying Revelations', *Globe & Mail*, 7 Oct. 2013; David Matas and David Kilgour, 'Calling China to Account', *Globe & Mail*, 30 May 2008; 'UN Panel Confronts China Over Reports That It Holds a Million Uighurs in Camps', *New York Times*, 10 Aug. 2018.

85 Paul Evans, *Engaging China: Myth, Aspiration, and Strategy in Canadian Policy from Trudeau to Harper* (Toronto: University of Toronto Press, 2014), 84; David Mulroney, *Middle Power, Middle Kingdom: What Canadians Need to Know about China in the 21st Century* (Toronto: Penguin, 2015), 289.

86 Renate Pratt, *In Good Faith: Canadian Churches against Apartheid* (Waterloo: Wilfrid Laurier University Press, 1997); John Saul, *On Building a Social Movement: The North American Campaign for South African Liberation* (Halifax: Fernwood, 2016).

87 'U of T Votes to Sell All Holdings in Firms Linked to South Africa', *Toronto Star*, 22 Jan. 1988; 'Court Rejects Ban on South African Ambassador's Speech', *Globe & Mail*, 16 Jan. 1986.

88 'Thousands Chant and Sing in Greeting to Mandela', *Toronto Star*, 19 June 1990.

89 'Bata Contravenes Ottawa Code on South Africa', *Globe & Mail*, 15 Feb. 1985.

90 Mulroney to Thatcher, 2 Oct. 1985, TNA, PREM 19/1644 f320; Powell, 'Prime Minister's Meeting with the Canadian Prime Minister: South Africa', 14 July 1986, TNA, PREM 19/1681 f19.

91 'Canada Can Do Much More to Oppose Apartheid, Says South African Bishop', *Ottawa Citizen*, 21 Dec. 1984; 'Tambo, Not Rambo: The ANC's President in Toronto', *Southern Africa Report*, Oct. 1987.

92 David Black, 'How Exceptional? Reassessing the Mulroney Government's Anti-Apartheid "Crusade" ', in *Diplomatic Departures: The Conservative Era in Canadian Foreign Policy, 1984–93*, ed. Nelson Michaud and Kim Richard Nossal (Vancouver: UBC Press, 2002).

93 'Opposes Sanctions, Suavé's Husband Director of Group Backing S. Africa, *Montreal Gazette*, 26 July 1985; Barbara Amiel, 'A Discordant Song of Sanctions', *Maclean's*, 18 Aug. 1986; 'Sanctions Still Lively Policy Debate', *Globe & Mail*, 12 Nov. 1990.

94 Michael Valpy, 'Brian Mulroney and Stephen Lewis on Principled Leadership in Foreign Affairs', *U of T News*, 15 Apr. 2014.

95 Doug Smith, 'An Awkward Visit', *Maclean's*, 23 March 1987; 'Indian Blanket, Aid Request Greet Babb at Peguis Reserve', *Globe & Mail*, 11 Mar. 1987.

96 'Indians Present Botha with Headdress', *Globe & Mail*, 19 Aug. 1987; 'Clark, Botha Stay at Odds over Release of Mandela', *Globe & Mail*, 15 Aug. 1987; 'Visiting Clark Told to "Get Lost" ', *Globe & Mail*, 14 Aug. 1987.

97 Ron Bourgeault, 'Canada Indians: The South African Connection', *Canadian Dimension*, Jan. 1988.

98 'Tutu Likens Native Fight to Blacks of South Africa', *Winnipeg Free Press*, 14 Aug. 1990; 'Tutu Makes Common Cause with Aboriginal Canadians', *Anglican News Service*, 14 Aug. 1990.

99 'Chiefs Urge Swift Recall of Parliament', *Globe & Mail*, 21 July 1990.

100 Audra Simpson, *Mohawk Interruptus: Political Life across Borders of Settler States* (Durham: Duke University Press, 2014).

101 RCAP *Report*, vol. 1: *Looking Forward, Looking Back* (Ottawa: Minister of Supply and Services, 1991), 610.

102 Special Joint Committee of the Senate and the House of Commons on Reviewing Canadian Foreign Policy, *Minutes of Proceedings and Evidence*, 9 June 1994, 36: 30.

103 'Canadian Apartheid Grabs Local Headlines', *National Post*, 31 Aug. 2001; 'Minister Demands Native Leader Apologize', *Toronto Star*, 1 Sept. 2001; 'Summit "not very useful", Chrétien says', *Toronto Star*, 7 Sept. 2001.

104 Jackie Hartley, Paul Joffe, Jennifer Preston, *Realizing the UN Declaration on the Rights of Indigenous Peoples: Triumph, Hope, and Action* (Saskatoon: Purich Publishing, 2010); Sheryl Lightfoot, 'Selective Endorsement without Intent to implement: Indigenous Rights and the Anglosphere', *International Journal of Human Rights* 16 (2012): 100–22.

105 Scott Gilmore, 'Canada's Race Problem? It's Even Worse than America's', *Maclean's*, 22 Jan. 2015.

106 Glen Sean Coulthard, *Red Skin, White Masks: Rejecting the Colonial Politics of Recognition* (Minneapolis: University of Minnesota Press, 2014).

107 Jeffrey Simpson, 'Too Many First Nations Live in a Dream Palace,' *Globe & Mail*, 5 Jan. 2013.

108 Marian Botsford Fraser, *Walking the Line: Travels Along the Canadian/American Border* (Vancouver: Douglas & McIntyre, 1989), 140.

109 'Canada Is Facing "Long Haul" Mission: Harper', *Ottawa Citizen*, 8 Sept. 2015.

110 Charles Foran, 'The Canada Experiment: Is This the World's First "Postnational" Country?' *The Guardian*, 4 Jan. 2017; Doug Saunders, *Maximum Canada: Why 35 Million Canadians is Not Enough* (Toronto: Knopf, 2017).

111 "Canada: 'A Model for the World', *Globe & Mail*, 2 Feb. 2002; 'Liberty Moves North: Canada's Example to the World', *The Economist*, 29 Oct. 2016.

112 Neil Bissoondath, *Selling Illusions: The Cult of Multiculturalism in Canada* (Toronto: Penguin, 1994).

113 Guy Lawson, 'Trudeau's Canada, Again', *New York Times Magazine*, 8 Dec. 2015.

114 Canada, *Canada in the World*.

115 See the 'Generations' special issue of *International Journal* 72 (2017).

116 Carol Off, *The Ghosts of Medak Pocket: The Story of Canada's Secret War* (Toronto: Random House, 2004), 29, 48–51.

117 Colin Freeze, 'The Khadr Effect', *Globe & Mail*, 3 Oct. 2005.

118 Stewart Bell, 'Blood Money: International Terrorist Fundraising in Canada', in *Canada among Nations 2002*, ed. Norman Hillmer and Maureen Appel Molot (Don Mills: Oxford University Press, 2002), 174; Stewart Bell, *Cold Terror: How Canada Nurtures and Exports Terrorism Around the World* (Toronto: Wiley, 2004).

119 Campbell Clark, 'Joe Clark's New Book: Canada Is the Country That "Lectures and Leaves"', *Globe & Mail*, 1 Nov. 2013; 'Scarborough Tamils Elated about Harper's Commonwealth Boycott', *Globe & Mail*, 15 Nov. 2013; Matthew Godwin, 'The War at Home: The 2009 Toronto Tamil Demonstrations', *Canadian Foreign Policy Journal* 18 (2012), 164–80; Steven Seligman, 'Exploring Canadian Foreign Policy Toward Sri Lanka Under the Harper Government', *International Journal* 71 (2016): 249–65.

120 House of Commons, Standing Committee on Justice, *Minutes of Proceedings and Evidence*, 16 June 1988.

121 John Ibbitson, 'She Is the New Canada', *Globe & Mail*, 5 Aug. 2005.

122 Bruno Dumons and Jean-Philippe Warren, *Les zouaves pontificaux en France, en Belgique et au Québec. La mise en récit d'une expérience historique, XIXe-XXe siècles* (Brussels: Peter Lang, 2015); Robert McLaughlin, *Irish Canadian Conflict and the Struggle for Irish Independence, 1912–1925* (Toronto: University of Toronto Press, 2013); Jaroslav Petryshyn, 'The "Ethnic Question" Personified: Ukrainian Canadians and Canadian-Soviet Relations 1917–1991', in *Re-Imagining Ukrainian Canadians: History, Politics, and Identity*, ed. Rhonda L Hinther and Jim Mochoruk (Toronto: University of Toronto Press, 2011); David Bercuson, *The Secret Army* (Toronto: Lester & Orpen Dennys, 1983).

123 Zuhair Kashmeri, *The Gulf Within: Canadian Arabs, Racism and the Gulf War* (Toronto: James Lorimer, 1991), 126.

124 John Ibbitson, 'What the Rise of Asia Means for Canadians', *Globe & Mail*, 24 Sept. 2012.

125 Jennifer Welsh, *The Return of History: Conflict, Migration, and Geopolitics in the Twenty-First Century* (Toronto: Anansi, 2016); Jennifer Welsh, *At Home in the World*; Margaret Macmillan, 'The Great War's Ominous Echoes', *New York Times*, 13 Dec. 2013; Chrystia Freeland, *Plutocrats: The Rise of the New Global Super-Rich and the Fall of Everyone Else* (Toronto: Penguin, 2012); Simon Lewsen, 'Chrystia Freeland Wants to Fix the Twenty-first Century', *The Walrus*, Mar. 2018.

126 Adam Lajeunesse, *Lock, Stock, and Icebergs: A History of Canada's Arctic Maritime Sovereignty* (Vancouver: UBC Press, 2016).

Index

Abyssinia, *see* Ethiopia
Acheson, Dean 135, 176
A Choice of Canada 173
Adams, Bryan 229
Adams, Howard 199, 200
Adbusters 242
Afghanistan 30, 210, 217, 232
    war in 206, 222–6, 227
Africa 2, 26–7, 45, 217, 232, 243
African National Congress 248
Afro-Asian Bloc 149, 153, 154, 155,
    156, 158
Aga Khan 252
Agence de coopération culturelle et
    technique 186
Agenda for Peace 211
AIDS 217, 243
Air Canada 192, 202
Air India bombing 254
Aird, John 194–5
Aitken, Max, *see* Beaverbrook
Akwesasne 201
Alaska 36, 56
Alaska Highway 126
Alberta 20, 55, 102, 111, 229
Alcatraz Island 201
Algeria 154, 183, 184, 202
d'Allemagne, André 183
Alliance laurentienne 183
al-Qaeda 237, 253
Aluminum Company of Canada
    (ALCAN) 195, 243, 248
Ambassador Bridge 88, 239
American Bell Telephone 54
American Federation of Labor 54
'American Woman' 174
Amery, Leo 94, 95
Amin, Idi 215
Amnesty International 216

Anglosphere 3, 8, 221, *see also* British
    World; Greater Britain; North
    Atlantic Triangle
Anglo-Saxon racial solidarity 49–50, 56,
    57, 71, 85, 124–5, 129, 178, 221,
    255
Angola 154, 194
Anicinabe Park 201
Annan, Kofi 218
anti-Americanism
    in Canada 53, 54–6, 90, 91–2, 160,
    171, 173–4, 226, 232
anti-communism 74, 103–4, 106, 128,
    131–2
anti-Semitism 102, 105–6, 107, 249
Anti-Terrorism Act 238
apartheid
    in Canada 156, 199, 201, 248–50
    in South Africa 143, 155–6, 192–3,
    199, 247–9
Arab Spring 226
Arar, Maher 238
Arbour, Louise 216, 227
Arcand, Adrien 105–6
Arctic Peoples Conference 201
Arctic sovereignty 255
Argentina 57, 191, 193, 194, 196
Arizona 234
Armenia 2, 229
    genocide in 82–3
Armenian Relief Association of Canada
    82
Arvida, Quebec 89
Asia 2, 29, 30, 41, 45, 46, 50, 80, 84,
    96, 108, 135, 139, 146–7, 148,
    200
    Canadian trade with 41, 42, 43, 109,
    166, 215, 241, 244, 245, 246
    development in 146–7, 181, 184, 200

immigration from 46–50, 75, 92, 110, 143–4
Southeast Asia 136, 146, 166, 176, 177
Asia-Pacific Economic Cooperation (APEC) 207, 216, 241, 242
Asiatic Exclusion League 48
Asquith, Herbert 62
Assembly of First Nations (AFN) 238, 249, 250
Association of Southeast Asian Nations (ASEAN) 241
Atlantic Charter 142, 144
Atlee, Clement 130
Atomic Energy Canada Limited (195–6)
Atomic Energy Commission 142
Australasia 27, 41
Australia 8, 21, 28, 43, 93, 95, 97, 112, 133, 145, 161, 163, 199, 200, 218
Austria-Hungary 8, 19
Auto Pact 231
AVRO Arrow 168–9
A.V. Roe Company 169
Axworthy, Lloyd 209, 214–15, 216, 218, 219, 220, 226, 227, 230, 238

Babb, Glenn 248
Baden-Powell, Lord 37
Baie-Comeau, Quebec 89, 232
Baku 67
Balfour Declaration 95–6
Balkans 77, 206, 211, 213, 218, 219, 223, 226
Ballistic Missile Defence 238
Bandung Conference 149, 158
Banff 234
Bangladesh 189
Bank of Canada 142
Bank of Nova Scotia 44, 194
Barbeau, Raymond 183
Barbie 172
Bata Shoes 248
The Beatles 163
Beaverbrook, Lord 44, 61–2, 165
Belgium 9, 60, 84, 129, 229
Bell Canada 54
Bennett, R. B. 92, 109
  and Britain 96, 164

and the Great Depression 97–8, 100–2, 104
and interwar international security 100, 108, 111
Berger, Thomas 201
Berlin 29, 107, 113, 122, 130
Berlin, Ontario 72
Berlin Olympics 107
Bermuda 44
Bethune, Norman 103
Biafra 188–9, 202, 219
Bieber, Justin 236
Big Bird 175
Bill of Rights 155
Birmingham, Alabama 156
von Bismarck, Otto 2
Bissett, James 218
Blair, Tony 217, 221, 241
Blake, Edward 57
Bliss, Michael 219
Bloc Québécois 224
Boer War 2, 32, 33–6, 37, 38, 49, 60, 61, 62, 206
BOMARC missile 169
Borden, Robert 39, 67, 73, 77, 80, 81
  and Canadian autonomy 63–4, 67–9, 70, 85, 94, 97
  and the First World War 59, 62–3, 64–5, 75
  and the United States 55–6, 78, 85, 234
  and the West Indies 44–5
Bosnia and Herzegovina 8, 211, 212, 217, *see also* Balkans
Bouchard, Charles 226
Bourassa, Henri 31–2, 35, 36, 61
Boutros-Ghali, Boutros 211
Bowell, Mackenzie 20, 28, 29
Boy Scouts 35, 37
Brand, R. H. 61
Brazil 43, 44, 89, 193, 194, 246
Brazilian Traction, Light and Power Company 44
Brebner, J. B. 85–6, 119
Brewin, F. Andrew 132
Britain 96, 100, 111, 115, 129, 133, 136, 152, 157, 163, 218, 220
  Canada, relations with 25–6, 27, 38, 63–4, 67–9, 87, 93–6, 99, 112,

114–15, 116, 123, 145, 152–3,
159–60, 163, 164
Europe and 160, 164–5
immigration to Canada from 20–1,
75, 163, 255
The Second World War and 120–1
The Suez Crisis and 149–52
British Army of the Rhine 134
British Broadcasting Corporation (BBC)
92
British Columbia 46, 65, 110
Confederation and 10, 41
indigenous peoples in 12, 13,
201–2
racism in 48–51, 66, 143–4
British Commonwealth of Nations, *see*
Commonwealth
British Commonwealth Air Training
Program 120
British Empire Expedition 95
British Empire Games 94
British Guiana, *see* Guyana
British Honduras 50
British Institute of International Affairs
77
British North America Act 9, 43, 187
British-North American Committee 178
British World 2, 3, 4, 22, 23–4, 29, 31,
32, 35, 37, 39, 40, 42, 60, 61, 62,
69, 75, 93, 94, 96, 99, 112, 113,
159, 163, 178
Broadway 90
Brown, George 8, 9, 54
Brown, George McLaren 61
Brussels Pact 129–30
Bryan, William Jennings 88
Bryce, R. B. 102
Brzezinski, Zbigniew 187
Buchanan, Patrick 236
Buck, Tim 104
Burkina Faso 243
Burma 30, 127
Burns, E. L. M. 151
Bush, George H. W. 207, 208, 209,
211, 213, 239
Bush, George W. 220, 221, 222, 238
Butler, Francis 21
Buy Nothing Day 242
Byng, Julian 95

Cadieux, Marcel 230
Cahan, C. H. 109
Calder, Frank 202
Cambodia 136, 176, 210
Campbell, Kim 235
Canada 1
Confederation of 8–9, 23, 24–5, 161
cultural nationalism in 90–1, 92–3,
160–3, 166, 172–3, 235–6
economic nationalism in 23, 36, 39,
55, 60, 123, 172–3
Election of 1891 23, 36, 55, 234
Election of 1911 39, 55, 60, 123,
231, 234
Election of 1917 65
Election of 1963 170
Election of 1988 234
Flag of 162
Relations with indigenous peoples
4, 8, 12–17, 72–3, 83–4, 156, 158,
198–202, 248–51
Canada 21 Council 214
Canada Asia Working Group 193
Canada China Business Council 245
Canada-China Legislative Association
245
Canada Council for the Arts 166
Canada Day 164
Canada Development Corporation
173
Canada Haiti Action Network 205
Canada Post 162
Canada-United States Free Trade
Agreement 233–4
Canada-United States Goodwill Week
91
Canadair 131
Canadian Alliance Party 222
Canadian Association in Support of the
Native Peoples 199
Canadian Authors Association 92
Canadian Broadcasting Corporation
(CBC) 92, 163, 229, 236
CBC-International Service 137
Canadian Chamber of Commerce 131
Canadian Citizenship Act 161
Canadian Committee for the Control of
Radiation Hazards 169
Canadian Council of Churches 193

Canadian Council for International Cooperation 193, 199, 243
Canadian Defence League 38
Canadian Encyclopedia 172
Canadian English 162
Canadian Expeditionary Force (CEF) 62–3, 65
  discrimination and 72
Canadian Exporters Association 241
Canadian Film Development Corporation 172
Canadian Historical Association 93
Canadian Institute of International Affairs (CIIA) 77, 78, 80–1, 92, 99, 102, 112, 140, 142, *see also* Canadian International Council
Canadian International Council 244
Canadian International Development Agency (CIDA) 197, 243
Canadian Jewish Congress 107
Canadian Labour Congress 156, 182
Canadian Legion, *see* Royal Canadian Legion
Canadian Nationalist Party 106
Canadian Olympic Committee 107
Canadian Pacific Railway (CPR) 7, 13, 19, 22, 26, 29, 42, 44, 47, 50, 53
  Canadian Pacific Steamship Company 42–3
Canadian Party 11
Canadian Peace Centenary Association 78
Canadian Peace Congress 133, 169, 233
Canadian Political Science Association 102
Canadian Radio Broadcasting Corporation (CRBC) 92, 97
Canadian Radio League 92
Canadian Radio and Television Commission (CRTC) 172
Canadian Red Cross 37, 63, 67, 82, 111, 188
Canadian Security Intelligence Service 254
Canadian-South African Society 248
Canadian-Soviet Friendship Society 132–3
Canadian Studies 172

Canadian Teachers' Federation 111
Canadian Union of Fascists 106
Canadian University Service Overseas (CUSO) 153
Canadian War Mission, Washington 67
Canadian Youth Congress (CYC) 108–9
CANDU reactor 195–6
Capone, Al 89
Cardinal, Harold 200
CARE 243
Caribbean 2, 28, 42, 43–4, 89, 126, 152, 157, 166, 193, 194–5, 196, 206, *see also* West Indies
Carnegie Endowment for International Peace 86, 119
Carnegie Corporation 86
Carnegie Steel 54
Carney, Mark 244
Carter, James (Jimmy) 187, 189
Castro, Fidel 189
Celil, Huseyin 253
Cellucci, Paul 220, 222, 237, 238
Central African Federation 152
Central America 210, 232, 240
Ceylon, *see* Sri Lanka 145
Chamberlain, Joseph 33, 36, 98
Chamberlain, Neville 97–8, 114
Chanak Crisis 93, 115, 150, 222, 227
Chapleau, Joseph-Adolphe 32
Charlesworth, Hector 97
Charter of Rights and Freedoms 188, 191
Chateau Frontenac 125
Cherry, Don 226
Chiapas 250
Chile 182, 191, 193–4, 202, 240
China 43, 46, 103, 110, 124, 156, 215, 241, 254
  Canada, relations with 133, 134, 136–7, 144, 156, 175, 189–90, 245–7, 253
  immigration from 47, 48, 75, 144, 190
  Japanese aggression toward 81, 100, 103, 109–10, 111–12
China Medical Aid Committee 111
Chinese Head Tax 47, 75
Chirac, Jacques 221
Chisholm, Brock 142

Chrétien, Jean 185, 214, 217, 219, 224,
    226, 231, 238, 253
  China and 245–6
  Iraq War and 206, 220–3
  trade and 239–40, 241
Christie, Loring 69
Chrysler 88
Churchill, Winston 67, 93, 119, 122,
    125, 127, 129
Citizens' Committee of 1,000 74
City of London 26, 37
Clark, James 'Champ' 55
Clark, Joe 209, 210, 229, 240, 245,
    249, 254
Clark, William 96
Clarkson, Adrienne 253
Clarkson, Stephen 175
Claxton, Brooke 133–4, 141
Clémenceau, Georges 23, 68
climate change 255–6
Clinton, Hillary 237
Clinton, William (Bill) 211, 241
Coca Cola 88
cold war 207–8
Colombia 244
Colombo Plan 146, 196
Colonial Conferences, see Imperial
    Conferences
Colonial Office 25, 26, 82, 95
colonialism 1, 2, 21
  and Canada 1–2, 7, 148, 152, 153,
    155, 158, 161, see also Settler
    colonialism
  Soviet colonialism 154, 166
Combined Allied Production
    Board 126
Combined Chiefs of Staff 126
Combined Food Board 126
Combined Universities Campaign for
    Nuclear Disarmament 169
Commercial Union League 54
Commission on International
    Development 196
Committee for an Independent Canada
    171
Committee to Aid Spanish Democracy
    103
Committee of Imperial Defence 39,
    112

Commonwealth 69, 93, 94, 95, 122,
    140, 144, 145, 146, 147, 157,
    164–5, 166, 194
  South Africa and 155–6, 192–3, 247,
    248
  Suez Crisis and 149–50, 152
Commonwealth Games 94, 192–3
Commonwealth Scholarships 153
Communication Security
    Establishment (CSE) 133
communism 74, 100, 102–3, 132–3,
    155, see also anti-communism
Communist Party of Canada (CPC), 74,
    102–3, 104
Conference on Safety of Life at Sea 28
Conference on Security and
    Co-operation in Europe (CSCE)
    192, 207, 212
Congo 151, 183
Conservative Party 97, 102, 111, 123,
    152, 166, 170, 207, 224, 225, 227,
    235, 243, 246
  First World War and 65
  Free trade and 55, 97, 234
Consolidated Mining and Smelting
    Corporation 87
Constitution Act 164, 202
Coolidge, Calvin 87
Coon Come, Matthew 238, 250
Cooperative Commonwealth
    Federation (CCF) 1, 102, 105, 115,
    123, 132, 155, 169, see also New
    Democratic Party (NDP)
Copps, Sheila 235
Corning, Sara 82
Coronation Street 163
Costa Rica 240
Côté-Harper, Gisèle 218
Couchiching Conferences 139
Coughlin, Charles 91
Council on Foreign Relations 77
Cree 201
Croatia 211–12, see also Balkans
Cruise missiles 232–3
Cuba 44, 69, 87, 108, 133, 183, 184
  relations with revolutionary Cuba
    156, 167–8, 175, 189, 190, 247
Cuban missile crisis 168, 187
Culhane, Clare 174

Cunard, Samuel 42
Currie, Arthur 62, 69, 80, 81
Cyprus 151, 202, 210
Czechoslovakia 100, 110, 114, 116, 122, 129, 190

Dafoe, John W. 69, 70, 79, 80, 114
Daladier, Édouard 114
Dalai Lama 246
Dallaire, Roméo 213, 216
Dandurand, Raoul 79, 107
Darfur 215
D'Arcy McGee, Thomas 10
Dartmouth College 159
Davis, T. C. 136
Day, Stockwell 205, 222
D-Day 124
De Chastelain, John 216
de Gaulle, Charles 121, 165, 184–6, 188
de-dominionization 160–2, 187–8
Declaration of the Rights of Canadian Youth 109
Dene 200
Denison, George 36, 61
Denmark 8, 141
Department of External Affairs 29, 45, 84, 96, 141, 161, 166
Department of Foreign Affairs and International Trade (DFAIT) 214, 223, 243
Department of Indian Affairs 15, 73
Department of National Defence 223
Department of Trade and Commerce 28
Deskaheh 83
Destroyers for Bases Agreement 127
Detroit 88, 173, 239
Detroit-Windsor Tunnel 88, 239
Development 146–7, 152–3, 156, 196–8, 243–4
  criticisms of 196–7, 198–9
Dexter, Grant 141
Diefenbaker, John 152, 247
  colonial questions and 153, 154, 155
  human rights and 154–5
  and the United Kingdom 164–5, 166
  and the United States 159–60, 165, 166, 167–9, 207

Dion, Celine 236
Disraeli, Benjamin 25
Dominican Republic 127
Dominion Day 162
Dominion Lands Act 13, 19
Dominion Order of King's Daughters 37
Dominions Office 95
Doukhobors 19
Dresden, Ontario 144
Drew, George 90, 108
Dufferin, Lord 25
Duke, James B. 89
Dulles, John Foster 88, 137
Dunn, Alexander 31
Duplessis, Maurice 102

Earth Summit 250
East Timor 189, 218
Eaton's 88
The Economist 140, 252
Edmonton 125, 126, 193
Egypt 87, 149, 151, 157, 209
Eisenhower, Dwight 137
El Salvador 127, 210, 227
Emerson, David 246
Empire Day 37
Endicott, James 124, 133, 137
Erasmus, Georges 249
Esquimalt 26, 38, 94
Ethiopia 111, 124, 137
  famine in 229, 243
Euler, William 107
Europe 8, 20, 41, 43, 45, 56, 60, 61, 66, 70, 72, 80, 85, 93, 100, 108, 109, 113, 116, 119, 121, 124, 127, 129, 131, 139, 144, 151, 164, 165, 186, 191–2, 199, 208, 255
  Canadian cold war commitment to 128, 130, 131, 133, 134, 146, 169, 208
  comparison with Canada 57, 58, 77–8, 79, 80, 101, 114
  immigration from 20, 50, 74–5, 103, 144, 157, 178, 254
  trade with Canada 28, 166, 244
European Economic Community (EEC) 160, 164–5
European Free Trade Area 244

European Union (EU) 58, 239, 244
Evans, Paul 247
Ewart, J. S. 35, 94
Expo 67 162–3, 185, 201
External Aid Office 152
Exxon Mobil 175

Fabre, Hector 28
Fairclough, Ellen 155
Fair Play for Cuba Committee 193
Falconbridge 248
Falconer, Robert 69, 79, 81, 108
Falun Gong 247
Fanon, Frantz 183
fascism 102, 105–7, 251–2
Fellowship for a Christian Social Order
   80
Fellowship of Reconstruction 80
Fenian Brotherhood 9–10
Fessenden, Clementina 37
First East Kootenay Anti-Imperialist
   Rifles 150
First World War 65–6, 77, 79–80, 101,
   115, 124, 229
   Canadian commitment 60–1, 62–3,
   64
   internal divisions caused by 61,
   64–5, 71–2, 100
Fisher, John 38
Flavelle, Joseph 61, 80
Fleming, Sandford 29
Florida 234
Food and Agriculture Organization
   (FAO) 142, 229
Ford, Gerald 232
Ford, Henry 89
Ford Motor Company 88, 248
Fordlandia 89
Fordney-McCumber Tariff 88
Foreign Affairs 187
Foreign Investment Review Agency
   (FIRA) 173, 233
Foreign Office 27, 83, 95, 161
Forsey, Eugene 160
Fort Garry 11
Foster, George 30
Fourth World 199
Fowler, Robert 216
France 28, 61, 84, 111, 115, 152, 222

cold war and 129, 131
Second World War and 121, 124, 133
Suez Crisis and 149–51
support of Quebec separatism
   184–6, 188
Franco, Francisco 103
La Francophonie 186
Fraser, Blair 140
Freeland, Chrystia 255
Free Trade 239–41, 244–5
   Canada and Britain 97–8, 164
   Canada and the United States 54–6,
   57, 98, 101, 123, 233–4, 239
   North American 239–40
Free Trade Agreement of the Americas
   (FTAA) 240
From Colony to Nation 148
Front de libération du Québec (FLQ)
   183–4, 191
Frost, Leslie 71
Frum, David 220
Fulford, Robert 161
Functional Principle 126, 127

Galt, Alexander 19, 27
Garner, Savile 'Joe' 165
Garreau, Joel 231
Garvey, Marcus 91
GATT-fly 193
Gaza 178
Gelber, Lionel 140
General Agreement on Trade and Tariffs
   (GATT) 240
General Motors 88
Generals Die in Bed 70
Geneva Accords 176
Gentlemen's Agreement 49, 50, 53
German-Canadian League 106
Germany 8, 19, 51, 61, 66, 84, 108,
   127, 208
   Nazi Germany 98, 99, 103, 107, 112,
   113–14, 115, 186, 241, 249
   Nazi influence campaign in Canada
   106–7
   Second World War and 120–1, 124,
   128
Ghadar Party 50–1
Ghana 152, 243
Girouard, Édouard Percy Cranwill 31

Gladstone, James 198
'God Save the Queen' 162
The Godfather 232
Goebbels, Joseph 99
Goering, Hermann 99
Golan Heights 210
Goldman, Emma 20
Gompers, Samuel 54
Gorbachev, Mikhail 207–8
Gordon, Alfred 70
Gordon, Walter 166, 172
Gotlieb, Allan 222, 234
Gould, Glenn 137
Gouzenko, Igor 128, 238
Graham, Bill 205, 220, 221
Granatstein, J. L. 222
Grant, George 171, 177
Grant, George Monro 21, 22, 30, 34,
    36, 41
Grant, Ulysses 54
Great Depression 81, 97, 98, 100–1
Great Recession 244, 246
Great War, *see* First World War
Greater Britain 21, 23–4, 29, 39, *see*
    also British World
Greece 129
Green, Howard 152, 153, 169–70
Greenpeace 198
Greenwich Village 174
Gretzky, Wayne 222
Groulx, Lionel 105
Group of 7 (G7) 208, 210, 232
Group of 8 (G8) 1, 220, 243
Group of 20 (G20) 241, 242
Group of Seven 92
Guantánamo Bay 253
Guatemala 44, 243
The Guess Who 174
Guinea-Bissau 182
Gulf War 209–10, 211, 255
Guyana 44, 46, 195
Gzowski, Peter 156

Haight-Ashbury 174
Haiti 69, 195, 205, 253, 254
Halibut Treaty 87
Halifax 26, 38, 66
Halifax, Lord 127
Hall, William 31

Ham, George 7
Hamilton, Ontario 37, 94, 242
Hankey, Maurice 112
Harding, Warren 79, 87
Harmon Air Force Base 127
Harper, Stephen 1, 222, 224, 225, 226,
    238, 239, 243, 245, 246, 252, 254
  trade promotion by 244–5
Hartt, Stanley 246
Haudenosaunee 34, 83–4, 202
Hawthorn, H. B. 199
Hawthorn Report 199–200
Heaps, A. A. 89, 96
Heeney, Arnold 136
Heinbecker, Paul 217
Helsinki Accords 191–2
Hemingway, Ernest 88
Hezbollah 253
High Commission, London 95, 112
Hill 70 64
Hill, James 53
Hillier, Rick 225
Hindustani Association (Vancouver)
    50
Hiram Walker 88
Hiroshima 125
Hitler, Adolf 71, 99, 106, 107, 113–14,
    127, 128, 129, 215
HIV 217, 243
HMCS *Niobe* 39
HMCS *Rainbow* 39, 51
Hollywood 90, 92, 166, 235
Holmes, John 132, 140, 145, 177
Holy Grail 164
Honduras 69, 244
Honest John rocket 169
Hong Kong 42, 51, 124, 241, 253
Hoover, Herbert 100, 101
Hopkins, J. Castell 53
Hopkinson, William 50–1
Howard, Esme 87
Howard, John 222
Hudson's Bay Company 10, 88
Hughes, Charles Evans 87
Hughes, William 68
Human Rights 142–3, 182, 219
  in Canada 143, 144, 154–5, 188
  Canadian foreign policy and 143,
    144, 156, 167, 175, 182, 188–90,

215–16, 217–18, 219, 241–2, 245–6, 247–8
Human Security 214–16, 217–19, 227
  criticisms of 217, 219
Human Security Network 215
Humphrey, John 143
Hundred Days Campaign 66
Hungary 149, 167
Hunter, Fraser 109
Hurtig, Mel 171
Hussein, Saddam 209, 210, 220, 221
Hutton, Edward 38
Hyde Park Agreement 122–3

IAMGOLD 243
Idle No More 251
If You Love This Planet 233
Ignatieff, Michael 206, 218, 219, 225
I'm Alone 89
immigration, 19–20, 52, 53, 145,
    157–8, 251–2, *see also* refugees
  Canadian restrictions on 47–9, 50–2,
    57, 75, 92, 144–5, 155, 157–8, 251
  China, immigration from 47, 48, 75,
    144, 190
  Europe, immigration from 20, 50,
    74–5, 103, 144, 157, 178, 254
  from Canada 52, 89–90, 234
  India, immigration from 50–1, 144–5
  Japan, immigration from 48–9, 50,
    157
  West Indies, immigration from 42,
    45, 47, 51–2, 145, 157
Imperial Conferences 28, 33, 38, 39,
    94, 95, *see also* Commonwealth
Imperial Economic Committee 94
Imperial Economic Conference 97–8
Imperial federation 29–30, 32, 44, 61,
    69
Imperial Federation League 30, 32
Imperial Munitions Board 61
Imperial Oil 54, 175
Imperial Order Daughters of the
    Empire (IODE) 37, 63, 91, 98, 131
Imperial Shipping Committee 94
Imperial War Cabinet 64, 68, 85, 125
Imperial War Graves Commission 94
Imperial Wireless Committee 94
India 18, 43, 51, 127, 157, 161, 210

Canada, relations with 135, 141,
    144–5, 148, 158, 195–6
  immigration to Canada from 50–1,
    144–5
Indian Act 15–16, 199, 200, 249
Indian Chiefs of Alberta 200
Indian Residential Schools 16
Indochina 146, 207, *see also* Cambodia;
    Laos; Vietnam
Indonesia 145–6, 189, 193, 215–16,
    241
'In Flanders Fields' 65, 70
Inland Fisheries Treaty 56
Institute of Economic and International
    Relations 80
Institute of Pacific Relations 77, 81
Inter-American Democratic Charter 240
Inter-Church Coalition on Africa 247
International Bank for Reconstruction
    and Development (IBRD) 142
International Boundary Commission
    56, 87
International Brigades 103
International Campaign to Ban Lands
    Mines 215
International Civil Aviation Organization
    (ICAO) 142
International Commission on
    Intervention and State
    Sovereignty 218
International Control Commission (ICC)
    176
International Criminal Court (ICC) 215
International Development Research
    Centre (IDRC) 197
International Harvester 54
International Joint Commission (IJC)
    56, 79, 109–10
International Labour Organization (ILO)
    69, 70
International Monetary Fund (IMF)
    142, 240
International Network on Cultural
    Policy 235
International NGO Conference on
    Discrimination Against Indigenous
    Populations in the Americas 201
International Nickel Company (INCO)
    54

International Radiotelegraphic
    Conference 28
International Security Assistance Force
    (ISAF) 223–4
Inuit 201, 250
Investment Canada 233
Iran 129, 136, 193, 210, 220, 253
Iraq 206, 209, 210, 215, 217, 200
Iraq War 216, 220–3, 227
Ireland 9, 65, 75, 183, 254, *see also*
    Northern Ireland
Irn-Bru 163
Islamophobia 238, 251–2
Israel 150, 151, 253
Italy 98, 108, 121, 124, 131, 141
    aggression in Ethiopia 111, 193
    fascist influence campaign in
        Canada 106
Íyotake, Tȟatȟáŋka 13

Jacobs, Margaret 8
Jamaica 44, 153, 157, 195
James Bay Cree 201
Japan 43, 66, 98, 110, 143–4, 231, 241,
    247
    aggression by 81, 98, 100, 108,
        109–10, 111–12, 193
    immigration to Canada from 48–9,
        50, 157
    relations with Canada 43, 48, 85,
        109–12
    and the Second World War 119, 124
Japanese Canadian internment 111,
    143–4
Jean, Michaëlle 1, 253
Jerusalem 150
Jesus Jones 209
Jeune Canada 105, 107
Jewett, Pauline 229
Jews 19, 28, 105, 107, 252
    activism by 107
    anti-Semitism 74–5, 102, 105–6,
        107–8
Johnson, Lyndon 174, 176
Jordan 151, 209, 244
Judicial Committee of the Privy
    Council 161
Judson, Wilfred 202
Juno Beach 121

Kabul 223, 224
Kahnawà:ke 249
Kandahar 224, 225
Kanehsatà:ke 249
Karelia 105
Kashmir 151
Kazemi, Zahra 253
Keenleyside, Hugh 141
Kellogg Company 88
Kellogg-Briand Pact 70, 86
Kennedy, John F. 165–6, 167–8, 170,
    177
Kennedy, W. A. 83
Kenora, Ontario 201
Kenyatta, Jomo 2
Keohane, Robert 231
Keynesianism 102
Khadr, Ahmed Said 253
Khard, Omar 253
Khartoum 26, 216
Kimberley Process 216
Kinai Nation 12
King, William Lyon Mackenzie 84, 109,
    119, 123, 128, 134, 141, 147, 207,
    210
    Britain and 82, 85, 86–7, 93–5, 96,
        100, 112, 113–14, 115, 123, 127
    immigration and 42, 49, 50, 107–8,
        144
    interwar international security and
        85, 86, 100, 108, 111, 112–15
    League of Nations and 79, 82, 84,
        111, 112, 128
    Nazi Germany and 113–14
    Second World War and 120–2, 124,
        126
    Soviet Union and 96, 105, 128–30
    the United States and 86–7, 101,
        122–3, 138
Kingston, Ontario 86, 88, 122
Kipling, Rudyard 34, 49
Kirkpatrick, George Macaulay 31
Kissinger, Henry 230
Kiwanis Club 91
Klein, Naomi 242
Knights of Labor 54
Komagatu Maru 51
Korea, North 134, 137, 215, 220, 238
Korea, South 196, 241, 244

Korean War 134–6, 138, 146, 176, 209, 210, 212, 221
Kosovo 217–18, 219, 222, 224, 226, 227
Kraft Foods 88
Kristallnacht 107, 108
Krokodil 167
Ku Klux Klan (KKK) 91
Kuala Lampur 152
Kurdi, Alan 227
Kuwait 209–10

Ladies Home Journal 90
Lalonde, Michèle 183
Lament for a Nation 171
Laos 87, 136, 176
Lapointe, Ernest 64, 84, 87, 111, 115
Las Vegas 234
Latin America 44, 69, 89, 96, 109, 141, 166, 184, 193–4, 197, 240
Latin America Working Group 194
Laurendeau, André 105, 116
Laurier, Wilfrid 19, 26, 32, 35, 36, 38, 44, 57, 81, 112
    First World War and 60, 65, 71
    immigration and 19–20, 48–9, 50, 52, 53
    reciprocity with the United States and 55
    relations with Britain 28, 32–3, 36, 38–9, 40, 93
Laut, Agnes Christina 37
Law, Andrew Bonar 62
Laxer, James 174
Leacock, Stephen 8, 20, 36
League Against War and Fascism 103
League for Social Reconstruction 80
League of Indians of Canada 73
League of Nations 68, 69, 70, 78, 79, 104
    Advisory Committee on the Traffic of Women and Children 84
    Canadian attitudes toward 81–2, 84, 96, 100, 109–11, 112
    Child Welfare Committee 84
    Commission on Deported Women and Children 83
    Health Committee 84
    Six Nations diplomacy toward 834, 202, 250

League of Nations Society 77, 78, 81, 111, 112, 142
Lebanon 151, 157, 210, 253
Léger, Jules 149
Lemieux, Rodolphe 49, 53
Lend-Lease 122–3
Lévesque, René 186–7
Lewis, David 175
Lewis, Stephen 174, 217, 229, 248
Liberal Party 95, 111, 120, 152, 155, 156, 160, 169, 170, 173, 209, 214, 217, 219, 224, 240–1, 252
    First World War and 64–5, 77
    free trade and 54–5, 234, 239–40
    nationalist criticisms of 54–5, 160, 170, 171
Liberia 68, 69, 219
Libya 206, 215, 226, 227
Lion's Club 91
Little Rock, Arkansas 156
Lloyd George, David 45, 64, 67–8, 70
Locarno Treaty 84–5
Loft, Frederick 72–3
Lombardo, Guy 91
Lorne, Marquess of 25
Lower, Arthur 110
Luxembourg 129

*M*A*S*H* 232
Macaulay, T. B. 44
MacDonald, Donald 182
Macdonald, Hugh John 74
Macdonald, James 52, 57, 79
Macdonald, John A. 22, 36, 47, 57, 81, 94
    indigenous peoples and 11–12, 14–16, 18
    as nation-builder 2, 7, 9, 10, 21, 24
    National Policy of 13, 19, 26, 54, 55
    relations with Britain and 23, 26–7, 33, 39, 97, 149
    relations with the United States and 23, 26, 36, 54–5, 234
MacEachen, Allan 172
MacGillivray, Donald 46
MacGillivray, Elizabeth 46
MacGuigan, Mark 191, 192
Mackenzie, Alexander 13, 15, 25, 54
MacKenzie, Lewis 206, 212

MacKenzie, Norman 110
Mackenzie, William 44
Mackenzie-Papineau Brigade 103, 177
Mackenzie Valley Pipeline 201
MacMechan, Archibald 90
Macmillan, Harold 155, 164, 165
Macmillan, Margaret 255
Macphail, Agnes 80, 105, 112, 116
Mair, Charles 32
Malaya 146, 152
Malaysia 152, 183
Manchuria 81, 109
Mandela, Nelson 247, 248
Manhattan Project 124–5
Manitoba 11, 17, 162
Manley, John 220, 224
Manuel, George 199, 201, 202
Mao Zedong 167
Maori 199
Marjie 172
Marmite 163
Martin Jr., Paul 216, 224, 238, 240, 241
Martin Sr., Paul 147, 148, 149, 175, 176, 177, 186, 194
Massey-Ferguson 248
Massey, Raymond 67, 91
Massey, Vincent 80, 87, 89, 96, 109, 126, 161, 166
  Massey Commission 166
Mawedipenais 14
McBride, Richard 66
McCall's 90
McCallum, John 221
McCarthy, Dalton 32
McCarthyism, *see* anti-communism
McClung, Nellie 108
McCrae, John 65
McDonald's 208
McDougall, Barbara 210, 212, 219
McGill University 183, 187
MacLaren, Roy 240
McLuhan, Marshall 181
McNamara, Robert 196
Meagher, Margaret 189
Medak 212
Médecins Sans Frontières (MSF) 243
Meighen, Arthur 74, 82, 85, 93, 95, 108

Merchant, Livingston 165
Métis 11, 12, 17–19, 27, 200, 227
Mexico 36, 43, 166, 232, 237, 239, 250
Meyer, Kurt 143
Middle Power 4, 69, 140–1, 145, 153, 158, 169
Middleton, Frederick 18
Miles for Millions Walkathon 202
Military Service Act 64
Military Voters Act 65
Millennium Development Goals 243
Milner, Lord 32, 68
Mines Action Canada 215
Minifie, James 169
Minto, Lord 35
missionaries 11, 12, 15–16, 21, 37, 45–6, 77, 82, 124, 133, 136–7, 194, 197, 246
Mississippi 174
Mistahimaskwa 14, 17
Mitsui, Tad 255
Moffett, Samuel 42
Mohawk 201, 249
Molson Canadian 236
Monnet, John 58
Monroe Doctrine 122
Mons 66
Montreal 7, 29, 32, 35, 43, 55, 65, 88, 105, 106, 107, 125, 142, 162, 183, 184, 185, 187, 192, 195, 221, 234, 235, 237, 252, 253
Montreal Olympics 192
Montreal Women's Anti-Reciprocity League 55
Morgan, J. P. 54
Morin, Claude 185, 186
Mormons 19
Morocco 147
Morris, Alexander 12
Morris, Jan 236
Morton, W. L. 160
Mowat, Oliver 48
Mozambique 154, 194
Muir, Alexander 32
Mulroney, Brian 207, 208, 209, 210, 211, 213, 228, 233, 235, 239–40, 241, 243, 245, 246
  South Africa and 247–9

Soviet Union and 207–8
the United States and 207, 208, 209, 232, 233–4, 238, 239
Mulroney, David 247
multiculturalism 252–3
Munich Settlement 114, 115, 137
Munk, Peter 243
Murmansk 67
Murray, Anne 229
Mussolini, Benito 106, 111

Naismith, James 53
Naked, General Butt 219
Namibia 210
Nasser, Gamal Abdel 149, 150
National Committee on Refugees and Victims of Political Persecution 108
National Council of Women 111
National Defence League 38
National Energy Program (NEP) 232, 233
National Film Board (NFB) 92, 233
National Indian Brotherhood 199
National Policy 13, 19, 26, 54, 55
National Research Council 133
National Resources Mobilization Act (NRMA) 121
National Unity Party (NUP) 106
Native Council of Canada 200
Native Sons of Canada 92
Natose-Onista 12
Nault, Bob 250
Naval Crisis 38–9
Navy League of Canada 38, 39
Nehru, Jawaharlal 2, 144
Neo-liberalism 240–3
Criticisms of 242
Netherlands 8, 129, 145
New Brunswick 9, 28
New Democratic Party (NDP) 169, 172, 175, 209, 217, 224, 234
Newfoundland 9, 62, 100, 125, 127, 161
New Iceland 19
New Left 171, 174, 177
New Nationalism 160, 171–2, 173–5, 177, 178–9, 210, 223, 230, 231, 236, *see also* Anti-Americanism

New Zealand 8, 18, 21, 28, 38, 93, 97, 112, 133, 161, 163, 192, 199, 218, 222
Newark 173, 178
Niagara Falls 88
Nicaragua 89
Nigeria 152, 188, 219
Nile Expedition 26–7, 33, 34, 60, 206, 227
The Nine Nations of North America 231
Nisga'a 201–2
Nixon, Richard 190, 231
Nkrumah, Kwame 2
Nobel Peace Prize 150, 171
Noranda 89
Norman, E. H. 132
North American Aerospace Defence Command (NORAD) 168, 169, 175, 187
North American Free Trade Agreement (NAFTA) 239, 240
North Americanism 57, 78–9, 85–6, 91, 98, 115, 116, 172, 231, 239
North Atlantic Coast Fisheries Agreement (1910) 56
North Atlantic Treaty Organization (NATO) 120, 134, 137–8, 141, 145, 146, 169, 175, 185, 187, 189, 192, 202, 208, 212, 224, 225, 226, 227, 255
Afghan War and 206, 223–5
creation of 130
Kosovo War and 217–18, 219, 222
North Atlantic Triangle 119–20, 125, 159–60, 178, 233
North Pacific Fur Seal Convention (1911) 56
North-West Mounted Police (NWMP) 12, 17, 18, 74, *see also* Royal Canadian Mounted Police
Northwest Passage 255
North-West Rebellion 17–18, 27, 34, 60, 62, 227
Northwest Staging Route 126
North-West Territories 10–11, 13, 15, 250
Northern Ireland 216
Northern Miner 89

Norton, Joseph 249
Nova Scotia 9, 28
Nuclear Non-Proliferation Treaty (NPT) 196, 208, 233
nuclear weapons 124–5, 168
    Canadian 125, 169–71, 174, 214
Numbered Treaties 13–14, 201
Nunavut 250
Nuremberg Trials 143
Nutt, Samantha 216
Nye, Joseph 214, 230–1

'O Canada' 162
Occupy Wall Street 242
October Crisis 184
Office of Strategic Services 124
Ogdensburg Agreement 122
Ojibway Warrior Society 201
Oka standoff 249
Oliver, Frank 20
On-to-Ottawa Trek 104
Ontario 9, 10, 45, 54, 82, 94, 162
Open Skies Agreement 234
Operation Apollo 224
Operation Athena 223–4
Operation Featherbed 132
Operation Picnic 132
Operation Profunc 132
Orange Order 32, 237
Organization of American States 201, 205, 207, 240, see also Pan-American Union
Oshawa, Ontario 88, 242
Ottawa 104
Ottawa Treaty 215
Ouellet, André 241
OXFAM Canada 188, 243

Paardeberg 34, 35
Pacifism 80
Packard 88
Pakistan 136, 145, 146, 157, 189, 195, 196, 210, 253
Palestine 150, 161, 184, 210, 250
Panama 69, 244
Pan-American Union 96
Paris 28, 67, 88, 96, 148, 152
Paris Club 193
Paris Peace Conference 67–9, 70, 71, 77, 79, 81

Park, Frank 133
Park, Libbie 133
Parkin, George 29, 41, 52
Parliamentarians for World Order 233
Parti national social chrétien 105–6
Parti Québécois (PQ) 186–7
Partners in Development 196
Pastor, Robert 239
Payipwat 174
Peace Bridge 88
Peace Corps 153
peacekeeping 149–50, 151–2, 202, 206
    post-cold war era 210–14, 223, 226, 227
Peacemaker or Powdermonkey? 169, 174
Pearl Harbor 125, 143
Pearson, Lester 125, 126, 217, 233
    cold war and 129, 130, 134, 135, 137, 139
    decolonization and 139, 145, 146, 149–50, 156–7
    de-dominionization and 162, 163
    development and 146, 196–7
    immigration and 145, 157–8
    interwar international security and 99, 109
    Quebec separatism and 185–6
    Suez Crisis and 149–50, 159
    United Nations and 130, 135, 151
    the United States and 135, 137–8, 170, 176–7
Pelletier, Gérard 184
People's Summits 242
Permanent Joint Board on Defence 122
Perry, A. B. 74
Persian Gulf 207, 223, see also Gulf War
Peru 243, 244
Peterson, Oscar 229
Petro-Canada 173, 233
Philadelphia 176
Philippines 49, 157, 241
Phillips, William 91
Phineas Finn 25
Pickford, Mary 91
Pictorial Review 90
Pîhtokahanapiwyin 14, 19
Pinochet, Augusto 215

Plummer, Christopher 235
Poland 8, 99, 115, 141, 176, 187, 192
Pol Pot 215
Pope, Joseph 45
Pope, Maurice 126
Posluns, Michael 199
Powell, Colin 221
Power, Charles 79, 82, 93
Prince Edward Island 9
Progressive Conservative Party, see
    Conservative Party
Project Ploughshares 233
Puerto Rico 44

Qaddafi, Muammar 226
Quebec 9, 28, 45, 54, 81, 89, 102, 103,
    105, 106, 108, 113, 188, 200, 201,
    231
  First World War and 65, 82
  international personality of 185,
    186–7
  Second World War and 120, 121
  separatism in 4, 178–9, 182–7, 194,
    202, 211, 231
  Tercentenary of 31
Quebec City mosque shooting 251
Queen's University 21, 30, 86

Rasminsky, Louis 142
Rassam, Ahmed 237
Rassemblement pour l'indépendance
    Nationale (RIN) 182
Reagan, Ronald 232, 233, 238, 248
reciprocity, see Free Trade
Red River Expedition 21, 25, 34
Red River Settlement 11
Redden, Jack 197–8
Refugee Convention 143, 190
Refugees 83, 108, 143, 190, 191
  Argentinian 191
  Armenian 83
  Chilean 190–1
  Chinese 190
  Czechoslovakian 190
  European 144
  Jewish 107–8, 190, 252
  Syrian 226–7, 252
  Tibetan 190
  Ugandan 190
  Uruguayan 191

Regina 18, 59, 104
Reid, Escott 80, 99
Resnick, Philip 194
Responsibility to Protect (R2P) 218–19,
    226
La Revue Socialiste 183
Rhodes, Cecil 2
Rhodesia 156–7, 183, 199, 201, 202
von Ribbentrop, Joachim 71
Riddell, W. A. 111
Rideau Canal 149
Riel, Louis 11, 15–18, 27
Rio Tinto 243
Ritchie, Charles 165
Robertson, Norman 108, 143, 151
Robinson, Svend 217
Roche, Douglas 133
Rockefeller Foundation 86
Romania 82, 196
Ronning, Chester 136
Roosevelt, Franklin Delano (FDR) 88,
    101, 121–3, 125
Roosevelt, Theodore 49, 50, 56
Root, Elihu 57
Rotary Club 91, 153
Round Table 30, 60, 65
Rowell, Newton 77–8, 81, 82
Roy, Raoul 183
Royal Bank of Canada 43, 195
Royal Canadian Air Force 124, 161
Royal Canadian Geographical Society
    92
Royal Canadian Legion 111, 114, 131,
    162, 226
Royal Canadian Mounted Police
    (RCMP) 83, 104, 132
Royal Canadian Navy 124, 161
Royal Commission on Aboriginal
    Peoples 250
Royal Commission on Canada's
    Economic Prospects 166
Royal Commission on National
    Development in the Arts, Letters
    and Sciences 166
Royal Commission on Publications 166
Royal Institute of International Affairs
    77
Royal Mail 162
Royal Military College of Canada
    (RMC) 25, 31

Royal Navy 39, 55, 94
Royal Proclamation of 1763 14
Rumsfeld, Donald 224
Rupert's Land 10, 11
Rush-Bagot Treaty 87
Rusk, Dean 177
Russia 8, 19, 28, 48, 57, 66, 208, 215,
  see also Soviet Union
  revolutions in 64, 66–7, 73, 74, 139
Rust Belt 231
Rwanda 8, 213, 218, 224, 226

St Laurent, Louis 123, 131, 145, 148,
  161, 167
  foreign policy of 129, 130, 134, 141,
    149, 233
  Suez Crisis and 149, 151, 159
St Lawrence Seaway 101
St Lawrence University 86
Sarajevo 212
Saskatchewan 20, 55, 167
Saturday Evening Post 90
Saudi Arabia 193
Schröder, Gerhard 221
Schwab, Charles 54
Scott, Duncan Campbell 73
Scott, Frank 92, 105
Seagram's 88
Sears and Roebuck 88
Seattle General Strike 73
Second World War 99, 120, 128, 137,
  163, 209
  Canadian commitment 123–4
  Canadian declaration of war 115–16
Secwepemc 199
Seeley, J. R. 21
Selma, Alabama 174
September 11 terror attacks 203, 220,
  237
Serbia 60, 217–18, see also Balkans
Sesame Park 172
Settler Colonialism 47, 155
  in Canada 8, 12–17, 21, 126–7, 155,
    158, 199–202, 250
Seward, William 10
Shanghai 42, 43, 51, 81
Sharp, Mitchell 173, 186
Shatner, William 235
Shawinigan, Quebec 231

Shotwell, James T. 70, 86
Shuster, Joe 91
Siberia 57
  Siberian expedition 67, 75
Siegfried, André 31, 53
Sierra Leone 218
Sifton, Clifford 19–20, 68
Sikh nationalism 254
Sinai 210
Singapore 29, 43, 192
Singer Sewing Machine Company 54
Sir George Williams Affair 195
Six-Day War 151
Six Nations, see Haudenosaunee
Skelton, O. D. 55, 76, 84, 96, 104, 111
  Britain, relations with 85, 95
  immigration and 51
  German aggression and 114
  Italian aggression and 111
  Japanese aggression and 109–10
Smith, Arnold 2, 157
Smith, Donald (Lord Strathcona) 18, 33
Smith, Goldwin 35–6, 41, 52, 55
Smoot-Hawley Tariff 97, 101
Smuts, Jan 64
Social Credit Party 102
Somalia 208, 211, 212–13, 217, 218,
  219, 224
Somalia Affair 212–13
South Africa 8, 21, 94, 95, 97, 143, 145,
  154, 155, 182, 247
  apartheid in 143, 155–6, 158, 175,
    192–3, 199, 201, 202, 247–9
South African Congress of Trade
  Unions Solidarity Committee 247
South African War, see Boer War
Soviet Union 96, 103, 104–5, 124, 133,
  149, 175, 208, 241, 245
  Canada, relations with 126, 128, 132,
    137, 154, 166–7, 189, 207–8
  cold war and 128–30, 131, 134,
    207–8
  colonialism of 154, 166, 187, 189,
    208, 255
Spain 81, 98, 103
  Civil War in 81, 103, 177
Spicer, Keith 196, 197
Sports Illustrated 235
Spry, Graham 81, 92

Srebrenica 212
Sri Lanka 145, 146, 196, 254
Stairs, William 31
Stalin, Josef 129, 133, 137
Standard Oil 54
Statute of Rome 215
Statute of Westminster 96, 99, 113, 116, 161
Stead, W. T. 41
Stephen, George 26
Stevenson, Louis 248
Stewart, Brian 229
Stratford Shakespearean Festival 235
Sudan, 17, 24, 26, 27, 60, 216, 254, *see also* Darfur; Nile Expedition
Studebaker 88
Sudbury 54
Suez Canal 27, 149
Suez Crisis 139, 149–50, 151–2, 155, 158, 159, 222
Suharto 215
Sukarno 146, 148
Summers, Larry 241
Summit Series 189
Sun Life Insurance 43, 44
Supreme Court of Canada 25, 161
Suzuki, David 221
Sweden 19, 141, 189
Switzerland 141
Syria 226–7, 238, 25

Taft, William Howard 55, 56
Taiwan 189
Taliban 224
Talisman Energy 216
Tambo, Oliver 248
Tamils 254
Tanzania 152
Tarr, Edgar 80
Task Force on Churches and Corporate Responsibility 247
Task Force on the Structure of the Canadian Economy 172
Taylor, Charles 219
'Tears Are Not Enough' 229
Temple University 176
Thailand 241
Thakur, Ramesh 218
Thatcher, Margaret 233, 248

Third Option 173, 193, 245
Thompson, Robert N. 124
Thousand Islands International Bridge 88
Tiananmen Square 245
Tibet 246
Tim Horton's 236
Time 235
Tin Pan Alley 90
Tolstoy, Leo 19
Tokyo 49, 96, 112, 143, 177
Tokyo War Crimes Trials 143
Toronto 11, 35, 36–7, 38, 44, 55, 59, 77, 88, 106, 107, 112, 174, 194, 215, 235, 252
Toronto Committee for the Liberation of Southern Africa 193
Toronto Stock Exchange 243
Trades and Labour Congress 111
Trail Smelter 87
Trans-Pacific Partnership 244–5
Trinidad 44, 46, 157, 195
Trollope, Anthony 25
Trotsky, Leon 66
Trudeau, Justin 1, 252, 253, 254
Trudeau, Pierre 105, 171, 173, 175, 178, 182, 184, 231
    China and 137, 189–90, 245
    human rights and 188–90, 191–3, 219, 248
    indigenous peoples and 200
    Quebec and 186–7, 188
    Third World and 181, 197
    the United States and 173, 207, 232
Tunisia 147, 148
Tupper, Charles 27
Turgeon, Adélard 31
Turkey 82, 93, 141, 209
Turks and Caicos 2
Tutu, Desmond 248, 249
TV Turnoff Week 242
Twain, Shania 236
Twinning Movement 233

Uganda 190
Uighur minority 247, 253
Ukraine 82, 208, 244
Ukrainian Canadians 20, 72, 74, 116, 154, 162, 202, 208, 252, 255

Underground Railroad 9, 237
Underhill, Frank 70, 111, 159
Union Government 65, 77
Union Nationale 102
Union of Soviet Socialist Republics
    (USSR), see Soviet Union
United Church of Canada 80, 255
United Kingdom, see Britain
United Nations (UN) 147, 149, 150,
    153, 201, 205, 213, 248
    Canada and 129, 134–5, 136, 140–1,
    142, 144, 148–9, 150, 153, 191, 202,
    207, 210, 212, 221, 222, 225, 227
    Charter of 142, 209, 210
    creation of 127–8
United Nations Association (UNA) 142,
    148
United Nations Declaration of the
    Rights of the Child 143
United Nations Declaration on the
    Rights of Indigenous Peoples
    (UNDRIP) 250
United Nations Economic and Social
    Council 128
United Nations Emergency Force
    (UNEF) 150, 151–2
United Nations High Commissioner for
    Refugees 191
United Nations Human Rights
    Commission 154
United Nations Protection Force
    (UNPROFOR) 211–12
United Nations Relief and
    Rehabilitation Administration 142
United Nations Relief and Works
    Agency for Palestine Refugees
    141–2
United Nations Security Council
    (UNSC) 128, 145, 221, 226
United Nations Technical Assistance
    Administration 141
United Nations Temporary Commission
    on Korea (UNTCOK) 134
United Nations Truce Supervisory
    Organization 151
United Nations World Summit 218
United States 100, 108, 120, 202, 215,
    239
    civil rights movement in 173–4

Civil War 9, 174
cold war and 130, 134–5, 167–8,
    207–8
Congress of 101, 167, 211, 234
Great Depression and 100, 101–2
investment in Canada 89, 231–2
Military cooperation with Canada
    122, 126, 168–9, 171
point of comparison with Canada 52,
    53–4, 152, 173–4, 178, 203, 236–7,
    251
post-cold war foreign policy 209,
    220–1, 227
prohibition in 88–9
Second World War and 121–3
Vietnam War and 173–5
United Task Force (UNITAF) 213
Universal Declaration of Human Rights
    (UDHR) 143, 144, 191, 219
Universal Negro Improvement
    Association 91
University of Edinburgh 172
Uruguay 191, 193, 194

Vallières, Pierre 183–4
Vancouver 29, 41, 42, 43, 46, 51, 66,
    79, 104, 198, 216, 235, 242, 252
    Asian community in 34, 46, 48–9, 51
Vancouver Trades and Labor Council
    47–8
Van Horne, William 42, 44, 48, 53
Verwoerd, Hendrik 155
Victoria, British Columbia 34, 43, 46,
    47
Vichy regime, see France
Vietnam 136
Vietnam War 173–7, 178, 202, 222,
    223, 237
Vimy Ridge 64, 70, 93, 185
Vladivostok 67
Voice of Women/La Voix des femmes
    (VOW) 169
Völkischer Beobachter 107

War of 1812 18, 57, 78
War Child 216
War Measures Act 72
Warner, Jack 91
Warnock, John 173

Wartime Elections Act 65
Washington Consensus 240
Washington, George 108
Washington Naval Conference 85, 93, 150
Washington Treaty of 1871 26, 36, 54
Watts, California 173
Welsh, Jennifer 219, 255
Wembley Park 95
'The West' 131
West Indies 42, 43–5, 152, 157, 194–5
    immigration to Canada from 42, 45, 47, 51–2, 145, 157
While Canada Slept 219
White Niggers of America 183
Who Killed the Canadian Military? 219
Wilgress, Dana 107, 120, 148
Wilson, Cairine 108
Wilson, Michael 233
Wilson, Woodrow 71, 83
Windsor, Edward 113
Windsor, Elizabeth 162, 163–4, 187
Windsor, George 113, 160
Windsor, Ontario 88, 239, 242
Winnipeg 20, 59, 88, 106
    General Strike 73–4, 104
Wolseley, Garnet 11
Women's International League for Peace and Freedom (WILPF) 80, 111, 169
Woodsworth, J. S. 80, 110, 112
    immigration and 20, 42, 52, 110
Workers' Economic Conference 98

World Alliance 80
World Bank 196, 240
World Conference against Racism 250
World Conference on Women 214
World Disarmament Conference (1932) 108, 109
World Economic Forum 242
World Federalists of Canada 198, 210
World Health Organization (WHO) 142
World Trade Organization (WTO) 235, 240, 242
World University Service of Canada 153
World Vision 243
Wray, Fay 91
The Wretched of the Earth (183)
Wrong, George 60, 69
Wrong, Hume 109, 126, 135, 136

Yakovlev, Aleksandr 207
Yip Sang 47
Yokohama 29, 42, 43, 51
Young Men's Christian Association (YMCA) 37
Young, E. R. 11
Young Socialists 163
Yugoslavia 208, 211–12, 213, 214, 228, 253, *see also* Balkans

Zambia 153
Zolf, Larry 173
Zouaves 254